Preface

Welcome to the exciting and rapidly evolving world of artificial intelligence (AI). This book, "Artificial Intelligence Tools: Unlocking the Power of Intelligent Systems," is designed to be your comprehensive guide to understanding, implementing, and leveraging the cutting-edge tools that drive the advancements in AI. Whether you are a seasoned professional in the field or a curious newcomer, this book aims to provide you with valuable insights and practical knowledge to navigate the multifaceted landscape of AI tools. From machine learning algorithms to neural networks, readers will gain insights into the core concepts that form the backbone of intelligent systems. We aim to make complex ideas accessible, ensuring that readers, regardless of their technical background, can grasp the essentials of AI.

Furthermore, we recognize the ethical implications and societal considerations surrounding AI. In a dedicated section, we address the responsible use of AI tools, discussing issues such as bias in algorithms, transparency, and accountability. It is crucial for individuals working with AI to understand the ethical dimensions of their work and strive towards the development of AI systems that align with human values and promote inclusivity. In addition to the technical aspects, this book emphasizes the importance of continuous learning and adaptation in the rapidly evolving field of AI. The final sections explore emerging trends, such as reinforcement learning, autonomous systems, and AI-driven creativity, offering readers a glimpse into the future of artificial intelligence.

Key Features

1. Extensive Theoretical Content: The book covers the full spectrum of topics, from fundamental concepts to advanced techniques. Each chapter is designed to build on the previous one, ensuring a logical progression and deep comprehension of the subject matter.

2. Online Test Papers: To reinforce your learning, we provide a series of online test papers that mimic real-world scenarios and challenges. These tests are designed to evaluate your understanding and help you identify areas that need further study.

3. Video Tutorials: Understanding concepts can sometimes be challenging through text alone. Our book includes links to a series of video tutorials that provide visual and auditory explanations of complex topics. These videos are created by experts and are intended to complement the written material, offering a more immersive learning experience.

4. Practical Applications: Each chapter includes real-world examples and case studies that illustrate how application is applied across different industries.

5. Self-Assessment Tools: At the end of each chapter, self-assessment questions and exercises allow you to test your understanding and track your progress. These tools are invaluable in helping you gauge your readiness and build confidence as you move forward.

Whether you are an aspiring data scientist, a business professional exploring AI application, or an academic researcher pushing the boundaries of knowledge, "Artificial Intelligence Tools" is crafted to be a valuable companion on your journey. As you embark on this exploration of artificial intelligence, we encourage you to engage with the content, experiment with the tools, and contribute to the ongoing dialogue surrounding the responsible development and application of intelligent systems. The future of AI is in your hands, and we are excited to be part of your learning journey.

Table of Contents

Chapter 1: Introduction to AI Tools

1.1 Evolution of AI in Various Domains

Artificial Intelligence (AI) has experienced significant evolution across various domains, transforming the way tasks are performed and problems are solved. The evolution of AI tools is evident in the following domains:

1. Natural Language Processing (NLP) and Content Creation Tools:

Early Stages: Initial AI tools focused on basic language processing tasks, such as rule-based chatbots and simple language translation.

Current State: Advanced NLP models, like OpenAI's GPT-3, enable sophisticated content generation, sentiment analysis, and language understanding. Tools like ChatGPT, Writesonic, and Wordtune showcase the evolution toward more natural and context-aware language processing.

2. Coding and Programming Tools:

Early Stages: Early coding tools employed basic algorithms and syntax checking functionalities.

Current State: The evolution is evident in tools like GitHub Copilot and TabNine, which utilize machine learning to assist developers in writing code snippets and enhancing productivity. These tools leverage vast code repositories and context-aware suggestions to streamline the coding process.

3. Meeting and Collaboration Tools:

Early Stages: Initial AI tools focused on basic meeting scheduling and reminders.

Current State: Advanced tools like Otter.ai and Fireflies use AI to transcribe meetings, extract actionable insights, and automate tasks related to collaboration. The evolution involves increased integration with natural language understanding to facilitate more effective communication and information retrieval during meetings.

4. Image Design and Editing Tools:

Early Stages: Basic image processing tools were rule-based and limited in functionality.

Current State: Evolution is evident in tools like DALL.E 2 and NightCafe, which use advanced AI models to generate and manipulate images creatively. These tools showcase the capability of AI to understand visual content, generate unique designs, and assist in creative processes.

5. Video Creation and Editing Tools:

Early Stages: Early video tools focused on basic editing functionalities.

Current State: Tools like Synthesia and Lumen5 leverage AI to generate realistic synthetic videos, automate video creation, and enhance the overall video editing process. This evolution involves the integration of AI to generate dynamic and engaging video content.

6. Customer Support and Sales Tools:

Early Stages: Initial AI tools in this domain focused on basic chatbots for customer interactions.

Current State: Advanced tools like SecondBrain, Chatfuel AI, and Conversica use AI to automate customer support, enhance sales interactions, and provide personalized experiences. The evolution involves more natural language understanding, sentiment analysis, and automation of complex customer interactions.

7. HR and Recruiting Tools:

Early Stages: Initial AI tools in HR focused on basic resume screening and candidate matching.

Current State: Evolution is evident in tools like Paradox and Textio, which use AI for advanced candidate assessments, cultural fit analysis, and personalized recruiting. These tools showcase the evolution towards more intelligent and data-driven HR and recruiting processes.

1.2 Impact of AI on Writing, Coding, Meetings, Design, Video, Customer Support, and HR

1. Writing:

AI has revolutionized the writing process by offering tools that assist in content creation, editing, and optimization. Writing AI tools like ChatGPT, Jasper, and Wordtune employ natural language processing (NLP) to enhance grammar, style, and overall coherence. They facilitate quicker ideation, generate creative content, and help writers refine their work efficiently.

2. Coding:

AI's impact on coding is significant, as seen in tools like GitHub Copilot and TabNine. These tools leverage machine learning to assist developers in writing code snippets, improving productivity, and reducing the time spent on repetitive tasks. AI coding tools also aid in catching errors and suggesting optimizations, streamlining the software development process.

3. Meetings:

AI tools for meetings, such as Otter.ai and Fireflies, utilize speech-to-text technology and natural language understanding to transcribe and analyze spoken words. This enhances collaboration by providing searchable and shareable meeting transcripts. Additionally, tools like Krisp use AI to remove background noise, improving the overall meeting experience.

4. Design:

In the realm of design, AI tools like DALL.E 2 and NightCafe are transforming how images are created. These tools use generative algorithms to produce unique and creative designs, automating certain aspects of the design process. This enables designers to explore new possibilities and iterate more rapidly.

5. Video:

AI's impact on video tools like Synthesia and Lumen5 is evident in the automation of video creation. AI-powered video tools can generate realistic avatars, automate video editing, and even synthesize human-like voices. This not only accelerates the video production process but also opens up new possibilities for personalized and engaging content.

6. Customer Support:

AI tools in customer support, such as Conversica and wARMER.ai, are transforming how businesses interact with customers. Chatbots powered by AI handle routine queries, provide instant responses, and learn from interactions to improve over time. This not only enhances customer satisfaction but also allows human support agents to focus on more complex issues.

7. HR:

In HR and recruiting, AI tools like Textio and HiredScore are streamlining talent acquisition. These tools analyze large datasets to identify suitable candidates, improve job descriptions, and enhance the overall recruitment process. AI in HR also aids in workforce management, employee engagement, and predictive analytics for talent retention.

1.3 Overview of AI Tools in Different Fields

Artificial Intelligence (AI) tools have made significant strides across various domains, revolutionizing the way tasks are performed and problems are addressed. Here's an overview of AI tools in different fields:

1. Writing and Content Creation Tools:

Purpose: These tools leverage natural language processing (NLP) and machine learning to assist users in creating high-quality content. From grammar checking to generating creative text, these tools streamline the writing process.

2. Coding Tools:

Purpose: Aimed at developers, coding tools employ AI algorithms to enhance coding productivity. They may offer code suggestions, auto-completion, and even generate entire code snippets, making the development process more efficient.

3. Meeting Tools:

Purpose: AI-powered meeting tools focus on automating and improving various aspects of meetings. This includes transcription services, intelligent note-taking, and features like noise cancellation, facilitating smoother communication.

4. Image Design Tools:

Purpose: AI is transforming graphic design by enabling tools that can generate images, assist in photo editing, and even create entirely new visual content. These tools often utilize advanced algorithms for image recognition and synthesis.

5. Video Tools:

Purpose: AI-driven video tools automate video creation, editing, and synthesis. They may include features like deepfake technology, video summarization, and content generation, catering to a wide range of applications from marketing to entertainment.

6. Customer Support and Sales Tools:

Purpose: AI tools in this category aim to enhance customer interactions, streamline support processes, and optimize sales strategies. They often include chatbots, automated responses, and analytics for customer engagement.

7. HR and Recruiting Tools:

Purpose: HR and recruiting tools utilize AI to streamline the hiring process. This includes resume screening, candidate matching, and even AI-powered virtual assistants for HR-related tasks.

Common Traits Across AI Tools:

1. Machine Learning: Many AI tools incorporate machine learning techniques to analyze data, recognize patterns, and improve their performance over time.

2. Natural Language Processing (NLP): Tools often leverage NLP for understanding and generating human language, enabling better communication and interaction.

3. Automation: A key characteristic of AI tools is their ability to automate repetitive tasks, saving time and reducing manual effort.
4. Personalization: AI tools often offer personalized experiences, tailoring outputs based on user preferences and historical interactions.
5. Data-driven Decision Making: AI tools rely on data analysis to make informed decisions and predictions, contributing to data-driven strategies.

Exercise

Exercise 1 – MCQ

Q 1. What does AI stand for?
A. Automated Intelligence
B. Augmented Intelligence
C. Artificial Intelligence
D. Adaptive Intelligence

Q 2. Which branch of computer science focuses on creating AI systems that can learn and improve from experience?
A. Robotics
B. Natural Language Processing
C. Machine Learning
D. Expert Systems

Q 3. What is the primary goal of AI tools in decision-making processes?
A. Minimizing Efficiency
B. Reducing Automation
C. Enhancing Human Involvement
D. Improving Accuracy and Efficiency

Q 4. Which type of AI system is designed to perform a specific task without human intervention?
A. Narrow AI (Weak AI)
B. General AI (Strong AI)
C. Superintelligent AI
D. Hyperintelligent AI

Q 5. What does NLP stand for in the context of AI?
A. Natural Language Programming
B. Network Language Processing
C. Neural Language Programming
D. Natural Language Processing

Q 6. In AI, what is the term for the ability of a machine to understand, interpret, and generate human-like language?
A. Cognitive Computing
B. Linguistic Processing
C. Sentiment Analysis
D. Conversational AI

Q 7. What does the term "Deep Learning" refer to in AI?
A. Shallow Neural Networks
B. Supervised Learning Techniques
C. Learning from Experience
D. Neural Networks with Multiple Layers

Q 8. Which industry commonly uses AI for fraud detection, market trends prediction, and investment optimization?
A. Healthcare
B. Finance
C. Retail
D. Education

Q 9. What is the purpose of a recommendation system in AI applications?
A. Identifying Security Threats
B. Automating Repetitive Tasks
C. Providing Personalized Suggestions
D. Simulating Human Emotions

Q 10. Which ethical consideration is crucial in the development of AI tools to avoid biased outcomes?
A. Security
B. Fairness
C. Efficiency
D. Transparency

Exercise 2 – True/ False

Q 1. AI tools are designed to replace human intelligence in all aspects of decision-making.
Q 2. Machine Learning is a subfield of AI that focuses on creating systems capable of learning from experience.
Q 3. Narrow AI, also known as Weak AI, is designed to perform a wide range of tasks without human intervention.

Q 4. Natural Language Processing (NLP) is the ability of a computer to understand, interpret, and generate human-like language.
Q 5. Deep Learning refers to the use of shallow neural networks with a limited number of layers.
Q 6. Supervised Learning is a type of machine learning where the algorithm learns from labeled training data.
Q 7. Quantum Computing is not closely related to AI, and the two fields operate independently.
Q 8. Chatbots and virtual assistants are examples of AI applications that do not involve Natural Language Processing.
Q 9. Bias in AI algorithms is an ethical consideration that developers need to address to ensure fair outcomes.
Q 10. Edge Computing involves processing data on centralized servers, away from the source of data generation.

Exercise 3 – Fill in the blanks
Q 1. Introduction to AI Tools welcomes users to the world of AI ____________.
Q 2. The overarching impact of AI on writing, coding, meetings, design, video, customer support, and HR is ____________.
Q 3. In healthcare and medicine, Gemini AI improves patient care, diagnoses diseases, and identifies potential ____________ with its advanced analytics.
Q 4. Gemini AI's Natural Language Processing enables users to effortlessly analyze and understand ____________ language in textual data.
Q 5. The Gemini AI tool is a game-changer, empowering individuals and organizations across various industries to elevate their ____________-making process.

Exercise 4 – Match case

1. Evolution of AI in Various Domains	A. Detailed analysis of AI tools in various domains
2. Impact of AI on Writing, Coding, Meetings, Design, Video, Customer Support, and HR	B. Historical development of AI within specific fields
3. Overview of AI Tools in Different Fields	C. Extends to various domains such as writing, coding, meetings, design, video, customer support, and HR
4. Introduction to AI Tools	D. Introduction to the world of AI tools
5. Create stunning visual representations of data for effective interpretation and communication.	E. Data Visualization

Exercise 5 – One word answer
Q 1. What is the focus of "Evolution of AI in Various Domains"?
Q 2. What is the primary influence of AI on various domains, according to the information?
Q 3. What kind of algorithms does Gemini AI leverage for solving complex problems?
Q 4. What does Natural Language Processing in Gemini AI enable users to analyze and understand effortlessly?
Q 5. What type of representations does Gemini AI help create for data in order to enhance interpretation?

Exercise 6 – Small answer
Q 1. What is the main theme of "Introduction to AI Tools"?
Q 2. What is the overall impact of AI on writing and coding?
Q 3. How can users get started with the Gemini AI tool?
Q 4. What is a key benefit of using Gemini AI?
Q 5. Name a use case where Gemini AI is applied in the financial industry.

Exercise 7 – Long answer
Q 1. Can you elaborate on the significance of "Evolution of AI in Various Domains" and its focus on historical development?
Q 2. How does "Overview of AI Tools in Different Fields" contribute to our understanding of AI tools, and what specific domains are covered?

Answers

Exercise 1 – MCQ
Ans: 1 C, 2 C, 3 D, 4 A, 5 D, 6 D, 7 D, 8 B, 9 C, 10 B

Exercise 2 – True/ False

Ans: 1 False, 2 True, 3 False, 4 True, 5 False, 6 True, 7 False, 8 False, 9 True, 10 False

Exercise 3 – Fill in the blanks

Ans: 1 Tools, 2 Diverse, 3 outbreaks, 4 human, 5 decision

Exercise 4 – Match case

Ans: 1 B, 2 C, 3 A, 4 D, 5 E

Exercise 5 – One word answer

Ans: 1 Historical, 2 Extension, 3 Deep Learning, 4 Language, 5 Visual

ONLINE RESOURCES

Practice Paper

Link https://forms.office.com/r/VHHdgTeP1E

QR Code

Video Content

Link https://www.youtube.com/playlist?list=PLzlh_31VWEFoGW10fGOcJlZBAhD9JtUwM

QR Code

Chapter 2: ChatGPT

2.1 Background and Overview

ChatGPT represents a milestone in the evolution of natural language processing (NLP) and artificial intelligence, developed by OpenAI. Building upon the success of its predecessor, GPT-3 (Generative Pre-trained Transformer 3), ChatGPT is designed to engage in dynamic and context-aware conversations, making it a powerful tool for a wide range of applications.

Background:

The foundation of ChatGPT lies in the continuous advancements in deep learning and transformer-based architectures. OpenAI's GPT series, which includes models like GPT-2 and GPT-3, has played a pivotal role in shaping the capabilities of language models. These models are pre-trained on vast datasets, learning intricate language patterns, context, and semantics from diverse sources on the internet. The success of GPT models paved the way for the development of ChatGPT, focusing specifically on improving conversational abilities.

Overview:

This writing tool uses artificial intelligence to create practically *anything*. Engage in conversation, explain complex topics, assist in research, and create content of any kind—even generate code. Its interface is simple in a "what you see is what you get" kind of way, but there's a lot going on beneath the surface to make ChatGPT so versatile and useful.

Introduction: ChatGPT, developed by OpenAI, represents a significant advancement in the field of natural language processing (NLP) and conversational artificial intelligence (AI). It is an iteration of the GPT (Generative Pre-trained Transformer) architecture, showcasing OpenAI's commitment to pushing the boundaries of AI capabilities. As of my last knowledge update in January 2022, ChatGPT has been designed to generate human-like text responses, making it a powerful tool for various applications.

ChatGPT is a language model that excels in understanding and generating human-like text in a conversational context. Unlike traditional chatbots that often produce rigid responses, ChatGPT leverages its extensive pre-training to provide nuanced and contextually relevant replies. It incorporates a transformer-based architecture, enabling it to capture long-range dependencies in text and exhibit a remarkable understanding of the intricacies of human language.

Key Components:

1. **Transformer Architecture:** ChatGPT's architecture is built upon transformers, which have proven to be highly effective in capturing contextual relationships in language. This architecture enables the model to process information in parallel, making it efficient in handling conversational nuances.
2. **Pre-training on Diverse Data:** The model undergoes pre-training on a diverse range of internet data, absorbing linguistic patterns, nuances, and contextual understanding. This extensive exposure contributes to its ability to generate coherent and context-aware responses.
3. **Fine-Tuning:** ChatGPT undergoes fine-tuning to enhance its performance for specific applications or domains. This process tailors the model to exhibit specialized behavior, making it adaptable for a variety of tasks.
4. **Dynamic Conversational Context:** What sets ChatGPT apart is its focus on dynamic conversations. It aims to provide responses that are not only accurate but also contextually appropriate, allowing for more natural and engaging interactions.

Applications:

ChatGPT finds applications in various domains, including customer support, content creation, language translation, and educational tools. Its versatility stems from its ability to adapt to different conversational scenarios, making it a valuable asset in both professional and personal contexts.

Ethical Considerations:

As with any advanced AI model, there are ethical considerations. OpenAI emphasizes responsible AI use and has implemented safety measures to mitigate potential risks, such as reducing biased behavior and avoiding inappropriate requests.

2.2 Key Features of ChatGPT

Here are the key features of ChatGPT:

1. **Context-Aware Conversations:** ChatGPT is designed to engage in dynamic conversations with a keen understanding of context. It processes and remembers the entire conversation, allowing it to generate responses that are not only contextually relevant but also coherent and natural. This context-awareness contributes to more fluid and human-like interactions.

2. Natural Language Understanding: One of the standout features of ChatGPT is its natural language understanding. It can comprehend the nuances of user inputs, deciphering the meaning behind complex sentences and accurately responding to a wide range of queries. This capability is crucial for creating a seamless and user-friendly conversational experience.

3. Text Generation: ChatGPT excels in text generation, producing coherent and contextually appropriate responses. Whether it's crafting creative content, answering s, or providing information, the model leverages its pre-trained knowledge to generate human-like text that aligns with the conversational context.

4. Multiturn Conversations: Unlike traditional chatbots that may struggle with multiturn conversations, ChatGPT is proficient in handling extended dialogues. It maintains a coherent thread of conversation, considering the full context of previous interactions. This makes it well-suited for applications where sustained engagement is crucial.

5. Versatility Across Domains: ChatGPT is versatile and adaptable across various domains and industries. Its language understanding and generation capabilities make it applicable in customer support, content creation, education, and more. This versatility is a testament to the model's ability to cater to diverse user needs and scenarios.

6. Transformer Architecture: Built on the transformer architecture, ChatGPT benefits from its ability to capture long-range dependencies in text. The transformer architecture enables efficient processing of information in parallel, making the model effective in understanding and generating complex conversational patterns.

7. Fine-Tuning for Specialized Tasks: ChatGPT undergoes fine-tuning to enhance its performance for specific tasks or domains. This process allows developers to tailor the model for specialized behavior, ensuring that it meets the requirements of diverse applications.

8. Dynamic Responses to User Inputs: User inputs can vary widely, and ChatGPT excels in dynamically responding to different prompts. Whether the input is a , a command, or a creative prompt, the model generates responses that align with the user's intent, showcasing its flexibility and adaptability.

9. User-Friendly Interactions: The user interface of ChatGPT is designed for user-friendly interactions. It allows users to have a conversation with the model in a simple and intuitive manner, contributing to a positive user experience.

10. Ongoing Research and Improvements: OpenAI emphasizes ongoing research and iterative improvements to enhance the capabilities and safety of ChatGPT. This commitment ensures that the model evolves with advancements in the field and continues to meet user expectations for high-quality conversational AI.

2.2.1 Language Understanding

Language understanding is a fundamental aspect of ChatGPT's capabilities, playing a pivotal role in its effectiveness across various applications. In this section, we delve into how ChatGPT excels in comprehending the nuances of human language, making it a versatile and powerful tool for diverse conversational scenarios.

1. Contextual Understanding:

ChatGPT is designed to understand language in context. Unlike traditional chatbots that might interpret each input in isolation, ChatGPT considers the entire conversation history. This contextual understanding allows the model to generate responses that are not only grammatically correct but also contextually relevant, contributing to a more natural and coherent conversation.

2. Semantics and Meaning Extraction:

Beyond mere syntactic understanding, ChatGPT excels in extracting the semantics and meaning embedded in user inputs. It can decipher the intent behind complex sentences, identify entities, and grasp the subtleties of language, enabling it to provide accurate and meaningful responses.

3. Handling Ambiguity:

Human language is often ambiguous, and understanding context is crucial for disambiguating meanings. ChatGPT tackles ambiguity by considering the broader conversation context. It leverages its pre-trained knowledge to discern the most likely interpretation of ambiguous phrases or words, ensuring more precise and relevant responses.

4. User Intent Recognition:

Recognizing user intent is a key component of language understanding. ChatGPT is adept at discerning the intent behind user inputs, whether it's a request for information, a command, or a casual conversation. This allows the model to tailor its responses to align with the user's goals and expectations.

5. Adaptability to User Style:

ChatGPT can adapt to diverse writing styles and linguistic preferences. Whether a user communicates formally or informally, in a technical or casual manner, the model adjusts its understanding to match the user's style. This adaptability enhances the user experience by creating a more personalized and engaging interaction.

6. Handling Complex Queries:

The model's language understanding capabilities shine when handling complex queries and multipart s. It can dissect intricate sentences, address multiple aspects within a single query, and maintain a coherent understanding of the overarching topic, facilitating in-depth and nuanced conversations.

7. Continuous Learning and Improvement:

While ChatGPT is pre-trained on a vast dataset, it also has the ability to learn from user interactions. The model continuously refines its understanding based on new inputs and adapts to evolving language patterns. This iterative learning process contributes to ongoing improvements in its language understanding capabilities.

8. Multilingual Competence:

ChatGPT's language understanding extends beyond English to multiple languages, showcasing its multilingual competence. This feature broadens its applicability, allowing users from different linguistic backgrounds to engage in conversations with the model.

2.2.2 Text Generation

Text generation is one of the cornerstone capabilities of ChatGPT, showcasing its ability to generate human-like and contextually relevant content in a variety of conversational scenarios. In this feature, we delve into the intricacies of ChatGPT's text generation and explore its implications for content creation and other language-related tasks.

1. Contextual Understanding:

ChatGPT's text generation capabilities are underpinned by its exceptional contextual understanding. Unlike simpler language models, ChatGPT processes input text holistically, taking into account the entire conversation history. This contextual awareness allows it to generate responses that are not only grammatically correct but also contextually coherent, maintaining the flow of the conversation.

2. Coherent and Natural Responses:

The model excels in crafting responses that mimic natural language patterns. It goes beyond mere grammatical correctness, considering the tone, style, and nuances present in the input. This results in coherent and contextually relevant responses that contribute to more engaging and human-like interactions.

3. Adaptable to Various Prompts:

Whether the input is a , a command, or a creative prompt, ChatGPT adapts to generate responses that align with the user's intent. Its versatility in handling diverse prompts makes it suitable for a wide array of language-related tasks, from answering queries to generating creative content.

4. Creative Content Creation:

ChatGPT's text generation capabilities have broad implications for content creation. Writers, marketers, and content creators can leverage the model to ideate, draft, and refine content for various purposes. From blog articles and marketing copy to creative writing, ChatGPT serves as a valuable assistant in the content creation process.

5. Language Variation and Style Matching:

The model is adept at capturing and replicating different language variations and styles. Whether it's formal language for professional contexts or more casual language for informal conversations, ChatGPT adjusts its output to match the desired tone and style specified by the user.

6. Context Retention Across Turns:

A notable feature of ChatGPT's text generation is its ability to retain context across multiple turns in a conversation. Each response is influenced by the entire conversation history, allowing the model to provide responses that not only make sense within the current context but also align with the preceding interactions.

7. Applications in Content Editing:

Beyond content creation, ChatGPT can also be utilized for content editing. Users can seek suggestions for rephrasing sentences, improving clarity, or enhancing the overall quality of written material. This makes it a valuable tool for refining and polishing text.

8. Continuous Learning and Adaptation:

ChatGPT's text generation capabilities are enhanced by its continuous learning and adaptation. The model is regularly updated and refined based on user interactions and feedback. This iterative improvement process ensures that ChatGPT stays current and effective in meeting user expectations.

9. Considerations for Accuracy and Ethical Use:

While ChatGPT's text generation is powerful, users should exercise caution and review the output for accuracy. It's essential to be mindful of ethical considerations, ensuring that the generated content aligns with ethical standards and does not promote misinformation or harmful messages.

2.2.3 Context Awareness

Context awareness is a fundamental aspect of ChatGPT that elevates its capabilities in engaging, dynamic conversations. This unique trait enables the model to maintain coherence and relevance throughout a conversation or text, allowing it to understand and respond to user inputs with a depth that goes beyond individual messages. Understanding context is pivotal for accurate and meaningful interactions, and ChatGPT excels in this area through the following mechanisms:

1. **Retaining Conversation History:** ChatGPT has the ability to retain and reference the entire history of a conversation. Unlike traditional chatbots that may only consider the latest input, ChatGPT stores and processes the full context. This includes user queries, system responses, and any other relevant information exchanged during the conversation.
2. **Long-Term Dependency Handling:** The model is designed to capture and understand long-term dependencies within a conversation. It doesn't just respond to the immediate input but considers the broader context of the dialogue. This allows ChatGPT to generate responses that align with the evolving narrative, providing a more coherent and natural conversation flow.
3. **User Prompt Understanding:** Context awareness in ChatGPT involves a deep understanding of user prompts. The model is trained to interpret and analyze user inputs in the context of the ongoing conversation. It identifies the intent behind each message and tailors its responses accordingly, contributing to more accurate and contextually relevant interactions.
4. **Dynamic Context Updating:** As the conversation progresses, ChatGPT dynamically updates its understanding of context. It adapts to changes in user intent, references previous messages, and incorporates new information to generate responses that align with the evolving discourse. This adaptability enhances the model's ability to generate contextually aware and situation-specific replies.
5. **Handling Ambiguity and Clarification:** ChatGPT is equipped to handle ambiguity and seek clarification when faced with unclear or ambiguous user inputs. It leverages context to make informed interpretations and, if necessary, prompts users for additional details to ensure accurate and meaningful responses.
6. **Conversational Coherence:** The focus on context awareness contributes to maintaining conversational coherence. ChatGPT's responses feel more natural and connected to the ongoing dialogue, resulting in interactions that resemble human-like conversations. This coherence enhances the user experience by providing meaningful and contextually relevant replies.
7. **Adaptability Across Domains:** The context awareness of ChatGPT makes it adaptable across various domains and topics. It can seamlessly transition between subjects, leveraging the context of the conversation to generate responses that align with the user's expectations and the conversational history.

2.2.4 Multimodal Capabilities

ChatGPT's multimodal capabilities represent a significant stride in expanding the model's proficiency beyond processing and generating text alone. This feature allows ChatGPT to process and understand multiple forms of data, including text, images, and potentially audio, opening up new possibilities for diverse and enriched user interactions.

1. **Text Understanding and Generation:** While the multimodal focus encompasses various data types, ChatGPT's foundation lies in its mastery of natural language understanding and generation. It excels in comprehending the nuances of textual input, producing coherent and contextually relevant responses. This ensures a strong base for conversations, even when other modalities are introduced.
2. **Image Processing:** One of the notable extensions of ChatGPT's capabilities is its ability to process and understand images. Users can input images along with text, allowing the model to consider visual information in its responses. This is particularly valuable in applications where textual descriptions alone might be insufficient, such as in content creation, image interpretation, or generating captions.
3. **Versatility in Applications:** The multimodal approach significantly enhances ChatGPT's versatility across various applications. For instance, in content creation, users can describe images they have in mind, and ChatGPT can generate corresponding text. In educational tools, the model can respond to queries related to visual content, providing a more comprehensive learning experience.
4. **Potential for Audio Input:** While the specific details may vary, the multimodal capabilities of ChatGPT may extend to audio processing. This could enable users to incorporate spoken language in their interactions with the model, broadening the scope of applications to include voice-based commands, language learning with pronunciation feedback, or even creative projects involving both text and audio elements.
5. **Enriching User Interactions:** The multimodal capabilities contribute to more immersive and enriched user interactions. Users can provide a combination of inputs, fostering a dynamic exchange of information. This enriches the overall conversational experience and opens avenues for creative collaboration between users and the model.

6. Contextual Understanding Across Modalities: ChatGPT's strength lies in its ability to maintain context across modalities. Whether transitioning from textual to visual input, the model retains an understanding of the ongoing conversation. This contextual awareness ensures coherent and meaningful responses, enhancing the overall quality of multimodal interactions.

7. Challenges and Considerations: While the multimodal capabilities of ChatGPT offer exciting possibilities, there are challenges to be addressed. Ensuring accurate interpretation of diverse inputs, handling potential biases in multimodal data, and refining the model's response generation for varied modalities are areas of ongoing research and improvement.

2.3 Applications of ChatGPT

ChatGPT, developed by OpenAI, has garnered attention for its advanced conversational abilities, opening up a plethora of applications across various domains. Its natural language understanding, context-awareness, and versatile responses make it a valuable tool in different fields. Here are some key applications of ChatGPT:

2.3.1 Conversational Agents and Chatbots

ChatGPT serves as a foundational technology for creating conversational agents and chatbots. Businesses can deploy these agents for customer support, guiding users through processes, and answering frequently asked s. The model's ability to comprehend user queries and provide relevant responses contributes to more effective and engaging interactions.

2.3.2 Content Creation and Writing Assistance

Writers, content creators, and professionals can leverage ChatGPT for content creation and writing assistance. The model generates ideas, refines language, and offers creative input, aiding users in overcoming writer's block and enhancing the overall quality of written content.

2.3.3 Customer Support Automation

In the realm of customer support, ChatGPT plays a crucial role in automating responses to user queries. It can provide instant and accurate information, troubleshoot common issues, and guide users through processes. This not only improves efficiency but also ensures consistent and reliable customer interactions.

2.3.4 Language Translation

ChatGPT's language understanding capabilities extend to translation tasks. It can assist in translating text from one language to another, facilitating cross-cultural communication and breaking down language barriers. This application is valuable for individuals and businesses operating in a global context.

2.3.5 Educational Tools

Within educational settings, ChatGPT can be employed to create interactive and engaging tools. It can serve as a virtual tutor, providing explanations, answering s, and facilitating learning in various subjects. The model's adaptability makes it a versatile educational companion.

2.4 How ChatGPT Works

Here's a step-by-step explanation:

1. Create an Account:

If the platform or application requires an account, you may need to sign up. This usually involves providing an email address, creating a username, and setting a password.

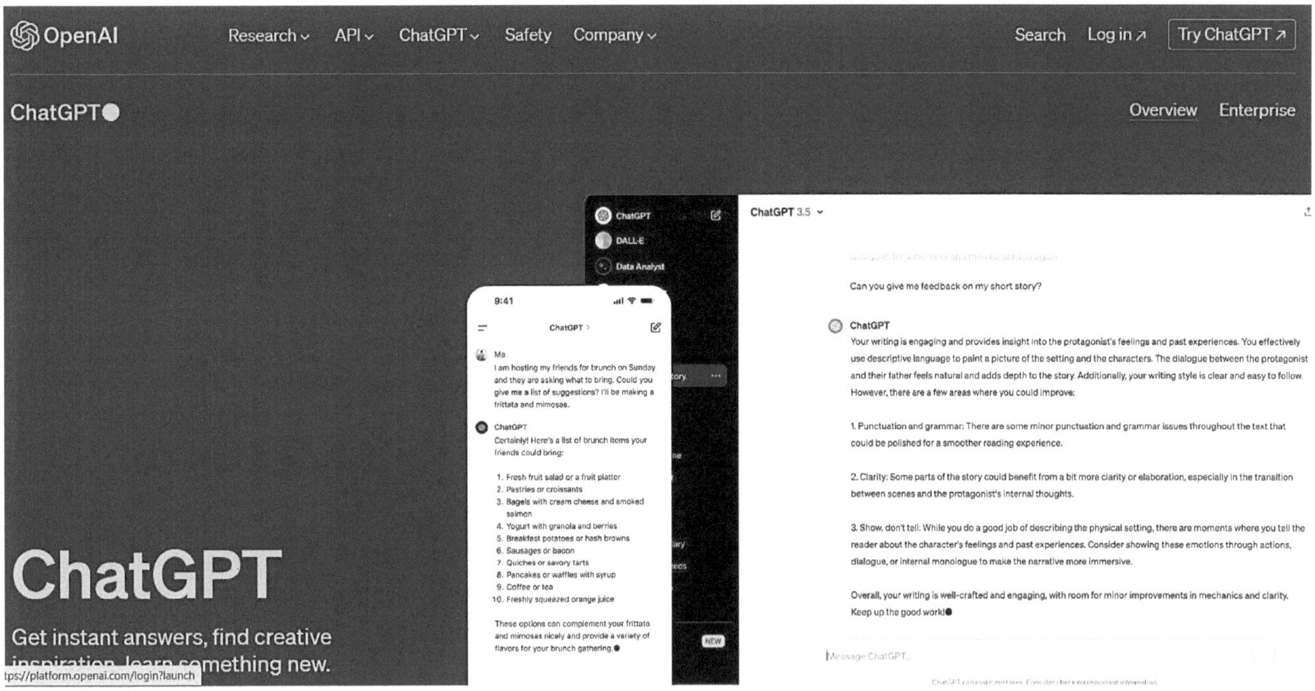

2. You can choose either Chatgpt or API.

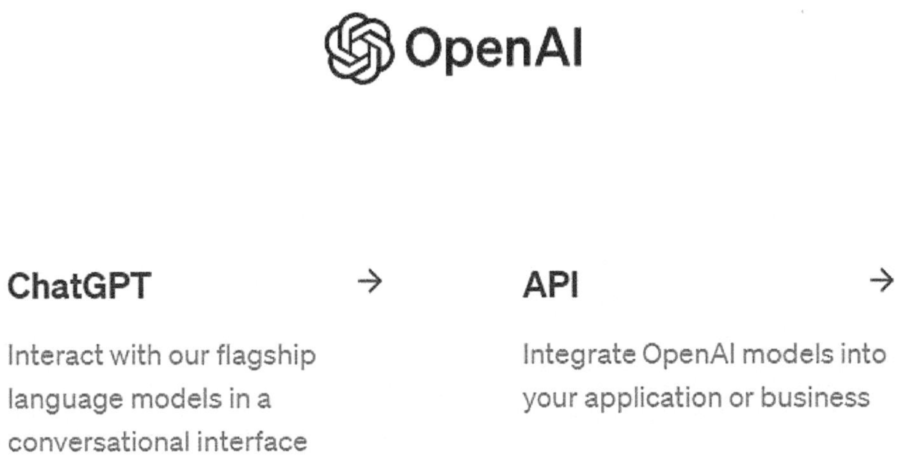

3. Login to Your Account:

1. After creating an account, log in using your credentials. This might involve entering your username or email and password.

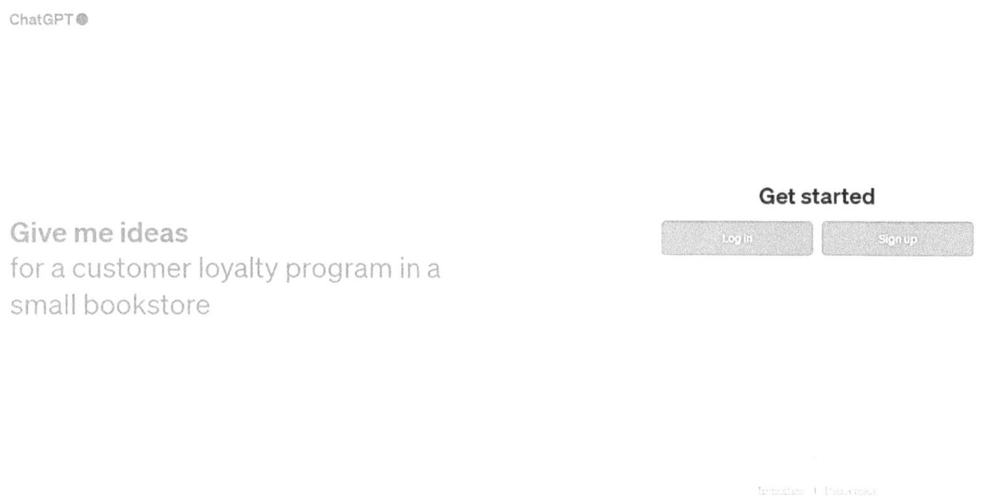

4. You Enter the Email Id and password and then you click the continue button.

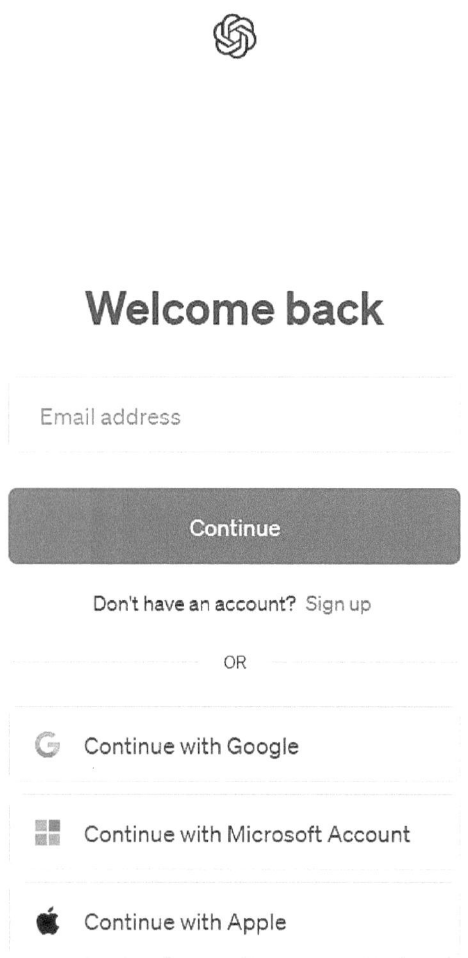

Access the ChatGPT Interface:
1. Once logged in, navigate to the section or interface where ChatGPT is implemented. This could be a chat window or another type of interface.

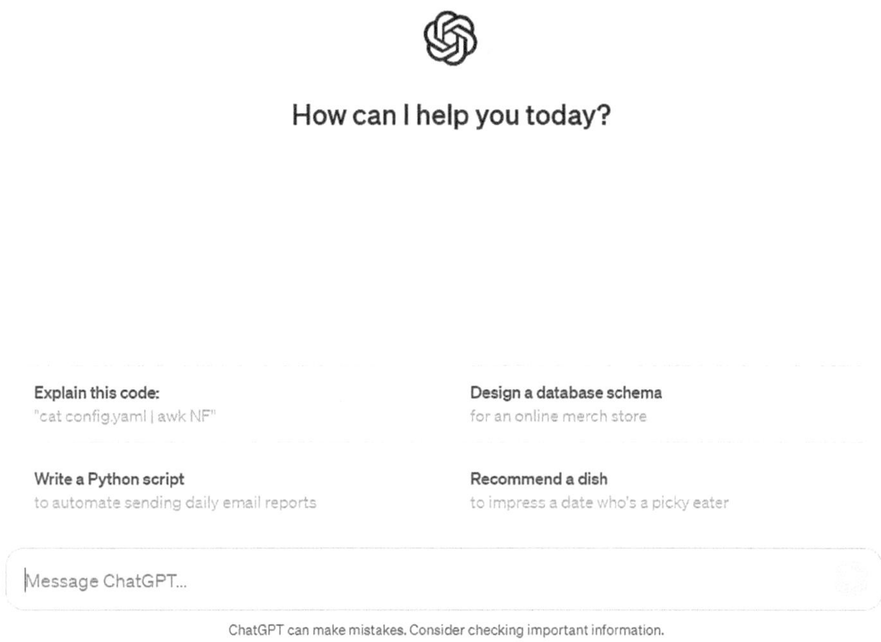

Start a Conversation:
1. Initiate a conversation by typing a message or a prompt. This is the input that the ChatGPT model will respond to.

2.4.1 Training Data and Datasets

ChatGPT is trained on diverse and extensive datasets to develop a broad understanding of language and context. OpenAI, the organization behind ChatGPT, utilizes a two-step process for training the model: pre-training and fine-tuning.

1. Pre-training: During the pre-training phase, ChatGPT is exposed to a massive corpus of publicly available text from the internet. The model learns to predict the next word in a sentence, acquiring an understanding of grammar, syntax, and contextual relationships. This pre-training phase is crucial for instilling general language knowledge and enables the model to generate coherent and contextually relevant text.

2. Fine-tuning: After pre-training, ChatGPT undergoes a fine-tuning process on custom datasets created by OpenAI. This step refines the model for specific applications and ensures that it aligns with OpenAI's goals and guidelines. Fine-tuning allows ChatGPT to exhibit more controlled behavior and adapt to specific use cases, making it more suitable for practical applications.

Considerations for Dataset Usage:

1. Diversity: The pre-training datasets are intentionally diverse to expose the model to a wide range of linguistic patterns, topics, and writing styles. This diversity helps ChatGPT develop a comprehensive understanding of language, enabling it to handle various user inputs.

2. Quality Control: OpenAI employs measures to filter and control the quality of training data. This involves excluding certain types of content or sources that may introduce biases or inappropriate behavior. The organization is committed to addressing concerns related to biases and ethical considerations.

3. Fine-Tuning for Specific Tasks: Fine-tuning involves training the model on custom datasets created by OpenAI to tailor its behavior for specific applications. This step is essential for ensuring that ChatGPT aligns with user expectations and adheres to ethical guidelines.

2.4.2 Fine-Tuning Process

The fine-tuning process in ChatGPT is a critical step that follows the initial pre-training phase. Fine-tuning allows OpenAI to customize the behavior of ChatGPT for specific use cases, ensuring that the model aligns with ethical guidelines, user expectations, and desired functionalities. Here is an overview of the fine-tuning process in ChatGPT:

1. Pre-training Setup:
2. Before fine-tuning, ChatGPT undergoes extensive pre-training on a diverse range of publicly available text from the internet. This initial phase helps the model develop a general understanding of language, syntax, and context.
3. Custom Dataset Creation:
4. OpenAI creates custom datasets for fine-tuning. These datasets are carefully curated and designed to address specific tasks or domains. The content of these datasets helps shape the model's behavior for practical applications.
5. Task-Specific Objectives:
6. During fine-tuning, the model is trained to perform task-specific objectives. For example, if ChatGPT is intended for customer support or code generation, the fine-tuning process focuses on refining the model's ability to generate contextually appropriate and relevant responses in those specific domains.
7. Adjusting Model Parameters:
8. Model parameters, such as weights and biases, are adjusted during fine-tuning to optimize the model's performance for the intended application. This involves modifying the model's internal representations to better align with the desired output.
9. Iterative Process:
10. Fine-tuning is often an iterative process. OpenAI conducts multiple rounds of fine-tuning, evaluating the model's performance and adjusting parameters to achieve the desired behavior. This iterative approach allows for continual improvement.
11. Addressing Biases and Ethical Considerations:
12. OpenAI actively works to address biases and ethical considerations during the fine-tuning process. This includes implementing measures to minimize biased behavior, preventing inappropriate outputs, and refining the model's responses to adhere to ethical standards.
13. User Feedback Incorporation:
14. OpenAI values user feedback to improve the model's behavior. Users are encouraged to provide feedback on problematic outputs or biases, and this information is used to make adjustments to the fine-tuning process.
15. Release and Deployment:
16. Once the fine-tuning process is complete and the model meets the desired standards, OpenAI releases the model for deployment. This can involve offering access to the model through APIs, making it available for developers to integrate into their applications.

2.4.3 Inference and Generation

In ChatGPT, the inference and generation process is the phase where the model takes user inputs and generates responses. This process involves applying the trained model to new, unseen data and producing output based on the learned patterns and context. Here's an overview of the inference and generation process in ChatGPT:

1. User Input:
2. The process begins with a user providing input to ChatGPT. This input can be a prompt, , or any textual information the user wants the model to respond to or generate content about.
3. Tokenization:
4. The input text is tokenized, meaning it is broken down into smaller units called tokens. Tokens can be words, subwords, or characters, depending on the tokenization scheme used during training.
5. Context Processing:
6. ChatGPT processes the input in the context of the conversation. Unlike single-turn models, ChatGPT maintains context over multiple turns, allowing it to consider the entire conversation history and generate responses that are contextually relevant.
7. Attention Mechanism:
8. The model uses attention mechanisms to assign different weights to different parts of the input sequence. This enables ChatGPT to focus on relevant information while generating responses, capturing long-range dependencies and context.
9. Probability Distribution:
10. After processing the input, ChatGPT generates a probability distribution over the vocabulary for the next token in the sequence. This distribution is based on the learned patterns during training and the contextual information provided by the input.
11. Sampling or Beam Search:
12. To generate the actual response, ChatGPT employs either sampling or beam search. Sampling involves randomly selecting a token from the probability distribution, introducing an element of creativity to the responses. Beam search, on the other hand, considers multiple possibilities and selects the most probable sequence of tokens.
13. Output Generation:
14. The selected tokens are concatenated to form the model's output. This output is the generated response to the user's input. The length of the output can be controlled based on the desired response length or the model's predefined maximum token limit.
15. Dynamic Conversational Context:
16. ChatGPT excels in maintaining a dynamic conversational context. It remembers and considers the entire history of the conversation, allowing for coherent and contextually aware responses. This context-awareness is a key feature that sets ChatGPT apart in conversational AI.
17. Real-time Interaction:
18. The inference and generation process happens in real-time, enabling users to interact with ChatGPT dynamically. As users input new information or queries, the model adapts its responses based on the evolving conversation context.
19. Post-Processing:
20. The generated output may undergo post-processing steps to ensure grammatical correctness and coherence. OpenAI implements measures to refine the model's outputs and improve the overall quality of generated text.

Exercise

Exercise 1 – MCQ

Q 1. What is ChatGPT?

A. Computer Hardware
B. Natural Language Processing Model
C. Robotics Technology
D. Programming Language

Q 2. Which organization developed ChatGPT?

A. Google
B. Microsoft
C. OpenAI
D. IBM

Q 3. What architecture is ChatGPT based on?

A. RNN (Recurrent Neural Network)
B. CNN (Convolutional Neural Network)
C. Transformer
D. LSTM (Long Short-Term Memory)

Q 4. How was ChatGPT trained initially?
A. Supervised Learning
B. Reinforcement Learning
C. Unsupervised Learning
D. Semi-Supervised Learning

Q 5. What is the primary purpose of ChatGPT?
A. Image Recognition
B. Speech Synthesis
C. Natural Language Understanding and Generation
D. Autonomous Driving

Q 6. What is the maximum token limit for a single interaction with ChatGPT as of the latest model (GPT-3.5)?
A. 1,024 tokens
B. 5,000 tokens
C. 10,000 tokens
D. 50,000 tokens

Q 7. How does ChatGPT handle sensitive or private information?
A. It stores information permanently.
B. It automatically anonymizes sensitive data.
C. It deletes all information after each interaction.
D. It shares information with third parties.

Q 8. Which version of the GPT series is ChatGPT based on?
A. GPT-1
B. GPT-2
C. GPT-3
D. GPT-4

Q 9. What programming language is primarily used for interfacing with ChatGPT API?
A. Java
B. Python
C. C++
D. JavaScript

Q 10. Can ChatGPT be fine-tuned by individual users as of the latest information?
A. Yes
B. No

Exercise 2 – True/ False

Q 1. ChatGPT is based on a transformer architecture.
Q 2. GPT-3.5, the latest version of ChatGPT, has a token limit of 10,000 tokens per interaction.
Q 3. ChatGPT primarily uses a supervised learning approach during its training process.
Q 4. Users can fine-tune ChatGPT to customize its behavior for specific applications.
Q 5. ChatGPT handles sensitive or private information by permanently storing it for future interactions.
Q 6. The underlying model architecture of ChatGPT, GPT-3, has fewer parameters than its predecessor, GPT-2.
Q 7. ChatGPT can perform tasks beyond natural language understanding and generation, such as image recognition.
Q 8. Developers can interact with ChatGPT using various programming languages, not limited to Python.
Q 9. ChatGPT is designed to keep a long-term memory of user interactions between conversations.
Q 10. ChatGPT is a product developed by IBM.

Exercise 3 – Fill in the blanks

Q 1. The main application of ChatGPT is natural language ________.
Q 2. ChatGPT's ability to generate human-like text responses is a result of its training with diverse and massive amounts of ________ data.
Q 3. ChatGPT's responses are influenced by the context provided in the ____________.
Q 4. The training of ChatGPT involves exposure to a diverse range of data to ensure ____________ understanding.
Q 5. OpenAI released ChatGPT to the public to gather user feedback and ____________ the model.

Exercise 4 – Match case

1. ChatGPT's underlying architecture	A. Artificial intelligence
2. ChatGPT's primary training approach	B. GPT-3
3. The main application of ChatGPT	C. Natural language conversation
4. The organization behind ChatGPT's development	D. OpenAI
5. ChatGPT's proficiency in generating human-like text	E. Unsupervised learning

Exercise 5 – One word answer

Q 1. What role does OpenAI play in the AI landscape?
Q 2. What kind of learning does ChatGPT undergo during training?
Q 3. What organization developed ChatGPT?
Q 4. How does users interact with ChatGPT?
Q 5. What influences ChatGPT's responses?

Exercise 6 – Small answer

Q 1. Who developed ChatGPT?
Q 2. How was ChatGPT primarily trained?
Q 3. What kind of patterns does ChatGPT use for text generation?
Q 4. Where can users experiment with ChatGPT's capabilities?
Q 5. What is the primary focus of ChatGPT's training?

Exercise 7 – Long answer

Q 1. Can you provide a detailed overview of the architecture on which ChatGPT is based?
Q 2. How was ChatGPT primarily trained, and what role does unsupervised learning play in its development?

Answers

Exercise 1 – MCQ

Ans: 1 B, 2 C, 3 C, 4 A, 5 C, 6 B, 7 C, 8 C, 9 B, 10 B

Exercise 2 – True/ False

Ans: 1True, 2 False, 3 False ,4 False ,5 False ,6 False ,7 False ,8 False ,9 False ,10 False

Exercise 3 – Fill in the blanks

Ans: 1 Conversation, 2 Textual, 3 Conversation, 4 Broad, 5 Improve

Exercise 4 – Match case

Ans: 1 E, 2 C, 3 D, 4 B, 5 A

Exercise 5 – One word answer

Ans: 1 AI research advancement, 2 Unsupervised, 3 Open AI, 4 Text, 5 Context

ONLINE RESOURCES

Practice Paper
Link
https://forms.office.com/r/9W80Eu4H7C
QR Code

Video Content
Link
https://www.youtube.com/playlist?list=PLzlh_31VWEFoLzaqayq06GM8O1ihO5enq
QR Code

Chapter 3: Bard AI: Understanding, Design, and Impact

3.1 Introduction

Bard is a generative AI developed by Google that uses machine learning and natural language processing techniques to generate human-like text responses to various prompts. The model is designed to mimic the style and structure of human writing. In order to do so, Bard was trained on a massive text-based data set and uses a deep neural network architecture, called transformers, to learn patterns in language, understand the context of the input text and generate appropriate output.

Bard is capable of generating contextually correct responses on a wide variety of topics including science, math, history, literature and religion. One of Bard's features is its ability to engage in multi-turn conversations wherein the AI can maintain a consistent topic and persona across multiple exchanges with a human user. This makes Bard particularly useful for applications like chatbots and virtual assistants.

Bard's ability to generate creative writing also has potential for website content generation or social media posts, thereby freeing up time for content creators to focus on other high-level tasks. Furthermore, we can use Bard as a tool for language learners to practice writing in a specific language because Bard can generate output in multiple languages and styles.

3.1.1 Background

Origins:

1. Conceptualized in 2022: Google AI was already deeply invested in large language models like LaMDA when the idea for Bard took root.
2. Initial codename: "Atlas" was the first internal name for the project, reflecting its ambitious nature.
3. 2023 - LaMDA to PaLM to Gemini: Bard initially ran on LaMDA, but quickly transitioned to the more powerful PaLM and later, Gemini, showcasing Google's rapid advancements in LLM technology.

Development and Release:

1. March 2023 - Limited launch: Recognizing the growing popularity of AI chatbots like OpenAI's ChatGPT, Google launched Bard in a limited capacity to gather feedback and refine its capabilities.
2. Initial reception: Reviews were mixed, with some praising its factual accuracy and others criticizing its lack of originality and personality.

3. Continuous improvements: Google AI actively iterated on Bard based on user feedback, gradually expanding its capabilities and addressing limitations.
4. May 2023 - Wider release: After months of refinement, Bard became available to a broader audience, gradually rolling out to more countries.

Current state:
1. Experimental phase: Bard is still considered an experiment, allowing Google AI to learn from user interactions and refine its approach to generative AI.
2. Focus on collaboration: Unlike some chatbots that mimic human conversation, Bard is designed as a collaborative tool, aiming to augment human creativity and productivity.
3. Evolving capabilities: Bard's features and functionalities are constantly being updated and expanded, with Google emphasizing responsible development and adherence to AI principles.
In essence, Bard's background reflects Google AI's commitment to pushing the boundaries of large language models. It's a constantly evolving platform designed to explore the potential of AI collaboration and empower users in various ways.

3.1.2 Purpose

Here are some of its key aims:
1. Information access and understanding:
- Providing factual and informative answers: Bard seeks to be a reliable source of information, drawing from its vast knowledge base and the power of Google Search to answer your s in a comprehensive and informative way.
- Summarizing complex topics: Bard can simplify complex information and present it in a clear and concise manner, making it easier to grasp new concepts and ideas.
- Multilingual communication: Bard understands and speaks multiple languages, facilitating communication and information access across various linguistic barriers.

2. Creativity and productivity enhancement:
- Generating different creative text formats: Bard can assist with writing poems, code, scripts, musical pieces, emails, letters, and more, providing a spark for your creative endeavors.
- Brainstorming and idea generation: Struggling for ideas? Bard can help you brainstorm and expand on existing concepts, opening up new possibilities for your projects.
- Problem-solving and decision-making: Bard can analyze information and suggest solutions to problems, aiding in informed decision-making and navigating complex situations.

3. Collaboration and communication:
- Facilitating effective communication: Bard can help you translate languages, find the right words to express yourself, and even suggest different communication styles for diverse audiences.
- Enhancing teamwork and collaboration: Bard can support teamwork by summarizing discussions, tracking tasks, and generating reports, improving efficiency and understanding.
- Promoting accessibility and inclusivity: Bard's multilingual capabilities and ability to explain complex concepts in simpler terms can bridge communication gaps and make information accessible to a wider audience.

4. Research and development:
- Advancing large language model technology: Bard is a platform for Google AI to explore the potential of LLMs, constantly learning and improving through user interactions and feedback.
- Responsible AI development: Google emphasizes responsible AI development with Bard, focusing on factual accuracy, bias mitigation, and user safety.
- Exploring new applications for LLMs: Bard's versatility allows it to be used in various domains, from education and healthcare to entertainment and scientific research, paving the way for future applications of AI technology.

3.1.3 Scope and Limitations

Scope:
1. Vast knowledge base: Trained on a massive dataset of text and code, Bard boasts a broad understanding of the world, covering scientific facts, historical events, current affairs, and more.
2. Multilingual communication: Bard understands and speaks numerous languages, facilitating communication and knowledge exchange across different cultures.

3. Creative potential: From writing poems and scripts to generating code and musical pieces, Bard can fuel your creative endeavors and assist in expressing your ideas in diverse formats.
4. Information access and understanding: Bard can help you access and synthesize information from various sources, simplifying complex topics and providing insightful summaries.
5. Collaboration and communication: Bard can enhance teamwork by facilitating discussions, translating languages, and suggesting effective communication styles.

Limitations:
1. Accuracy and bias: While striving for factual accuracy, Bard can still be susceptible to biases present in its training data. It's crucial to critically evaluate its responses and consult additional sources for verification.
2. Originality and critical thinking: Though creative, Bard primarily generates derivative content based on its training data. It can't truly "think critically" or come up with entirely original ideas.
3. Common sense and reasoning: Understanding and applying common sense in real-world situations is still a challenge for Bard. It may struggle with implicit information or nuanced contexts.
4. Misinformation and manipulation: Like any AI tool, Bard can be misused for spreading misinformation or generating harmful content. It's important to use it responsibly and ethically.
5. Evolving nature: Bard is constantly learning and improving, but its capabilities remain under development. Some features may be limited or not yet available, and its responses can sometimes be unpredictable.

3.2. Foundations of Bard AI

Bard's foundations rest on a complex interplay of technical and philosophical pillars, each contributing to its unique capabilities and limitations. Here's a deeper dive into these foundational elements:

Technical Foundations:
1. Large Language Models (LLMs): Bard belongs to the family of LLMs, trained on massive datasets of text and code. These neural networks learn to recognize patterns and relationships within the data, enabling them to generate text, translate languages, and answer your s in a seemingly intelligent way.
2. Transformer Architecture: Bard's core architecture is based on the Transformer, a groundbreaking neural network model designed for natural language processing (NLP). This architecture allows Bard to attend to different parts of an input sequence and understand the relationships between them, crucial for comprehension and generation tasks.
3. PaLM/Gemini Model: Unlike its initial LaMDA version, Bard runs on Google's more powerful PaLM and Gemini models. These models boast a significantly higher number of parameters and advanced training techniques, contributing to Bard's improved factual accuracy, reasoning abilities, and overall performance.
4. Data Sources: Bard's vast knowledge base is built on a diverse set of sources, including books, articles, code repositories, and other forms of text and code. This broad training data allows Bard to cover a wide range of topics and domains.

Philosophical Foundations:
1. Human-AI Collaboration: Unlike some chatbots solely mimicking human conversation, Bard is designed as a collaborative tool. It aims to augment human creativity, improve productivity, and facilitate information access, rather than replace human interaction.
2. Responsible AI Development: Google emphasizes ethical considerations in Bard's development. Principles like factual accuracy, fairness, and transparency guide the model's training and application to minimize bias and potential harm.
3. Continuous Learning and Improvement: Bard is not a static entity but a constantly evolving platform. User feedback and interactions continuously shape its development, refining its capabilities and addressing limitations. This iterative approach allows Bard to adapt to changing needs and user preferences.
These foundations, both technical and philosophical, provide the bedrock for Bard's existence and evolution. Understanding these core principles offers a deeper appreciation for its capabilities and potential impacts, while also highlighting the areas of ongoing development and responsible use.

3.2.1 Understanding Artificial Intelligence

- The Language Learning Machine: At its core, Bard is a large language model (LLM). Imagine a vast library, not of books, but of text and code, encompassing articles, novels, poems, scripts, and even programing languages. Bard has devoured this library, learning the intricate patterns and relationships within language. This allows it to understand the meaning of words, sentences, and entire paragraphs, recognizing the nuances of grammar, context, and even sentiment.

- **The Power of Transformers:** But Bard isn't simply a passive reader. It utilizes a sophisticated neural network architecture called the Transformer. This network acts like a translator, deciphering the complex relationships between words within a sentence. It can attend to different parts of the input simultaneously, understanding how each word interacts with its neighbors to convey a specific meaning. This "attention" mechanism is crucial for Bard's ability to comprehend your s, translate languages, and even generate creative text formats.
- **Beyond Facts and Figures**: Though grounded in factual knowledge, Bard's intelligence extends beyond mere recall. It can reason and infer, drawing connections between seemingly disparate pieces of information. This allows it to answer open-ended s, summarize complex topics, and even brainstorm new ideas. However, it's crucial to remember that Bard's reasoning abilities are still under development. While it can analyze information and suggest solutions, its conclusions should be evaluated critically and cross-checked with other sources.
- **The Human Connection:** Unlike some AI chatbots mimicking human conversation, Bard recognizes the value of collaboration. It seeks to be a partner in your endeavors, a tool that augments your creativity and enhances your productivity. Its understanding of human language allows it to adapt its responses to your specific needs and preferences, making it a versatile companion for diverse tasks.
- **Learning and Growing**: Bard is not a static entity; it's constantly evolving with every interaction. The feedback you provide helps it refine its responses, identify areas for improvement, and even learn new things. This ongoing learning process ensures that Bard adapts to changing needs and remains relevant in a dynamic world.
- **Limitations and Biases:** Like any AI tool, Bard has its limitations. Its knowledge base, though vast, is not infinite. It can fall prey to biases present in its training data, leading to inaccuracies or skewed responses. Additionally, its understanding of common sense and real-world contexts is still under development, making it susceptible to misinterpretations in certain situations.
- **Transparency and Responsibility:** Recognizing these limitations, Google, the creators of Bard, prioritizes transparency and responsible AI development. Bard's responses are designed to be clear and understandable, highlighting the sources of its information and allowing you to assess its accuracy. Additionally, Google is committed to mitigating bias and ensuring that Bard is used ethically for the benefit of all.
- A Glimpse into the Future: Understanding the AI behind Bard offers a glimpse into the future of human-computer interaction. LLMs like Bard hold immense potential to revolutionize various fields, from education and healthcare to research and creative endeavors. The ability to access and process information, generate creative text formats, and collaborate with AI tools on complex tasks opens up exciting possibilities for human progress.

3.2.2 History and Evolution

The Birth of Bard AI: A Journey into Creative Writing and Storytelling

In the realm of artificial intelligence, the journey of Bard AI began as a response to the growing demand for innovative tools capable of harnessing the power of machine learning and natural language processing for creative endeavors. The need for a tool that could assist and inspire writers, poets, and storytellers led to the conceptualization and development of Bard AI.

Early Beginnings (Year 1-2):

The first iterations of Bard AI emerged as experimental projects within a dedicated team of AI researchers and language enthusiasts. These early versions focused on basic language generation tasks, attempting to create coherent and grammatically sound sentences based on predefined rules. These foundational models laid the groundwork for future advancements.

Introduction of NLP Techniques (Year 3-4):

As natural language processing (NLP) techniques gained prominence in the AI community, Bard AI underwent a significant transformation. Developers integrated sophisticated NLP algorithms, allowing the system to understand context, semantics, and even subtle nuances in language. This marked a turning point as Bard AI evolved from simple sentence generation to more contextually aware content creation.

Machine Learning Enhancements (Year 5-7):

To enhance its creative capabilities, Bard AI embraced machine learning algorithms. The system was trained on vast datasets containing a diverse range of creative writing examples – from classic literature to contemporary poetry. This training empowered Bard AI to learn intricate patterns, styles, and themes inherent in different forms of writing.

Generative Models Take Center Stage (Year 8-10):

The introduction of generative models, inspired by advanced architectures like the Transformer, catapulted Bard AI to new heights. These models allowed the system not only to understand language intricacies but also to generate entirely new and contextually relevant content. Users witnessed the emergence of Bard AI's ability to craft poetic verses, compelling narratives, and imaginative prose.

Context Maintenance and Conversational AI (Year 11-12):

Recognizing the importance of context in creative writing, Bard AI delved into the realm of conversational AI. The system became adept at maintaining context over extended interactions, enabling users to engage in dynamic and evolving conversations. Writers could now explore complex storylines, characters, and dialogues with Bard AI as their creative companion.

User Interaction and Feedback Integration (Year 13-15):

A crucial phase in Bard AI's evolution involved increased emphasis on user interaction and feedback. Developers implemented a feedback loop where users could actively contribute to the system's learning process. This iterative cycle allowed Bard AI to adapt to individual writing styles, preferences, and creative inputs, making it a more personalized and collaborative tool.

Ethical Considerations and Bias Mitigation (Year 16-18):

As Bard AI gained popularity, ethical considerations took center stage. Developers worked rigorously to address biases that might inadvertently surface in generated content. Transparency became a key principle, and users were provided with tools to understand and control the ethical dimensions of Bard AI. Privacy safeguards were reinforced, ensuring responsible and secure usage.

Integration of Multimodal Capabilities (Year 19-20):

In response to the evolving landscape of AI, Bard AI expanded its horizons to include multimodal capabilities. The tool could now process not only text but also images, allowing writers to draw inspiration from visual prompts or incorporate multimedia elements into their creative projects. This holistic approach marked a milestone in Bard AI's versatility.

Global Adoption and Community Engagement (Year 21-23):

By its third decade, Bard AI had become a global phenomenon, adopted by writers, educators, and creative enthusiasts worldwide. A vibrant community emerged, sharing stories, collaborating on projects, and providing valuable insights for continuous improvement. Bard AI's developers actively engaged with the community, fostering a culture of creativity and exploration.

Future Horizons (Year 24 and Beyond):

As Bard AI looks toward the future, the journey continues with a commitment to pushing the boundaries of creative AI. Plans include exploring emerging technologies, refining user experiences, and venturing into new frontiers of artistic expression. Bard AI envisions a world where human creativity is elevated and augmented by the possibilities unlocked through AI collaboration.

3.3. Bard AI Architecture

3.3.1 System Overview

The Bard AI architecture is designed to facilitate creative writing, storytelling, and content generation. It leverages advanced natural language processing (NLP) techniques, machine learning algorithms, and generative models to understand user input and generate contextually relevant and creative outputs.

At its core, Bard AI is built upon a scalable and modular architecture that allows for seamless integration of various components, ensuring flexibility and adaptability to evolving creative writing needs.

3.3.2 Components and Modules

a) Natural Language Processing (NLP) Module:

1. Responsible for parsing and understanding user input. This module employs state-of-the-art NLP techniques to extract meaning, context, and nuances from textual prompts.

b) Generative Model Module:

1. Incorporates advanced generative models, potentially based on transformer architectures. This module generates creative content based on learned patterns and styles from diverse training datasets, ranging from classical literature to contemporary writing.

c) Context Management Module:

1. Maintains context over multiple turns in a conversation or writing session. This module ensures that the generated content remains coherent and contextually aligned with the user's input.

d) User Interaction and Feedback Module:

1. Enables a dynamic feedback loop with users. Users can provide feedback on generated content, allowing the system to adapt and refine its models over time. This module fosters a collaborative and iterative creative process.

e) Multimodal Integration Module:

1. Allows the incorporation of multimedia elements, such as images or visual prompts, into the creative process. This module expands the range of inspirations and possibilities for writers using Bard AI.

f) Ethical AI and Bias Mitigation Module:

1. Addresses ethical considerations and mitigates potential biases in generated content. Transparency tools empower users to understand and control ethical dimensions, ensuring responsible and fair use.

g) User Interface (UI) Module:

1. Provides an intuitive and user-friendly interface for interacting with Bard AI. The UI module facilitates a seamless experience, allowing users to input prompts, view generated content, and engage in creative collaborations.

3.3.3 Data Flow

a) User Input Flow:

1. The data flow begins with the user input, where writers provide prompts or engage in a conversation with Bard AI. The NLP module processes this input, extracting key information, and understanding the user's creative intent.

b) Contextual Data Flow:

1. The context management module ensures the continuity of the creative context. It considers the entire conversation or writing history, allowing Bard AI to generate content that aligns with the evolving context.

c) Generative Model Flow:

1. The processed input, along with contextual information, is fed into the generative model module. This module leverages pre-trained models and generates creative writing based on learned patterns from extensive datasets.

d) User Feedback Loop Flow:

1. Users can provide feedback on the generated content through the user interaction and feedback module. This feedback loop contributes to the system's learning and adaptation, enhancing its ability to cater to individual writing styles.

e) Ethical AI and Bias Mitigation Flow:

1. The ethical AI module monitors the generated content for potential biases and ensures that ethical guidelines are followed. Transparent feedback is provided to users, giving them insights into the ethical considerations of the AI-generated content.

f) Multimodal Integration Flow:

1. If users incorporate multimedia elements, the multimodal integration module allows the system to process and integrate visual prompts, expanding creative possibilities.

g) User Interface Interaction Flow:

1. The UI module facilitates a smooth interaction between users and Bard AI. Writers can input prompts, navigate through generated content, and engage in a collaborative and creative writing process.

3.4. Bard AI Capabilities

1. Creative Writing Assistance:

Description: Bard AI excels in providing assistance to writers and storytellers by generating creative and contextually relevant content.

How It Works: The system uses advanced natural language processing (NLP) and generative models to understand prompts and produce imaginative writing, including poetry, stories, and narratives.

2. Contextual Understanding:

Description: Bard AI demonstrates a strong ability to maintain context over extended interactions or writing sessions.

How It Works: Context management modules allow the system to remember and consider the entirety of the conversation, ensuring coherence and relevance in the generated content.

3. Multimodal Integration:

Description: Bard AI goes beyond text-based interactions by incorporating multimedia elements like images or visual prompts.

How It Works: The system integrates multimodal capabilities, allowing users to draw inspiration from visual stimuli and enhancing the creative process with a broader range of artistic elements.

4. User Interaction and Feedback:

Description: Bard AI engages users in a dynamic feedback loop, fostering a collaborative and iterative creative process.

How It Works: Users can provide feedback on generated content, and the system adapts and refines its models over time based on user interactions. This ensures a personalized and evolving writing experience.

5. Generative Models for Diverse Content:

Description: Bard AI leverages generative models to produce diverse forms of creative content, spanning various genres and writing styles.
How It Works: The system is trained on extensive datasets that include examples of classical literature, modern poetry, and diverse writing styles, enabling it to generate content across a spectrum of creative expressions.
6. Ethical AI Practices:
Description: Bard AI is designed with a focus on ethical considerations, ensuring responsible and fair use of AI in creative writing.
How It Works: Ethical AI modules monitor content for potential biases and provide transparency tools to users, allowing them to understand and control the ethical dimensions of the AI-generated content.
7. Adaptive Learning and Personalization:
Description: Bard AI adapts to individual writing styles and preferences through an adaptive learning mechanism.
How It Works: The system continuously learns from user feedback, refining its models to better cater to the unique creative preferences of each user. This results in a more personalized and enjoyable writing experience.
8. User-Friendly Interface:
Description: Bard AI features an intuitive and user-friendly interface for seamless interactions.
How It Works: The user interface (UI) module provides an accessible platform for writers to input prompts, navigate through generated content, and actively participate in the creative process.
9. Collaborative Writing Support:
Description: Bard AI facilitates collaborative writing efforts, allowing multiple users to contribute to a shared creative project.
How It Works: The system can handle collaborative inputs and generate content that maintains coherence and context in group writing scenarios.
10. Privacy and Security Measures:
Description: Bard AI prioritizes user privacy and incorporates security measures to protect sensitive information.
How It Works: Stringent privacy measures are implemented to ensure the secure handling of user data and to build trust among users.

3.5. Use Cases and Applications

Here are some speculative use cases:

1. Content Creation and Writing Assistance:
Bard AI can be employed to assist writers and content creators in generating engaging and contextually relevant text for various purposes, including blog posts, articles, and marketing materials.
2. Storytelling and Narrative Generation:
Authors and storytellers can leverage Bard AI to collaboratively develop plotlines, characters, and dialogues, exploring new narrative possibilities and enhancing the storytelling process.
3. Educational Tools for Creative Writing:
Bard AI can serve as an educational tool to support students and aspiring writers in developing their creative writing skills. It can provide guidance, suggestions, and feedback on writing assignments.
4. Interactive Game Narratives:
Game developers can integrate Bard AI to dynamically generate and adapt storylines within interactive games. This application allows for personalized and evolving narratives based on player choices.
5. Chatbots with Creative Personality:
Businesses looking to create engaging and creative chatbots for customer interaction can utilize Bard AI to infuse personality and creativity into automated responses, providing a unique and enjoyable customer experience.
6. Multimedia Content Creation:
Bard AI's multimodal capabilities make it suitable for generating creative content beyond text, such as assisting in the creation of multimedia presentations, incorporating visuals, and even suggesting music or artistic elements.
7. Collaborative Writing Platforms:
Collaborative writing platforms can integrate Bard AI to enable multiple users to co-author content seamlessly. The system ensures coherence and context in group writing endeavors, fostering collaborative creativity.
8. Poetry Generation and Exploration:
Poets and enthusiasts can use Bard AI to explore diverse poetic styles, generate unique verses, and experiment with language, providing inspiration and expanding the boundaries of poetic expression.
9. Scriptwriting Assistance:
Screenwriters and playwrights can benefit from Bard AI's capabilities in generating dialogues, developing characters, and assisting in the creative process of scriptwriting for films, plays, or other productions.

10. AI-Enhanced Virtual Writing Workshops:
Bard AI can be integrated into virtual writing workshops, providing real-time feedback, suggesting writing exercises, and facilitating interactive discussions to enhance the overall learning experience.
11. Personal Journaling and Reflection:
Individuals looking for a creative outlet or personal reflection tool can use Bard AI to assist in journaling. The system can offer prompts, generate reflective passages, and serve as a virtual companion for self-expression.
12. Language Learning Support:
Bard AI can aid language learners in developing their language skills by providing creative prompts, generating language exercises, and offering contextually relevant content for language practice.

Here are some Application of Bard AI:

3.5.1 Conversational Agents

Bard AI emerges as a unique and imaginative tool for fostering creative dialogues. Writers and users can engage with Bard AI in dynamic conversations, seeking inspiration, brainstorming ideas, or co-authoring content. The system's contextual understanding and generative capabilities come together to generate creative responses that align with the evolving narrative. Whether it's crafting compelling dialogues, exploring character interactions, or collaboratively shaping a story, Bard AI serves as a conversational companion that enhances the creative writing process. Its ability to maintain context, adapt to user feedback, and integrate multimodal elements adds a layer of depth to conversational interactions, making it an engaging and innovative application of AI in the domain of interactive and creative conversations.

3.5.2 Creative Writing Assistance

Bard is designed to generate creative writing like poetry, short stories and articles. This makes Bard an ideal tool for those experiencing writer's block, authors who want to experiment with new writing styles or topics or those looking to optimize their writing processes.

3.5.3 Educational Applications

We can use Bard in educational settings to teach students about creative writing, literature and language. Teachers can use Bard to generate writing prompts, create examples of different writing styles and structures, and provide feedback on student writing. Additionally, we can use Bard as a virtual tutor or mentor to help students with specific s or challenges related to STEM subjects. The model could provide explanations, examples and feedback in real-time. Bard can also adjust its approach to the student's level of understanding.

Exercise

Exercise 1 – MCQ

Q 1. What type of large language model is Bard?
A) Generative Adversarial Network (GAN) B) Transformer-based model
C) Recurrent Neural Network (RNN) D) Rule-based system

Q 2. What is one of Bard's key strengths in text generation?
A) High factual accuracy B) Humor and wit
C) Long-form storytelling D) Emotional intelligence

Q 3. Which of the following tasks can Bard NOT perform?
A) Translating languages B) Writing different kinds of creative content
C) Answering your s in an informative way D) Performing surgery

Q 4. What are some potential ethical concerns surrounding the use of large language models like Bard?
A) Bias and discrimination B) Job displacement
C) Spread of misinformation D) All of the above

Q 5. How can developers mitigate the risks of bias in large language models?
A) Use diverse training data B) Implement fairness algorithms
C) Allow for user feedback and corrections D) All of the above

Q 6. What is the name of the AI research lab that developed Bard?
A) DeepMind
B) OpenAI
C) Google AI
D) Facebook AI Research

Q 7. What are some potential applications of Bard in the field of education?
A) Personalized learning experiences
B) Language learning assistance
C) Automatic grading and feedback
D) All of the above

Q 8. How can Bard be used to improve communication and collaboration in the workplace?
A) Generating meeting summaries and action items
B) Facilitating brainstorming sessions
C) Translating languages for multilingual teams
D) All of the above

Q 9. What are some limitations of Bard and other large language models?
A) Lack of common-sense reasoning
B) Difficulty understanding context and nuance
C) Susceptibility to adversarial attacks
D) All of the above

Q 10. What do you think is the most important thing to remember about Bard and other large language models?
A) They are powerful tools, but not without limitations.
B) They should be used responsibly and ethically.
C) They are still under development and constantly learning.
D) All of the above

Exercise 2 – True/ False

Q 1. Bard is primarily designed for code generation and debugging.
Q 2. Bard's responses are always guaranteed to be accurate and factually correct.
Q 3. Bard can hold its own in a philosophical debate.
Q 4. Bard's development solely relies on Google AI engineers.
Q 5. Bard can learn and adapt based on user feedback.
Q 6. Bard is completely unbiased in its outputs.
Q 7. Bard is capable of independent thought and creativity.
Q 8. Bard's potential applications are limited to entertainment and personal use.
Q 9. Bard's development poses no ethical concerns.
Q 10. Bard will eventually be able to replace human interaction and communication.

Exercise 3 – Fill in the blanks

Q 1. In Bard AI, "Design" encompasses both the ________ structure and the user ________.
Q 2. Bard AI aims to contribute to AI development by balancing technological advancements with ________ benefit.
Q 3. The tool emphasizes the importance of ____________ in the development and deployment of AI systems.
Q 4. Bard AI contributes to enhancing the ____________ of AI applications.
Q 5. Users can leverage Bard AI to gain a deeper understanding of the ____________ behind AI decisions.

Exercise 4 – Match case

1. Understanding" in Bard AI.	A. Ethical considerations in AI development
2. Design" in Bard AI.	B. Balancing technological advancements with societal benefit
3. Impact" in Bard AI.	C. Maximizing profits for businesses
4. Addressing ethical considerations" in Bard AI.	D. Algorithmic structure and user interface
5. Bard AI contributes to enhancing the societal impact of AI applications."	E. Impact Focus

Exercise 5 – One word answer

Q 1. What is Bard AI's focus on comprehending complex concepts?
Q 2. What is one of the key objectives of Bard AI related to ethical considerations?
Q 3. What does Bard AI promote in AI system development?
Q 4. What ethical practices does Bard AI encourage in AI?
Q 5. What cultural aspects does Bard AI prompt users to consider in AI technologies?

Exercise 6 – Small answer
Q 1. What does "Design" in Bard AI encompass?
Q 2. How does Bard AI aim to contribute to AI development?
Q 3. What does Bard AI emphasize in AI system development?
Q 4. What do users gain insights into regarding AI decisions using Bard AI?
Q 5. What does Bard AI promote in AI system development?

Exercise 7 – Long answer
Q 1. Can you provide an in-depth overview of Bard AI's approach, covering its three core aspects: Understanding, Design, and Impact?
Q 2. Could you elaborate on what Bard AI specifically means by "Design" and how it integrates algorithmic structure and user interface considerations in its development?

Answers

Exercise 1 – MCQ
Ans: 1 B, 2 A, 3 D, 4 D, 5 D, 6 A, 7 C, 8 D, 9 D, 10 D
Exercise 2 – True/ False
Ans: 1 False, 2 False, 3 True, 4 False, 5 True, 6 False, 7 False, 8 False, 9 False, 10 False
Exercise 3 – Fill in the blanks
Ans: 1 Algorithmic, interface, 2 Societal, 3 Ethics, 4 Impact, 5 Rationale
Exercise 4 – Match case
Ans: 1 D, 2 A, 3 B, 4 C, 5 E
Exercise 5 – One word answer
Ans: 1 Understanding, 2 Ethics, 3 Transparency, 4 Responsibility, 5 Cultural implications

ONLINE RESOURCES

Practice Paper
Link
https://forms.office.com/r/kTfGgP5SDr
QR Code

Video Content
Link
https://www.youtube.com/playlist?list=PLzlh_31VWEFoAEiQsraGzQlgT80FGJIce
QR Code

Chapter 4: Exploring Gemini AI Tool

4.1. Introduction

Gemini is a new and powerful artificial intelligence model from Google that can understand not just text but also images, videos, and audio. As a multimodal model, Gemini is described as capable of completing complex tasks in math, physics, and other areas, as well as understanding and generating high-quality code in various programming languages.

Who made Gemini?

Gemini was created by Google and Alphabet, Google's parent company, and released as the company's most advanced AI model to date. Google DeepMind also made significant contributions to the development of Gemini.

Are there different versions of Gemini?

Google describes Gemini as a flexible model that is capable of running on everything from Google's data centers to mobile devices. To achieve this scalability, Gemini is being released in three sizes: Gemini Nano, Gemini Pro, and Gemini Ultra.

1. **Gemini Nano:** The Gemini Nano model size is designed to run on smartphones, specifically the Google Pixel 8. It's built to perform on-device tasks that require efficient AI processing without connecting to external servers, such as suggesting replies within chat applications or summarizing text.
2. **Gemini Pro:** Running on Google's data centers, Gemini Pro is designed to power the latest version of the company's AI chatbot, Bard. It's capable of delivering fast response times and understanding complex queries.
3. **Gemini Ultra:** Though still unavailable for widespread use, Google describes Gemini Ultra as its most capable model, exceeding "current state-of-the-art results on 30 of the 32 widely-used academic benchmarks used in large language model (LLM) research and development." It's designed for highly complex tasks and is set to be released after finishing its current phase of testing.

4.2. Key Features

1. Multimodal dialogue:

In the first segment, the user draws on a piece of paper and asks Gemini to guess what it sees. The A1 model keeps guessing the image as the user continues to add more complexities to it. At each step, Gemini is capable of offering a reasonable analysis of the drawing and providing additional information about the object. It also recognized objects and offered information about what they might be made up of.

2. Multilinguality

In the second segment, the user asks the A1 to tell him how to pronounce a word in a different language. Not only does the A1 show the response in text format, but it also offers an audio response to help the user pick up the dialect. It also helped him with the pronunciation.

3. Game creation

In the third segment, the user puts a world map and a rubber duck on the table and asks the A1 to create a fun game based on it and to use emojis for the game. Gemini obliges and creates a country guessing game where the user will have to guess the name of the country based
on three emojis.

4. Visual puzzles

In the next segment, the A1 is put to the test and is asked to solve some puzzle presented to it in the real world. The video shows it to be capable enough to easily follow the puzzles in real time and solve them.

5. Making connections

In the next segment, the user keeps two random objects on the table and asks Gemini what it sees. Based on the visual context, the A1 is able to make a connection between the two objects and categorize them. The user keeps switching out objects, but each time it is able to find a correct category to group the items together.

6. Image and text generation

Next, the user keeps two balls of yarn of different colors on the table and asks the A1 to suggest what could be made using them. The AI comes up with different things that can be made. While the primary response is in text format, it also shows an A1-generated reference image to help the user visualize the final result.

7. Logic and spatial reasoning

The A1 is also shown to be comfortable with answering logic-based visual puzzles and correctly identifying various aspects of it before offering a solution.

8. Translating visuals

In the last segment, Google Gemini is asked to identify what the user is drawing. As he draws a guitar, the A1 identifies it and plays Al- generated guitar music. The user keeps adding more instruments and themes, and the A1 is able to change the music based on the new elements added.

4.3. Use Cases

Here are some common use cases for artificial intelligence in various industries:

1. Natural Language Processing (NLP):

Chatbots and Virtual Assistants: AI-powered chatbots are used in customer service to handle routine inquiries and provide assistance.

Language Translation: AI is employed for real-time language translation, breaking down language barriers in communication.

2. Computer Vision:

Image and Object Recognition: AI can analyze and recognize objects, patterns, and faces in images or videos, leading to applications in security, healthcare, and retail.

Autonomous Vehicles: Computer vision is a crucial component for enabling self-driving cars to navigate and perceive their environment.

3. Healthcare:

Diagnostic Assistance: AI systems can assist medical professionals in diagnosing diseases by analyzing medical images and data.

Drug Discovery: AI is used to accelerate drug discovery processes by analyzing complex biological data.

4. Finance:

Fraud Detection: AI algorithms can identify patterns indicative of fraudulent activities in financial transactions.

Algorithmic Trading: AI is utilized for analyzing market trends and executing trades in financial markets.

5. Manufacturing and Robotics:

Quality Control: AI-powered systems can inspect and identify defects in manufacturing processes.

Robotic Automation: AI enables robots to perform tasks in manufacturing, logistics, and other industries with precision and efficiency.

6. Marketing and Advertising:

Personalized Marketing: AI analyzes user behavior and preferences to deliver personalized content and advertisements.

Predictive Analytics: AI algorithms predict customer behavior, helping businesses make data-driven decisions.

7. Education:

Adaptive Learning Platforms: AI can personalize learning experiences by adapting to individual student needs and learning styles.

Automated Grading: AI tools can assist in grading assignments and providing feedback.

4.3.1 Content Generation

1. Blog Post Creation: Automatically generate blog posts, articles, or other written content based on specified topics or keywords.

2. Product Descriptions: Generate unique and compelling product descriptions for e-commerce websites.

3. Social Media Posts: Create engaging social media content for various platforms.

4.3.2 Sentiment Analysis

1. Customer Feedback Analysis: Analyze customer reviews and feedback to determine sentiment and gauge overall satisfaction.

2. Social Media Monitoring: Monitor social media channels to understand public sentiment toward a brand, product, or topic.

3. Employee Feedback: Evaluate sentiment in employee surveys to gauge morale and identify areas for improvement.

4.3.3 Text Summarization
1. Document Summarization: Automatically generate concise summaries of lengthy documents or articles.
2. Meeting Summaries: Summarize meeting transcripts or minutes to capture key points and action items.
3. News Article Summaries: Provide condensed versions of news articles for quick consumption.

4.3.4 Language Translation
1. Real-Time Translation: Translate text from one language to another in real-time for communication or content localization.
2. Multilingual Customer Support: Assist in providing customer support in multiple languages.
3. Global Collaboration: Facilitate collaboration among international teams by translating documents and communications.

4.3.5 Code Generation
1. Auto-Completion: Assist developers by automatically generating code snippets or completing code lines based on context.
2. Prototype Development: Quickly generate basic code structures for prototyping applications.
3. Code Refactoring: Offer suggestions and generate refactored code for improved efficiency and readability.
How to get started with Gemini API?
In order to get started with the Gemini API, you will first need to go over to their website that is found on the following link:

https://www.gemini.com/

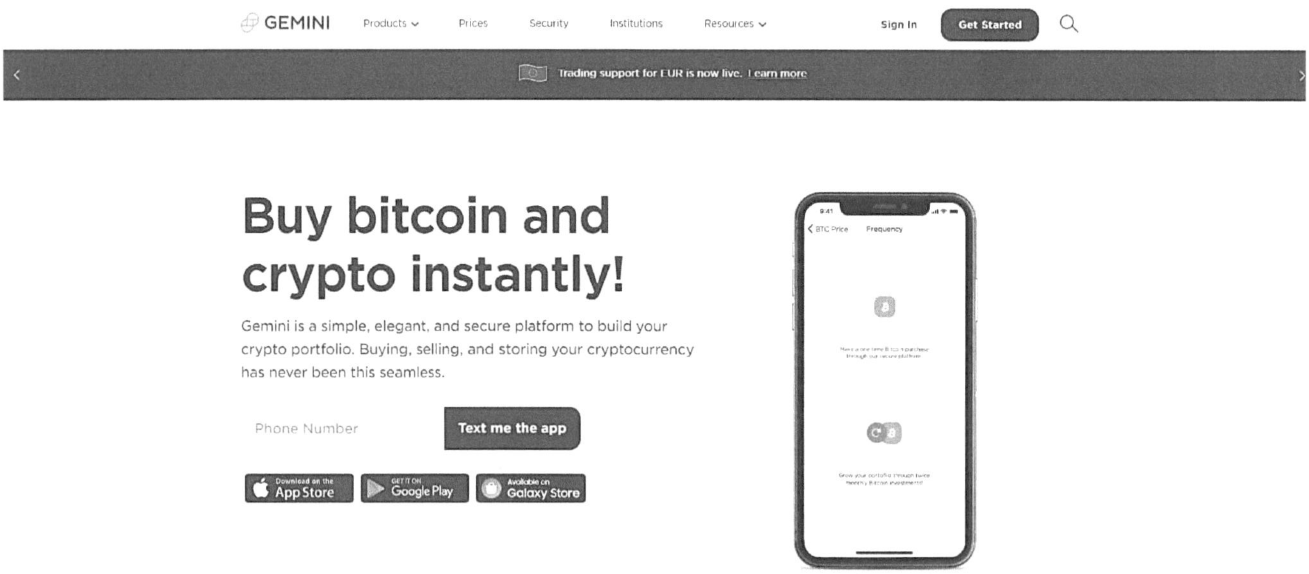

The next thing will be to sign up. For this, click on the "Get Started" icon and the Gemini will take you through the sign up process. Be prepared to give a lot of personal information such as your phone number and ID card as Gemini is a US regulated exchange.
For the purpose of this article, I will use Gemini's sandbox environment that is aimed for API testing. It has a separate sign up process so let's go over it together.
The first thing to do is to visit the following link that will take us to the sign up screen:
https://exchange.sandbox.gemini.com/
There you will simply inter your first and last name, email and password.

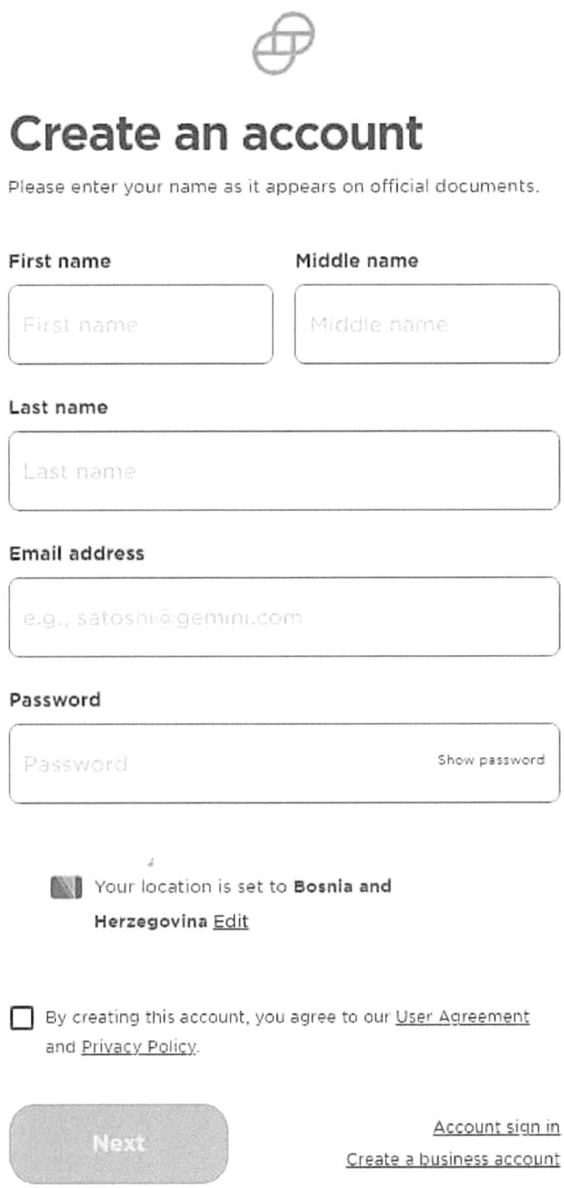

After completion you will need to enter in your phone number for the verification step. After entering the SMS code, you will be brought to a screen that looks like the following:

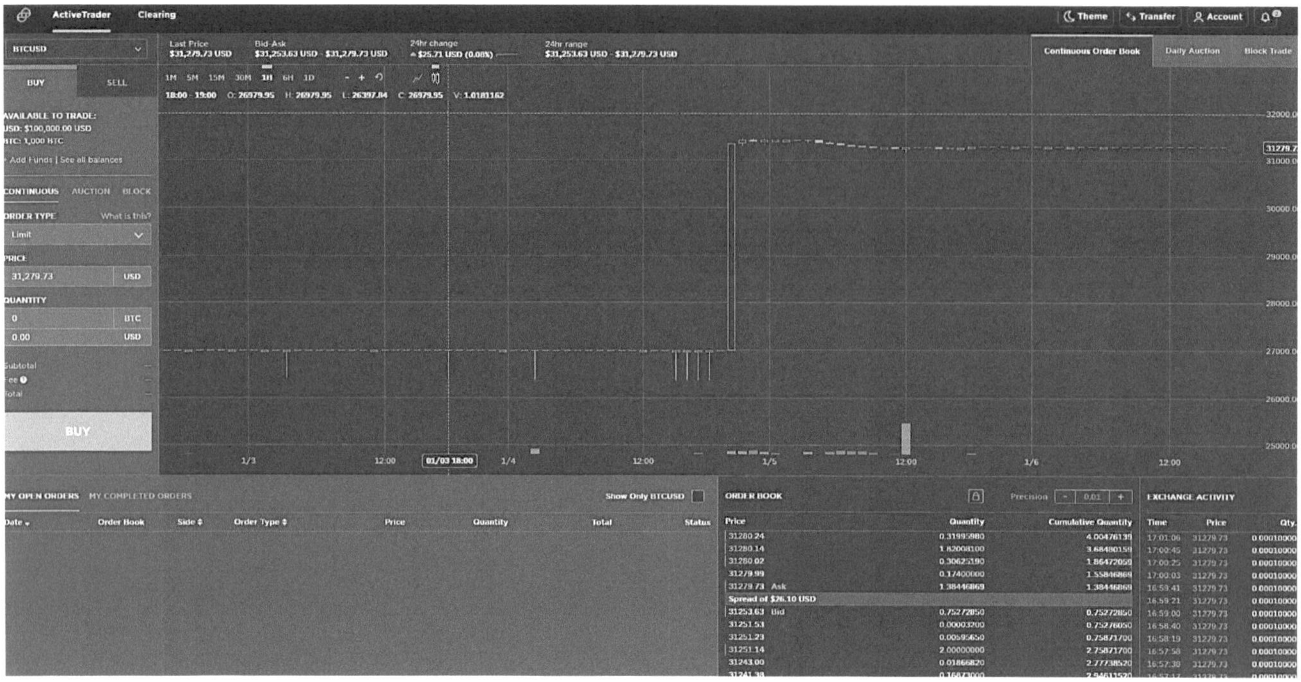

Click on your account icon that is found in the upper-right corner and go to settings. Then navigate the newly opened tab to the API icon that is found on the left side:

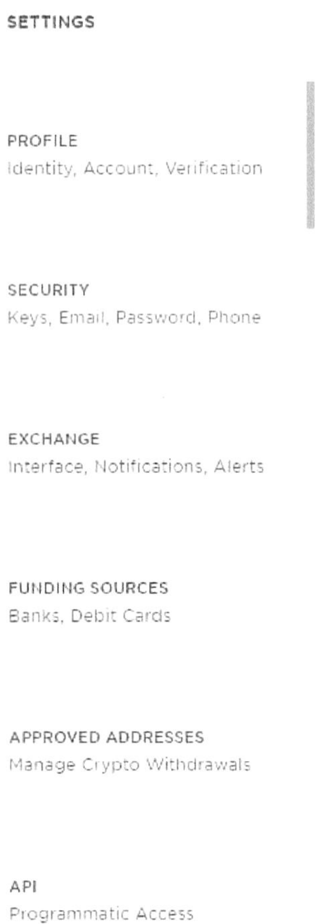

When there, click the "CREATE A NEW API KEY" button. A pop-up will prompt you to enter a key that was sent to your phone via SMS. After entering it you will state what kind of an API Key you want.

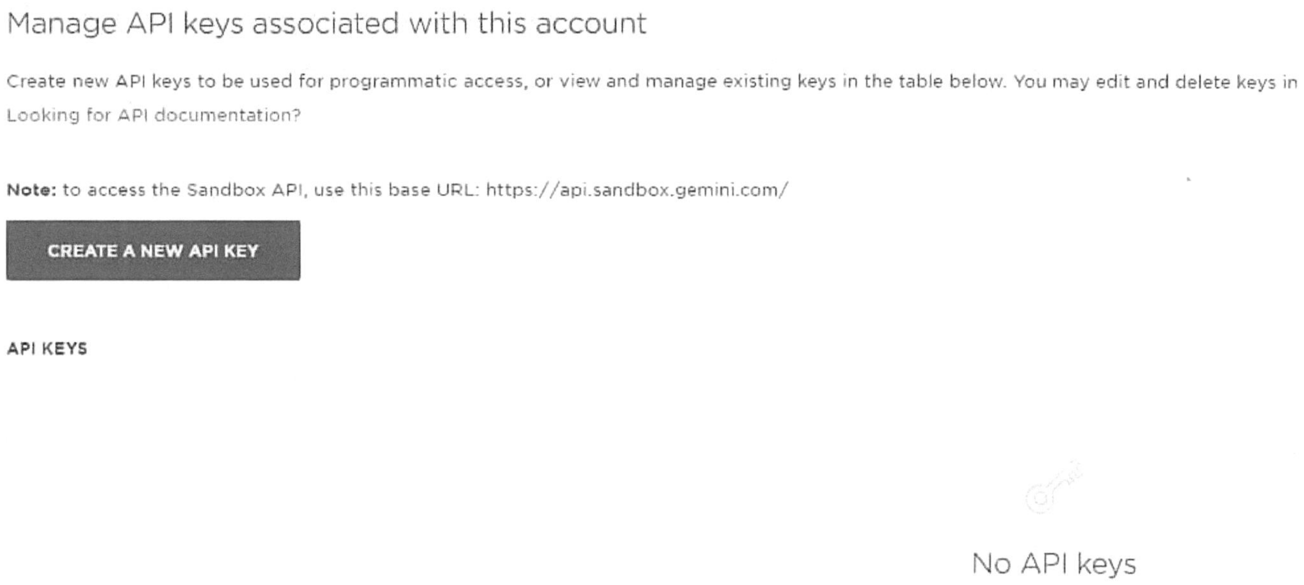

You can pick either the Master or Primary API Key option. The main difference between them is that the Master API Key has more options in terms of regulation between your accounts. I will pick this one.
Then you will be presented with your API Key and API Secret. Be sure to safely store them as you won't see them again. Also, don't forget to name your API Key and give it permissions in the API Key Settings.

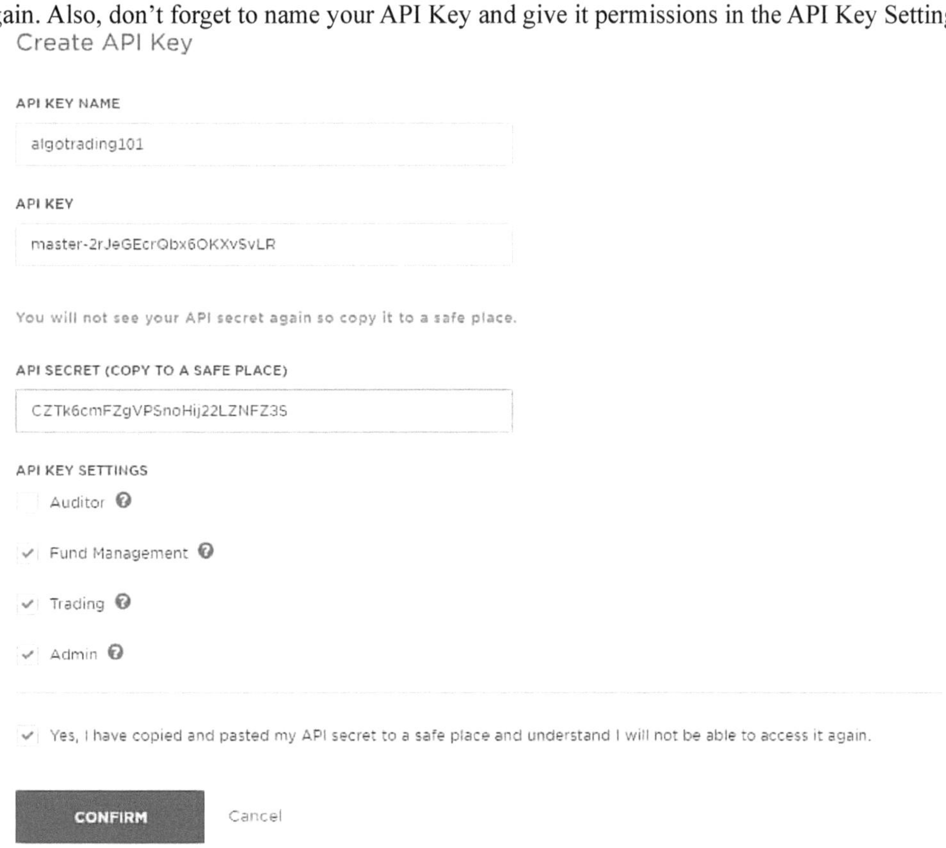

All done. Now, let us install the python library for the Gemini API using the following command:
pip install gemini_python

Exercise

Exercise 1 – MCQ

Q 1. What type of technology is Gemini AI based on?
A) Rule-based system
B) Deep learning neural network
C) Symbolic reasoning engine
D) Both B and C

Q 2. What is one of Gemini AI's key features?
A) Code generation from natural language descriptions
B) Fact-checking and information verification
C) Automatic essay writing and poetry composition
D) Personalized chatbot interaction with emotional intelligence

Q 3. What programming languages can Gemini AI currently generate code for?
A) Python, Java, and C++ only
B) A limited range of popular languages
C) Any major programming language with enough training data
D) It cannot directly generate code, but provides pseudocode suggestions

Q 4. What are some potential applications of Gemini AI beyond software development?
A) Scientific research and data analysis
B) Educational tools and personalized learning assistants
C) Creative writing and artistic expression
D) All of the above

Q 5. What are some limitations of Gemini AI that users should be aware of?
A) Limited accuracy and potential for generating buggy code
B) Difficulty understanding complex or ambiguous requirements
C) High computational requirements and resource overhead
D) All of the above

Q 6. How can users provide feedback to improve Gemini AI's accuracy and performance?
A) Reporting bugs and suggesting improvements through dedicated channels
B) Upvoting and downvoting generated code outputs
C) Providing additional training data specific to their needs
D) All of the above

Q 7. What is the relationship between Gemini AI and Bard, another AI tool from Google?
A) Gemini AI is a subset of Bard with narrower functionalities.
B) Bard is a more advanced version of Gemini AI with additional features.
C) They are completely separate AI tools with distinct purposes.
D) They collaborate and share information to enhance each other's capabilities.

Q 8. What are some ethical considerations to keep in mind when using Gemini AI for code generation?
A) Potential for bias and unintended consequences in generated code
B) Importance of attributing generated code and respecting intellectual property rights
C) Responsibility for ensuring the safety and security of code produced
D) All of the above

Q 9. What is the future potential of Gemini AI and similar code-generation tools?
A) Democratizing software development and making coding accessible to everyone
B) Automating routine coding tasks and increasing developer productivity
C) Facilitating human-AI collaboration and fostering innovation in software development
D) All of the above

Q 10. What is the most important thing to remember when exploring Gemini AI and other AI tools?
A) They are powerful tools, but their outputs should be carefully reviewed and validated.

B) Understanding their limitations and using them responsibly is crucial.
C) They are still under development and their capabilities will continue to evolve.
D) All of the above

Exercise 2 – True/ False

Q 1. Gemini AI is only able to generate code in Python.
Q 2. Gemini AI can understand and fulfill complex, open-ended coding requests.
Q 3. Generated code by Gemini AI will always be bug-free and run perfectly.
Q 4. Exploring and experimenting with Gemini AI can be valuable for anyone interested in software development, even without prior coding experience.
Q 5. You can provide your own training data to Gemini AI to improve its understanding of specific domains or libraries.
Q 6. Gemini AI has access to and can utilize the knowledge and information present in Google Search results.
Q 7. Using Gemini AI automatically grants you ownership and intellectual property rights over the generated code.
Q 8. Gemini AI is primarily designed to replace human programmers and make software development obsolete.
Q 9. Integrating Gemini AI into existing development workflows involves complex technical configurations and requires extensive coding expertise.
Q 10. The ethical implications of using AI tools like Gemini AI for code generation are minimal and need not be a major concern.

Exercise 3 – Fill in the blanks

Q 1. The Gemini AI tool harnesses the power of ____________ and ____________ to solve complex problems.
Q 2. Data visualization in Gemini AI helps create stunning visual representations to interpret and communicate ____________ information effectively.
Q 3. Gemini AI contributes to the evolution of ___________ technologies.
Q 4. The ethical framework of Gemini AI prioritizes transparency and ___________.
Q 5. Gemini AI aims to deliver a seamless and user-friendly ___________ experience.

Exercise 4 – Match case

1. Deep Learning and Neural Networks in Gemini AI	A. Includes improved efficiency and accurate predictions
2. Natural Language Processing in Gemini AI	B. Analyzes and understands human language in textual data
3. Data Visualization in Gemini AI	C. Creates stunning visual representations of data
4. Benefits of Using the Gemini AI Tool	D. Automates decision-making processes

Exercise 5 – One word answer

Q 1. What is Gemini AI designed to enhance?
Q 2. What does Gemini AI leverage to solve complex problems?
Q 3. Gemini AI capabilities?
Q 4. Gemini AI applications?
Q 5. Gemini AI limitations?

Exercise 6 – Small answer

Q 1. How does Gemini AI solve complex problems?
Q 2. What does Natural Language Processing enable Gemini AI to analyze?
Q 3. What role does data play in Gemini AI?
Q 4. How does Gemini AI encourage collaboration?
Q 5. What is the focus of Gemini AI's development?

Exercise 7 – Long answer

Q 1. How does Gemini AI leverage deep learning and neural networks to solve complex problems, and what distinguishes this approach in addressing intricate challenges?
Q 2. In what ways does Gemini AI utilize Data Visualization, and how does this capability contribute to the interpretation and communication of complex information effectively?

Answers

Exercise 1 – MCQ

Ans: 1 D, 2 A, 3 C, 4 D, 5 D, 6 D, 7 D, 8 D, 9 D, 10 D

Exercise 2 – True/ False

Ans: 1 False, 2 False, 3 False, 4 True, 5 True, 6 True, 7 False, 8 False, 9 False, 10 False

Exercise 3 – Fill in the blanks

Ans: 1 Artificial Intelligence, machine learning, 2 Complex, 3 Cutting-edge, 4 Accountability, 5 Interface

Exercise 4 – Match case

Ans: 1 D, 2 C, 3 B, 4 A

Exercise 5 – One word answer

Ans: 1 Decision - making, 2 Learning, 3 Versatile, 4 Diverse, 5 Context

ONLINE RESOURCES

Practice Paper
Link https://forms.office.com/r/mkK4hj3P2r
QR Code

Video Content
Link https://www.youtube.com/playlist?list=PLzlh_31VWEFqpMMEpvwQ9-mh2my6hrM3d
QR Code

Chapter 5: Writing and Content Creation Tools

5.1 ClickUp

- ClickUp is the only productivity software powerful enough to bring all of your work together across apps into one centralized work hub. With hundreds of flexible project management features, a vast Template Library, and a range of integrations, ClickUp has long been the ideal destination for teams to streamline and manage every inch of their work.
- Now, ClickUp is taking that sentiment even further with the launch of ClickUp AI.
- ClickUp AI is the only role-based AI solution with research-backed prompts to help you reach your best results faster. ClickUp's AI technology is deeply integrated into its platform to meet you almost anywhere within your Workspace, but its power comes to life in ClickUp Docs. Simply choose your role, select your use case, and ClickUp AI will take it from there!
- Still, there's so much more to explore with ClickUp AI. Translate text in over 10 languages, summarize lengthy documents in seconds, and watch as ClickUp continues to refine your experience with new AI updates released each week.

Here we started the ClickUp AI tool Steps are given below:-

here's a step-by-step explanation:

Step 1: Sign Up and Log In

1. Visit the ClickUp website.

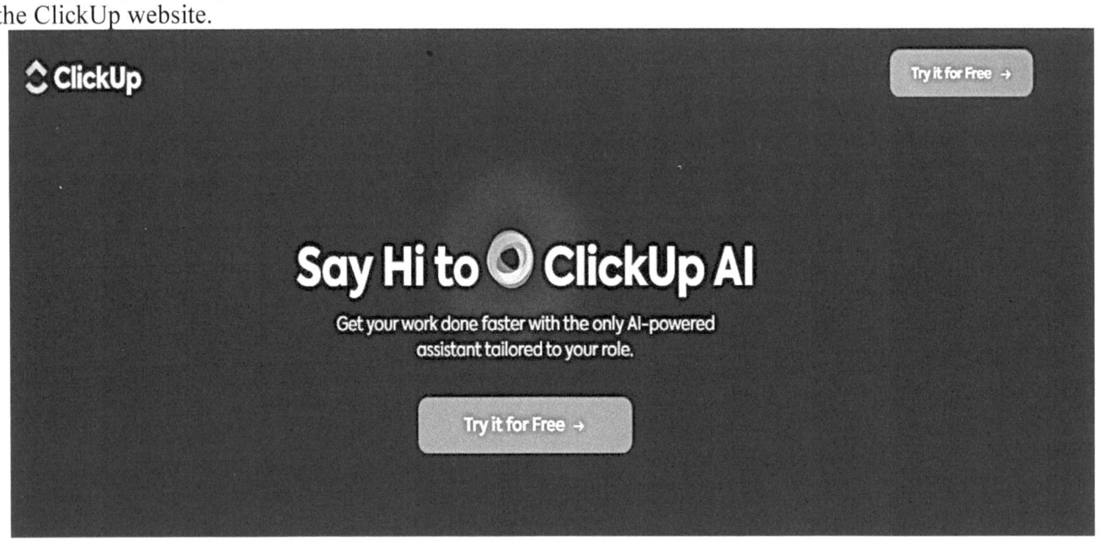

2. Sign up for an account using your email address or other authentication options.

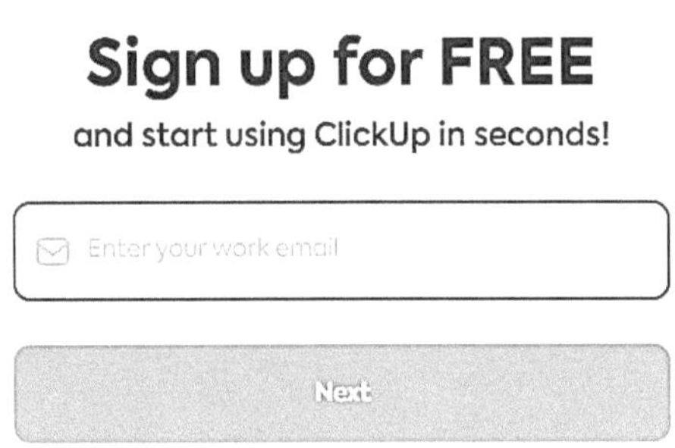

3. Log in to your newly created account.

Step 2: Create a Workspace

1. After logging in, create a workspace. Workspaces are top-level containers that house all your projects and tasks.

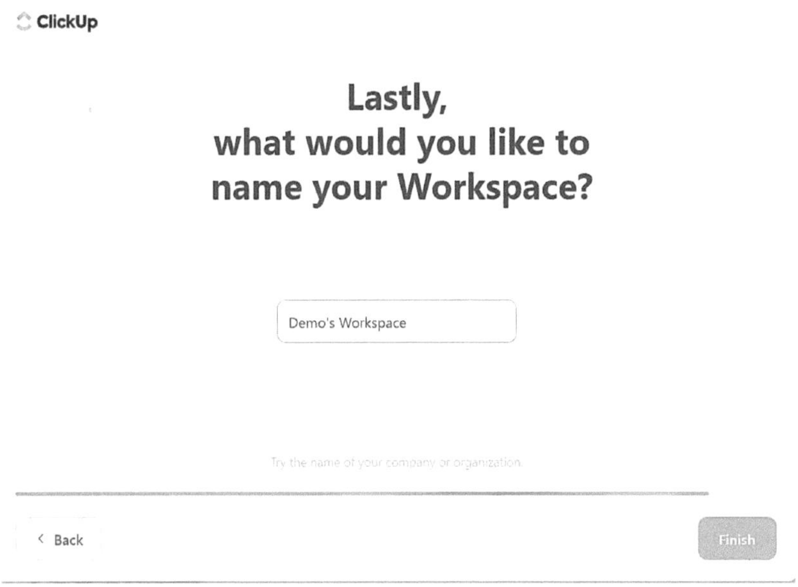

2. Name your workspace based on your team, department, or project.

Step 3: Create Projects

1. Within your workspace, create projects. Projects help you organize tasks around a specific goal or objective.
2. Assign team members to each project and set project details.

Step 4: Create Lists and Tasks

1. Inside each project, create lists to further categorize tasks. Lists are collections of related tasks.
2. Add tasks within lists. Tasks represent individual actions that need to be completed.

Step 5: Customize Task Details

1. Add details to tasks, such as due dates, priorities, and attachments.
2. Use custom fields to tailor task information to your specific needs.

Step 6: Collaboration and Communication

1. Use comments to communicate with team members on tasks and projects.
2. Attach documents, images, or links to provide additional context.
3. Mention team members to notify them of updates or specific information.

Step 7: Time Tracking and Workload Management

1. Utilize time tracking features to monitor how much time is spent on tasks.
2. Manage workloads by assigning tasks evenly and avoiding overloading team members.

Step 8: Dashboards and Reporting

1. Explore dashboards to visualize project progress.
2. Generate reports to analyze team performance and project metrics.

Step 9: Integrations

1. Integrate ClickUp with other tools your team uses, such as Google Drive, Slack, or Trello.
2. Streamline workflows by automating processes through integrations.

Step 10: Explore Advanced Features (if applicable)

1. If ClickUp has introduced AI features, explore them based on the specific documentation provided.
2. This could include AI-driven task prioritization, smart scheduling, or predictive analytics.

Step 11: Training and Support

1. Familiarize yourself with ClickUp's knowledge base and support resources.
2. Attend training sessions or webinars provided by ClickUp to enhance your understanding of the platform.

ClickUp Overview:

1. Project Management:
2. ClickUp serves as a comprehensive project management tool, allowing users to create and manage tasks, set due dates, assign responsibilities, and organize projects in a hierarchical manner.
3. Task and Time Tracking:
4. Users can track time spent on tasks, set priorities, and monitor progress. This feature aids in assessing project timelines and individual workloads.

5. Collaboration:
6. ClickUp emphasizes collaboration by providing features such as comments, file sharing, and real-time editing. This enhances team communication and ensures everyone is on the same page.
7. Customization:
8. ClickUp is highly customizable, allowing users to adapt the platform to their workflow. Users can create custom fields, templates, and views tailored to their specific project needs.
9. Integrations:
10. ClickUp supports integrations with various third-party applications and services, enhancing its functionality. Integrations may include communication tools, file storage services, and more.
11. Dashboards and Reporting:
12. ClickUp offers dashboards and reporting features to provide insights into project progress. Users can generate custom reports and visualizations to track key metrics.
13. Accessibility:
14. ClickUp is accessible across different devices and platforms, enabling users to manage projects and tasks on the go.

ClickUp best features
1. Over 100 role-based AI-powered prompts are built into ClickUp AI to reach targetted results on the first try every time
2. Reprompting functionality to fine-tune your results with conversational feedback and requests to "make it funnier" or sound more creative
3. A Translate action to bridge the gap between any language barriers and render near-perfect interpretations of your text in 12 languages
4. Thread summaries to quickly grab the key points of lengthy comment conversations in both Docs and tasks
5. More than 15 customizable project views, including Gantt, List, AI calendar, Timeline, and Kanban-like Board view to manage your work from every angle
6. Custom and pre-built Automations to eliminate repetitive action items and save valuable time
7. Whiteboards, Docs, Mind Maps, and Chat built directly into the platform
8. Over 1,000 integrations with other leading work tools
9. An ever-growing Template Library of pre-built and customizable resources to kickstart any process in ClickUp

ClickUp limitations
1. ClickUp is loaded with hundreds of powerful features that can take a bit of time to master. Luckily, ClickUp offers webinars, support, and Help Docs to ease your onboarding experience
2. Not all views are available via the mobile app yet
3. AI-powered project summaries, task and subtask creation, and mobile access are not yet available—but coming soon!

ClickUp pricing
ClickUp offers a free trial to give every person the opportunity to test drive ClickUp AI, regardless of whether you're a new user or on its Free Forever Plan. When you're ready to commit, you can add ClickUp AI to any paid Workspace for just $5 per member, per month.
On top of this perk, ClickUp also offers a handful of feature-rich pricing plans:
1. Free Forever Plan: Unlimited free plan members, no credit card required
2. Unlimited Plan: $7 per member, per month
3. Business Plan: $12 per member, per month
4. Enterprise Plan: Contact ClickUp for custom pricing options

2.2 Jasper
1. Official Documentation and Websites: Visit the official website of the company or organization behind Jasper, if applicable. Check for documentation, user guides, and release notes that may provide details about the tool's features, functionalities, and use cases.
2. Company Announcements and Press Releases: Look for any announcements or press releases related to the launch or updates of Jasper. Companies often share detailed information about their products and their intended applications in these communications.

3. Online Reviews and Articles: Explore reputable tech news websites, blogs, and forums for reviews or articles discussing Jasper. Users and experts often share their experiences and insights into the tool's capabilities and use cases.
4. Community Forums: If Jasper has a user community or forums associated with it, consider checking those platforms. Users often discuss their experiences, share tips, and ask s that can provide valuable information.
5. Social Media: Companies often share updates and engage with their audience on social media platforms. Check the official social media accounts of the organization behind Jasper for any relevant information.
Now, if Jasper is a popular tool in 2023, and you're looking for a hypothetical overview based on common trends and patterns in AI tools, here's a speculative example:

Hypothetical Overview of Jasper AI:
Jasper AI is an advanced artificial intelligence tool designed to excel in natural language processing and understanding. Developed by a team of experts, Jasper leverages state-of-the-art machine learning algorithms to offer a range of functionalities.

Key Features:
1. Natural Language Processing (NLP): Jasper is equipped with advanced NLP capabilities, enabling it to understand and generate human-like language. This makes it suitable for applications such as chatbots, virtual assistants, and sentiment analysis.
2. Multimodal Capabilities: Beyond text, Jasper can process and understand multimedia data, including images, videos, and audio. This makes it versatile for applications that require analysis of diverse data types.
3. Customizable Machine Learning Models: Jasper allows users to customize and fine-tune machine learning models to meet specific use case requirements. This flexibility makes it adaptable to various industries and applications.
4. Scalability and Integration: The architecture of Jasper is designed for scalability, allowing seamless integration into existing systems and workflows. This ensures that businesses can leverage AI without major disruptions.

Use Cases:
1. Virtual Assistants: Jasper powers advanced virtual assistants capable of engaging in natural, context-aware conversations and providing intelligent responses to user queries.
2. Content Generation: Content creators can use Jasper to automate parts of the content generation process, such as writing articles, creating product descriptions, or generating marketing copy.
3. Healthcare Applications: In the healthcare sector, Jasper assists with medical documentation, transcription services, and contributes to diagnostic processes by analyzing medical records.
4. Customer Support: E-commerce platforms can implement Jasper to enhance customer support through intelligent chatbots that understand and respond to customer inquiries effectively.
5. Financial Analysis: Jasper's machine learning capabilities make it suitable for financial institutions to analyze market trends, predict investment outcomes, and automate routine financial tasks.
If you're looking for more coherent and engaging responses from your AI writing tool, Jasper might be your best bet. Jasper specializes in creating long-form content like blog articles, scripts, outlines, and more.

Jasper best features
1. Quickly create detailed in your own voice outlines and even let Jasper fill in the rest from there
2. Easy-to-navigate UI
3. You can tailor your responses to any kind of tone, including professional, academic, or technical writing
4. Generate ideas quickly and in your own voice with the Chat feature

Jasper limitations
1. Long-form writing can be tricky and even Jasper's content will require an additional read-through for edits, accuracy, and tone
2. A limited free trial can make it difficult to decide the tool's worth in your tech stack before committing to a paid plan

Jasper pricing
1. Creator: $49 per month for one user, billed annually
2. Teams: $125 per month for three users, billed annually

3. Business: Contact for pricing

Here step by step explaination-

Here's a brief tour of the Jasper platform, and how to use each feature.

A quick tour of the platform

https://www.jasper.ai/

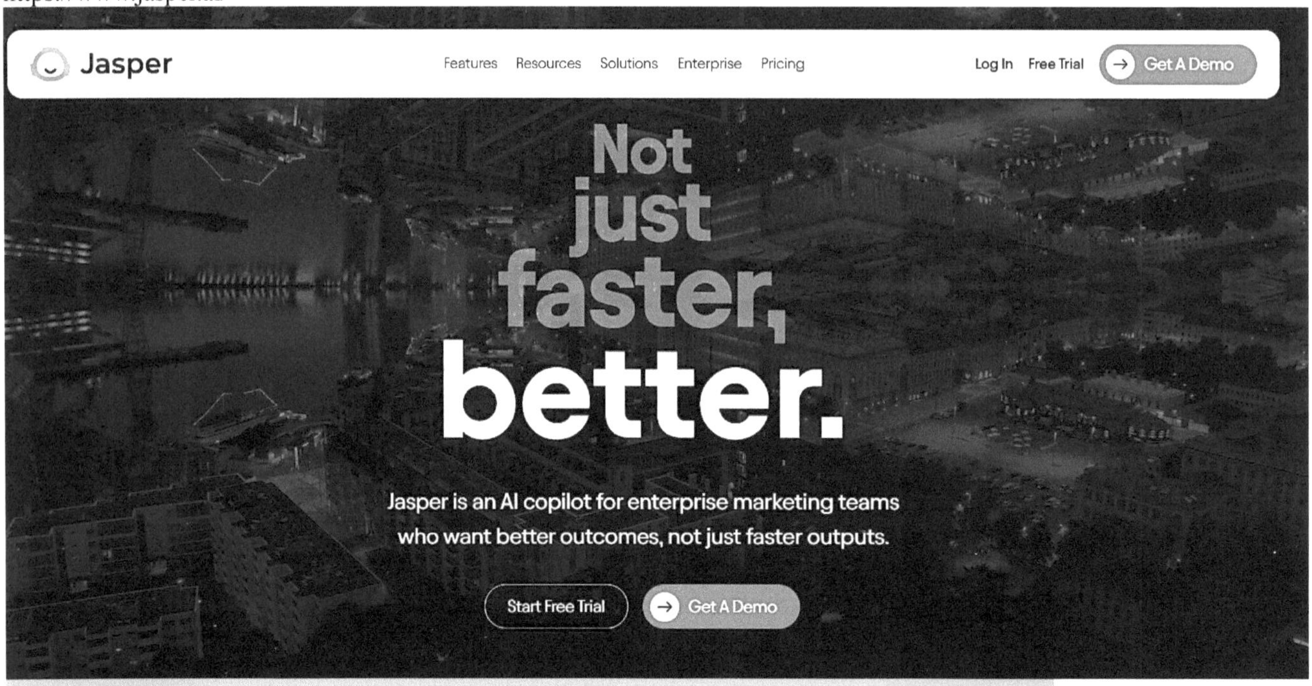

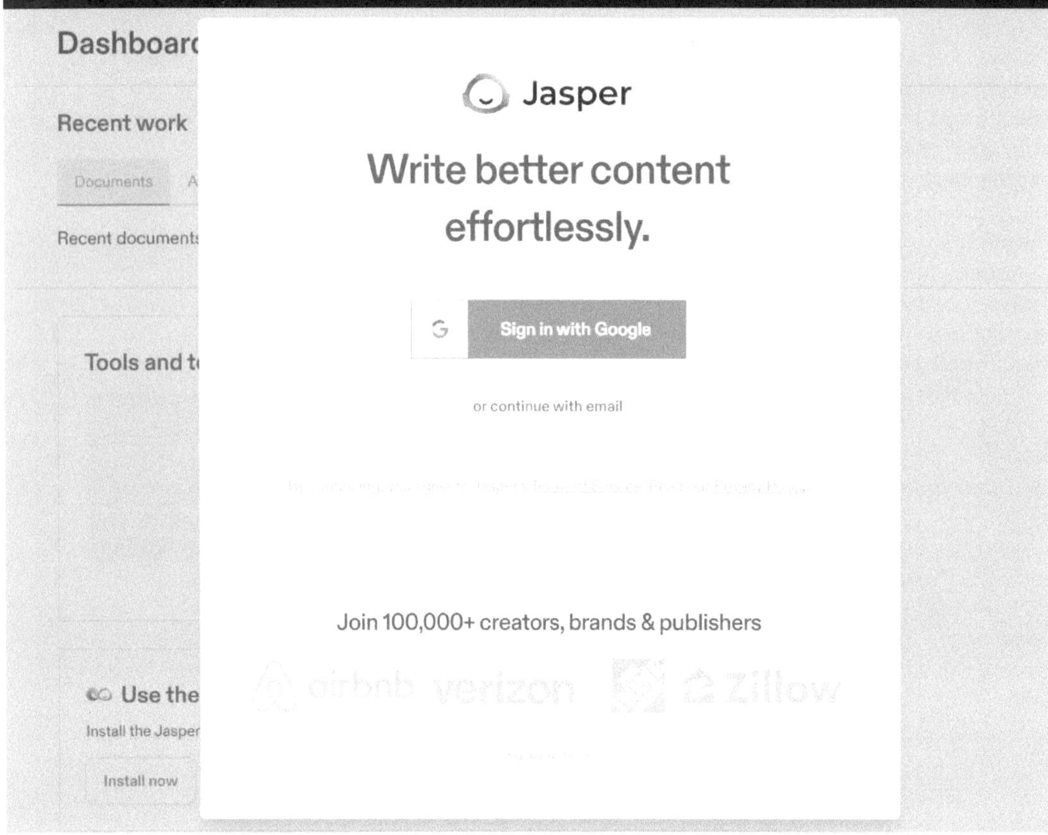

Here's a quick tour around the Jasper dashboard:

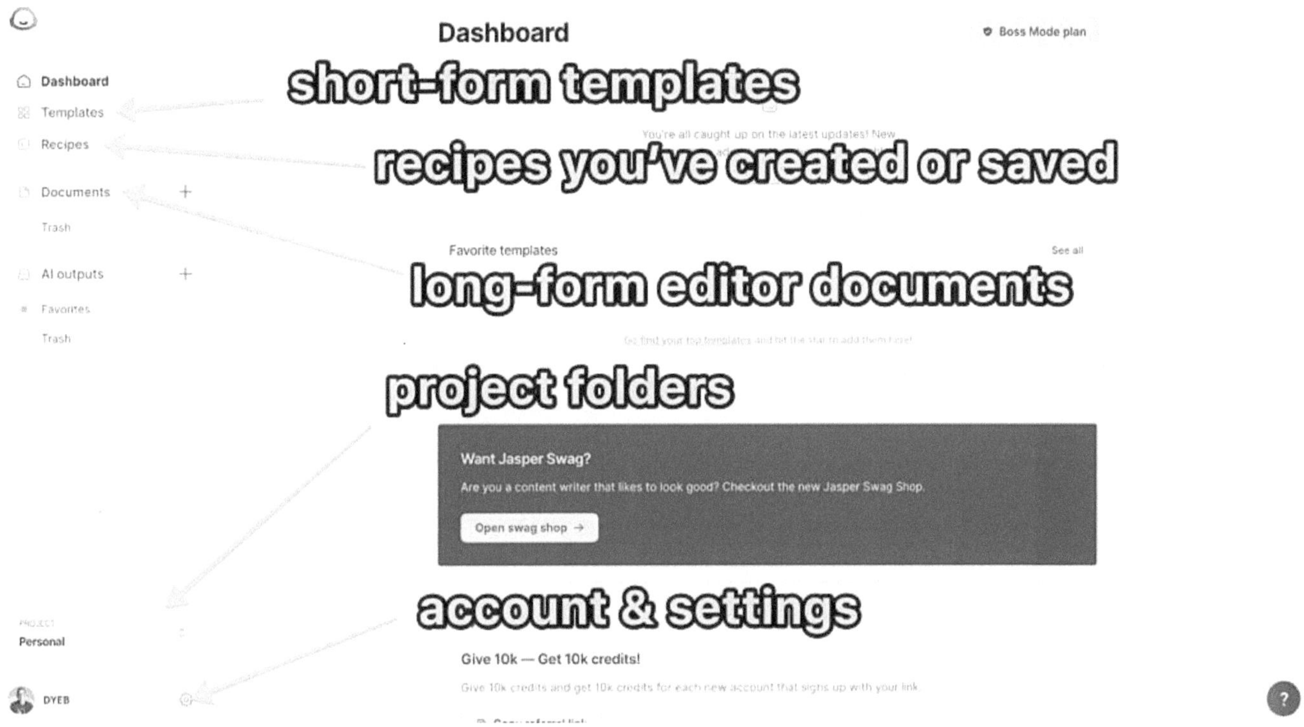

The dashboard is simple and straightforward, usually showing you a bit of news, how many credits you've used recently, etc.

How to use Jasper Templates

"Templates" in Jasper are simply pre-made programs to accomplish a **specific, short-form copy.**

1. Facebook Ad headlines
2. Blog post outlines
3. YouTube video outlines
4. dozens more.

Here's how templates work:

1. You open the Jasper template you want
2. Jasper will **prompt you for a specific type of input** (for example, "Blog post title" or "product name" or "benefits of product."
3. You'll set the tone of voice (optional)
4. You'll select how many different outputs you want (I suggest 1-2)
5. Hit "Generate AI content"
6. Jasper spits options out

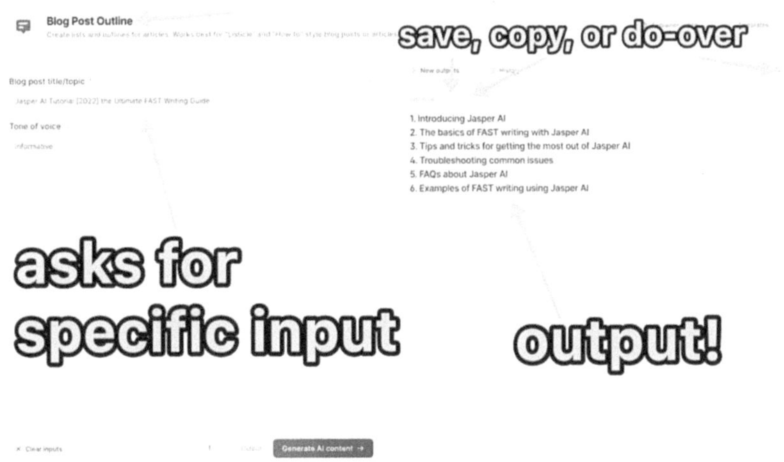

With some outputs, you can choose to copy them, "star" them for later use, or regenerate more copy.
There are a few basic "categories" of templates that Jasper offers…
Here are some blogging Templates:
1. Paragraph Generator (NEW in April 2022): You give an idea of what to write, and Jasper will spit out a paragraph (or more) of content for you to use!
2. Long-form assistant: This template walks you through, step-by-step, of what to include in your blog post (introduction, conclusion, etc.)
3. Blog Post Outline: This is just what it sounds like…Jasper will help you create an outline for your blog post!
4. Blog Post Topic Ideas: Jasper will help you brainstorm ideas for your next blog post.
5. Blog Post Intro: Jasper writes an intro to your blog post
6. Blog Post Conclusion Paragraph: Jasper writes a nice little summary conclusion.
7. Creative Story: You'll give Jasper some input, and the AI will write a story that engages readers.
There are a few more that relate to long-form articles, but those are the bigger ones.

Copywriting Templates:
1. AIDA Framework: AIDA stands for Attention, Interest, Desire, Action. Give Jasper info about your product, and it'll output the framework used by copywriters around the world to write effective sales pages, landing pages, etc.
2. PAS Framework: A similar framework to give sales copy, PAS stands for Problem, Agitation, Solution.
3. Facebook Ad: You'll give Jasper info about your product and target market, and it'll write ad copy! **THIS IS GOLD** for FB ad people–mostly due to the fact you generally need SEVERAL ads to test.
4. Google Ads: Same thing, but for Google Ads!
5. Product Description: You'll give Jasper info about your product, and it writes a description for you to use on e-commerce platforms, etc.
SUMMARY: Templates are pre-made formulas for a specific, short-form copywriting objective! They're available on all Jasper plans.
How to Use the Jasper Long-Form Document Editor
The long-form editor is one of my FAVORITE features of Jasper.
It's an AI-powered writing document that makes it easy to write long-form content like blog posts, articles, and even books!
This is where I spent 95% of my time in Jasper.
1. Access to Jasper's commands (more on this below)
2. Content "lookback," meaning Jasper reads the previous words to better understand what you're writing.
3. SEO mode and power mode, etc.

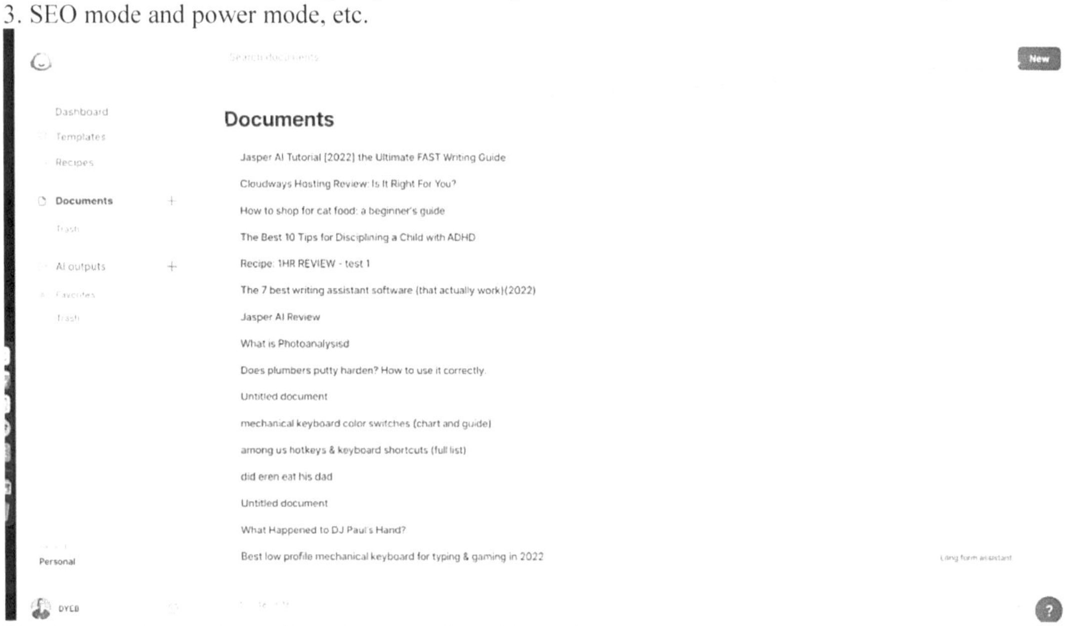

Here's a quick overview of how to use the long-form editor:

1 – Create a new document

First, create a new document (either from scratch, or you can use the "long-form blog post" prompts to help you get started. That basically just helps you whip up the title, outline, and intro to your post–but you can also just do this in the blank editor).

2 – Optionally, just start writing!

Honestly, it's a pretty decent text editor even apart from AI tools. Personally, I like to write a little bit on my own just to help give Jasper more CONTEXT for what we're writing about.

PRO TIP: The more you write, the better Jasper gets! At saying the "right" content, adapting to your tone and formatting, everything.

3 – Use a recipe or template (in Power Mode) to get started.

If you want to kick off your document with a title, outline, content brief, or intro, etc…

You have access to all of Jasper's templates right in the long-form editor (accessed via the "power mode" button).

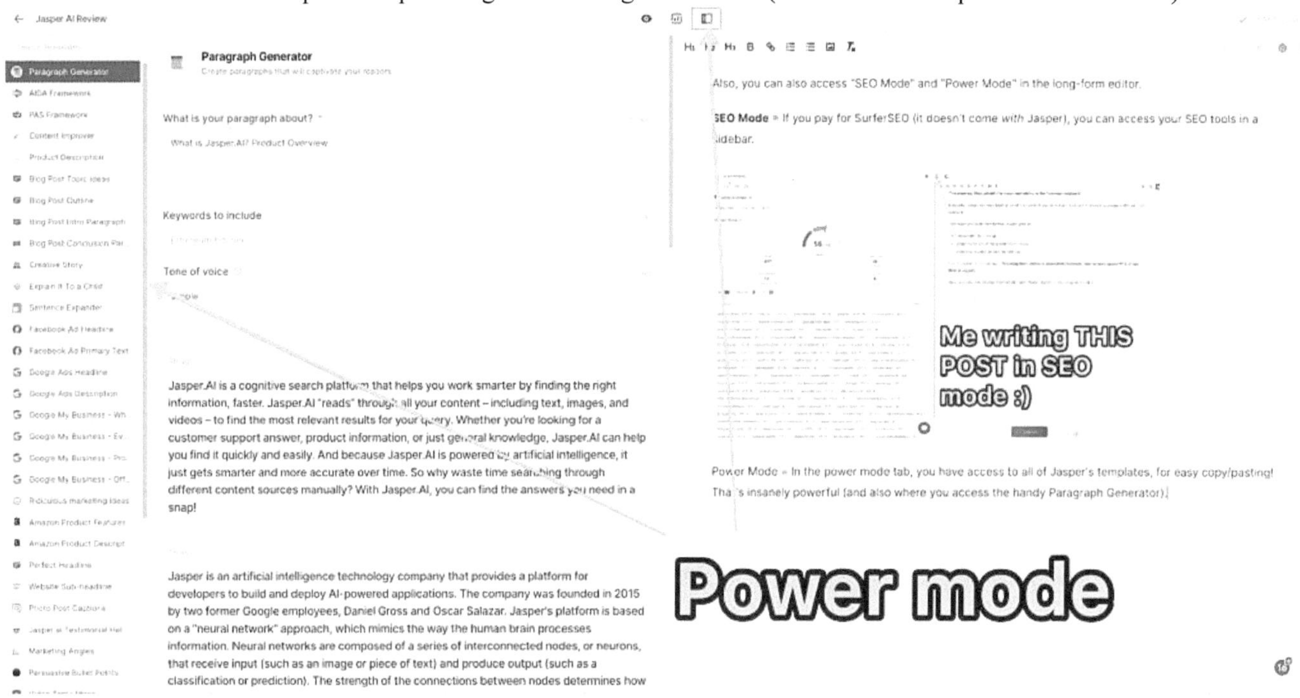

4 – Don't forget to add a title, and optionally a "content brief" to Jasper

While you don't have to do this, it's generally a good practice to fill in the title and description boxes to help Jasper better understand what to create (especially at the beginning of a long-form document BEFORE Jasper can look back!).

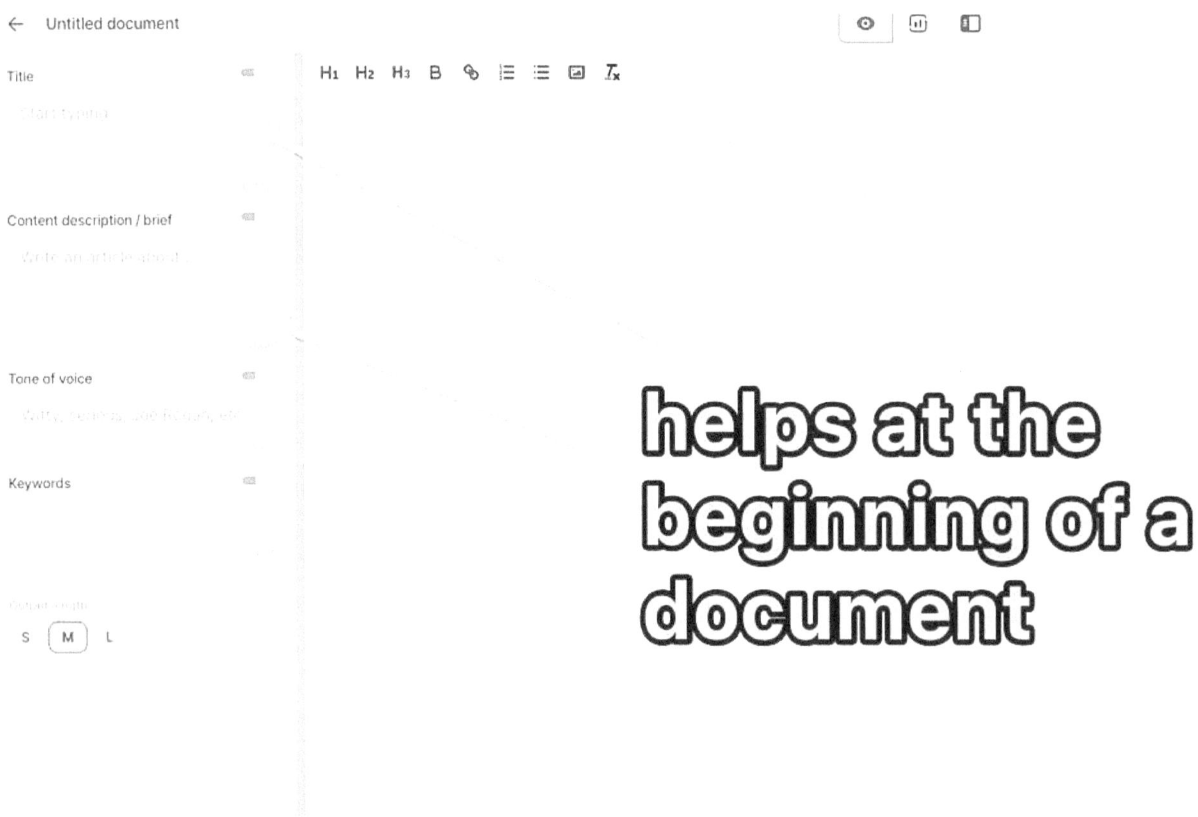

5 – Use Jasper Commands

In the long-form editor, you'll see a "compose" button that will run your instructions for Jasper to analyze and give output.

However, there is another approach to instruct Jasper on what to create—through "commands."

Basically, you can "command" Jasper with natural language processing (i.e. you say "write a blah blah"), and it follows your orders.

Boss Mode Command Ideas

With Boss Mode, you can create content simply by giving Jasper a command and then hitting CMD + Enter or CTRL + Enter on PC.

While there's literally no limit to what you can ask Jasper for, there are some commands he currently understands better than others. He's always improving and learning more and more commands every day, but here are some initial ideas to get you started.

Jasper Commands To Try

Blog Posts

• Set the tone of voice to second-person expert friend.
• Write four blog post titles based on [topic and keywords).
• Write a content brief about [topic, title, and keywords].
• Write an outline that covers [list the main outline topics].
• Write a list of section headings about [topic).
• Make a list of [topic]. (ex. Make a list of auto manufacturers).
• Write an introduction for a blog post titled (title) using keywords [keywords).
• Write an introduction about [section heading).
• Write a paragraph of content about [topic].
• Rephrase the content above.
• Expand on and explain [specific topic / context] in more depth including the keywords [keywords).

Summarizing and conclusion

• Summarize what we will cover in this content based on [outline title 1), [outline title 21, [outline title 3), etc.
• Write a blog conclusion on
• Write a conclusion about the above content. (Likely to write a conclusion paragraph).

You can easily use "natural language processing, " i.e. just telling Jasper what to do in plain English.
Here are some examples of commands you can give Jasper:
1. "Create an outline for my post."
2. "Write a paragraph on the benefits of black garlic."
3. "Give me three ideas for blog post titles."
4. "Add a section on 'how to use black garlic.'"

6 – If you're a SurferSEO user, you can use the SEO mode

Note: SurferSEO is a separate, paid tool for SEO bloggers.
You can open the SEO mode sidebar and get access to all your NLP tools to help you optimize your document for SEO (and it updates in real-time!)

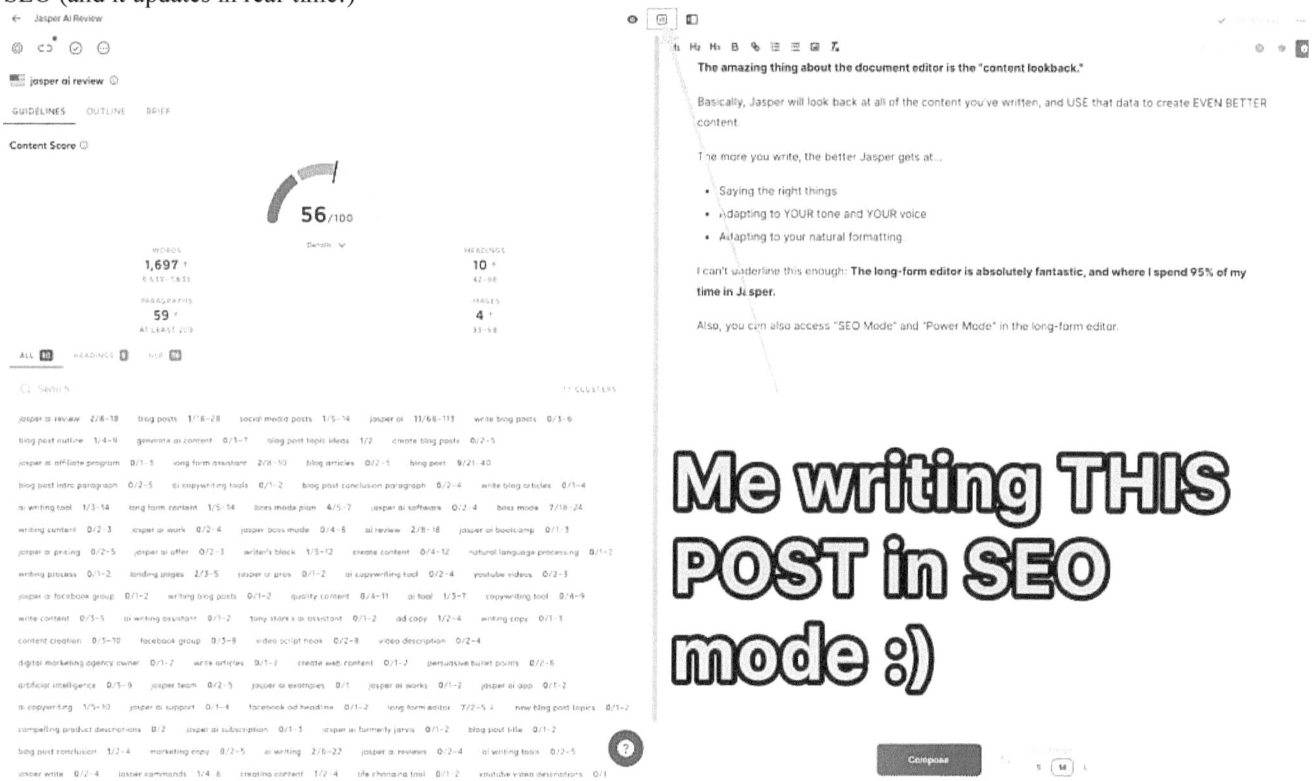

7 – Use the "compose" button to fill in the gaps.

When you need to quickly finish a thought, sentence, or paragraph, tap the compose button (or use the keyboard shortcut) to quickly tell Jasper to start writing.
Note: You'll end up deleting a LOT of what the AI writes, but that's normal–see my tricks below…

8 – See my tips & tricks below…

Below I'll share even more tricks to making the Jasper long-form editor work SWIMMINGLY.

Jasper Recipes: What They Are and How to Use Them

Next up are Jasper's long-form recipes.
These use the long-form editor ONLY (and so they only make sense for the Boss Mode Jasper plan).
Jasper Recipes are community-made templates for different types of content that you can deploy into the long-form editor with one click.

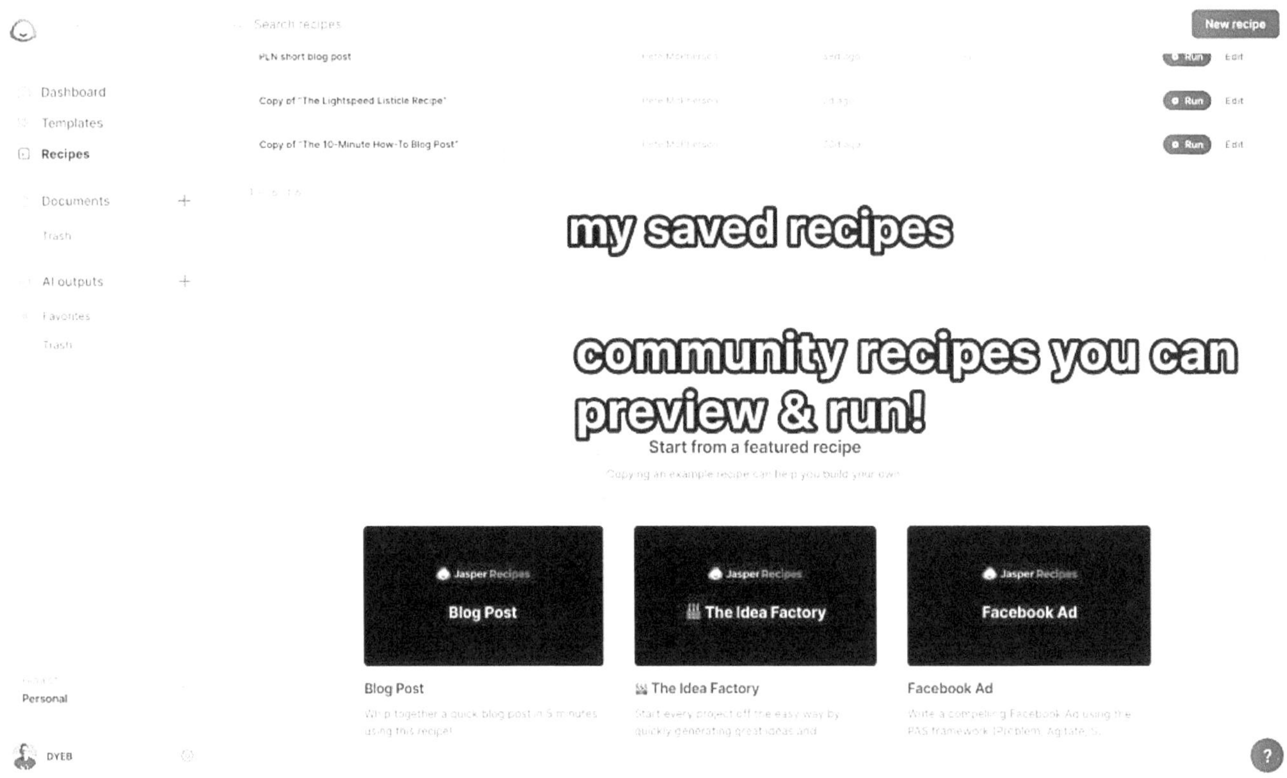

To create a reusable Jasper recipe:

1. Click "recipes" and then "new"
2. Fill in the name and description of your recipe (you can make these public or private btw)
3. Fill in the recipe! This is what will be deployed directly to the long-term editor when you run your recipe.
4. Save it.

You can then "deploy" the recipe to the long-form editor, complete with the variables and commands you wrote in the recipe.

Once the recipe is run, you'll simply go through the recipe and…

1. Replace the variables you created
2. Run the Jasper commands you wrote

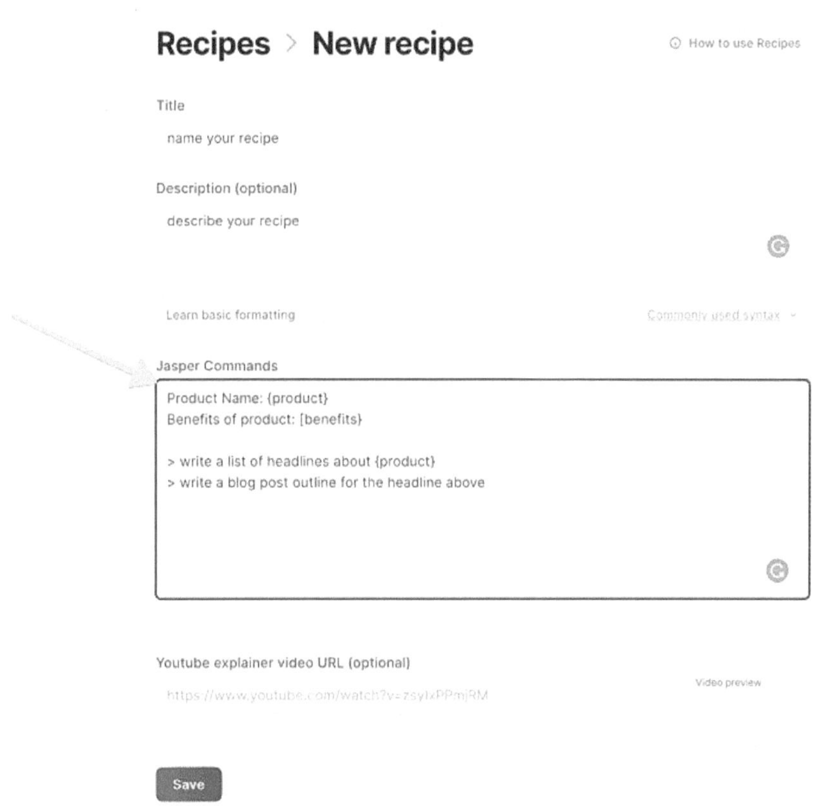

9 Tips and Tricks for Making Jasper Work Better
Believe it or not, that's pretty much it as far as the Jasper platform…
1. You give Jasper inputs (either in specific templates or in the long-form editor)
2. Jasper analyzes its database on the internet
3. Jasper gives you outputs.
That's the easy part. The HARD PART is figuring out how to get Jasper to actually produce GOOD content! And it can take a while to learn.

Here are my top tips for making Jasper work better & faster:

1 – Think of Jasper as an ASSISTANT
Jasper is NOT a completely one-click "done for you" type of tool, but rather an assistant that can help you get your work done faster and better.
If you think of Jasper as your assistant, not a human mind that KNOWS WHAT YOU WANT.
You have to give Jasper SPECIFIC Instructions–else it's going to be useless for you.
And…the more specific you are with your instructions, the better Jasper will be able to help you.

2 – Edit as you go
Again, the more you GIVE Jasper, the better he gets.
It's vitally important to edit Jasper's outputs as you go.
1. Correct the INFORMATION first and foremost
2. Format the content the way you like (Jasper picks up on this!)
3. Delete bad or unneeded content
THEN get back to letting Jasper create outputs. **This is the most important tip in this entire article.**
Many new Jasper users think Jasper's going to do ALL the work for them. It won't.
Let it create content, then edit, then go again.

3 – Get used to constantly deleting Jasper's work.

Speaking of which–don't be worried if you find yourself constantly deleting Jasper's outputs.
It's completely normal.
In fact, the more you use Jasper, the more you'll find yourself doing this.
Jasper gives you a lot of content. Most of it will be unusable. That's just the way it is.
The key is to get used to editing and deleting quickly so quickly that Jasper starts to pick up what you're doing–faster.
Towards the end of a blog post–I usually find that Jasper is MUCH better at anticipating what I want it to do.

4 – "Pre-load" Jasper with facts and opinions!

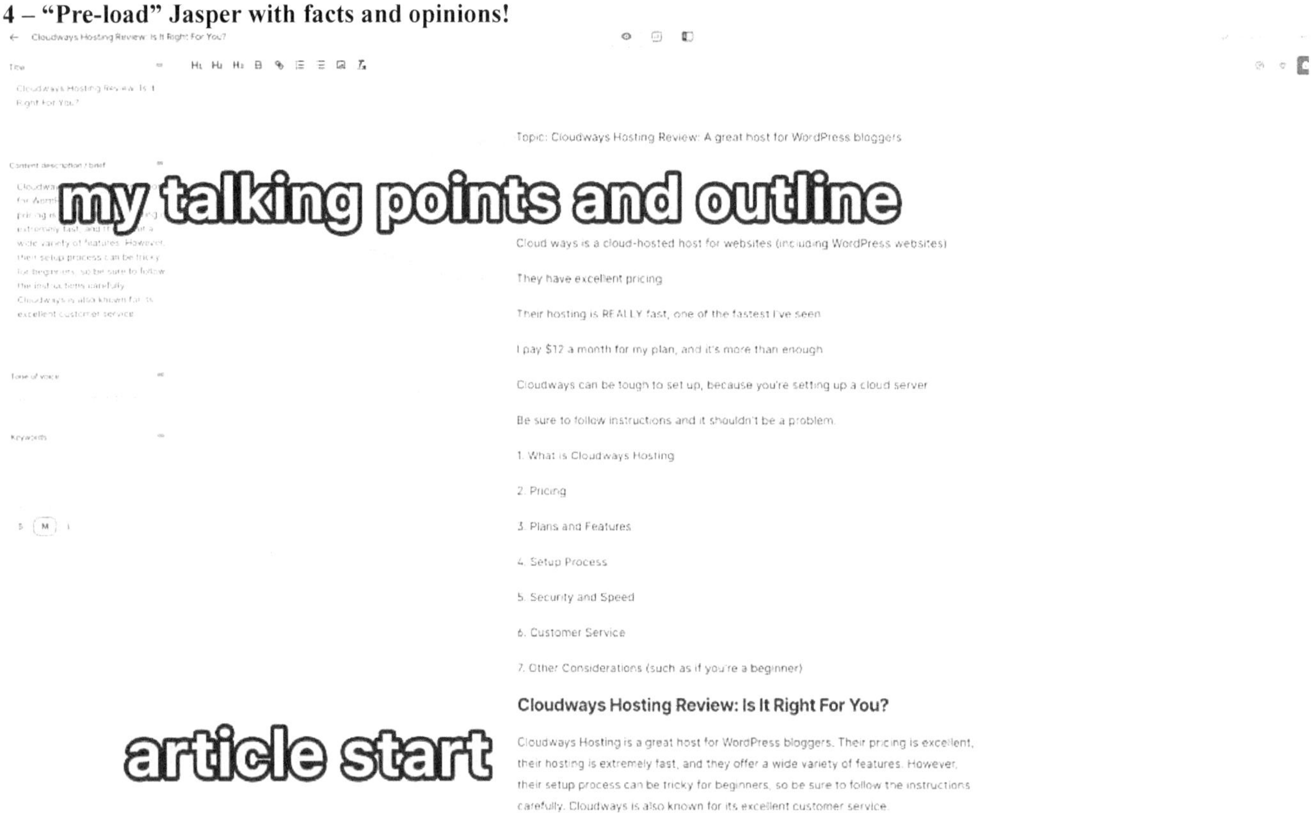

If there's one thing Jasper DOES NOT do well, it's come up with your opinions or accurate facts.
You have to give Jasper those.
The best way to do this is to "pre-load" him with information before you start writing.
For example, if I'm going to write a post about "essential oils for men," here's what I'd do:
1. Google the search term and open the top results
2. Go through each post BRIEFLY, and make notes
3. Collect the accurate data, reviews, product info, etc, that I need
4. Come up with my overall opinion on the topic
5. COPY AND PASTE MY TALKING POINTS RIGHT INTO THE TOP OF THE JASPER EDITOR.

Then I'll start writing and using Jasper. I basically just TOLD him the facts and opinions about the product, and now he'll USE that info in his outputs.
This makes fact-checking and editing so much easier.

5 – Limit Jasper outputs to 1 or 2

Whenever you hit "compose," Jasper will, by default, give you 3 outputs to choose from.
This is great if you want QUICK options, but it also eats up a ton of word credits.
I generally leave my outputs set to 1 or 2, to save credits. You can always re-do it if you don't like those.

6 – Don't give up on Jasper! It gets easier (and way faster)

Like any new software, it will take a hot minute to "figure things out" on the Jasper platform!
All of the AI tools are new, so there's a bit of a learning curve.

I remember when I first started using Jasper, it was SLOW and painful (I literally went through 3 different free trials, before I became a full-time paying user lol).
I'd have to edit EVERYTHING it wrote, and it would take me forever to get a post done.
But little by little, I started discovering these tricks and tips, and Jasper became exponentially more useful to me.

7 – Use the 3 asterisks shortcode
Sometimes, you'll want to tell Jasper to IGNORE certain sections of your content, and that's where the three asterisks come into play.

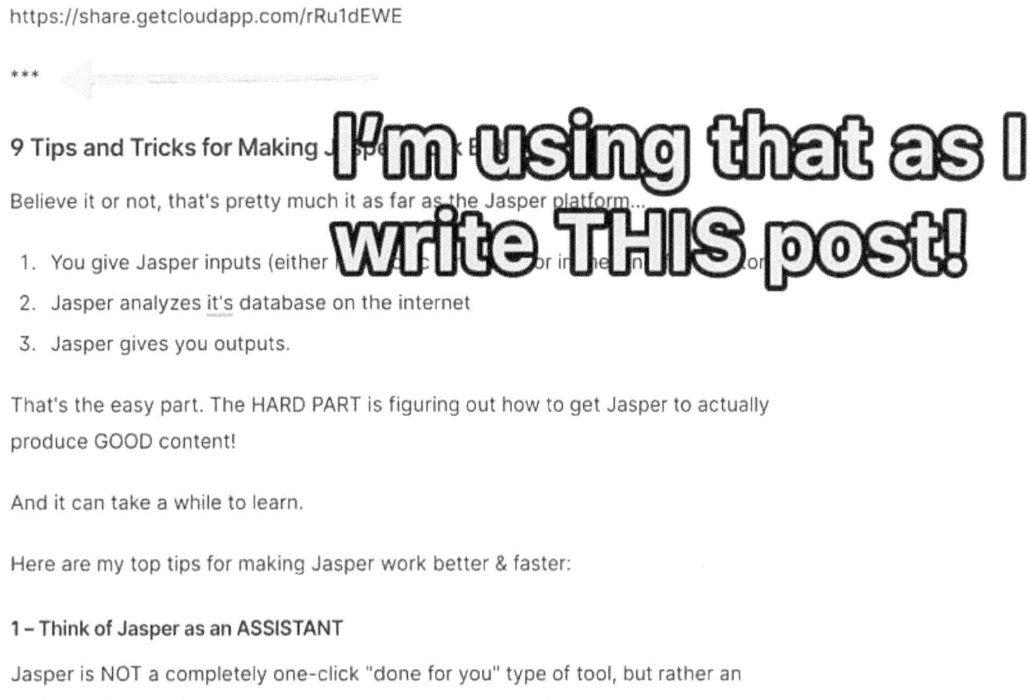

Just put those on a line in the long-form editor, and Jasper will ignore all the content above it.
This will help the AI avoid duplicating content it's already written, and keep it more focused!

8 – Use voice dictation to speed up the process even more
This isn't really a Jasper trick, but more of a writing trick in general.
Look up the keyboard shortcut on your computer to enable voice dictation (it's different from Mac and Windows).
This will allow you to SPEAK your content, rather than type it.
You can even speak Jasper commands. It's almost like talking to a real AI, right??

9 – ALWAYS use the built-in plagiarism checker

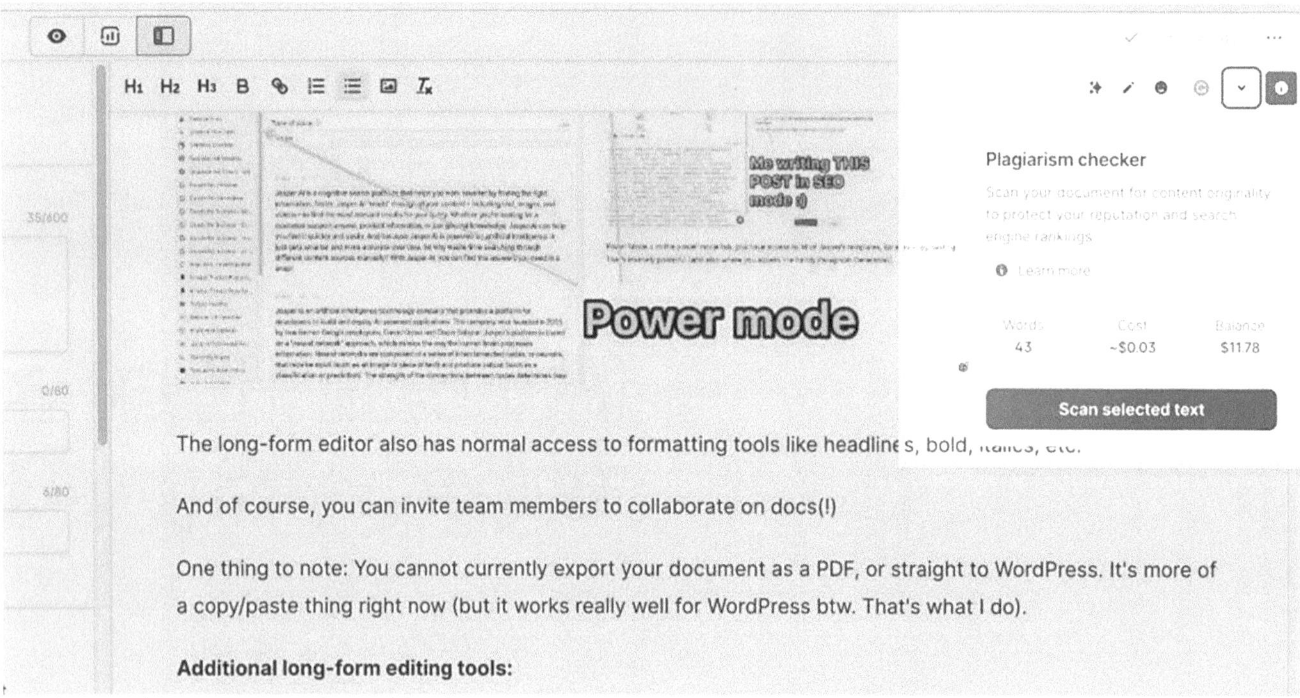

This is one of those "do NOT forget this" tip.
The built-in plagiarism check actually uses Copyscape, a popular plagiarism detection tool.

2.3 GrammarlyGO

GrammarlyGO is a writing assistance tool powered by AI that enables users to generate text instantly, revise existing text, brainstorm ideas, and respond to emails with the support of artificial intelligence. Students, writers, marketers, and other business professionals can use GrammarlyGO to automate their tedious and repetitive tasks.

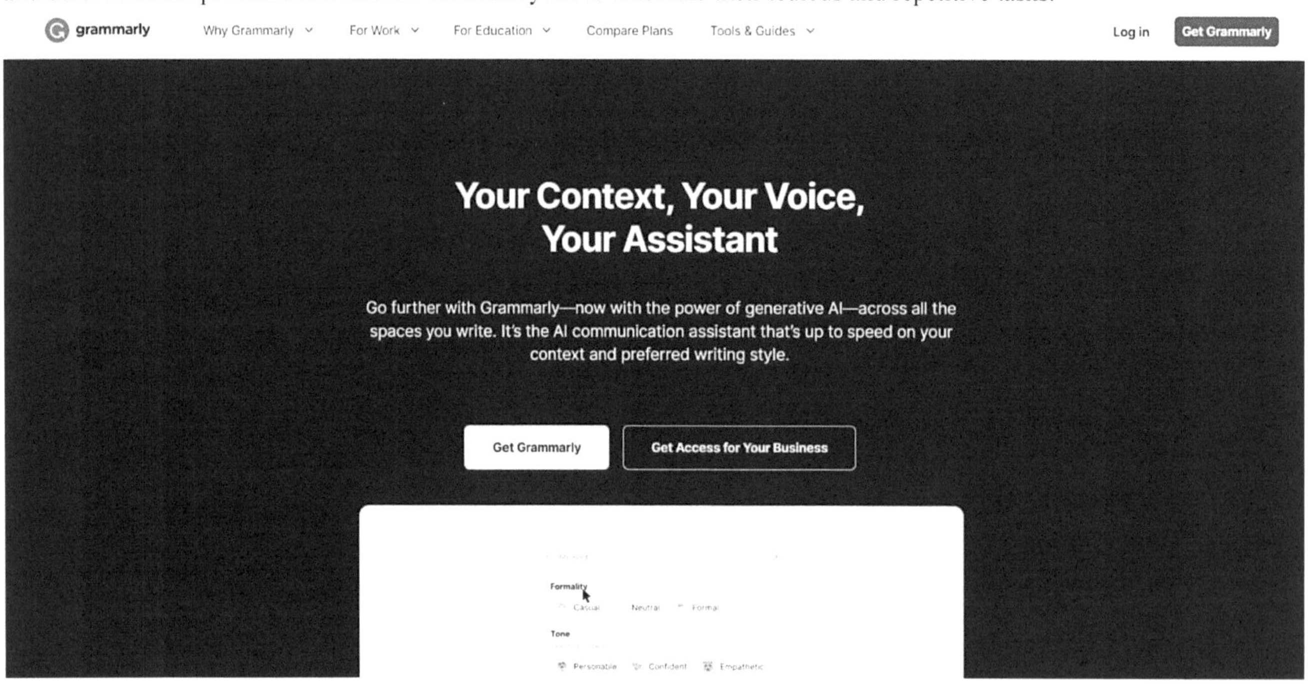

Paraphrase

GrammarlyGo makes paraphrasing content easier, saving time and reducing frustration. It's excellent for users like students, bloggers, and professionals who want to improve their writing.

The tool uses intelligent algorithms to analyze text and offer alternative ways to say things that keep the original meaning but make it more transparent, shorter, and better in style.

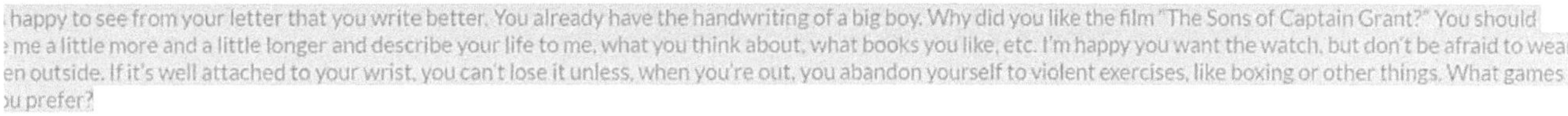

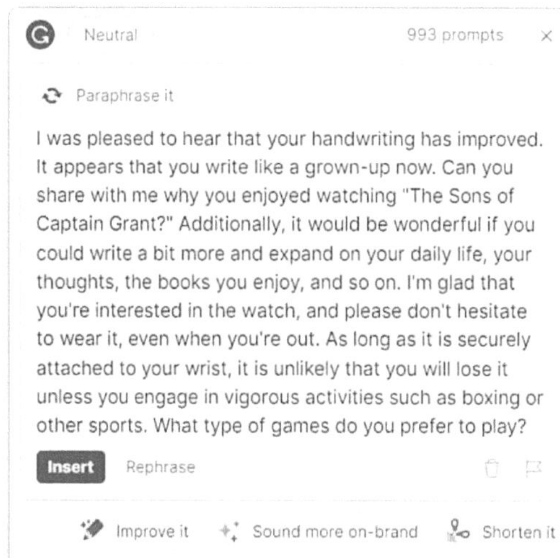

GrammarlyGO best features
1. Produce content in seconds using your own unique prompts or one of Grammarly's suggestions
2. Specify the degree of formality and tone to align your content with your written voice
3. A built-in plagiarism detector for proper attribution and originality
4. It can be used with other work tools, including Microsoft Word and other browser-based apps like Google Docs, ClickUp Docs, LinkedIn, and more

GrammarlyGO limitations
1. GrammarlyGO only currently supports the English language
2. You are limited to a pre-set number of prompts per month based on your pricing plan
3. Since it only offers general writing assistance, this tool might not be the most reliable option for highly specialized or technical fields

GrammarlyGO pricing
1. Free
2. **Premium:** $12 per month for individual use
3. **Business:** $15 per member, per month for teams

2.4 Copy.ai
AI-powered copywriting tools are innovative solutions that leverage artificial intelligence and natural language processing technologies to assist users in creating compelling and effective written content. These tools are designed to streamline the content creation process, providing assistance with tasks such as generating marketing copy, creating social media posts, composing blog articles, and more.

One of the key advantages of AI-powered copywriting tools is their ability to analyze input prompts and produce contextually relevant and coherent text. These tools often incorporate machine learning algorithms that learn from vast datasets, enabling them to understand language patterns and generate content that matches user preferences and objectives.

Write a Twitter thread in a snappy, fun, and conversational tone. It should contain a least 3 tweets highlighting best practices featured in this blog post: https://www.copy.ai/blog/sales-marketing-ai-prompts

Scanning https://www.copy.ai/blog/sales-marketing-ai-prompts

Sure, here's a snappy, fun, and conversational Twitter thread summarizing the best practices featured in the blog post you provided:

1/ Hey, marketers! Want to supercharge your sales & marketing teams? Check out these AI prompts that can help you streamline processes and generate more usable responses. #AI #sales #marketing

2/ Garbage in, garbage out, folks! The quality of the output depends entirely on the input. So, before you get started with AI prompts, clarify your desired outcome and take the time to flesh out your prompts. #marketing #sales #AI

3/ Feeling stuck? No problem! ABT: Always Be Testing. Prompt iteration—tweaking, testing, and refining different types of instructions—will help generate more usable responses over time. Plus, you can stop blank screen syndrome with the right prompts! #sales #marketing #AI

Copy Add to Editor

Copy.ai is an AI-assisted writing tool for producing virtually any kind of content. Its advanced AI language model lends itself to more creative and unique content than its competitors, making it a go-to tool for everything from social media posts to product descriptions.

Copy.ai best features

1. Machine-learning technology to produce error-free creative content
2. AI copywriter is known to generate a wider range of content in comparison to other artificial intelligence tools
3. Its interface is straightforward and easy to use for a smooth user experience
4. It can provide AI-generated suggestions if you're suffering from writer's block

Copy.ai limitations

1. Copy.ai level of service often fluctuates between GPT-3 and GPT-4
2. It doesn't offer the most supportive customer service resources

Copy.ai pricing

1. **Free:** Up to 2,000 words per month

2. **Pro:** $49 per month, with unlimited words (limited to 1 user)
3. **Enterprise:** Contact Copy.ai for pricing

Unlocking Copy.AI: The Login Process

Accessing Copy.AI is a breeze. Here's how you can log in:

- Visit the Copy.AI website and click on "Login" at the upper right corner.
- On the registration page, enter your email address or use your Google email for a simplified registration process.
- Click "Continue" and verify your email using the provided verification code.
- Return to the login page, click "Continue," and start exploring the Copy.AI service.

2.5 Wordtune

Wordtune is a writing enhancement tool that leverages artificial intelligence to assist users in refining their written communication. Whether users are crafting business emails, academic papers, blog posts, or social media content, Wordtune aims to provide intelligent suggestions for improving grammar, style, and overall clarity.

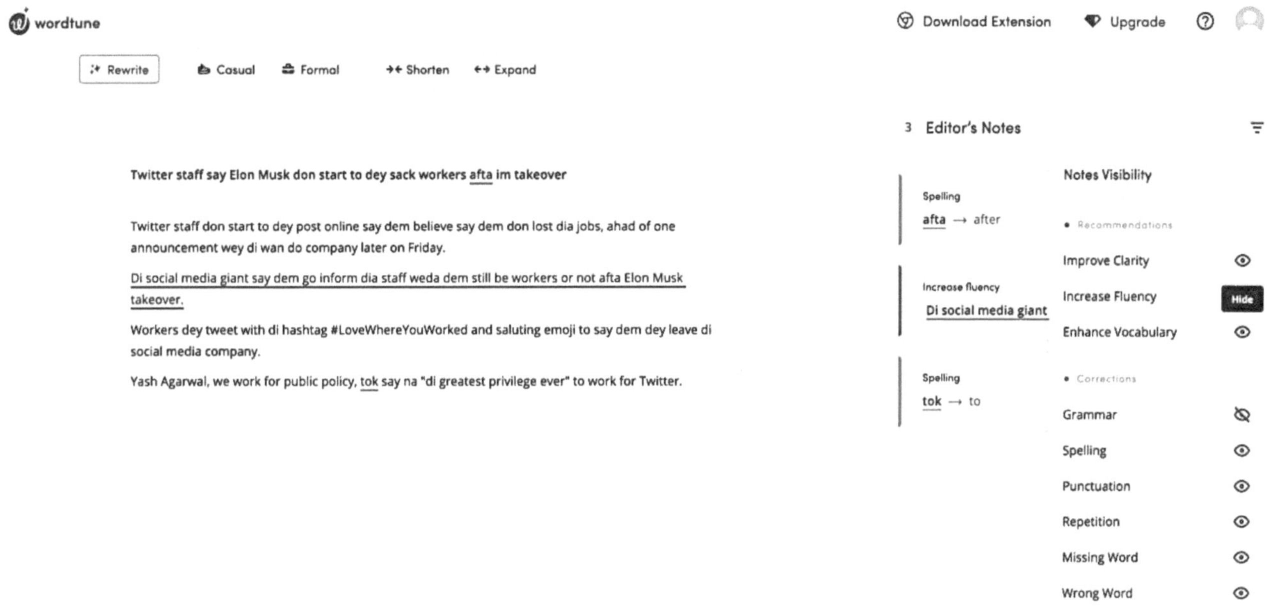

If you're looking for an AI writing assistant without all the bells and whistles, give Wordtune a try. This tool takes a casual and simple approach to its UI so you can focus on what matters most—saving time and staying under budget while crafting the perfect content.

Wordtune best features

1. Wordtune integrates with common work tools like Microsoft Word, iOS, and Google Chrome for an even faster editing and writing experience
2. Its synonyms feature helps you find new ways to say different words and phrases
3. You can easily repurpose video content into written blogs using the YouTube summarization feature

Wordtune limitations

1. Wordtune lacks more advanced functionality, including additional voice setting features and templates
2. Its rephrasing feature sometimes changes the meaning of the original text

Wordtune pricing

1. **Free**: $0 with 10 iterations per day
2. **Premium**: $9.99 per month with unlimited content creation for one user
3. **Premium for teams**: Custom pricing for content creator teams

Potential Use Cases:

1. Business Communication: Wordtune can assist professionals in creating clear, concise, and impactful business emails, reports, and other written communications.
2. Academic Writing: Students and researchers can use Wordtune to refine their academic papers, ensuring that their writing is not only grammatically correct but also clear and coherent.
3. Content Creation: Bloggers, content creators, and journalists can benefit from Wordtune's suggestions for improving the style, tone, and overall quality of their articles.
4. Resume Writing: Job seekers can use Wordtune to optimize their resumes, ensuring that they present their skills and experiences in the most compelling way.
5. Social Media Posts: Wordtune can assist users in generating engaging and well-crafted social media posts for platforms like Twitter, Facebook, and LinkedIn.

Challenges and Considerations:
While Wordtune and similar tools offer valuable assistance, users should be mindful of certain considerations:
1. Overreliance: It's essential to maintain a balance between using AI suggestions and preserving a personal touch in writing. Overreliance on AI-generated content may result in a loss of individuality.
2. Context Understanding: While AI tools like Wordtune are sophisticated, they may not fully grasp the nuances of specific contexts or industries, requiring users to exercise judgment.
3. Editing for Accuracy: Users should carefully review AI-generated suggestions to ensure accuracy, relevance, and alignment with their intended message.

2.6 Writesonic

Writesonic is an AI-powered content generator that creates engaging copy within minutes and only a few inputs. It's a great tool for anyone who wants to bring more variety and authenticity to their blog, newsletter, or other types of content.
If you're looking to create more unique content, but don't have the time to write it, Writesonic may be the perfect tool for you! If you want to create more original content, but don't know where to start, or if you just don't have the time to do it, then Writesonic is the perfect tool for you! Writesonic allows you to create fresh, unique, and engaging content in just a few clicks.

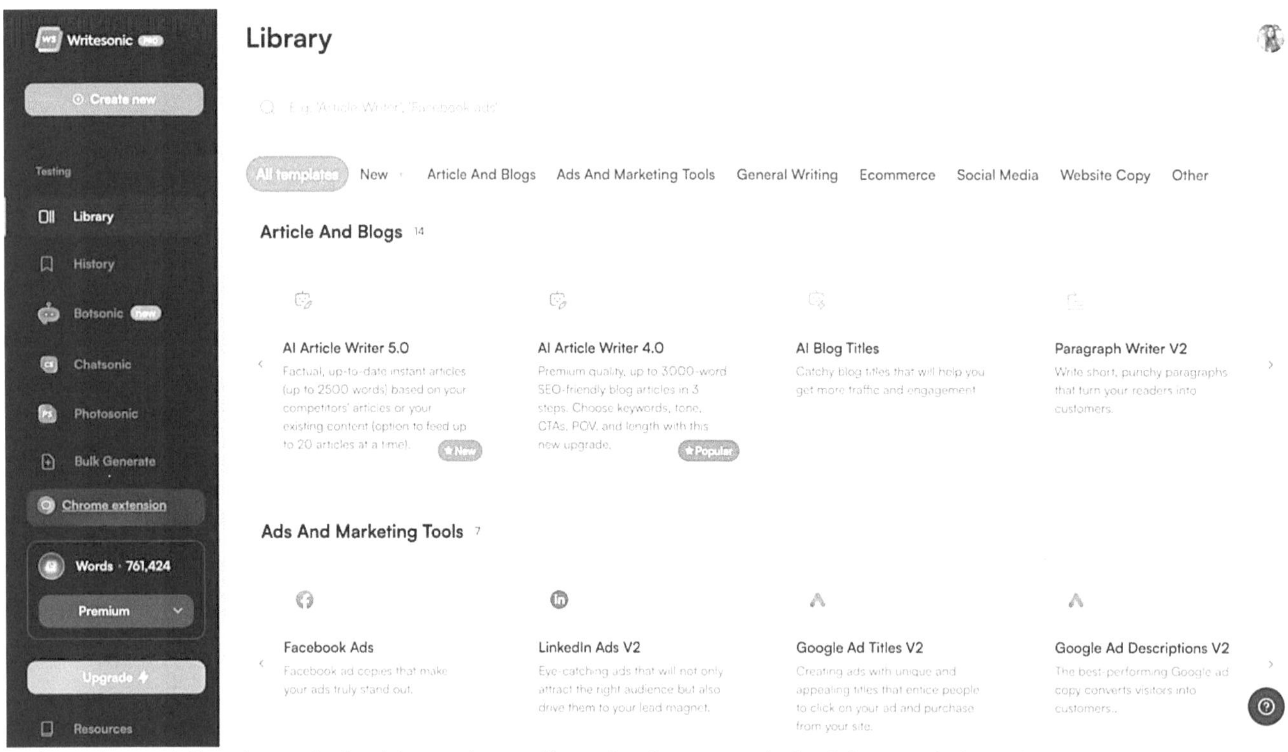

Writesonic specializes in producing blogs, ads, emails, and webpages optimized for search from the jump. This tool runs on OpenAI's GPT-4 model and also offers a chatbot called Chatsonic to specifically fill the gaps left by ChatGPT.

Writesonic best features
1. Writesonic's paid plans use upgraded GPT-4 technology
2. You can repurpose content across social media platforms with Twitter and LinkedIn integrations
3. Advanced features, including voice commands and plagiarism detection

Writesonic limitations
1. The free trial is limited to one user and word count restrictions
2. Writesonic operates on a credit system which requires some strategizing ahead of time to ensure you'll get all of the content you need

Writesonic pricing
1. **Free trial**: For your first 10,000 words
2. **Pro:** Starts at $12.67 per month
3. **Enterprise:** Contact for pricing

Potential Use Cases:
1. **Marketing Copy:** AI writing tools can assist businesses in creating persuasive and engaging marketing copy for advertisements, product descriptions, and promotional materials.
2. **Social Media Posts:** Content creators and marketers can use AI tools to generate catchy and shareable content for platforms like Twitter, Facebook, Instagram, and LinkedIn.
3. **Blog and Article Writing:** Writers and bloggers can utilize AI writing tools to generate ideas, headlines, and even entire articles, helping to overcome writer's block.
4. **Email Campaigns:** AI tools can streamline the creation of email campaigns by generating subject lines, body content, and calls-to-action, enhancing the effectiveness of email marketing efforts.
5. **SEO Content Creation:** Writers and website owners can use AI writing tools to generate SEO-friendly content that ranks well in search engine results.
6. **Brand Messaging:** These tools can assist in developing and refining brand messaging by providing consistent and coherent language that aligns with the brand's identity and values.

Challenges and Considerations:
While AI writing tools offer numerous benefits, users should be aware of certain challenges:
1. **Quality Control:** The generated content may lack the nuanced creativity of human writing. Users need to review and edit the output to ensure it aligns with their voice and intentions.
2. **Ethical Use:** Users should be mindful of ethical considerations, ensuring that the generated content aligns with ethical standards and does not promote misinformation or harmful messages.
3. **Overreliance:** Depending too heavily on AI-generated content may result in a loss of a personal touch or unique voice. Striking a balance between automation and human creativity is important.

Here step by step explanation:

STEP 1 - Go to Writesonic's dashboard and select "Make your own AI."
If case you don't have an account, sign up for free today!

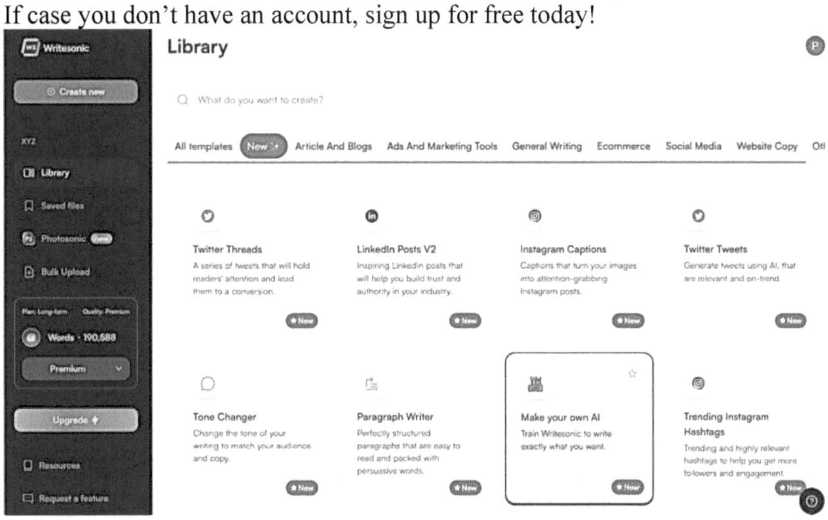

STEP 2 - Add some background information regarding the type of content you want to generate. Try to mention the points that you want to be included in the content piece and be as descriptive as possible.

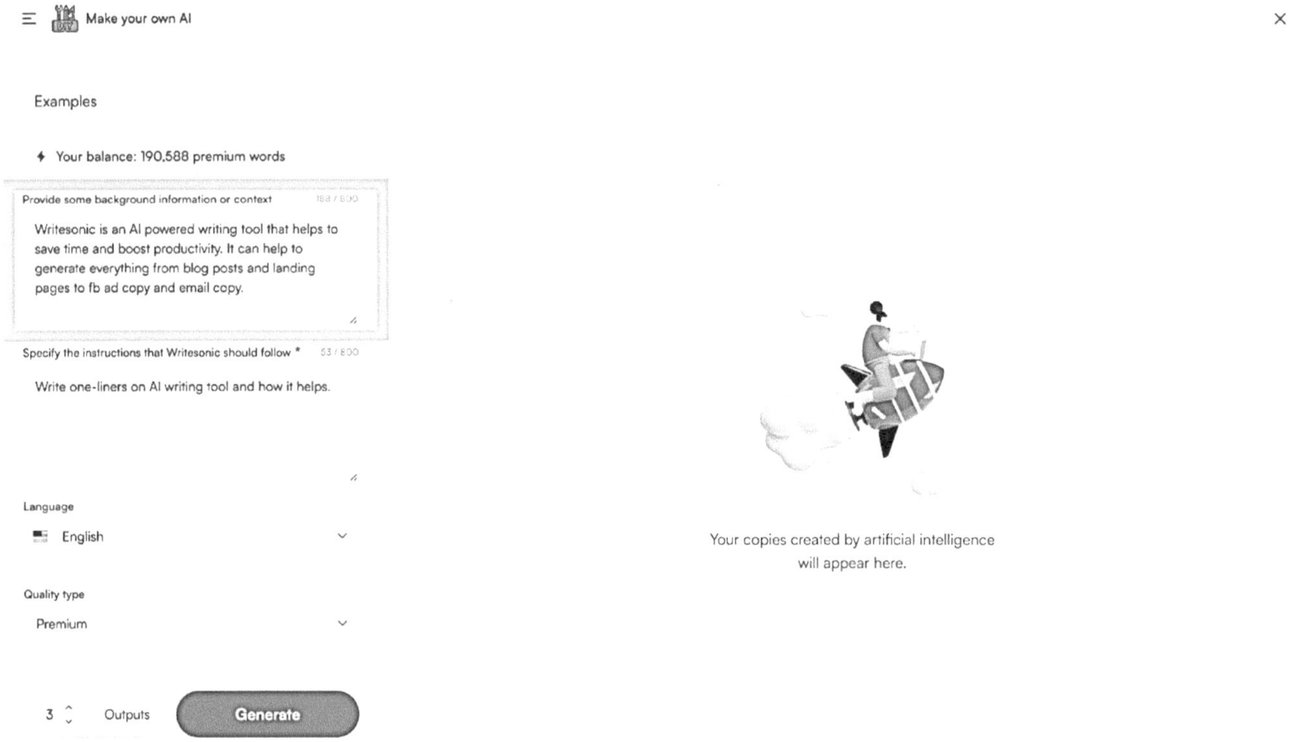

STEP 3 - Specify the instructions that you want Writesonic to follow. For example, what you want to generate, how long it needs to be, the tone of voice, and so on. Be specific about what you would like to generate.

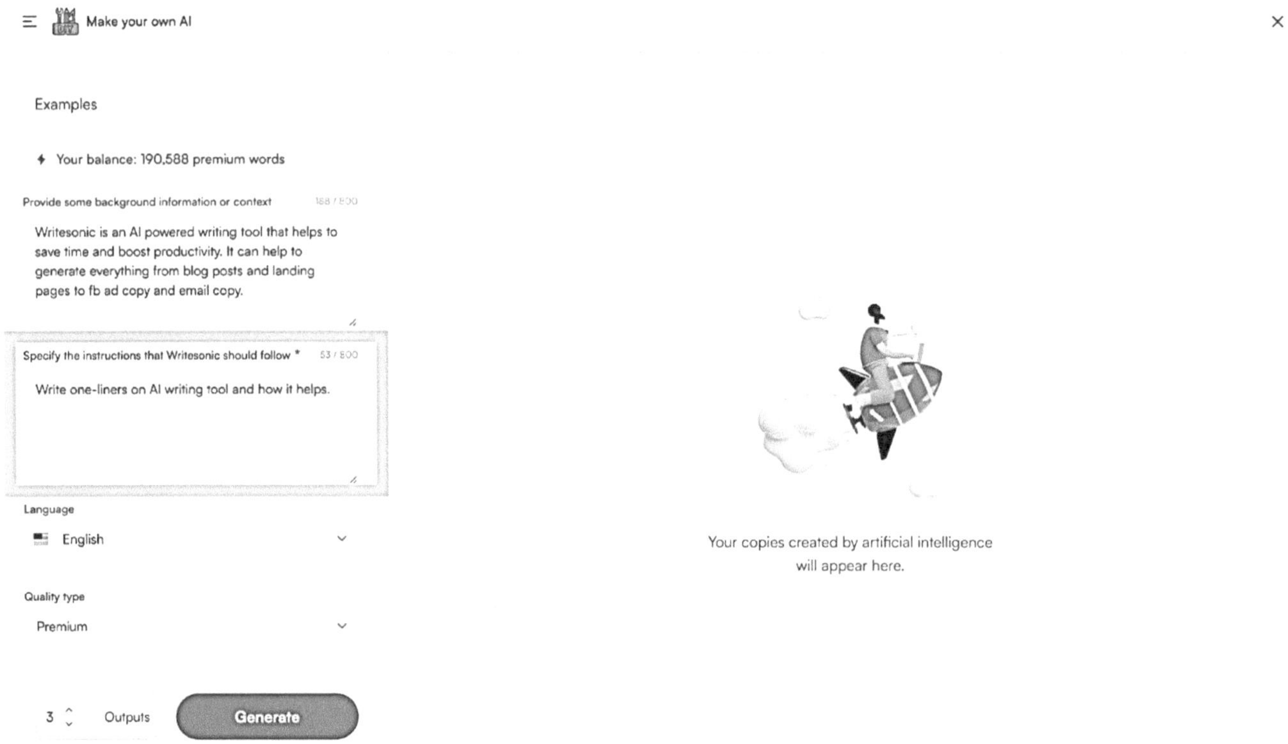

STEP 4 - Next, select the language you want. Writesonic supports 25+ languages that you can choose from. Then, choose the quality type you want (Premium, Good, Economy Average). It is better to keep the quality type as premium for better results.

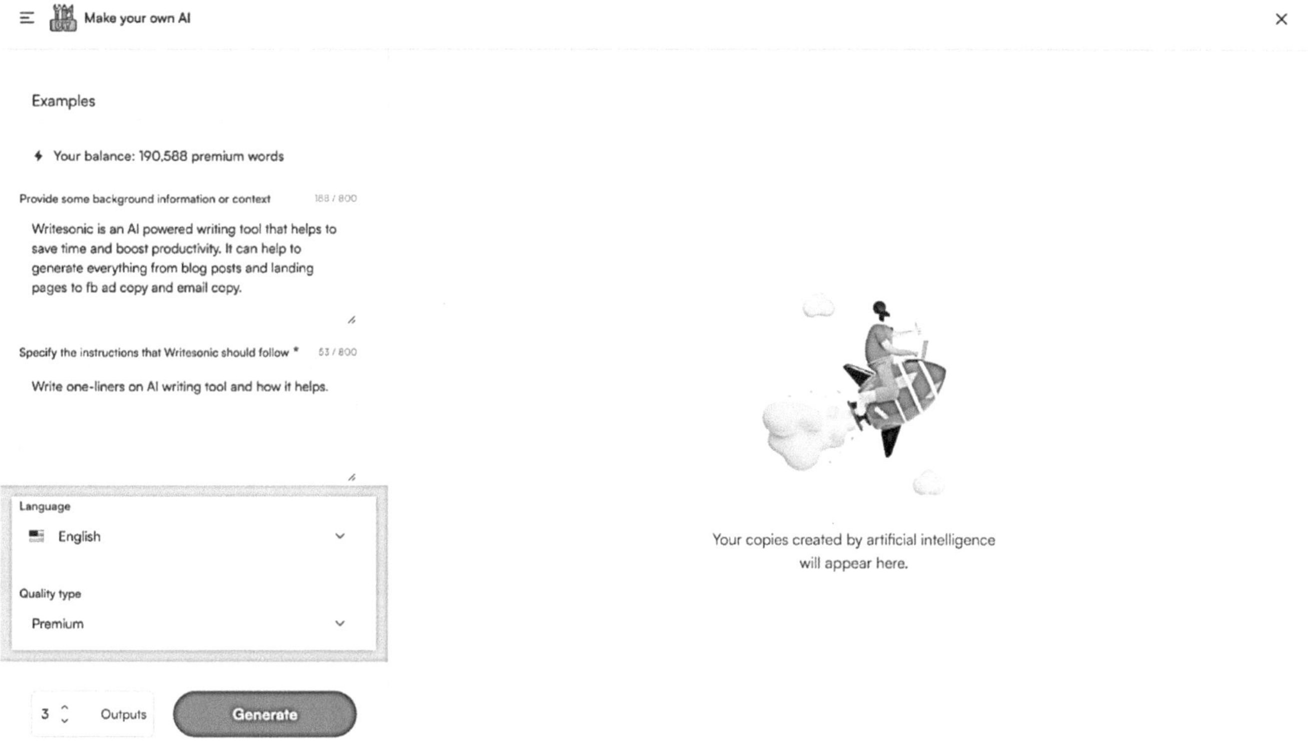

STEP 5 - Finally, hit generate button. And boom! Writesonic's Make Your Own AI generates 3 variations that you can choose from.

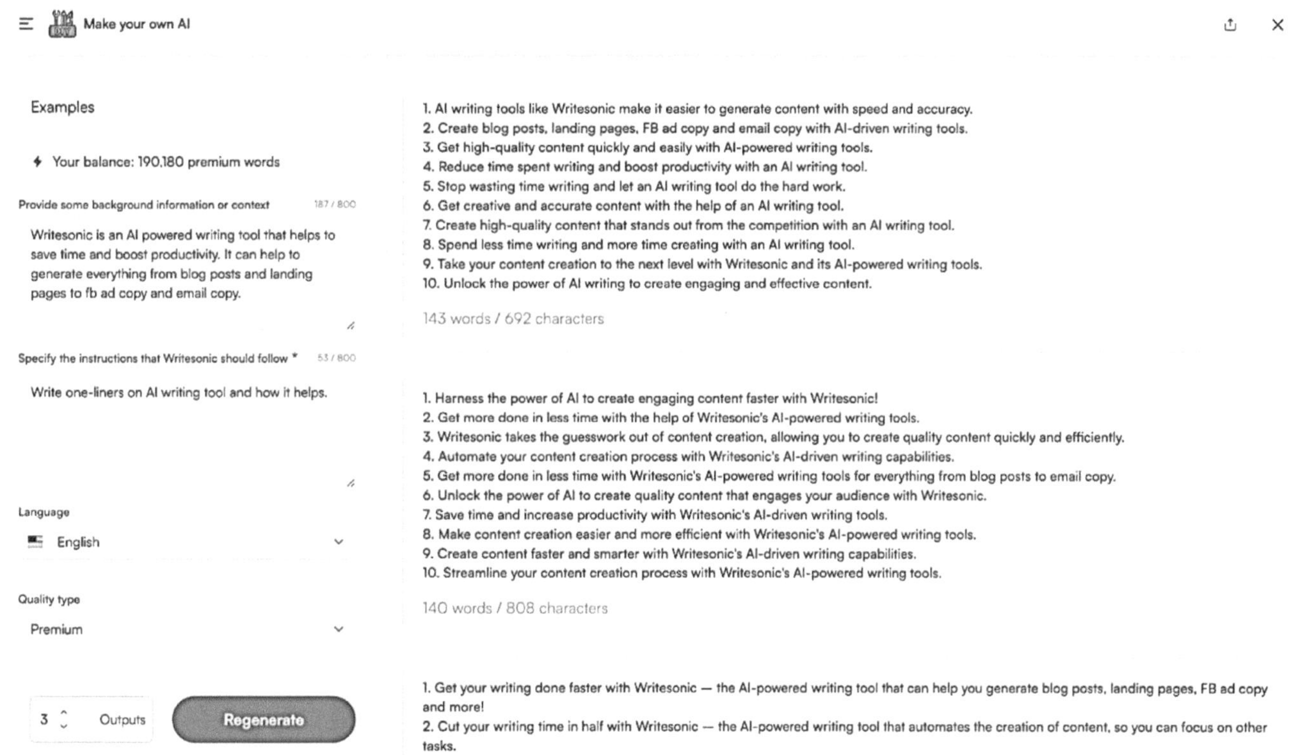

If you want more variations, hit the generate button again.

2.7 Rytr

Rytr creates engaging, SEO-optimized content in seconds using its robust machine-learning capabilities. You can use this powerful AI writing tool to check your academic and professional writing for any mistakes before a major deadline or create net-new drafts of any kind.

Rytr is an online AI writing tool that lets you generate unique, original text for personal and business use. It relies on artificial intelligence for writing and user inputs to ensure the generated text is original, on-topic, covers all the key points, and addresses the topic appropriately.

You can use the Rytr AI copy generator to:

1. Generate content briefs
2. Create long-form or short-form blog posts or articles
3. Instantly get copy variations for ads
4. Get text for email marketing campaigns
5. Use it as an AI essay writer for college assignments — but only for inspiration, of course

The options are truly endless with Rytr, so if you're looking for an AI writing assistant to help you create content ten times faster without breaking a sweat, look no further.

What is Rytr.ai Used For?

There are many use cases for Rytr, ranging from creating high-quality content for your blog and writing the copy for your advertising campaigns to creating cover letters and emails.

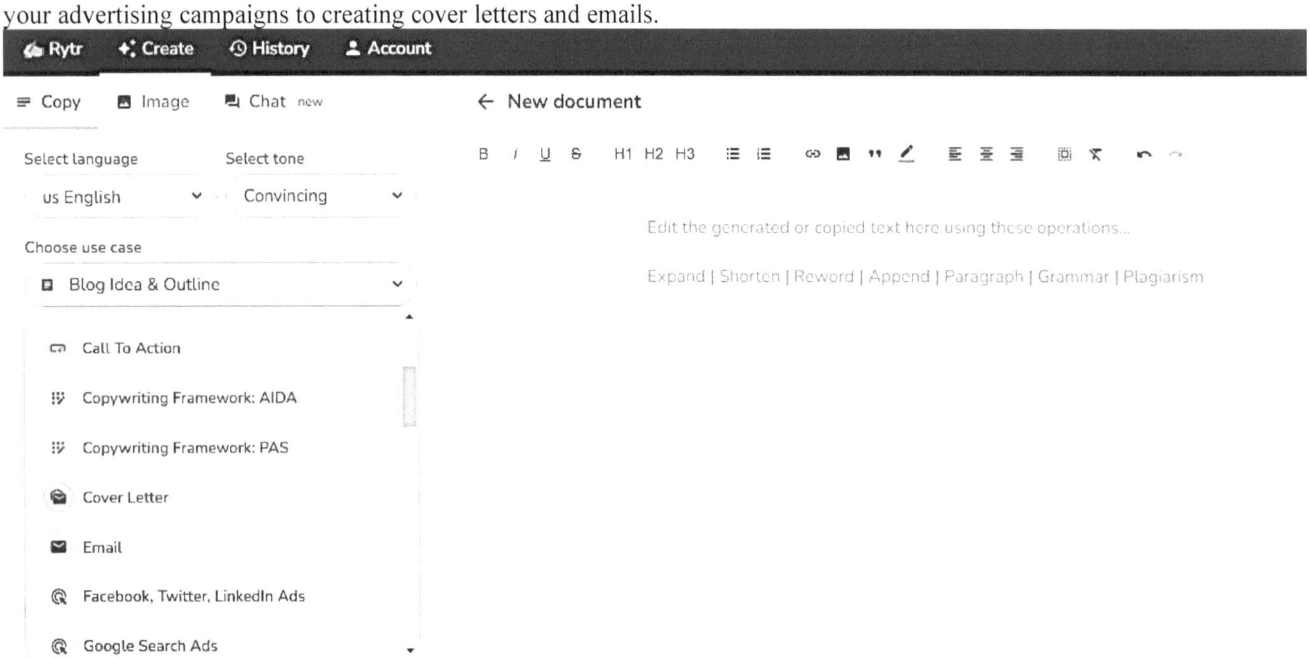

Here's a quick breakdown of the most common uses for Rytr.ai:

1. Content ideas — Rytr can help generate content ideas on virtually any topic. You could use the tool to get ideas for your blog, including full article outlines, or YouTube videos for video content creators.

2. Long-form content — In addition to blog ideas, Rytr can generate text for blog posts. All you need to do is provide it with instructions and keywords, and it will instantly generate up to three variants.

3. Copy — Instantly create multiple variations of ad copy, email subject lines, and Calls to Action (CTAs), then simply choose the one you like the best.

4. Job descriptions — Companies often use the Rytr app to create compelling job descriptions for roles in ads so they can attract top talent.

5. **SEO metadata** — If you don't want to bother with SEO meta titles and meta descriptions but still want to rank high on Google, you can have Rytr create SEO-optimized metadata for you.

6. Product descriptions — For ecommerce stores with thousands of items, it would take weeks to create unique product descriptions for every item. Rytr can do it in seconds.

Rytr best features
1. Various writing modes to generate blogs, social media posts, product descriptions, and more
2. Its UI is intuitive and easy to learn, so you can focus on creating content ASAP
3. It supports multiple languages to make your content more accessible
4. Grammar and spell-checking features to catch mistakes before your content goes live

Rytr limitations
1. Content from Rytr sometimes needs additional editing to smooth out awkward phrasing
2. Word count limitations on every pricing plan, even its "unlimited" option

Rytr pricing
1. Free plan
2. Saver Plan: $9 per month or $90 per year
3. Unlimited Plan: $29 per month or $290 per year

How to Use Rytr — A Quick Guide
To round out this Rytr review, we'll show you just how easy it is to get started with this tool. Follow the step-by-step guide below, and you can start creating engaging, compelling content and copy with Rytr.ai in minutes.

Step 1: Get Started With a Free Plan
Rytr.ai offers a free plan that you can use to try out the tool in practice. It requires zero commitment, and you won't even have to provide your credit card information to test it out.
Keep in mind that the free plan is limited to 10,000 characters each month, equal to around 1,500 to 2,500 words. While this will suffice to test Rytr on one full long-form piece of content, you'll have to upgrade to a paid plan if you want to continue using it on a daily basis.
To get started, visit the official Rytr.ai website and click the Start Ryting button.

Rytr.ai sign up
Then, log in using one of your existing accounts. The available options are for Google, LinkedIn, and Facebook.

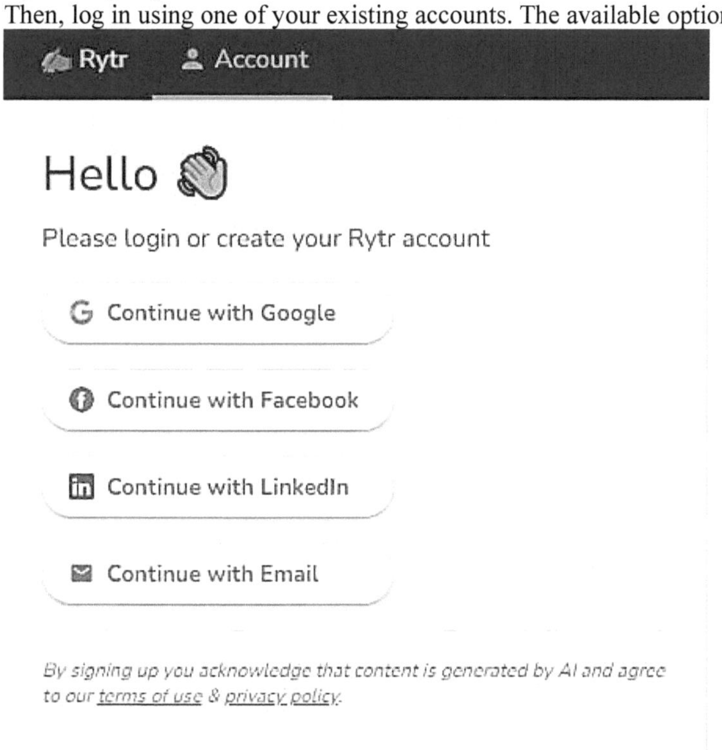

Alternatively, you can use your email address to create an account and use your Rytr login in the future to access the tool.

Step 2: Select a Use Case

Once you log into the dashboard, you'll need to select a Use Case. Put simply, you need to choose what kind of text you want Rytr.ai to generate.

There are currently 35 different use cases to choose from, ranging from blogs and ad copy to job descriptions, keyword generation, and YouTube video ideas.

With a paid plan, you'll also have the opportunity to create your own use case and have Rytr.ai writing any kind of text you need, such as a short story or even a video script.

Step 3: Provide Detailed Instructions to Rytr.ai

After selecting the type of text you want the tool to generate, you need to feed it crucial information for it to know what to focus on.

This includes selecting the tone for the generated text, with options including convincing, informative, casual, and passionate, stating what topic the tool should cover, and providing keywords that Rytr.ai should include in the text.

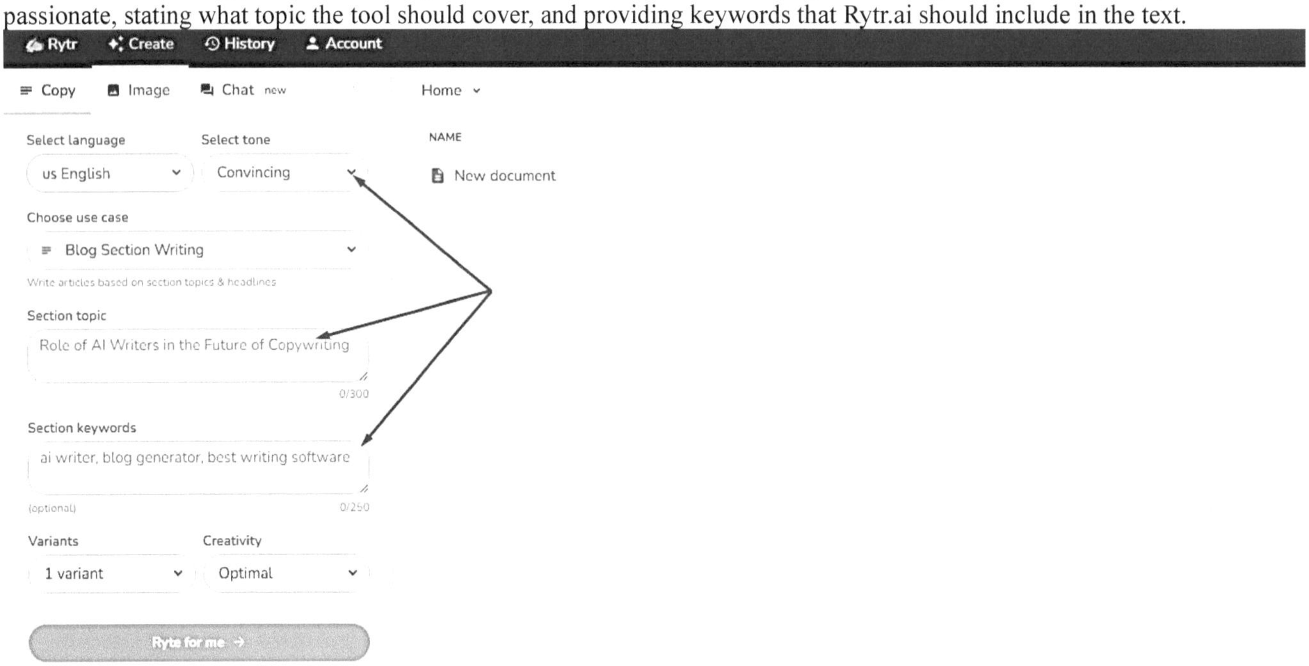

You can also choose how many variants of the text you'd like Rytr to generate — one, two, or three. Keep in mind that with three variants, you're burning through your monthly character limit three times as fast.

So, if you want to fully utilize this feature, we recommend the Unlimited subscription plan, which removes all limitations regarding the amount of generated text.

Step 4: Fine-Tune the Generated Text
Rytr will generate the variations in a couple of seconds, and you'll see all the content right there in the dashboard. You can then select sentences or phrases and use the Improve or Rephrase function to force it to generate that particular section again until you're satisfied with the result, as seen in our previous cat food example.

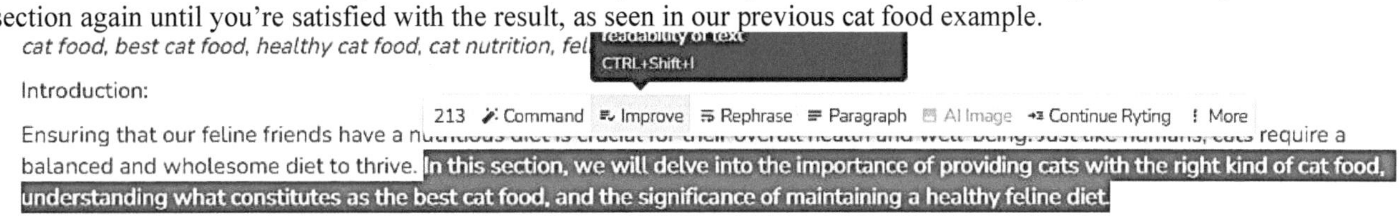

Rytr improve

Naturally, you can also manually edit the text, rewrite parts of it, reorganize paragraphs to your liking, and edit the text as you see fit.

Step 5: Publish the Article
After you're done editing and are satisfied with the final version of the text, you can simply copy-paste it into WordPress or any other content management platform you're using and publish it right away.
The same goes for ad copy. All you need to do is paste the generated text into your campaign and add product images, and you're good to go.

Exercise

Exercise 1 – MCQ

Q 1. What is the primary function of ClickUp in the context of writing and content creation?
A. Grammar checking B. Project management
C. AI-powered writing D. Content optimization

Q 2. Which tool is known for AI-powered writing and content generation?
A. Jasper B. GrammarlyGO
C. Copy.ai D. Rytr

Q 3. GrammarlyGO is specifically designed for:
A. Project management B. Grammar checking on the go
C. AI-powered content creation D. Code editing

Q 4. Copy.ai is recognized for its capabilities in:
A. Project management B. AI-powered writing and content creation
C. Grammar checking D. Data analysis

Q 5. Wordtune is a tool primarily focused on:
A. Project management B. Grammar checking
C. AI-powered writing enhancement D. Social media management

Q 6. Writesonic is known for:
A. Project management B. Social media management
C. Grammar checking D. AI-powered content generation

Q 7. What type of tool is Jasper in the realm of writing and content creation?
A. Social media management B. Grammar checking
C. AI-powered writing assistant D. Project management

Q 8. Rytr is often used for:
A. AI-powered content creation B. Grammar checking
C. Project management D. Social media analytics

Q 9. In the context of content creation, what is one of the key features of Writesonic?
A. Advanced project management
B. AI-generated code snippets
C. Social media analytics
D. AI-driven content suggestions

Q 10. Which tool among the listed options is specifically associated with improving written language skills?
A. Rytr
B. GrammarlyGO
C. Writesonic
D. Wordtune

Exercise 2 – True/ False

Q 1. ClickUp is primarily known as a Writing and Content Creation Tool.
Q 2. Jasper is an AI-powered writing assistant.
Q 3. GrammarlyGO is designed for grammar checking on the go, targeting mobile users.
Q 4. Copy.ai is focused on project management and collaboration.
Q 5. Wordtune is an AI-powered tool that enhances written language skills.
Q 6. Writesonic is known for its capabilities in social media management.
Q 7. Rytr is primarily used for AI-powered content creation.
Q 8. ClickUp is widely recognized for its grammar checking features.
Q 9. GrammarlyGO is specifically designed for code editing purposes.
Q 10. Wordtune focuses on providing AI-generated code snippets.

Exercise 3 – Fill in the blanks

Q 1. ClickUp is a versatile platform that helps users with ___________ and project management.
Q 2. Jasper is known for its advanced capabilities in ___________ and natural language generation.
Q 3. GrammarlyGO is a tool that primarily focuses on enhancing ___________ in written content.
Q 4. Copy.ai utilizes artificial intelligence to generate ___________ for various purposes.
Q 5. Wordtune is designed to assist users in improving the ___________ of their writing.

Exercise 4 – Match case

1. Match the tool with its focus on task organization and project management	A. Wordtune
2. Connect the tool known for its natural language generation and text summarization	B. Copy.ai
3. Pair the tool that focuses on enhancing grammar and language correctness	D. GrammarlyGO
4. Match the tool that utilizes AI to generate copywriting content	C. Jasper
5. Associate the tool designed to assist users in improving the tone and style of their writing	E. ClickUp

Exercise 5 – One word answer

Q 1. ClickUp?
Q 2. Jasper?
Q 3. GrammarlyGO?
Q 4. Copy.ai?
Q 5. Wordtune?

Exercise 6 – Small answer

Q 1. What is the primary focus of ClickUp?
Q 2. What distinguishes Jasper in content creation?
Q 3. Which aspect of writing does GrammarlyGO primarily enhance?
Q 4. What is the main function of Copy.ai?
Q 5. How does Wordtune help users improve their writing?

Exercise 7 – Long answer

Q 1. What are the key features and functionalities that ClickUp offers for task and project management, and how does it contribute to improving team collaboration and productivity?
Q 2. Could you elaborate on Jasper's capabilities in natural language generation and text summarization, and how these features contribute to content creation and automation?

Answers

Exercise 1 – MCQ

Ans: 1 B, 2 D, 3 B, 4 B, 5 C, 6 D, 7 C, 8 A, 9 D, 10 D

Exercise 2 – True/ False

Ans: 1 False, 2 True, 3 False, 4 False, 5 True, 6 False, 7 True, 8 False, 9 False, 10 False

Exercise 3 – Fill in the blanks

Ans: 1 Task organization, 2 Text Summarization, 3 Grammar and language correctness, 4 Copywriting content, 5 Tone and style

Exercise 4 – Match case

Ans: 1 E, 2 C, 3 D, 4 B, 5 A

Exercise 5 – One word answer

Ans: 1 Organization, 2 Summarization, 3 Grammar, 4 Copywriting, 5 Style

ONLINE RESOURCES

Practice Paper

Link https://forms.office.com/r/ar4wgbF1PY

QR Code

Video Content

Link https://www.youtube.com/playlist?list=PLzlh_31VWEFqEXMOclSf0Tt_udPnWJtr4

QR Code

Chapter 6: Coding Tools

6.1 GitHub Copilot

- Introduction: Understanding GitHub Copilot

GitHub Copilot is not your ordinary code autocomplete tool. It is a revolutionary coding assistant powered by artificial intelligence (AI) that can transform the way we write code. In this section, we'll delve into the core concepts and features that make Copilot a game-changer in the world of software development.

- What Is GitHub Copilot?

GitHub Copilot is an AI-powered coding assistant developed collaboratively by GitHub and OpenAI. It's built on the foundation of the GPT (Generative Pre-trained Transformer) technology, which enables it to understand natural language descriptions and generate code based on context.

Unlike traditional code autocomplete tools (such as those found in common code editors like VSCode), Copilot goes beyond simple suggestions by offering complete lines, functions, or even entire code blocks based on your coding context and intentions.

- Supported Languages and IDEs

GitHub Copilot supports a wide range of programming languages, including JavaScript, Python, Ruby, Go, and more. It is designed to cater to the diverse needs of developers across various technology stacks.

It's compatible with popular Integrated Development Environments (IDEs) such as Visual Studio Code (VS Code). This means we can seamlessly integrate Copilot into our preferred development environment, enhancing our coding experience.

- Licensing and Pricing

GitHub Copilot comes with its own licensing and pricing model. While specifics might change over time, it's important to understand the terms and costs associated with using Copilot in your projects.

Typically, Copilot is offered through GitHub's pricing plans, which include both free and paid tiers. The paid plans often provide additional features and support for commercial use.

Keep in mind that GitHub Copilot might have different licensing agreements for personal and commercial use, so it's essential to review the terms based on your project's requirements.

- Capabilities and Limitations

GitHub Copilot has impressive capabilities, but it's not perfect. It excels in generating code based on context and descriptions, but developers should exercise caution and review its suggestions to ensure correctness, security, and adherence to project-specific standards.

While Copilot is proficient in understanding natural language, it will not fully replace a developer's expertise, especially for intricate or domain-specific tasks.

- Community and Ecosystem

Copilot benefits from the vast GitHub community and ecosystem. Developers worldwide contribute to its improvement by providing feedback, creating plugins, and sharing their experiences.

GitHub Copilot integrates with GitHub's code repositories, making it a valuable tool for collaborative development. It can assist in pull request reviews, suggesting changes and enhancements.

By grasping these fundamental aspects of GitHub Copilot, we can harness its potential. In the following sections, we'll explore how to get started with Copilot, integrate it into our development environment, and utilize its features to become a more efficient developer.

Getting Started with GitHub Copilot

In this section, we'll walk you through the initial setup process, linking Copilot to your GitHub account, and ensuring you have the necessary permissions.

Installation and Setup

1. Step 1: Install a Supported IDE: To get started with GitHub Copilot, you'll need an Integrated Development Environment (IDE) that supports it. Visual Studio Code (VS Code) is one of the most popular choices. Ensure that you have VS Code installed or choose another supported IDE according to your preference.

2. Step 2: Install the GitHub Copilot Extension: Once your IDE is set up, you can install the GitHub Copilot extension. In VS Code, visit the VS Code marketplace and search for "GitHub Copilot." Click the "Install" button to add the extension to the IDE.
3. Step 3: Sign in to GitHub: Launch your IDE, and you'll be prompted to sign in with your GitHub account. If you don't have one, you'll need to create an account on GitHub. This step is essential to link Copilot to your GitHub repositories.

Linking to GitHub

1. Step 4: Authorize GitHub Copilot: After signing in, GitHub Copilot will request permission to access your GitHub account. Authorize the extension to connect to your account.
2. Step 5: Repository Access: Copilot needs access to your repositories to understand your project's context. Ensure that you grant the necessary permissions for the specific repositories you plan to work on with Copilot.

Authentication and Permissions

1. Step 6: Set Up SSH or Personal Access Tokens: Depending on your GitHub settings and security preferences, you might need to set up SSH keys or generate personal access tokens to authenticate your IDE with GitHub. These credentials ensure secure communication between Copilot and your repositories.
2. Step 7: Configure Repository Access: In your GitHub account settings, navigate to "Developer Settings" and configure repository access for Copilot. Ensure that Copilot can read and write to repositories as needed for your projects.

With these steps completed, you're ready to start using GitHub Copilot within your development environment. It's important to note that Copilot's effectiveness is closely tied to the repositories it has access to, so be sure to configure permissions appropriately.

In the upcoming sections of this tutorial, we'll delve into how to use Copilot effectively, from basic code generation to advanced techniques. You'll soon discover how Copilot can become an invaluable coding companion, improving your productivity, and helping you write high-quality code more efficiently.

Using GitHub Copilot Effectively

Now that you have GitHub Copilot installed and linked to your GitHub account, it's time to harness its full potential. In this section, we'll explore the several ways you can use Copilot effectively to boost your productivity, adhere to best practices, and even debug your code.

Basic Code Generation

Code Autocompletion: Copilot excels at code autocompletion. As you type, it suggests code snippets, function definitions, and variable names that are contextually relevant to your current coding task.

Code Blocks and Functions: To create a new function or code block, start typing the function name or code structure and Copilot will provide suggestions. Accepting these suggestions can save you time when writing boilerplate code.

Natural Language Assistance

Descriptive Comments: One of Copilot's powerful features is its ability to generate code from natural language descriptions. You can write comments in plain English describing what you want to achieve, and Copilot will generate the corresponding code.

Conversational Programming: You can engage in conversational programming with Copilot by asking s or providing descriptions of your solution requirements. Copilot responds to your natural language input with code suggestions.

Coding Best Practices

Coding Standards: Copilot can help you adhere to coding standards and best practices. It suggests code that follows industry conventions, improving the readability and maintainability of your code.

Error Handling: When writing error-handling code, Copilot can provide suggestions for catching exceptions, logging errors, and handling them gracefully.

Debugging and Error Handling

Troubleshooting: If you encounter an error in your code, you can use Copilot to assist in debugging. To do this, write a description of the issue in a comment, and Copilot may suggest debugging strategies or solutions.

Test Case Generation: Copilot can also help generate test cases or unit tests based on your code. This can be valuable for maintaining code quality and ensuring that your code works as expected.

Incorporating Copilot into your coding workflow involves embracing its assistance when it's helpful and critically evaluating its suggestions to ensure they align with your project's requirements and coding standards.

Tips for Effective Copilot Usage:

1. Review Suggestions: Always review Copilot's suggestions. While it's a powerful tool, it's fallible, and you should ensure that the generated code meets your project's specific needs.
2. Provide Clear Context: When using natural language input, provide clear and concise descriptions of your coding intentions. The more context you provide, the more accurate Copilot's suggestions will be.

3. Use Custom Snippets: Consider creating custom code snippets for your project's unique patterns or frequently used code structures. Copilot can learn from these snippets and provide more tailored suggestions.
4. Collaborate and Learn: Collaborate with team members who use Copilot and share your experiences. It can be a valuable tool for learning and improving your coding skills.
5. Stay Security-Conscious: Be mindful of security best practices. Copilot may not always generate secure code, so it is essential to review and validate code for potential vulnerabilities.
By using GitHub Copilot effectively, you can significantly enhance your coding experience, improve code quality, and accelerate your development process. In the next section of this tutorial, we will explore advanced techniques and tips for taking your Copilot usage to the next level.

Advanced Techniques and Tips

GitHub Copilot is a versatile tool that can adapt to various coding scenarios and workflows. In this section, we will explore advanced techniques that can help you maximize the benefits of Copilot for more complex projects and collaborative development.
1. Custom Code Snippets
- Creating Custom Snippets: GitHub Copilot allows you to create and save custom code snippets. This is especially valuable for frequently used patterns, project-specific code, or complex logic that you want Copilot to generate accurately.
- Teaching Copilot: By using custom snippets, you can effectively teach Copilot your project's coding conventions and unique patterns. Copilot will learn from these snippets and offer more contextually relevant suggestions.
2. Working with Frameworks and Libraries
- Leveraging Frameworks: If you are developing with a particular framework or library, Copilot can assist by providing code snippets and function calls specific to that framework. This can significantly speed up your development process.
- Integrating with APIs: When working with external APIs or services, Copilot can generate code for making API requests, handling responses, and integrating data seamlessly into your application.
3. Code Reviews and Collaboration
- Code Review Assistance: GitHub Copilot can be an asset during code reviews. It can suggest code improvements, point out potential issues, and help ensure that the code adheres to best practices.
- Collaborative Development: When collaborating with team members, Copilot can assist in maintaining code consistency across the project. It helps ensure that everyone follows the same coding standards and conventions.
4. Automating Repetitive Tasks
- Task Automation: Copilot can automate repetitive coding tasks, such as data serialization, file handling, or database queries. By generating this code, you can focus on higher-level aspects of your project.
- Boilerplate Code: Copilot is excellent at generating boilerplate code for new components or modules. It can save you time when setting up the initial structure of your code.
5. Enhancing Productivity
- Code Generation in Batches: If you need to generate a significant amount of code quickly, Copilot can assist by providing code in batches. This can be useful when scaffolding multiple similar components.
- Code Refactoring: Copilot can help with code refactoring tasks by suggesting improvements to existing code, making it more maintainable and efficient.
6. Contribute to Copilot's Learning
- Provide Feedback: As you use Copilot, consider providing feedback on its suggestions. GitHub encourages user feedback to improve Copilot's accuracy and utility.
- Share Knowledge: Sharing your experiences and knowledge with the GitHub Copilot community can help others learn how to use it effectively and discover unique use cases.
7. Stay Security-Conscious
- Security Awareness: When using Copilot for security-related code, be especially vigilant. Review generated code for potential security vulnerabilities and follow security best practices.
- By embracing these advanced techniques and tips, you can take full advantage of GitHub Copilot's capabilities and elevate your coding experience. Remember that Copilot is a versatile tool that can adapt to your specific needs, making it an asset for both individual and team-based development projects.

Let's show you how to do that.

Step 1. Install Copilot Labs
Make sure you have GitHub Copilot installed*. If you have access to Copilot, you'll also be able download and install GitHub Copilot Labs.

Step 2. Choose code to explain
Open your VS Code editor and open a file with code you want explained.
Also, make sure you have Copilot turned on. You can find the Copilot icon in the bottom tray on the left hand side. Click it, and sure you select "Enable".

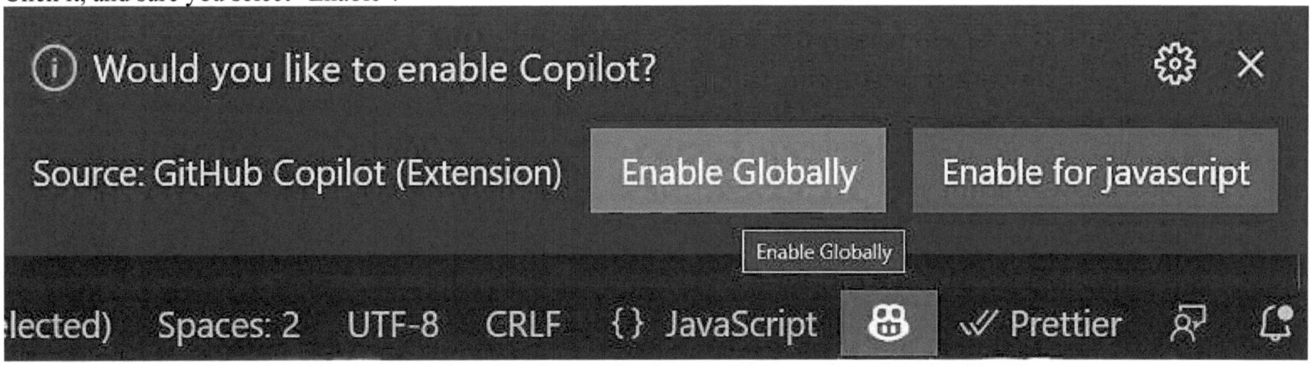

I always click "Enable Globally" because then Copilot works for everything and not just the file I have open.

Step 3. GitHub Copilot Labs sidebar
The GitHub Copilot Labs sidebar has everything you need to explain and translate code. You'll find the toolbar on the left side of the screen. If you can't see it, click the ellipses and you'll find a list of any additional extensions you have installed.

The GitHub Copilot Labs icon will only appear if you have installed GitHub Copilot Labs. Click the icon and it will toggle open a new pane. If you still have your code highlighted, your screen should look something like:

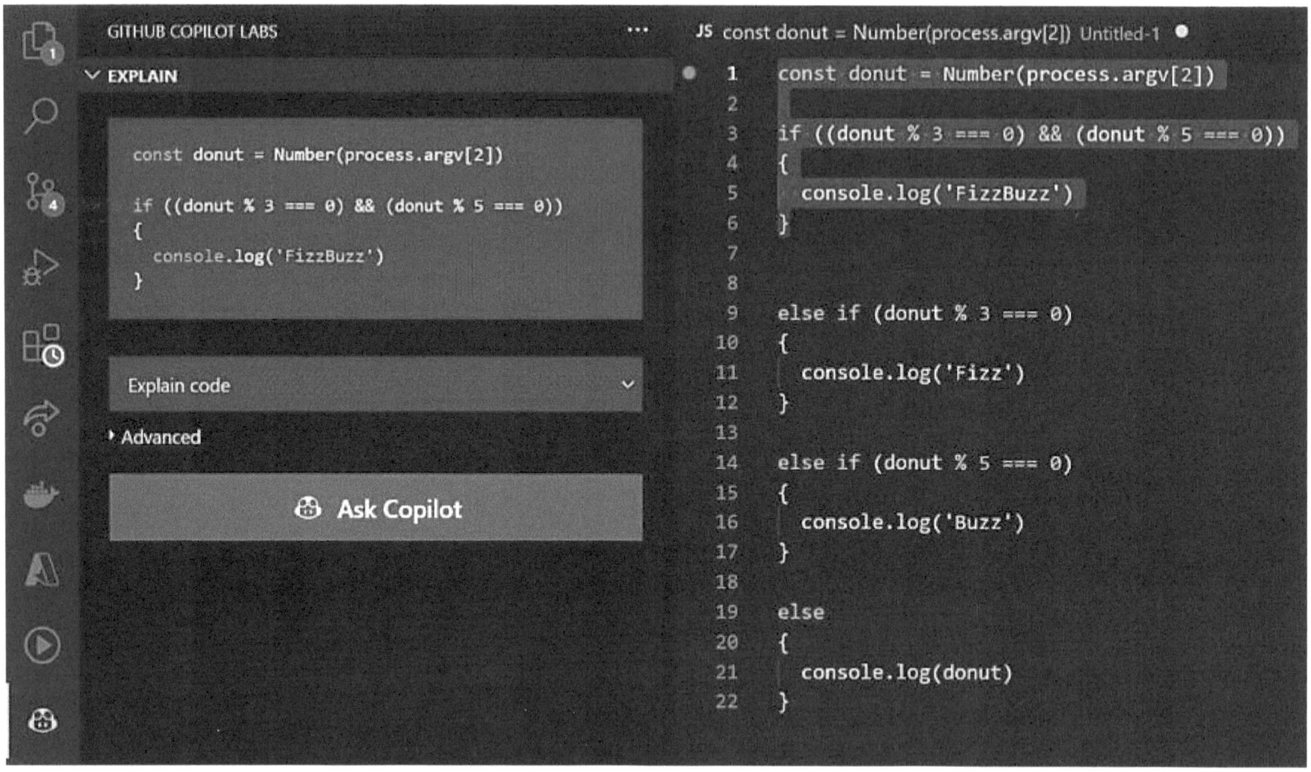

Step 4. Highlight Code
Now that you have the Copilot Labs sidebar open, highlight the chunk of code you'd like to better understand.

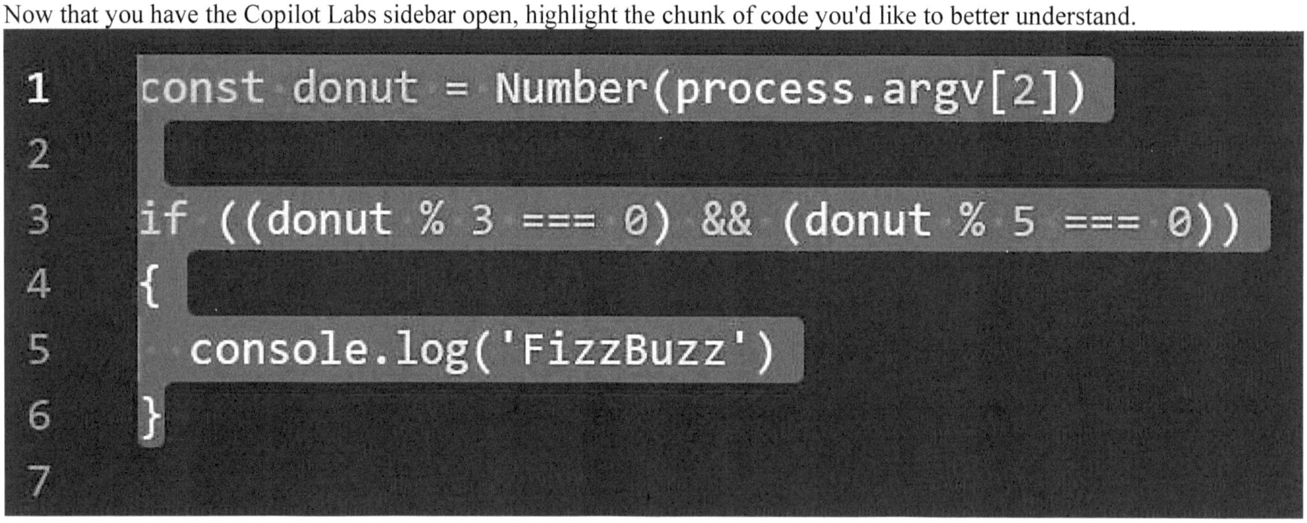

Step 5. Explain Code
The GitHub Copilot Labs pane will show a section called "Explain". Under this section, your highlighted code will appear, along with a box saying "Explain code".

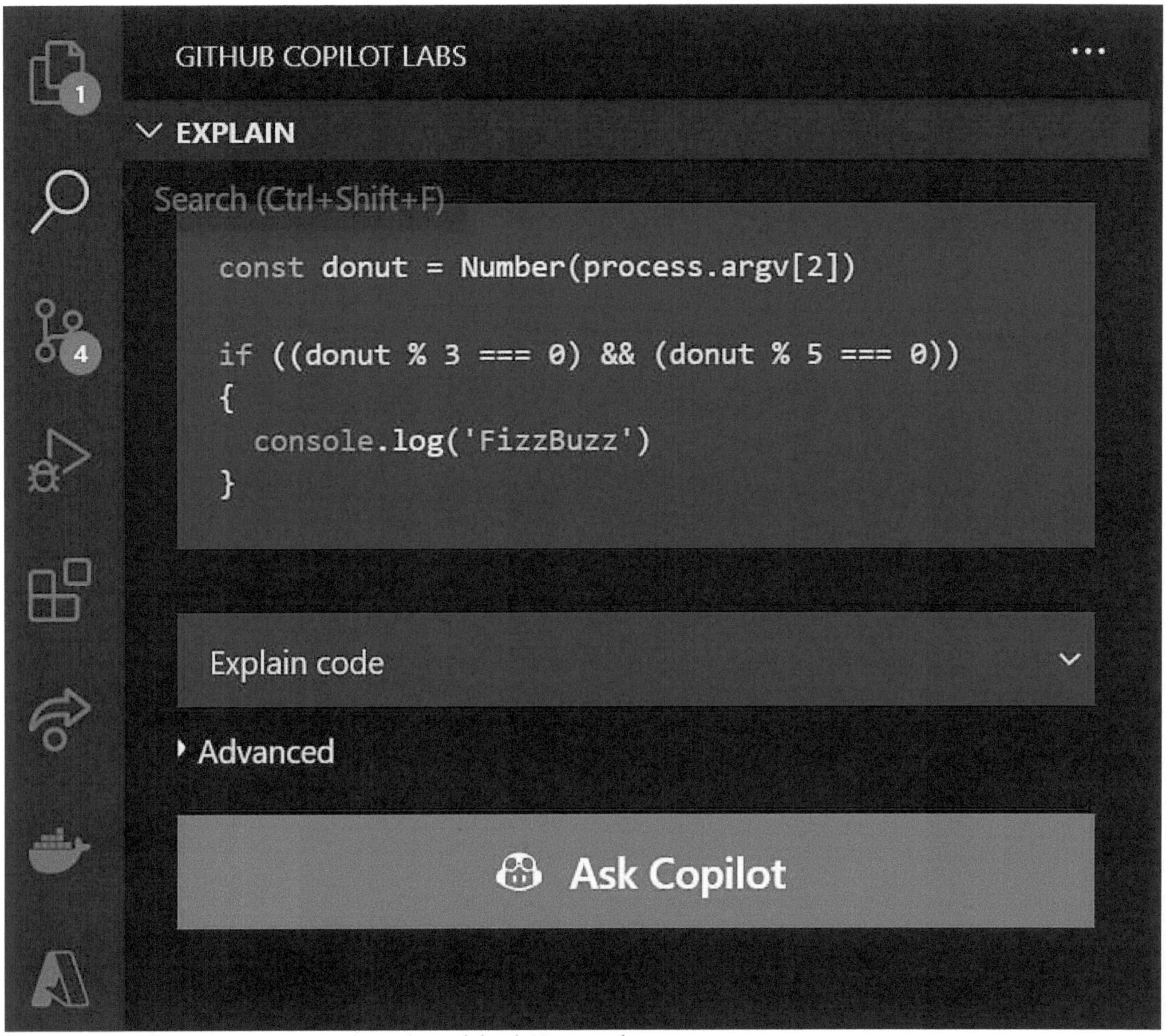

Here, you can choose how you want the code explained. You can choose:

1. "Explain code": step by step what the code is checking for and what it is outputting.
2. "Code does following": brief summary of what the code is does.
3. "Code does following (English)": detailed explain (in plain English) of what the code does.
4. "Show example code": provides an input example and shows how the code calls a function and works.

Select one, and click "Ask Copilot". Your result will be immediately displayed:

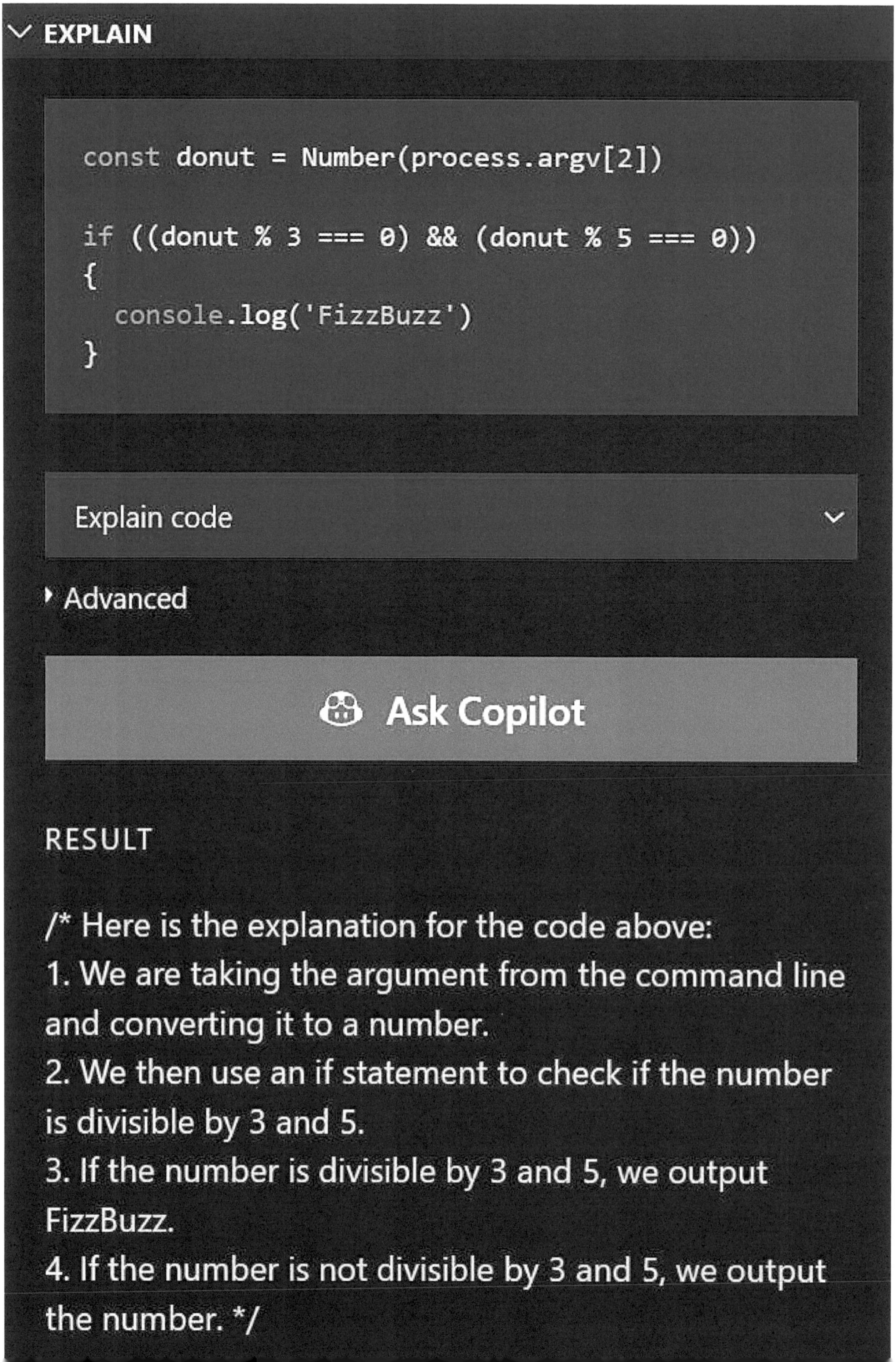
EXPLAIN
const donut = Number(process.argv[2])
if ((donut % 3 === 0) && (donut % 5 === 0))
{
console.log('FizzBuzz')
}
Explain code
Advanced
Ask Copilot
RESULT
/* Here is the explanation for the code above:
1. We are taking the argument from the command line and converting it to a number.
2. We then use an if statement to check if the number is divisible by 3 and 5.
3. If the number is divisible by 3 and 5, we output FizzBuzz.
4. If the number is not divisible by 3 and 5, we output the number. */

Since this is a learning tool, you might be shown a slightly different result each time you "Ask Copilot". Experiment with various languages and compare the different results. This is a great way to learn and understand your code better.

Step 6. Feedback
GitHub Copilot and GitHub Copilot Labs are very new features. They are both in technical preview stage. After your code has been explained you'll be able to provide feedback on how well Copilot did.

You can read more about how GitHub Copilot works and the training set t

GitHub Copilot best features
1. Multiple programming languages, including Python, JavaScript, TypeScript, Go, and C++
2. AI pair programming to generate relevant solutions using machine-learning technology and conversational prompts
3. Tons of integrations with tools like Visual Studio Code, JetBrains IDEs, and Neovim

GitHub Copilot limitations
1. Copilot may require a bit of time to learn your processes
2. Its real-time AI feature creates code at a slower pace than other similar tools
3. GitHub provides some debugging assistance but lacks in-depth support

GitHub Copilot pricing
1. Individual: $10 per month
2. Enterprise: $19 per user, per month

6.2 aiXcoder

aiXcoder is a powerful code completion and code search engine based on state-of-the-art deep learning technology. It can be used as a plugin for various IDEs like IntelliJ and JetBrains, making it easily integrated into your programming workflow. Here's a breakdown of its key features:
Intelligent Code Completion:
1. Predicts and suggests your next line of code based on context and grammar, allowing you to write code faster and with fewer errors.
2. Generates complete function bodies from natural language descriptions, saving you time and effort.
3. Supports multiple programming languages, including Python, Java, JavaScript, and Golang.
Advanced Code Search:
1. Helps you find relevant code examples on GitHub based on your current code context.
2. Utilizes natural language processing to understand your search query and find the most relevant results.
3. No need to sift through vast amounts of code, aiXcoder efficiently identifies the solutions you need.
Additional Features:
1. Remote and local modes – run aiXcoder on your local machine for faster response times or use the remote server for more complex tasks.
2. Customizable settings – adjust the sensitivity and level of detail in code suggestions to match your preferences.
3. Continuous updates – aiXcoder regularly receives new features and improvements based on user feedback and advancements in deep learning technology.
4. Intelligent code completion: aiXcoder can predict the programmer's intent and automatically complete the subsequent code snippets, saving developers valuable time.
5. Virtual programming expertise: Trained with professional code from various sectors, this tool serves as a virtual programming expert, assisting programmers in their tasks.

6. Enhanced efficiency: By streamlining repetitive tasks, this tool significantly improves coding efficiency, enabling developers to focus on more complex aspects of their projects.

Here is a step-by-step guide on how to use aiXcoder:

1. Install the aiXcoder plugin for your IDE. Supported IDEs include Visual Studio Code, IntelliJ IDEA, Eclipse, and more. To install the aiXcoder plugin, follow these steps:
2. Open your chosen IDE.

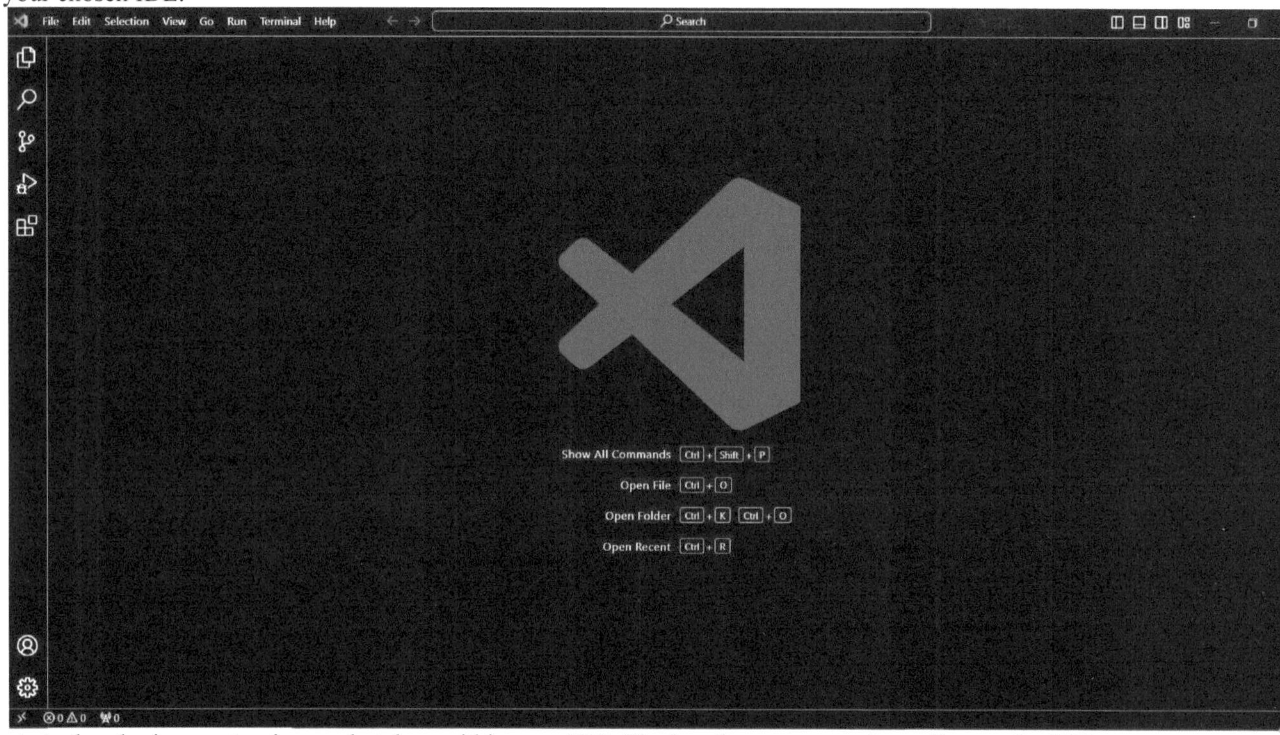

3. Navigate to the plugin or extension marketplace within your IDE. The location may vary depending on the IDE you're using.

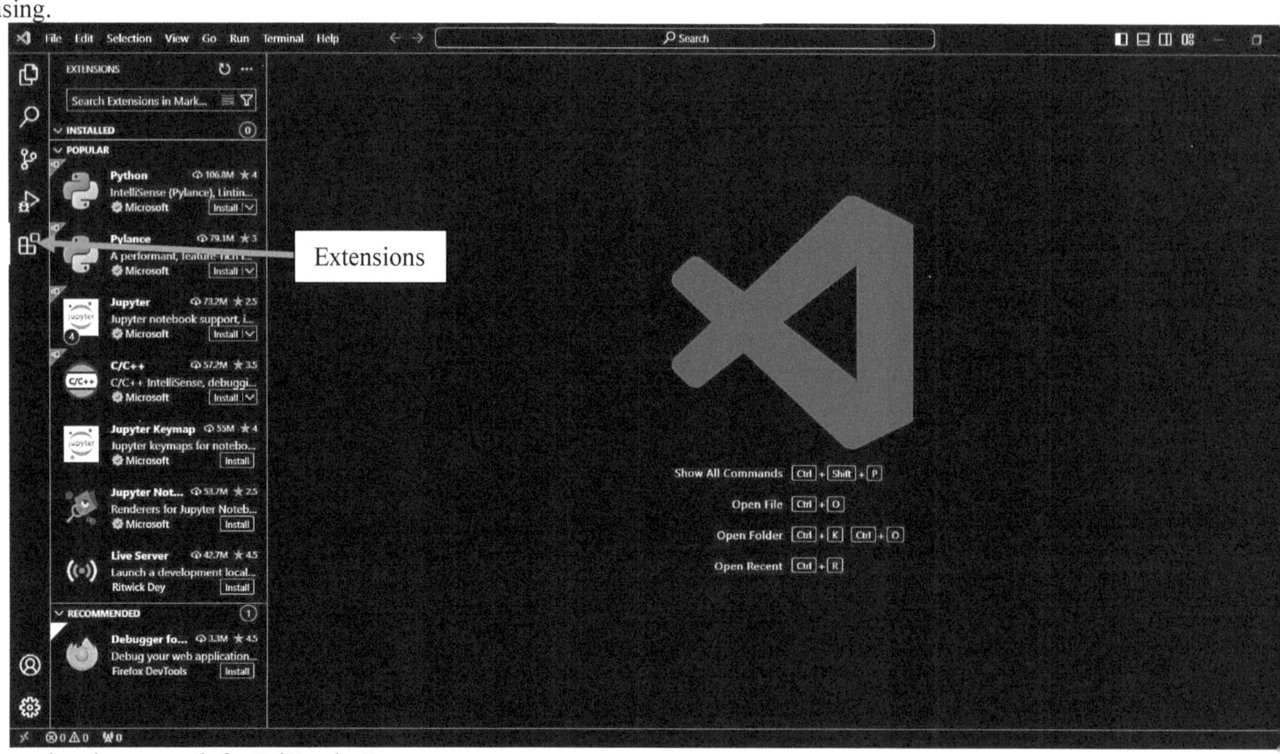

4. In the marketplace, search for "aiXcoder."

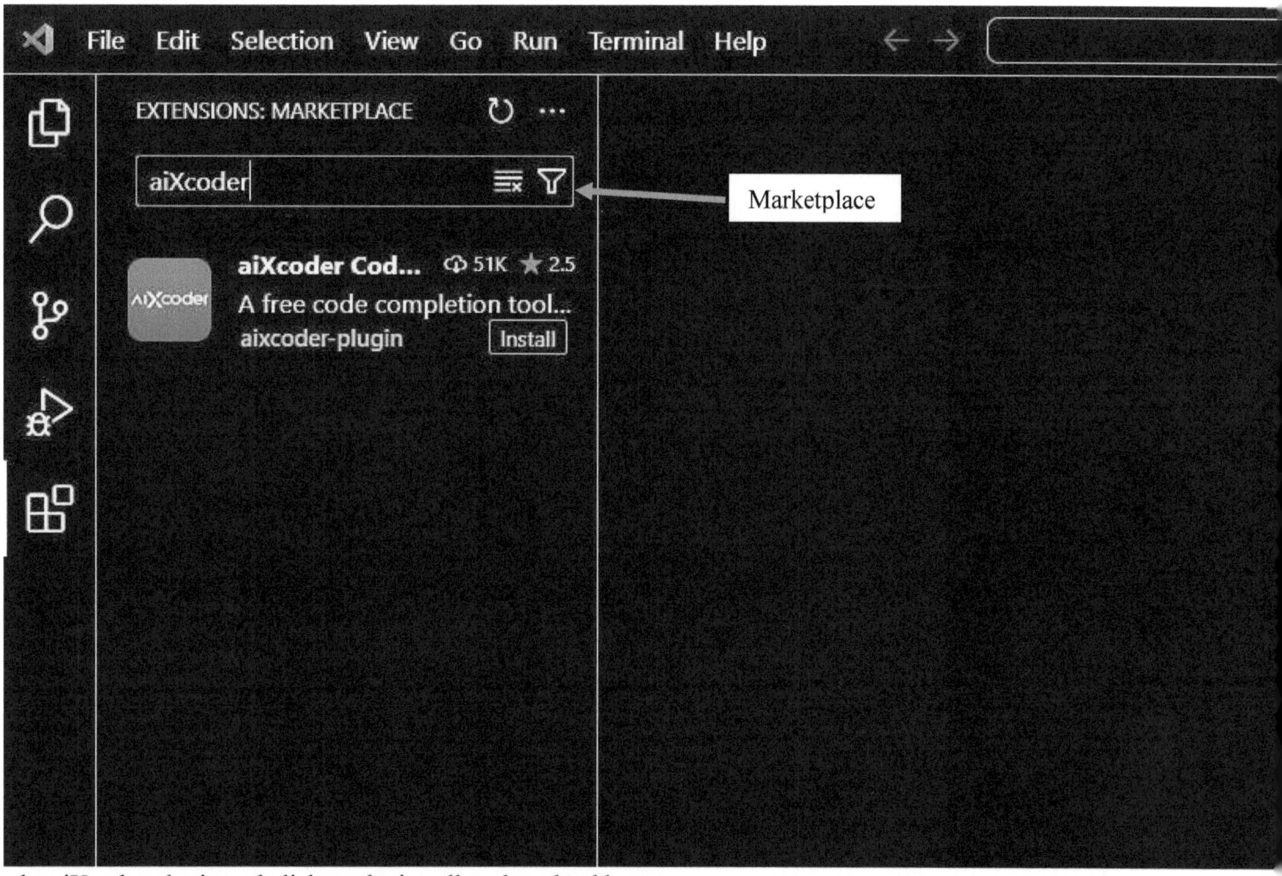

5. Locate the aiXcoder plugin and click on the install or download button.

6. Restart your IDE. After successfully installing the aiXcoder plugin, it's essential to restart your IDE to activate the new functionality. This step ensures that aiXcoder seamlessly integrates with your coding environment.

7. Start writing code with aiXcoder. Once your IDE has been restarted, you're ready to start writing code with the assistance of aiXcoder. Begin by opening or creating a code file in your IDE, and aiXcoder will automatically activate as you type. As you write code, aiXcoder will analyze your code context and provide intelligent code completion suggestions, enhancing your coding efficiency and accuracy.
8. Select code completion suggestions. As aiXcoder offers code completion suggestions, you have the flexibility to accept or reject them based on your coding preferences and requirements. To accept a code completion suggestion, you can press the Tab key to insert the suggested code. For more information, you can visit this link.

6.3 TabNine

1. Tabnine is an AI assistant that helps developers code faster and better. It uses deep learning to provide code completions, chat, and code generation in various programming languages and IDEs. Tabnine can also learn from your own codebase and adapt to your coding style and preferences. Tabnine is trusted by millions of developers worldwide and supports all major programming languages.
2. Tabnine is an AI-powered autocompletion and code suggestion tool designed to assist software developers in their coding workflows. It utilizes machine learning algorithms to analyze code and predict what the developer is likely to type next, providing intelligent suggestions and accelerating the coding process. Tabnine aims to enhance developer productivity and efficiency by reducing the time spent on manual typing and increasing the accuracy of code completion

Some additional information that you might find useful are:

1. Tabnine is not a code editor, but a plugin that works with your existing IDE. You can install Tabnine from its website or from your IDE's plugin marketplace

Here are some key features and aspects of Tabnine:

1. AI-Powered Code Completion:

1. Tabnine uses machine learning algorithms to analyze code patterns and predict what a developer is likely to type next.
2. The AI model is trained on a vast dataset of publicly available code repositories, enabling it to understand and suggest relevant code snippets.

2. Cross-Language Support:

1. Tabnine supports a wide range of programming languages, making it versatile for developers working with multiple technologies.
2. It provides suggestions for languages such as JavaScript, Python, Java, C++, HTML, CSS, and more.

3. Context-Aware Suggestions:

1. The tool takes into account the context of the code, including variable names, function names, and surrounding code, to offer more contextually relevant suggestions.
2. Context-aware suggestions help reduce the need for manual typing and make the coding experience more efficient.

4. Integration with Popular Editors:

1. Tabnine integrates with various popular code editors and IDEs, including Visual Studio Code, IntelliJ IDEA, Atom, Sublime Text, and others.
2. The integration is seamless, allowing developers to use Tabnine's features directly within their preferred development environment.

5. Real-Time Feedback:

1. Suggestions from Tabnine appear in real-time as developers type, providing immediate feedback and reducing the cognitive load associated with remembering syntax and code structures.

6. Personalization:

1. Over time, Tabnine learns from a developer's coding style and adapts its suggestions to better match individual preferences.
2. The tool aims to provide a personalized and efficient coding experience tailored to each user.

7. Code Snippet Expansion:

1. Tabnine can suggest entire code snippets or blocks, not just individual keywords or functions, further accelerating the coding process.

8. Privacy and Security:

1. Tabnine often emphasizes privacy and security by ensuring that code analysis is performed locally on the user's machine, without sending code to external servers.

Here's a step-by-step guide TabNine using Visual Studio Code:

1. Install Visual Studio Code:
If you don't have Visual Studio Code installed, download and install it from the official website: Visual Studio Code.
2. Open Visual Studio Code:
Launch Visual Studio Code on your computer.
3. Install the TabNine Extension:
- Open the Extensions view by clicking on the Extensions icon in the Activity Bar on the side of the window or use the shortcut **Ctrl+Shift+X**.
- Search for "TabNine" in the Extensions view search box.
- Install the TabNine extension by TabNine.
4. Configure TabNine:
- After installation, you may want to configure TabNine based on your preferences. Access the settings by clicking on the gear icon in the Extensions view.
- Adjust settings such as enabling/disabling specific features, changing keybindings, or setting up any additional configurations.
5. Restart Visual Studio Code:
After installing and configuring TabNine, it's a good idea to restart Visual Studio Code to ensure that the changes take effect.
6. Start Coding:
- With TabNine installed and configured, start coding in your preferred programming language.
- TabNine should provide intelligent code completion suggestions as you type, helping you write code more efficiently.
7. Explore Features:
Explore additional features provided by TabNine, such as documentation lookup, multi-line suggestions, and other intelligent code completion capabilities.
8. Stay Updated:
- Check for updates to the TabNine extension regularly. Extensions are often updated to include new features, improvements, and bug fixes.

Once you've joined your team's Tabnine account, the next step is to install Tabnine from the VSCode marketplace.

Install from the VSCode Marketplace

1. 1. In your VSCode IDE, go to **Extensions**
1. 2. Search for ***Tabnine Enterprise (Self-Hosted)*** (Do not mix with the other Tabnine extension)
1. 3. Install the extension

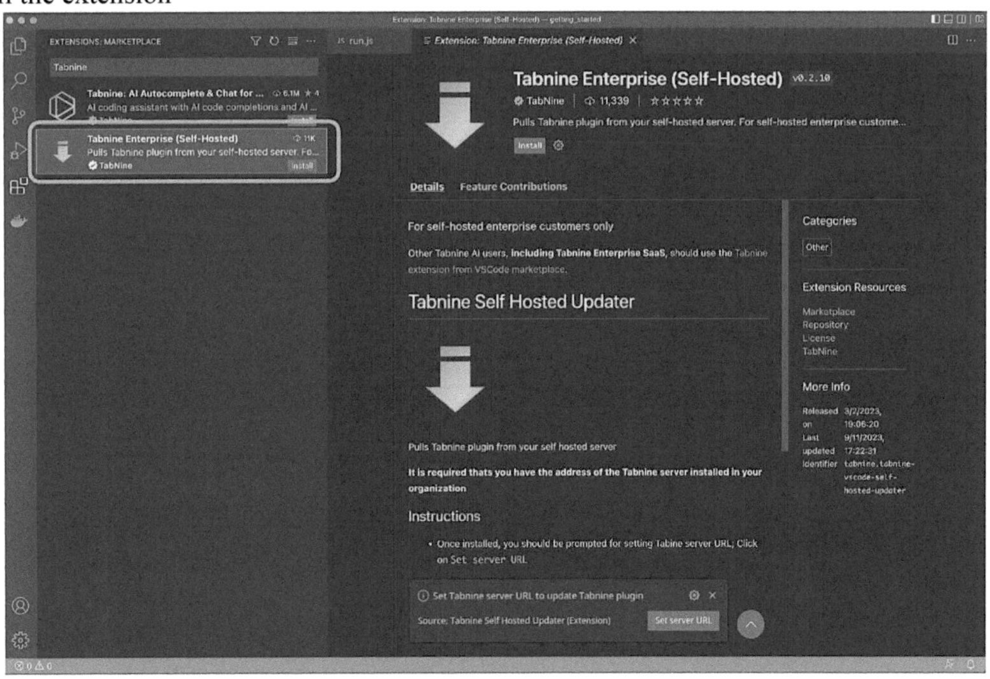

Configure the Tabnine Server URL
Once you restart the IDE and the extension is initialized, you'll be prompted to set the URL of your Tabnine Enterprise Server.
If you don't have the URL, contact your Tabnine admin within your organization.

1. Click **Set server URL** and enter the Tabnine server URL. Tabnine will update itself to the latest version according to your organization's instance.

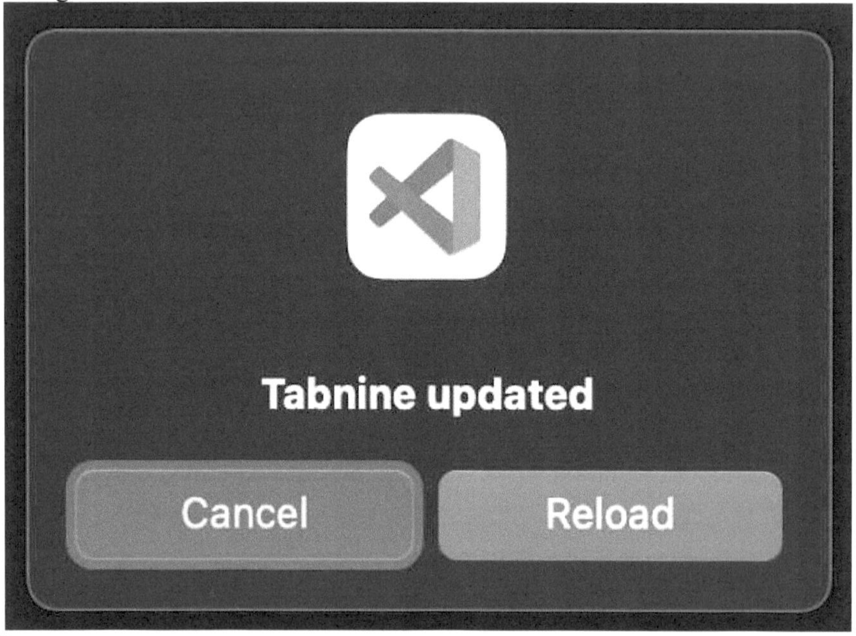

2. Click **Reload**
3. When you see the following prompt, click **Sign in**

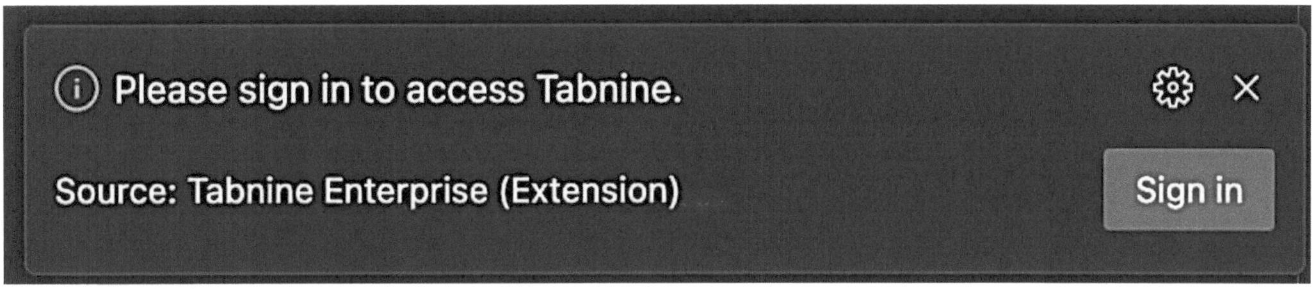

Sign in to Tabnine

Next, a browser window will open and you'll be prompted to log in to Tabnine.

Click **Sign In.**

If your organization doesn't have SSO, you'll see the following screen. Sign in using your Tabnine user credentials

Once you've successfully signed in, you'll see the following message:

Once you see this confirmation screen, close the browser, return to your IDE, and start using Tabnine!

6.4 Figstack

Figstack is a powerful suite of code generators designed to help developers quickly understand, document, and optimize their code. Powered by AI and trained with billions of lines of code, Figstack offers a range of features including Explain Code, Language Translator, Docstring Writer, and Time Complexity functions. With Figstack, users can read and write code in any language, and benefit from detailed docstrings and time complexity analysis. Whether you're a seasoned developer or just starting out, Figstack makes it easy to explore and test your code, and to optimize it for maximum efficiency.

Figstack is an AI-powered tool suite designed to supercharge your coding experience across various languages.

It uses machine learning trained on billions of lines of code to offer a range of features that help you:

1. Understand Code:

1. Explain Code: Figstack translates complex code into plain English, making it easier to grasp the logic and purpose of any code snippet.
2. Code Documentation: Generate detailed docstrings automatically, saving you time and ensuring proper documentation for your code.

2. Improve Performance:

1. Language Translation: Easily convert code from one language to another, facilitating collaboration and code reuse.
2. Time Complexity Analysis: Measure the efficiency of your code and identify potential bottlenecks for optimization.

3. Boost Productivity:

1. Context-aware Suggestions: Get relevant code completion suggestions and refactorings based on your coding context.
2. Improved Debugging: Identify and understand bugs faster with AI-powered analysis and suggestions.

4. Additionally:

1. Supports multiple languages: Python, Java, JavaScript, Go, and many more.
2. Integrates with popular IDEs: VSCode, IntelliJ IDEA, PyCharm, Eclipse, etc.
3. Offers a Free plan: Get started with core features for free.

Overall, Figstack acts as your personal AI assistant, assisting you throughout the coding process from understanding existing code to writing efficient and documented new code.

Here are some specific use cases for Figstack:
1. Onboarding new developers: Quickly grasp the codebase with Figstack's explanations and documentation tools.
2. Working with unfamiliar languages: Translate code to your preferred language for easier understanding and modification.
3. Optimizing code performance: Identify and improve bottlenecks with time complexity analysis.
4. Maintaining clean and consistent code: Generate comprehensive docstrings and adopt best practices through AI suggestions.

Figstack best features
1. Figstack's Explain Code feature can understand any programming language and translate code between languages instantly
2. It provides code functionality assistance to help users operate the tool more efficiently
3. It can generate code documentation on the spot, saving developers critical time

Figstack limitations
1. Figstack's assistance isn't as consistent or reliable if the code is unclear or lacks proper documentation
2. It doesn't always reflect real-time updates to account for new releases or changes in the data it's been trained on

Figstack pricing
1. Free trial
2. Contact Figstack for all other pricing information

Figstack can be used in a variety of ways to improve your coding experience, here are some specific uses:
Understanding Code:
1. Explaining complex code: If you're struggling to understand a piece of code, Figstack can break it down into plain English, explaining the logic and purpose of each line.
2. Generating documentation: Figstack can automatically generate detailed docstrings for your functions, saving you time and ensuring your code is well-documented.
3. Debugging: Figstack can help you identify and understand bugs faster by analyzing your code and suggesting potential causes.
Improving Code Performance:
1. Code review: Figstack can highlight potential issues in your code, such as inefficiencies or security vulnerabilities.
2. Time complexity analysis: Figstack can measure the efficiency of your code in Big O notation, helping you identify potential bottlenecks for optimization.
3. Refactoring: Figstack can suggest alternative ways to write your code that are more efficient and readable.
Boosting Productivity:
1. Context-aware suggestions: Figstack can provide relevant code completion suggestions and refactorings based on the context of your code.
2. Language translation: Figstack can translate code from one language to another, making it easier to collaborate with other developers or reuse existing code.
3. Automating repetitive tasks: Figstack can automate some of the more tedious tasks involved in coding, such as generating boilerplate code or formatting your code.
Additionally:
1. Learning new languages: Figstack can help you learn new programming languages by providing explanations and suggestions as you code.
2. Pair programming: Figstack can be a valuable tool for pair programming, helping both developers to understand the code and identify potential issues.
3. Sharing code: Figstack can help you share your code with others by generating clear and concise explanations and documentation.
Whether you're a beginner or an experienced developer, Figstack can be a valuable tool to help you improve your coding skills, write better code, and be more productive.

Here are some specific examples of how developers use Figstack in their daily work:
1. A front-end developer who is new to JavaScript can use Figstack to understand the logic of a complex script.

2. A back-end developer who is working on optimizing a critical piece of code can use Figstack to analyze its time complexity and identify potential bottlenecks.
3. A team of developers working on a large project can use Figstack to share code and ensure everyone understands the different parts of the system.

Figstack offers various functionalities, so the exact steps depend on what you want to achieve. Here's a breakdown for using Figstack for different purposes:

1. Code Explanation and Documentation:

a. Website:
1. Go to the Figstack website (https://www.figstack.com/).
2. Click "Explain Code" or "Generate Docstrings" depending on your need.
3. Paste your code snippet in the provided box.
4. Choose your programming language (if not automatically detected).
5. Click "Go."
6. Figstack will analyze your code and provide an explanation in plain English (for Explain Code) or generate comprehensive docstrings for each function/class (for Generate Docstrings).

b. IDE Plugins:
1. Install the Figstack plugin for your IDE (VS Code, IntelliJ IDEA, etc.).
2. Open your code file in the IDE.
3. Select the code snippet you want explained or documented.
4. Use the Figstack plugin commands (e.g., right-click and choose "Explain Code" or "Generate Docstrings").
5. Figstack will display the explanation or generated docstrings directly in your IDE.

2. Code Review and Optimization:

a. Website:
1. Go to the Figstack website and click "Code Review."
2. Upload your code file (supported formats: .py, .java, .js, etc.).
3. Choose your programming language.
4. Click "Get insights."
5. Figstack will analyze your code and provide a report highlighting potential issues like inefficiencies, security vulnerabilities, and best practice violations.

b. IDE Plugins:
Similar to explaining code, use the Figstack plugin commands within your IDE to trigger code review and receive insights.

3. Language Translation and Refactoring:

a. Website:
1. Go to the Figstack website and choose "Translate Code" or "Refactor Code."
2. Choose your source and target programming languages (for translation) or select the code snippet you want to refactor.
3. Click "Translate" or "Refactor."
4. Figstack will provide the translated code or suggest alternative ways to write your code for improved efficiency and readability.

b. IDE Plugins:
Some IDE plugins allow direct translation and refactoring functionalities within your coding environment. Check your plugin's documentation for specific instructions.

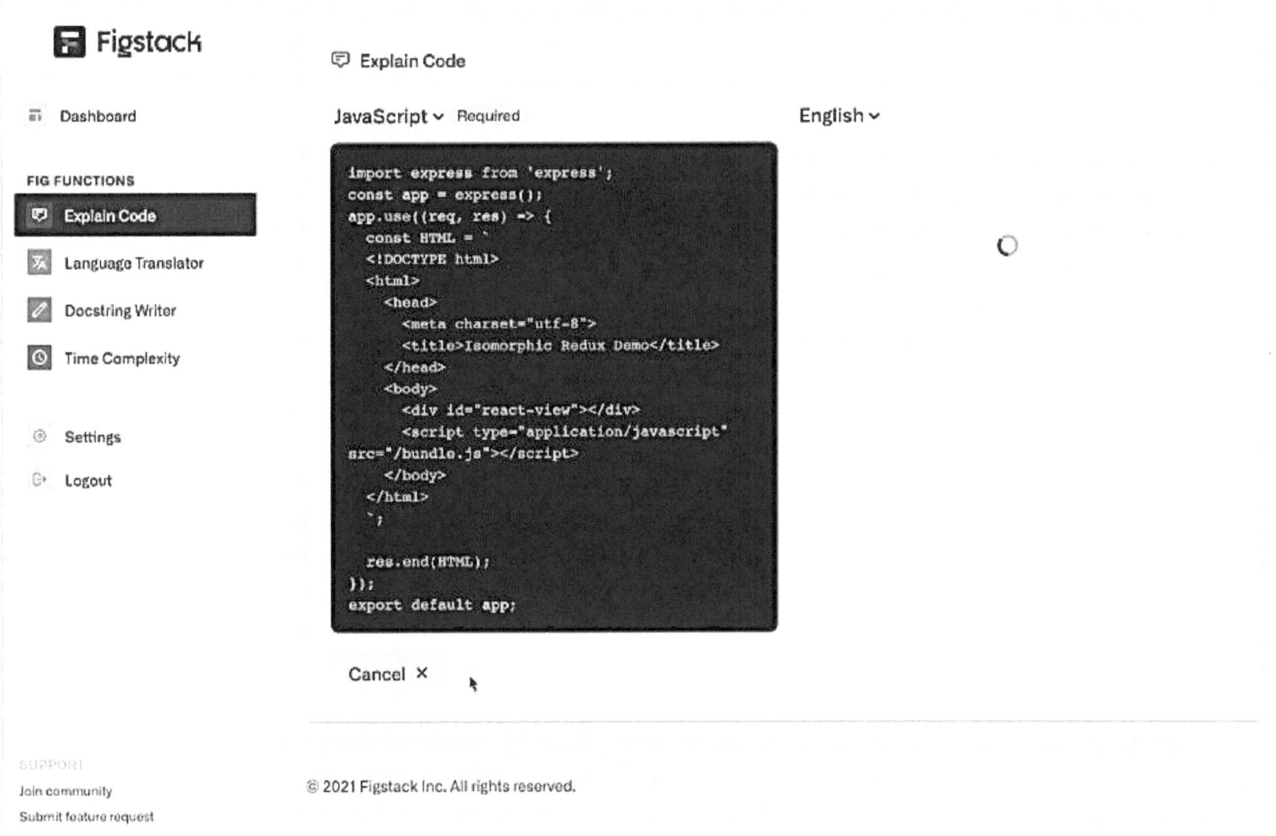

6.5 Cody by Sourcegraph

Cody is a free and open-core AI coding assistant that writes, fixes, and maintains your code. Cody understands your entire codebase by leveraging the power of Code Graph to gather context, which assists you in writing accurate code. Cody connects seamlessly with codehosts like GitHub, GitLab and IDEs like VS Code and JetBrains. Once connected, Cody acts as your personal AI coding assistant, equipped with a comprehensive understanding of the following three crucial elements:

1. Your entire codebase
2. Vast knowledge of open source code
3. Extensive training data for code understanding and problem-solving

Follow these steps to install the Cody AI extension for VS Code:

Open VS Code editor on your local machine

Click the Extensions icon in the Activity Bar on the side of VS Code, or use the keyboard shortcut Cmd+Shift+X (macOS) or Ctrl+Shift+X (Windows/Linux)

Type Cody AI in the search bar and click the Install button

After installing, you may be prompted to reload VS Code to activate the extension

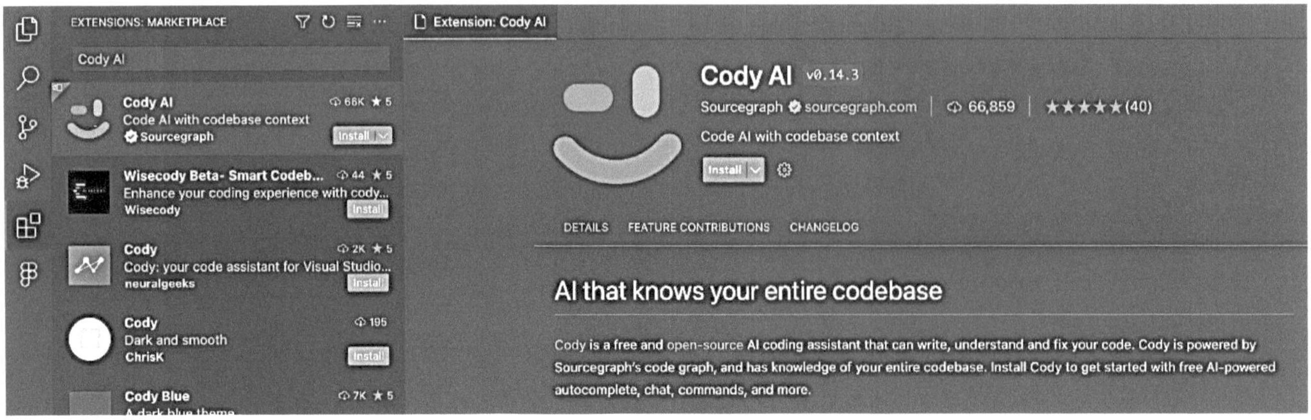

Connect the extension to Sourcegraph

After a successful installation, the Cody icon appears in the Activity sidebar. Cody Free and Cody Pro users can sign in to their Sourcegraph.com accounts through GitHub, GitLab, or Google.

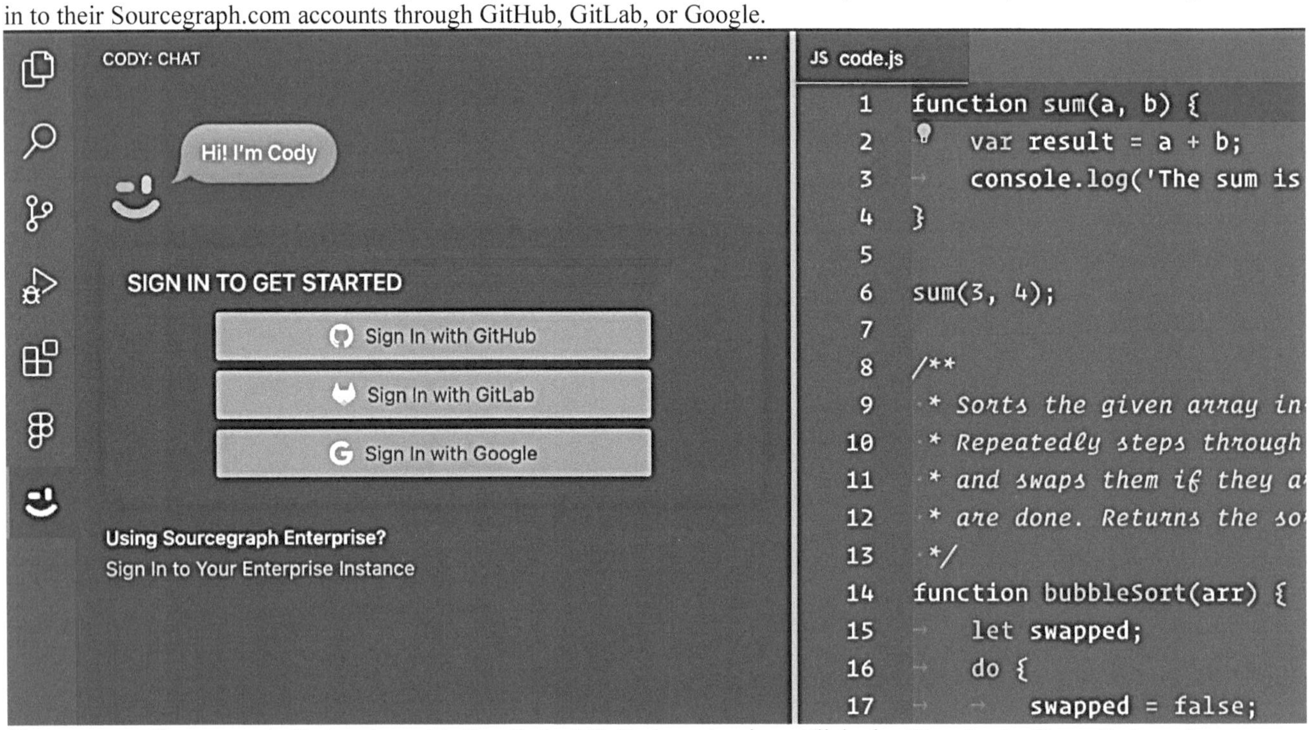

You can use Sourcegraph Enterprise with the Cody VS Code extension. Click the **Sign In to Your Enterprise Instance**, and it connects to your enterprise environment. For Enterprise users, please sign in with your custom Sourcegraph instance URL and access token.

Verifying the installation

Once connected, click the Cody icon from the sidebar again. The Cody extension will open in a configurable side panel.

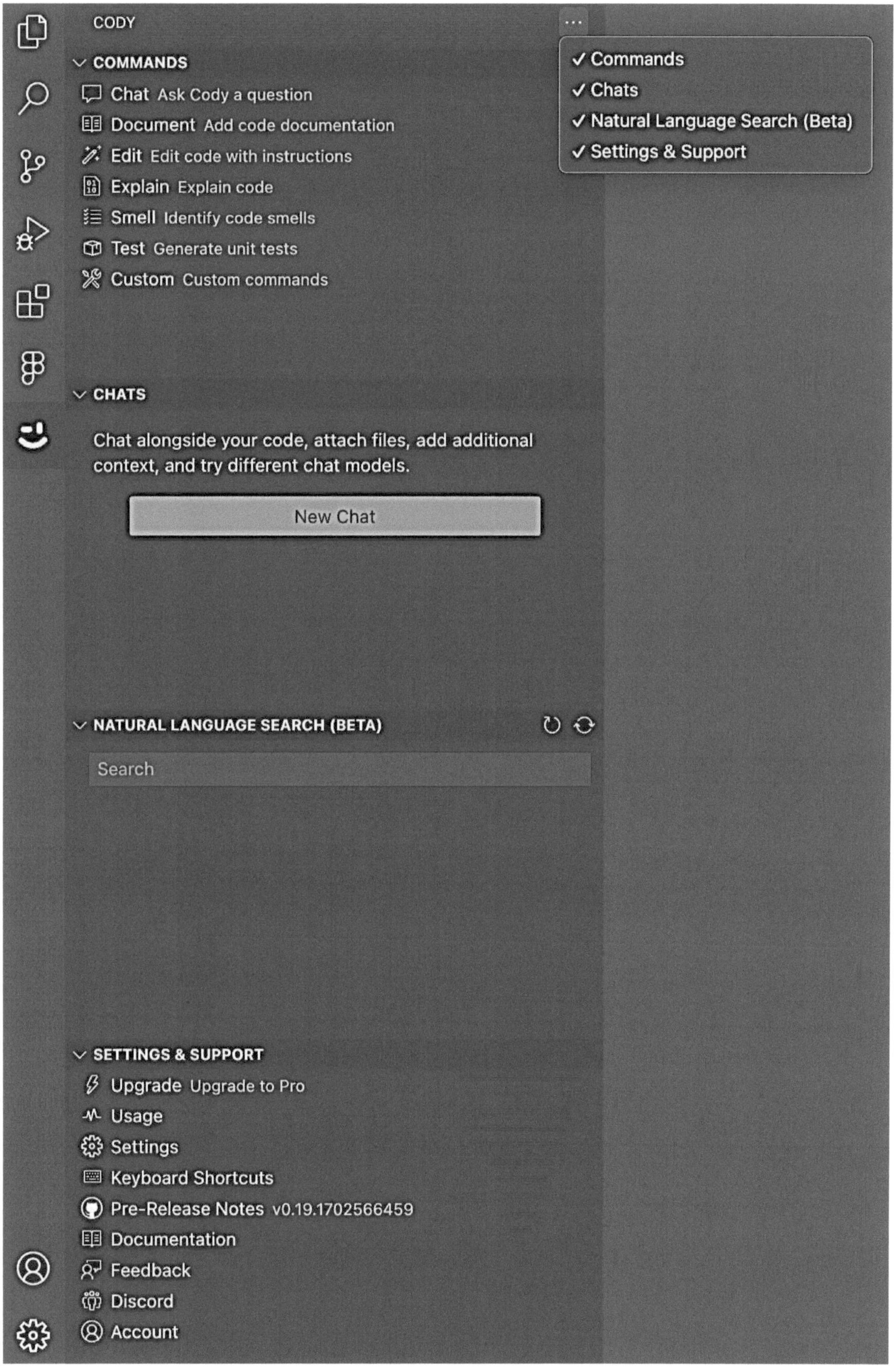
CODY
COMMANDS
Chat Ask Cody a question
Document Add code documentation
Edit Edit code with instructions
Explain Explain code
Smell Identify code smells
Test Generate unit tests
Custom Custom commands
✓ Commands
✓ Chats
✓ Natural Language Search (Beta)
✓ Settings & Support
CHATS
Chat alongside your code, attach files, add additional context, and try different chat models.
New Chat
NATURAL LANGUAGE SEARCH (BETA)
Search
SETTINGS & SUPPORT
Upgrade Upgrade to Pro
Usage
Settings
Keyboard Shortcuts
Pre-Release Notes v0.19.1702566459
Documentation
Feedback
Discord
Account

Let's create an autocomplete suggestion to verify that the Cody extension has been successfully installed and is working as expected.
Cody provides intelligent code suggestions and context-aware autocompletions for numerous programming languages like JavaScript, Python, TypeScript, Go, etc.
1. Create a new file in VS Code, for example, code.js
2. Next, type the following algorithm function to sort an array of numbers

```
function bubbleSort(array){
```

1. As you start typing, Cody will automatically provide suggestions and context-aware completions based on your coding patterns and the code context
2. These autocomplete suggestions appear as grayed text. To accept the suggestion, press the Tab key

Cody best features
1. Inline chat to quickly fix and optimize your code using conversational language
2. Ready-made workflows to expedite your work with Cody. Choose whether you need the code explained in detail, improved variable names, translations, change summaries, or notes generated
3. Real-time autocomplete to write code in seconds

Cody limitations
1. Cody's UX is not the most user-friendly

Cody pricing
The Cody app is free for any Sourcegraph users on a paid plan:
1. Business plan: $99 active user, per month
2. Enterprise: Contact for custom pricing

6.6 SpellBox

1. SpellBox is a versatile AI coding assistant that caters to a wide range of users, from hobbyist coders to professional software developers. It provides a simple and efficient solution to coding problems, helping users to improve their coding skills. Whether you're dealing with simple or complex algorithms, SpellBox can generate the code you need from simple prompts, saving you hours of frustrating coding. For professional developers, SpellBox reduces the time spent on routine coding tasks, allowing more focus on developing high-quality software. For students and learners, it makes the process of coding easier and more efficient by providing instant solutions to common coding problems. This not only saves time but also allows users to focus on understanding the concepts behind the code.
2. So, let's dive into the specifics of SpellBox. One of the great things about this tool is its versatility. It supports major programming languages like Python, JavaScript, C++, Java, MATLAB, Excel, and Go. This means that no matter which language you're working with, SpellBox has got you covered. It's a one-stop solution for all your coding needs.
3. Another standout feature of SpellBox is its code generation capability. With just a prompt or description of what you need, SpellBox can generate the code for you. This is incredibly useful when you're dealing with complex algorithms or trying to solve a specific coding problem. It saves you the time and effort of writing code from scratch and allows you to focus on the logic of your program.
4. In addition to code generation, SpellBox also provides code explanation. This feature allows you to quickly gain a deep understanding of the code you're working with. It saves you from spending hours researching or studying documentation. Whether you're a beginner looking to improve your coding proficiency or an experienced developer who wants to quickly understand a piece of code, SpellBox's code explanation feature is a valuable tool.
5. One more feature worth mentioning is bookmarking. With SpellBox, you can easily save and organize your favorite code snippets or solutions. This makes it convenient to refer back to them later, saving you time and effort in searching for the same solution again.
6. While SpellBox is a powerful tool, it's important to note that it is an AI assistant and not a substitute for learning how to code. It can provide instant solutions and generate code, but it's still essential to understand the underlying concepts and logic. SpellBox is best used as a learning aid and a productivity tool to enhance your coding skills.
7. As for pricing, SpellBox makes it straightforward. It's a one-time payment of $40 for a one-year license, which is not too bad, considering you the license lets you generate as much code as you want with the AI. However, it's worth noting that the tool doesn't offer any free trials or free plans. You have to pay upfront to use it.

Overall, SpellBox is a valuable tool for anyone who needs to write code. It simplifies the coding process, saves time, and helps users improve their coding skills. Whether you're a student, a hobbyist coder, or a professional developer, SpellBox can be a game-changer in your coding journey.

Key Features of SpellBox:

1. Versatile AI coding assistant
2. Generates code from simple prompts
3. Supports major programming languages
4. Code bookmarking feature for quick access
5. Code explanation feature for deep understanding
6. Standalone desktop versions for Windows and macOS
7. VS Code extension for integrated coding experience

SpellBox:

You can invoke SpellBox's features in various ways:

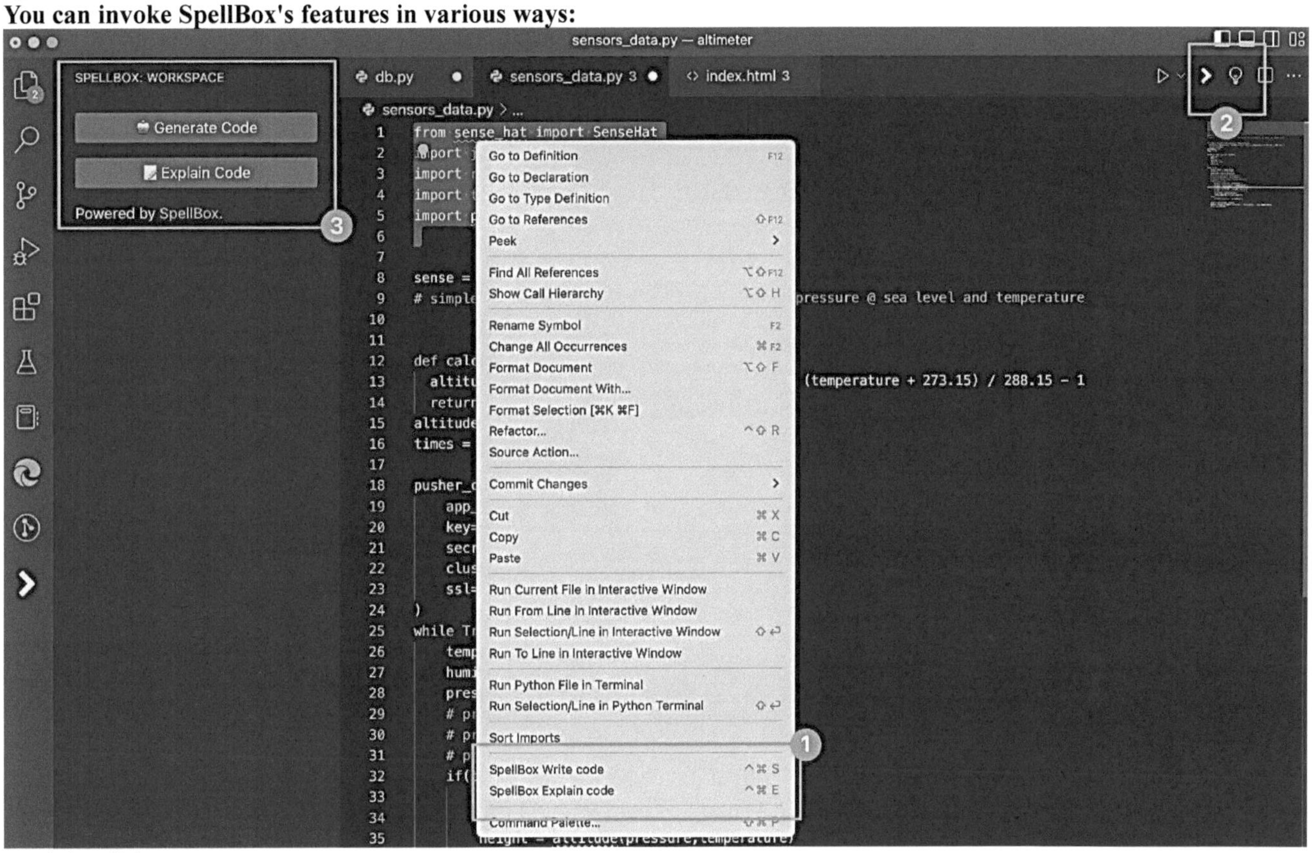

1. Right-click
2. Toolbar menu:
3. Carret: Write code
4. Light bulb: Explain code
5. Workspace

You can also invoke SpellBox using the command panel:

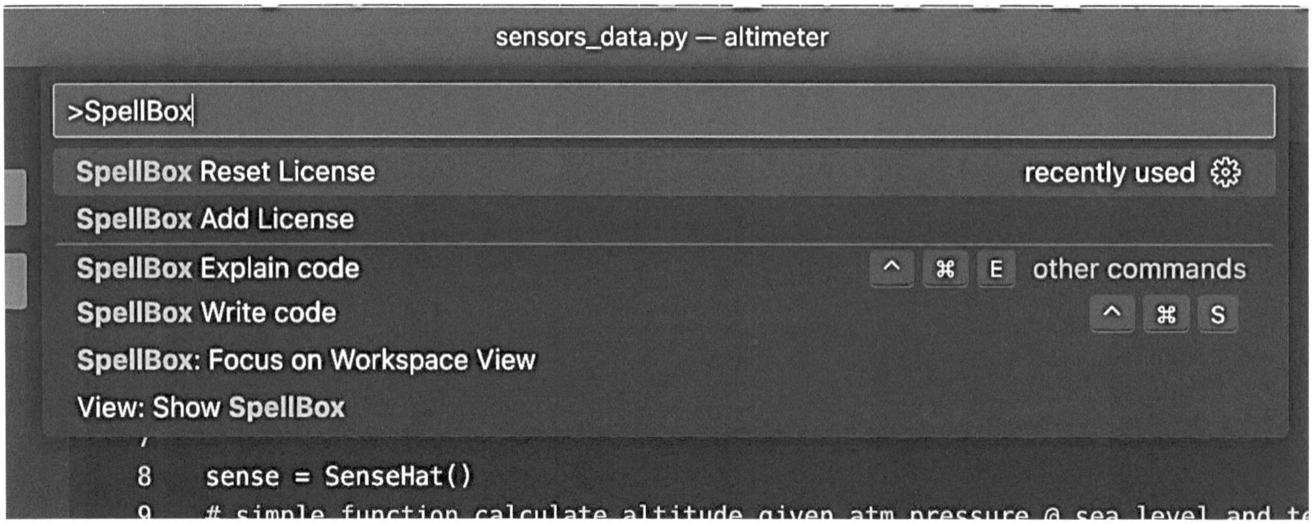

Documentation:
Please click here to go to SpellBox's documentation: https://docs.spellbox.ai
Languages supported
1. JavaScript
2. TypeScript
3. MATLAB
4. Excel
5. HTML
6. CSS
7. Swift
8. Go
9. C#
10. C++
11. Java
12. Rust
13. Python
14. Ruby
15. PHP

6.7 AskCodi

1. AskCodi is a tool designed to make the life of developers easier by eliminating redundant tasks. It's all about helping you code faster, easier, and better. The tool is built with AI capabilities, allowing it to provide precise and to-the-point answers to your coding queries in real-time. This means less time spent searching for solutions and more time spent actually coding. In addition to its time-saving features, AskCodi also integrates with popular editors like Visual Studio, VS code, and IntelliJ suite. This means you can stay in your coding zone while getting the support you need. And the best part? It's continually improving, with plans to support other IDEs in the future. So, if you're a developer looking for a tool that can help you code more efficiently and effectively, AskCodi might just be what you need.
2. AskCodi is like having a coding assistant that's always ready to help you out. The tool is designed to provide precise and to-the-point answers to your coding queries in real-time. This means you spend less time searching for solutions and more time actually coding.
3. One of the best things about AskCodi is its integration with popular editors like Visual Studio, VS code, and IntelliJ suite. This means you can stay in your coding zone while getting the support you need. It's like having a coding assistant that's always ready to help you out.
4. However, it's not all sunshine and rainbows. Some users have reported that AskCodi can be slow to respond at times, which can be frustrating when you're in the middle of trying to solve a problem. Additionally, it can be difficult to know how to format your query properly. There are a lot of different programming languages, and each one has its own specific syntax that can be difficult to remember.

5. Despite these minor drawbacks, AskCodi is a tool that's worth considering if you're a developer. It's a time-saver, a problem-solver, and a great companion for any developer or even for a no-code entrepreneur. It's continually improving, with plans to support other IDEs in the future.
AskCodi offers a free forever plan as well as two different paid plans. The free plan is a great way to test out the tool and see if it's right for you. If you decide to upgrade to the Premium plan, you'll get access to more features and benefits for a monthly cost of $9.99. Power users can opt for the Ultimate plan, priced at $29.99 per month, for even more advanced features.

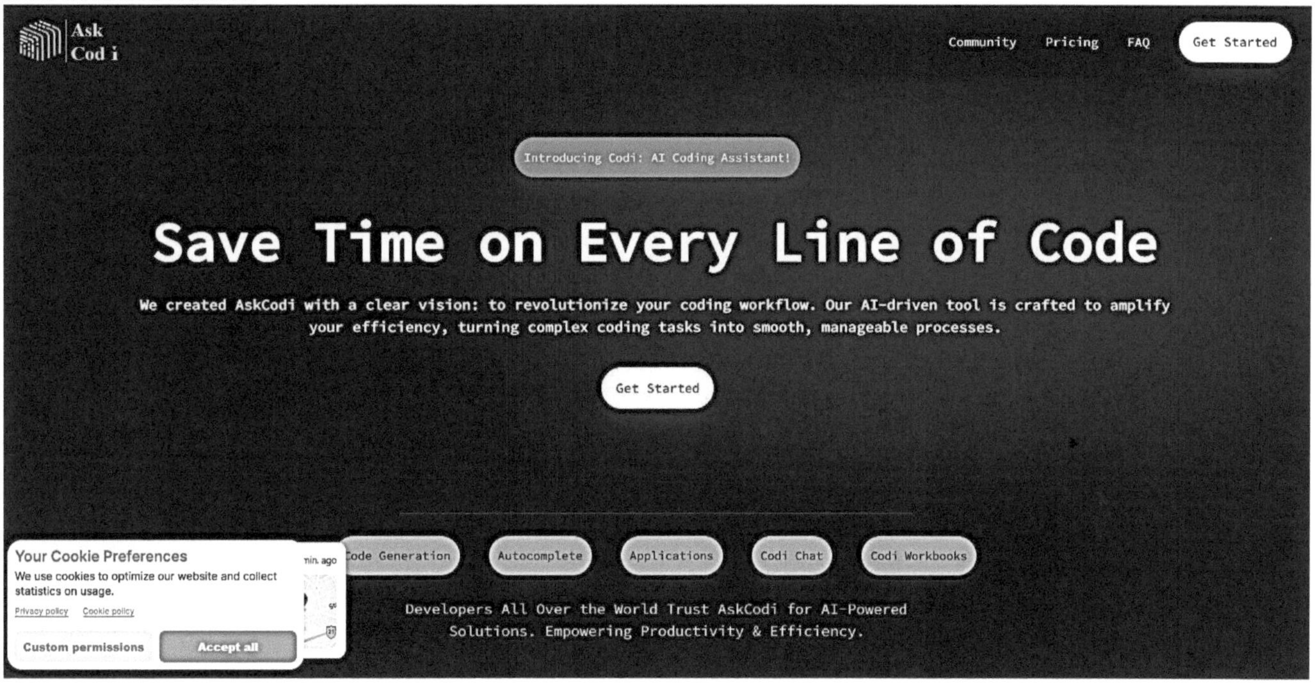

Here step by step explanation how to create account and how can we work on this platform:
1. Create an AskCodi user account
Go to AskCodi login page and create an account.

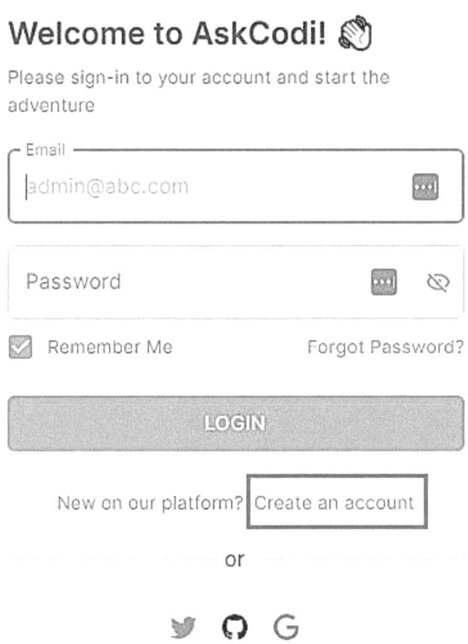

2. Provide your email and create a password. Next, click the sign up button.

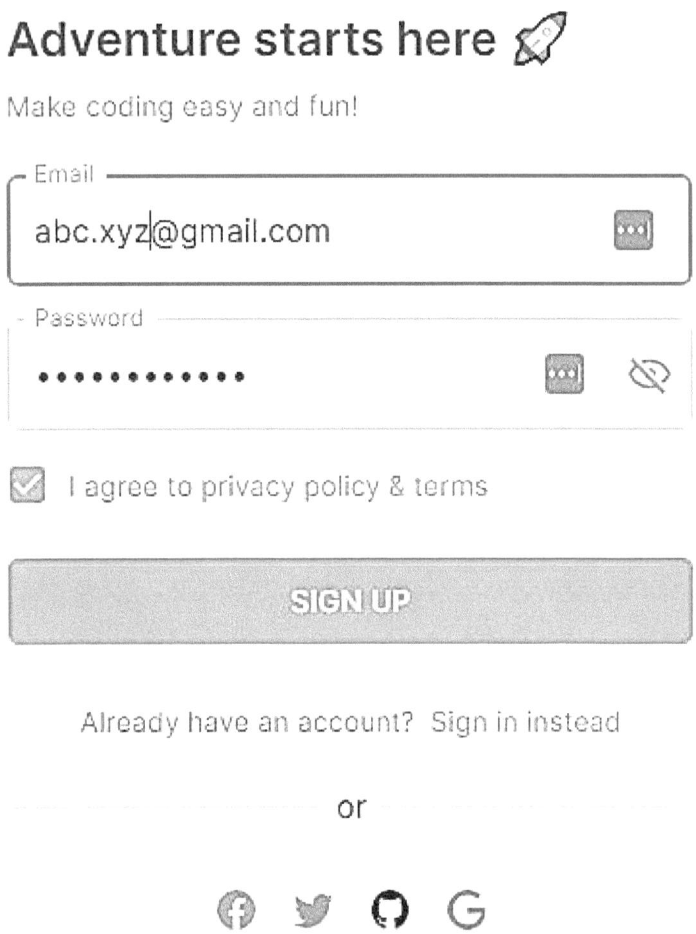

3. **Optionally**, you can create a project and test AskCodi application on the browser itself.

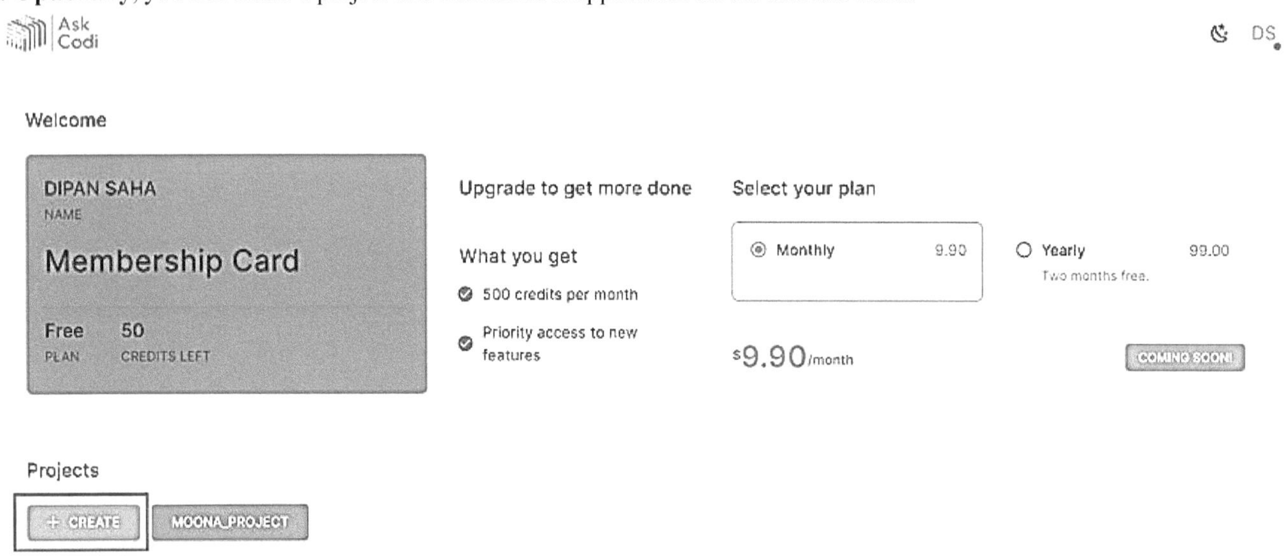

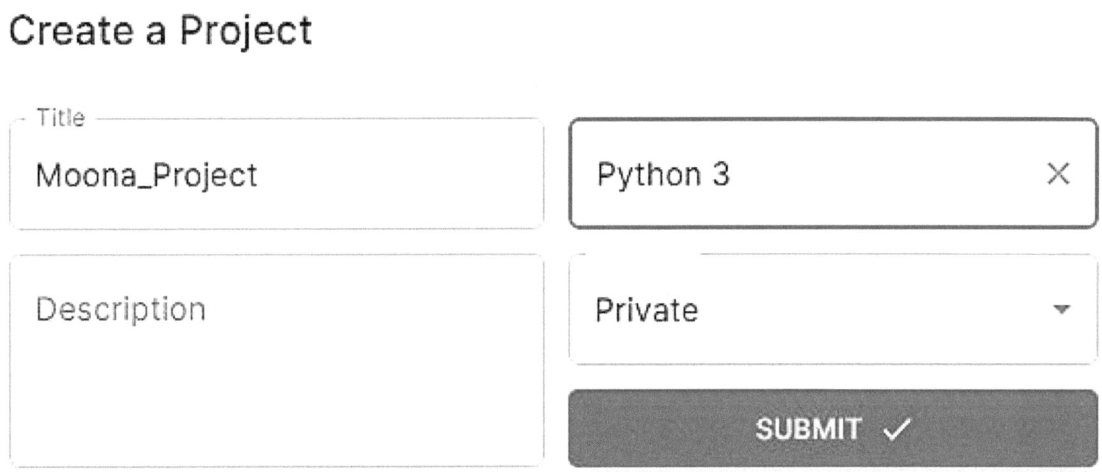
Create a Project
Title
Moona_Project
Python 3
Description
Private
SUBMIT

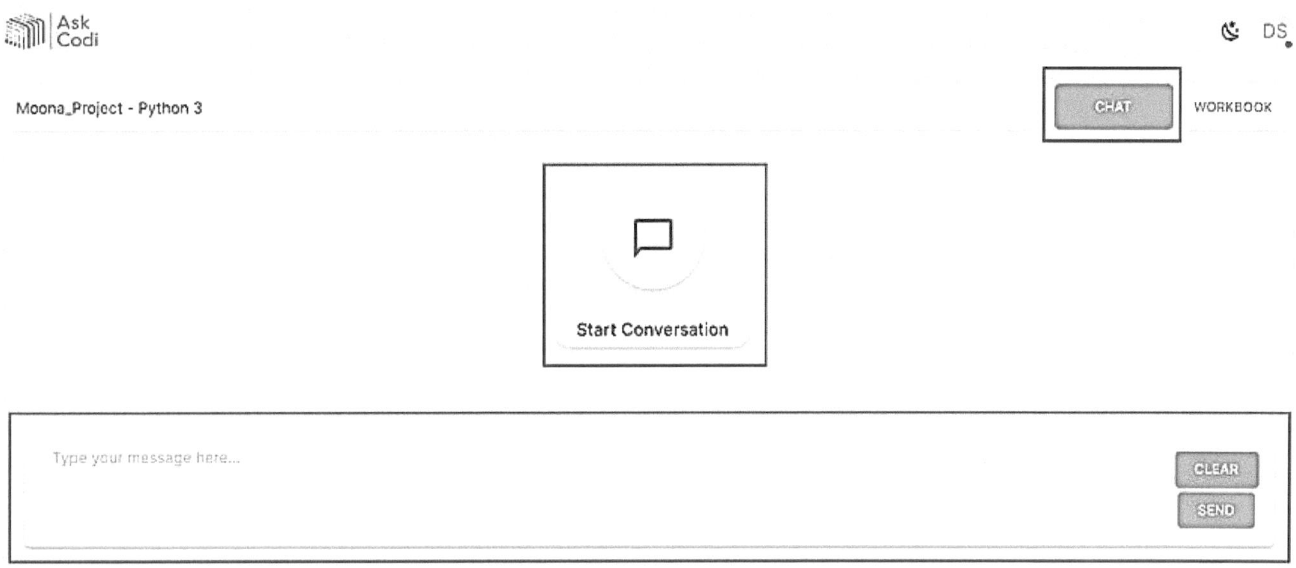
Ask Codi
DS
Moona_Project - Python 3
CHAT
WORKBOOK
Start Conversation
Type your message here...
CLEAR
SEND

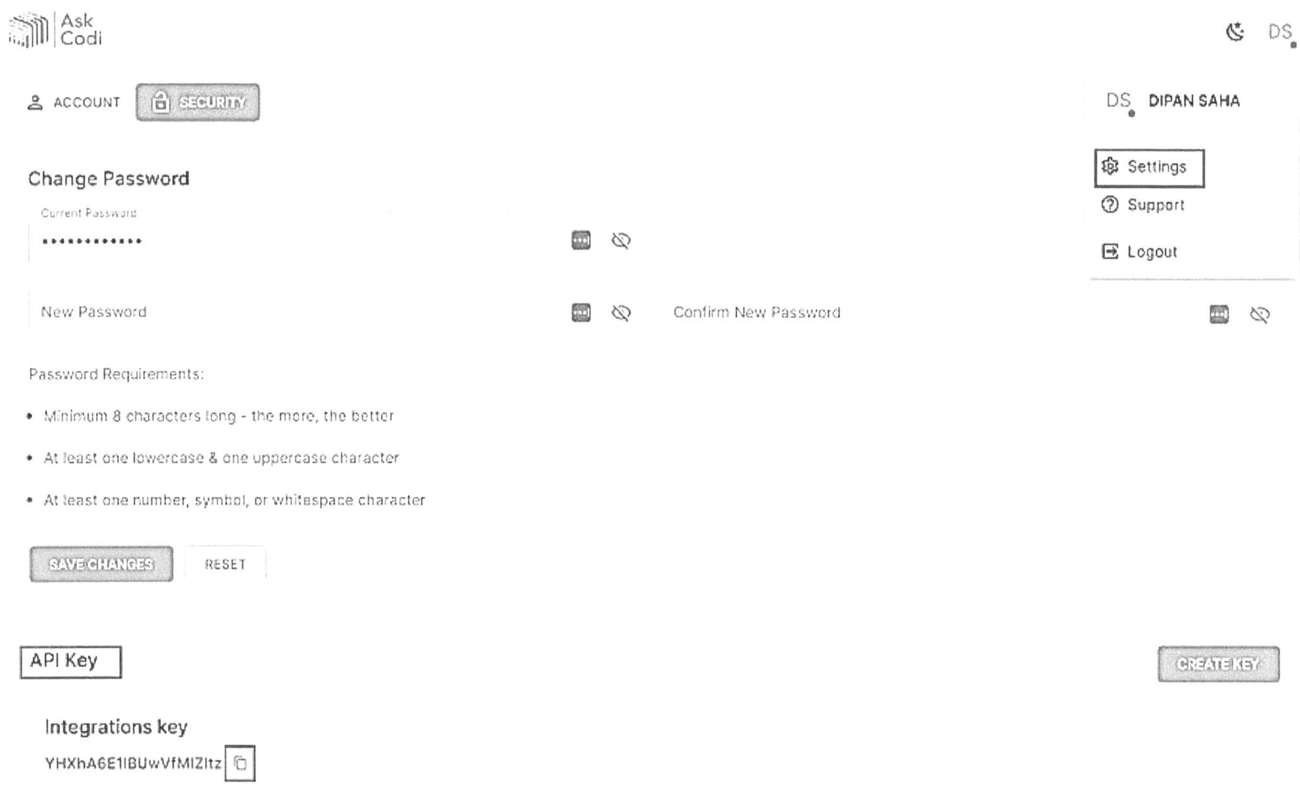

4. Now, go to **Settings** and copy the API Key.

5. Add AskCodi extension to VSCode
Install the AskCodi extension from VSCode extension marketplace.

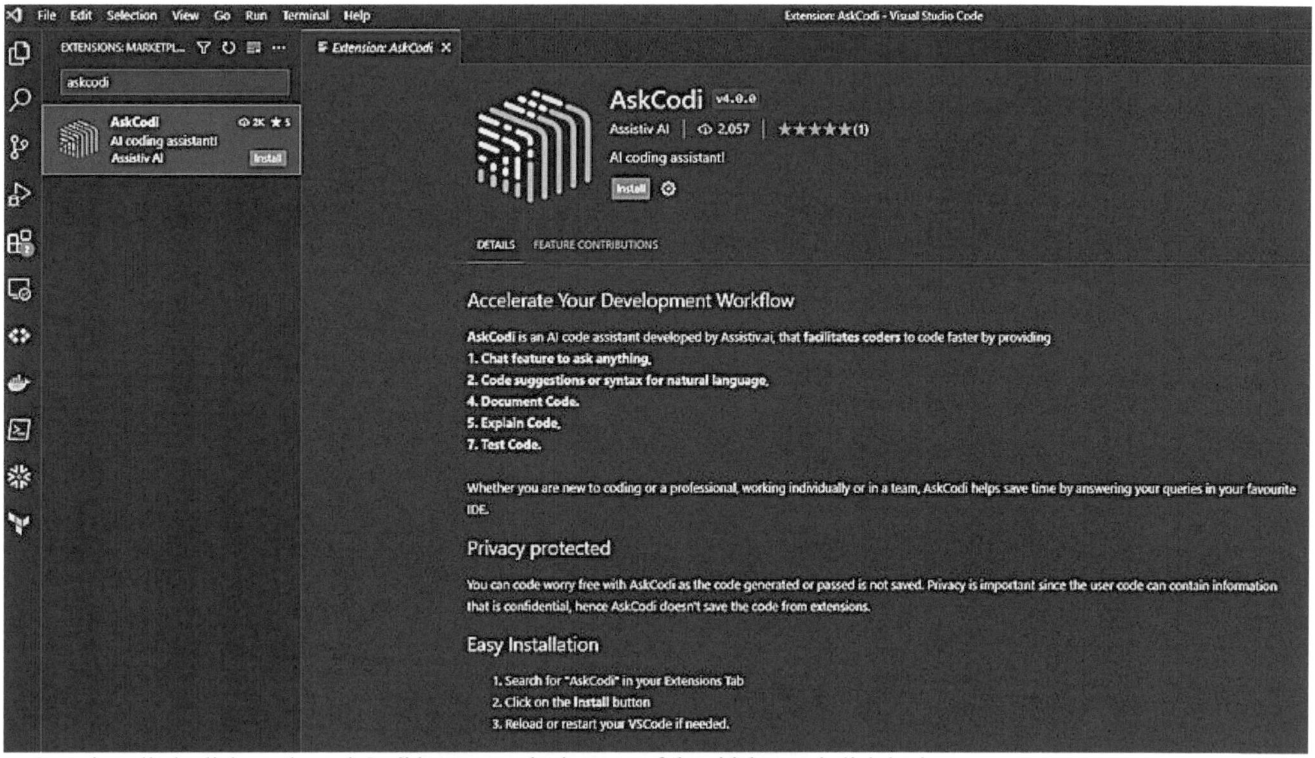

6. Once installed, click on the AskCodi button on the bottom of the sidebar and click login.

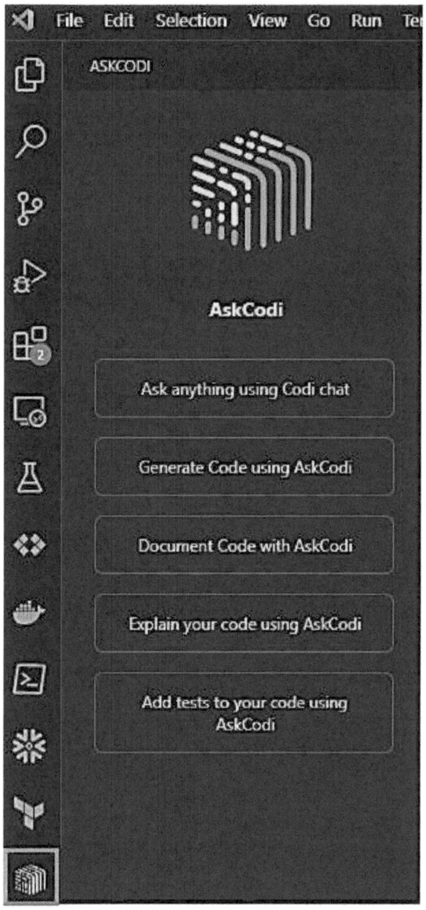

7. This will open a prompt which will ask you store the API key.

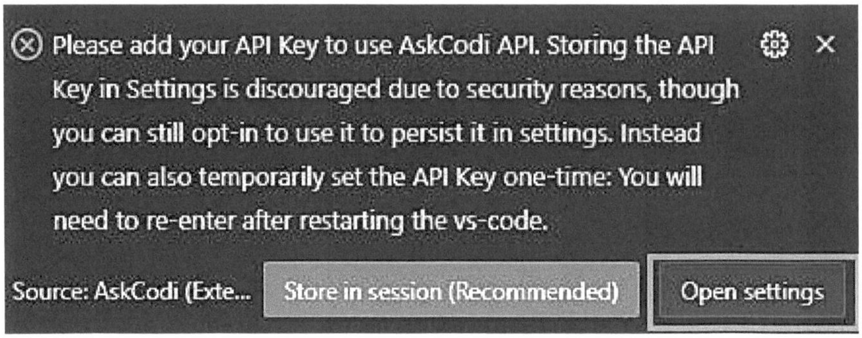

8. Save the copied API code.
9. Next, click on the Login button once again. You should now be logged in using the API key.
10. Use the AskCodi extension to generate code

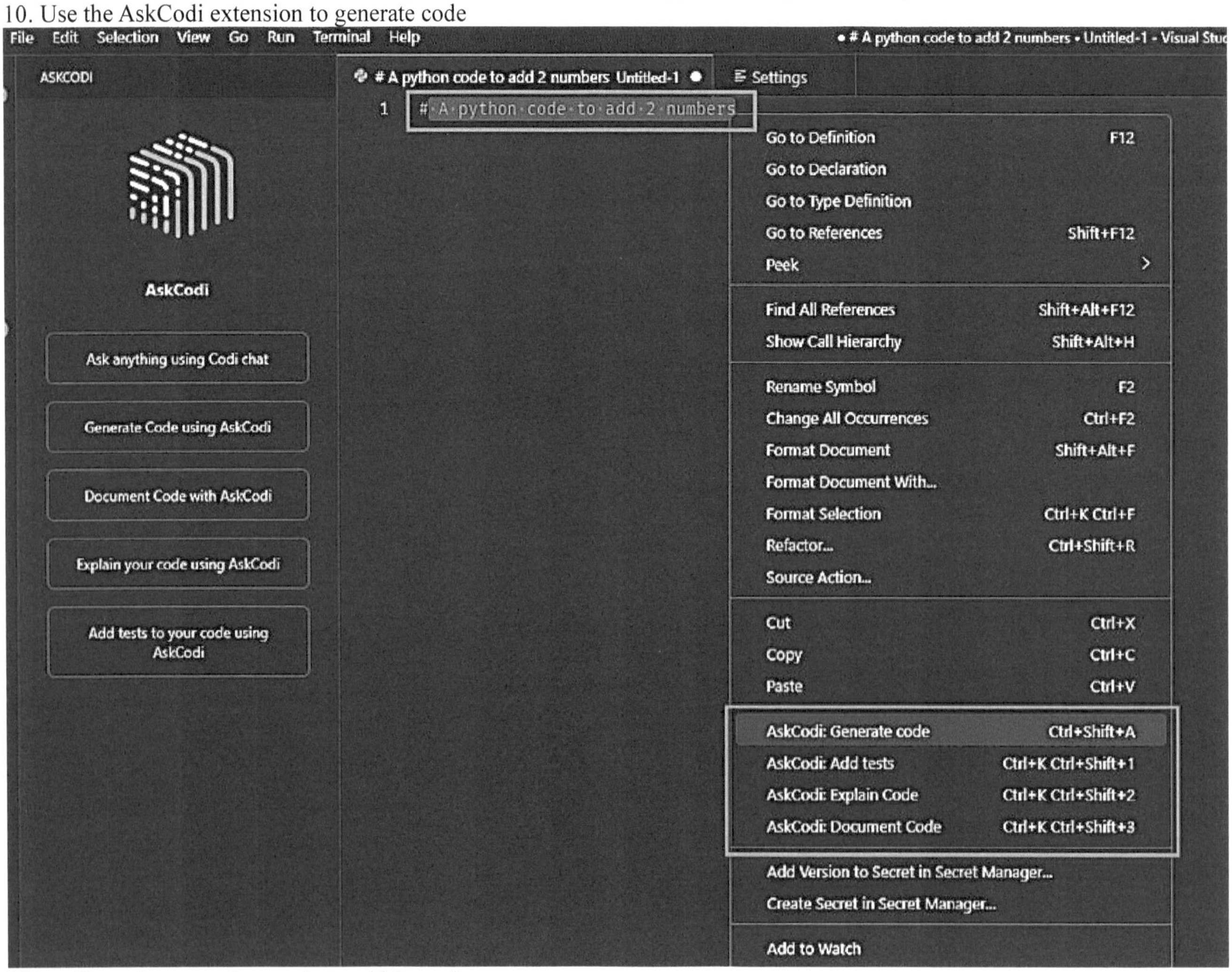

This will produce a python code to add 2 numbers.

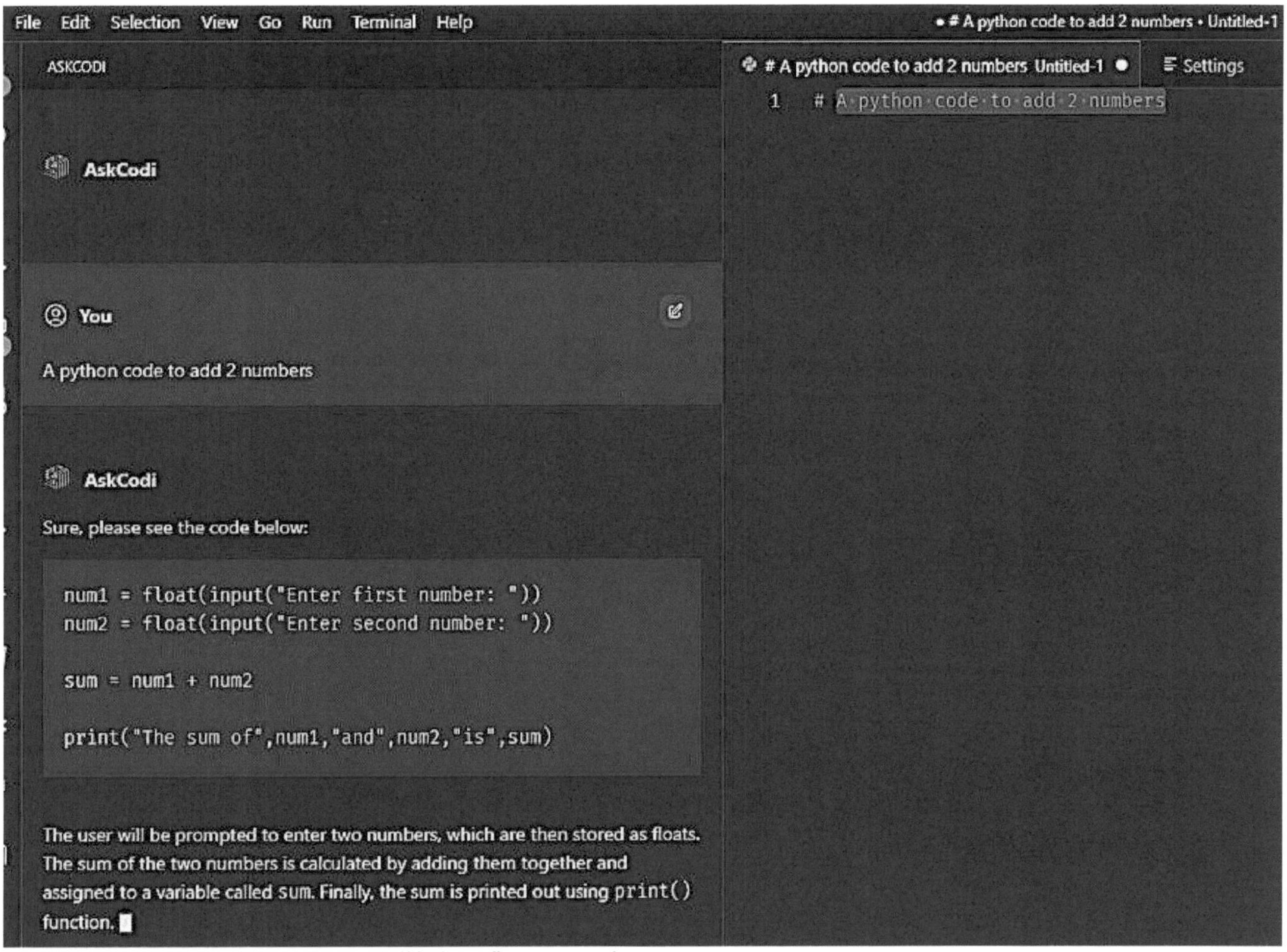

You can now use this code as is or modify it to fit your needs.

Use the AskCodi extension to document code

Here, I have written a sample code (on the right-hand side) and selected the 'AskCodi: Document Code' option. You will notice that on the left-hand side, it has produced the documentation for the same code.

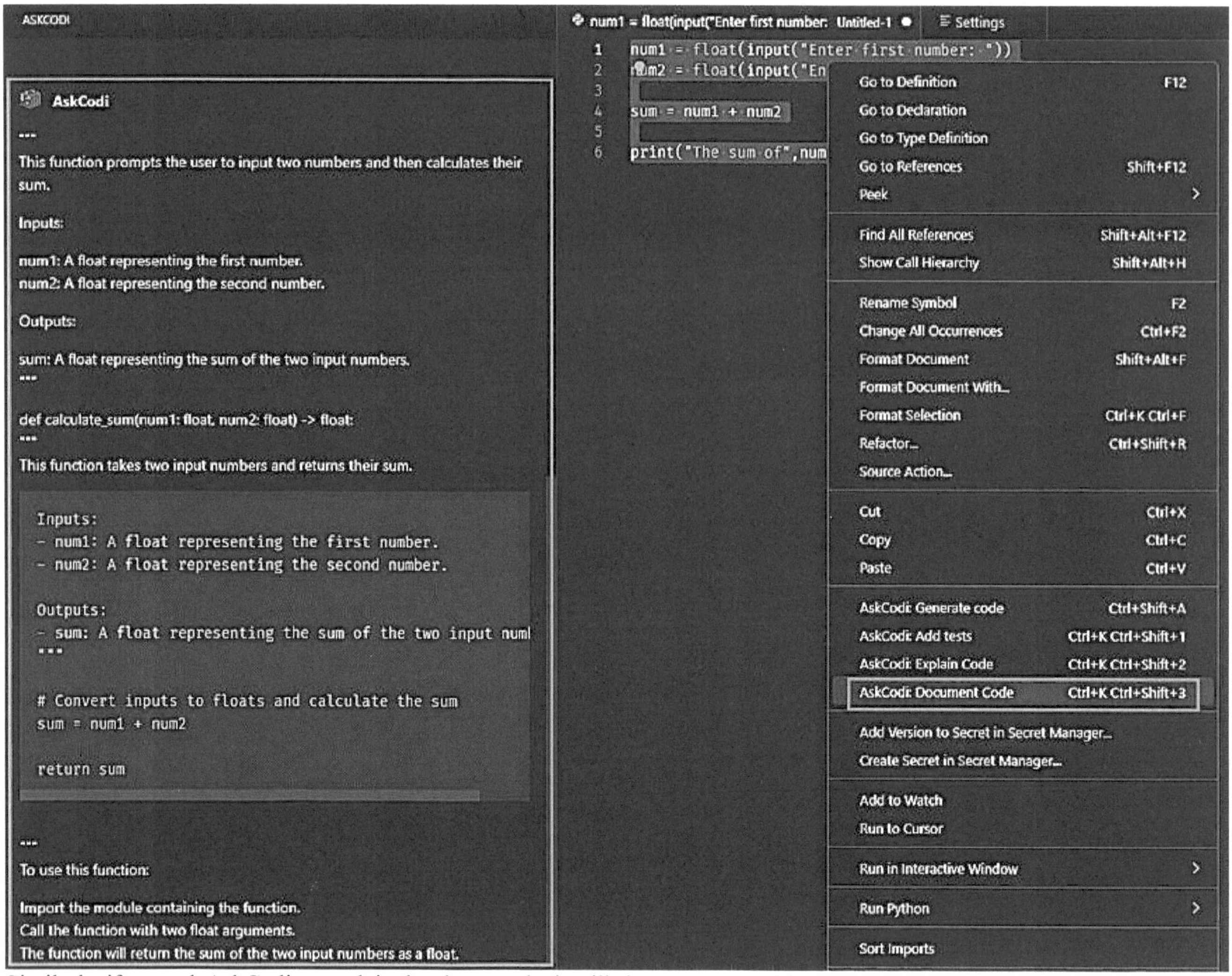

Similarly, if you ask AskCodi to explain the above code, it will show you something like below:

AskCodi

This is a simple Python program that prompts the user to input two numbers, and then calculates and displays the sum of those numbers.

The first line defines a variable `num1` to store the first number that the user will input, and requests the user to enter a number with the `input()` function. The `float()` function is used to convert the input to a floating-point number since the input function returns a string by default.

The second line is similar to the first line but defines the second number variable, `num2`.

The third line calculates the sum of `num1` and `num2` by adding them together with the + operator. The result is stored in the variable `sum`.

The last line uses the `print()` function to output a message to the user displaying the sum of the two numbers. The message is constructed using string concatenation, which combines the strings and variables using the + operator.

The output will look something like this:

```
Enter first number: 5
Enter second number: 3.2
The sum of 5.0 and 3.2 is 8.2
```

There are no apparent performance or security considerations with this code since it only performs basic arithmetic operations and user input is limited to numbers.

Use AskCodi to generate Java code

Here is a nice example to showcase the java code generation capabilities of AskCodi.

Benefits of using AskCodi

There are many benefits to using AskCodi, including:

1. Increased productivity: AskCodi can help you write code faster and more efficiently. This can free up your time to focus on other tasks, such as design and architecture.

2. Improved quality: AskCodi can help you improve the quality of your code by finding potential errors and style issues. This can help you avoid bugs and improve the maintainability of your code.

3. Enhanced collaboration: AskCodi can help you collaborate with other developers more effectively. For example, you can use AskCodi to generate documentation or unit tests for your code.

4. Reduced costs: AskCodi can help you reduce the costs of hiring and training new developers. This is because AskCodi can help you automate many of the tasks that are typically performed by developers.

Privacy protection
You can code worry free with AskCodi as the code generated or passed is not saved. Privacy is important since the user code can contain information that is confidential, hence AskCodi doesn't save the code from extensions.

6.8 BlackBox

This refers to AI-powered tools specifically designed for programmers, often as plugins or extensions within existing IDEs. They leverage machine learning models trained on massive codebases to offer features like:
1. Code Completion: Suggest relevant code snippets based on your current context, saving time and reducing errors.
2. Code Generation: Automatically generate entire functions, classes, or boilerplate code according to your specifications.
3. Code Search: Efficiently search through your codebase or external repositories for specific code elements.
4. Refactoring: Propose alternative ways to write your code for improved efficiency and maintainability.
5. Debugging Assistance: Analyze error messages and suggest potential causes and solutions.

Examples of Blackbox AI tools for programmers include:
1. Copilot by GitHub: Integrates with popular IDEs and offers context-aware code completion, generation, and refactoring suggestions.
2. Kite: Provides code completion and documentation suggestions on various platforms.
3. TabNine: Focuses on intelligent code completion and syntax prediction based on deep learning models.

2. Blackbox AI as a General Term:
In a broader sense, Blackbox AI refers to any AI system whose internal workings and decision-making processes are opaque and difficult to understand. This lack of transparency raises concerns about accountability, bias, and potential misuse.
While Blackbox AI tools for programmers often aim for explainability and user control, the term itself carries this connotation of hidden complexity and raises ethical s, especially when applied to AI systems used in high-stakes contexts like healthcare or finance.
Therefore, understanding the context when encountering the term "Blackbox AI" is crucial. For programming tools, it generally signifies powerful AI assistance, but in broader contexts, it highlights the need for ethical considerations and responsible development of AI technologies.

Define: -
BlackBox AI is a platform that allows you to create AI models without writing complex code. It uses pre-built libraries and algorithms to simplify the AI development process. You can use BlackBox AI to code faster, debug easier, and build smarter applications.
To use BlackBox AI, you need to install the BlackBox AI extension for Visual Studio Code. Then, you can ask BlackBox AI s or commands in natural language, and it will generate the code for you. You can also use BlackBox AI to suggest the next lines of code based on your project context.
Here are the steps to get started with BlackBox AI:

Step by Step
To start this demo I'll assume that you have your preferred IDE already installed, for me, I choose VScode as a text editor.
1- Add blackbox extension to VSCode(see the link below the image)

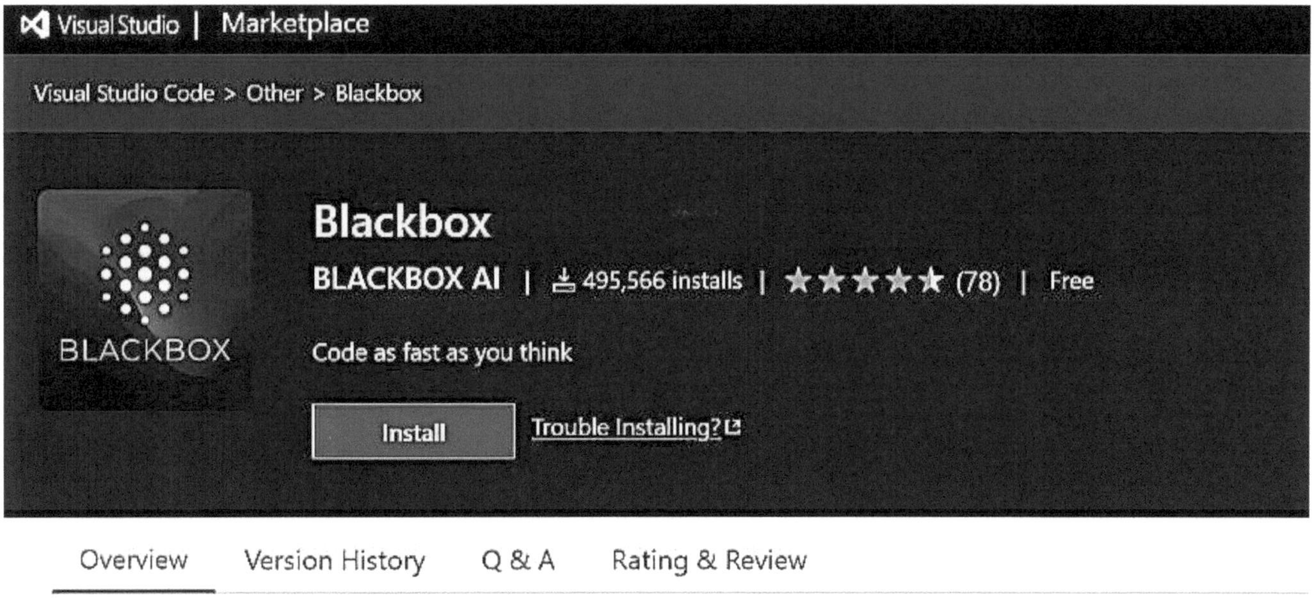

Blackbox — Visual Studio Marketplace

2- the letter "B" will be added left your VsCode

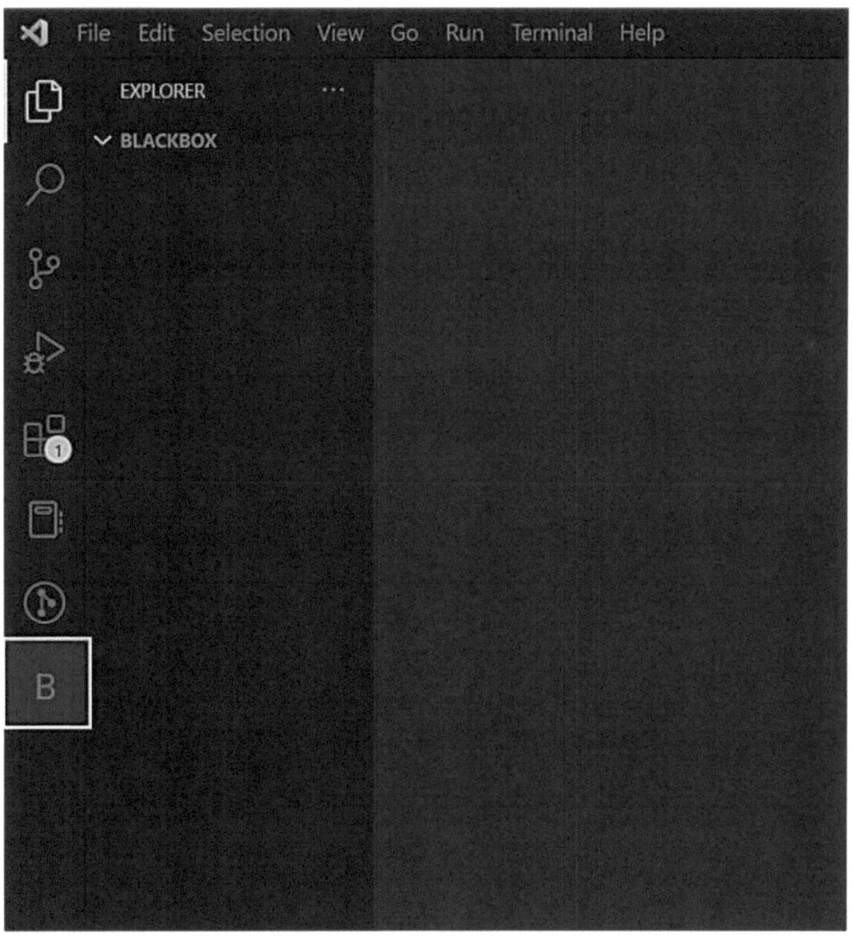

3- start coding

Suppose we want to code with python, let's see what blackbox can do for us.

```
lst = [1,2,3]
# print list in python?
```
first of all I declared a list of numbers then I asked blackbox to print it for me, here is the answer
```
print(*myList, sep='\n')
for p in myList: print p
print '\n'.join(str(p) for p in myList)
```
4. Wait for the installation process to complete.
5. Start a new project or open an existing one in VS Code.
6. In the bottom right corner, click on the BlackBox AI icon to activate it.
7. In the top right corner, click on the microphone icon to enable voice input, or use the keyboard shortcut Ctrl+Shift+B to open the BlackBox AI chat window.
8. BlackBox AI will generate the code for you and display it in the editor. You can edit, run, or debug the code as usual.

The Blackbox AI tool boasts several key features that can drastically improve your coding workflow. Here are some highlights:

Code Completion and Editing:

1. Autocompletion: Suggests relevant code snippets, functions, and variables as you type, saving you time and effort.
2. Context-aware suggestions: Adapts its suggestions based on the context of your code and the programming language you're using.
3. Multi-line editing: Completes entire lines or blocks of code based on your intent and surrounding code.
4. Error detection and correction: Flags potential errors and suggests fixes, improving code accuracy.

Debugging and Refactoring:

1. Interactive debugging: Helps you step through code, identify bugs, and understand their underlying causes.
2. Refactoring capabilities: Restructures and improves your code for better readability, maintainability, and efficiency.
3. Test generation: Automates the creation of unit tests for your code, ensuring robustness and quality.

Additional Functionality:

1. Extract code from sources: Pulls out code from images, videos, or PDFs, reducing tedious manual work.
2. Support for various languages: Works with over 20 programming languages, including Python, JavaScript, Java, C++, and more.
3. Intuitive interface: Easy to use and navigate, even for beginners.
4. Open-source and free: You can contribute to its development and use it for personal and commercial projects without any costs.

However, it's important to consider the limitations of Blackbox AI:

1. Black box nature: While powerful, its internal workings are opaque, making it challenging to understand why it suggests certain actions.
2. Potential for errors: As with any AI tool, it might occasionally suggest inaccurate or suboptimal solutions.
3. Overreliance: Overdependence on Blackbox can hinder your own code comprehension and development skills.

Exercise

Exercise 1 – MCQ

Q 1. GitHub Copilot is known for:
A. Project management
B. AI-driven code completion
C. Code version control
D. Automated testing

Q 2. What is the primary function of aiXcoder?
A. Code review and collaboration
B. Code debugging
C. AI-powered code generation
D. Project documentation

Q 3. TabNine is recognized for its capabilities in:
A. Code completion using machine learning
B. Real-time code collaboration
C. Automated code testing
D. Code refactoring

Q 4. Figstack is a tool primarily used for:

A. Code version control
B. Code documentation
C. Visual testing of UI components
D. Code profiling

Q 5. Cody by Sourcegraph is known for:
A. AI-powered code suggestions
B. Gamification of coding challenges
C. Automated code deployment
D. Cloud-based IDE

Q 6. SpellBox is a coding tool designed for:
A. Automated spell checking in code
B. Code profiling and optimization
C. AI-driven code generation
D. Automated code formatting

Q 7. AskCodi is primarily focused on:
A. AI-driven code completion
B. Code documentation
C. Real-time code collaboration
D. Code-related Q&A

Q 8. BlackBox is known for its capabilities in:
A. Automated code testing
B. Code obfuscation
C. Code version control
D. Code security analysis

Q 9. Which coding tool is specifically designed for enhancing accessibility in code?
A. GitHub Copilot
B. aiXcoder
C. Figstack
D. SpellBox

Q 10. Which tool provides AI-driven suggestions for writing SQL queries in natural language?
A. GitHub Copilot
B. aiXcoder
C. TabNine
D. AskCodi

Exercise 2 – True/ False

1. GitHub Copilot utilizes artificial intelligence to suggest and complete code snippets.
2. aiXcoder primarily focuses on code review and collaboration features.
3. TabNine uses machine learning to provide intelligent code completion suggestions.
4. Figstack is a coding tool primarily designed for automated code testing.
5. Cody by Sourcegraph introduces gamification elements into coding challenges.
6. SpellBox is an AI-powered coding tool that automatically checks for spelling errors in code.
7. AskCodi focuses on real-time code collaboration and pair programming.
8. BlackBox is known for its capabilities in code obfuscation and security analysis.
9. GitHub Copilot offers features for enhancing the accessibility of code.
10. SpellBox provides AI-driven suggestions for writing SQL queries in natural language.

Exercise 3 – Fill in the blanks

Q 1. GitHub Copilot is an AI-powered coding tool that assists developers by generating ___________.
Q 2. aiXcoder is known for its AI-driven features that enhance developer ___________ and efficiency.
Q 3. TabNine is a coding tool that uses advanced ___________ to provide context-aware code completions.
Q 4. Figstack is a tool designed for collaborative ___________ and sharing of visual elements in code.
Q 5. Cody by Sourcegraph is a coding tool that focuses on improving ___________ for developers.

Exercise 4 – Match case

1. Match the coding tool known for generating code snippets and suggestions using AI	A. Cody by Sourcegraph
2. Connect the coding tool recognized for enhancing developer productivity through AI-driven features	B. aiXcoder
3. Pair the coding tool that utilizes machine learning for context-aware code completions	C. TabNine
4. Match the tool designed for collaborative designing and sharing of visual elements in code	D. Figstack
5. Connect the coding tool focused on improving code search for developers	E. GitHub Copilot

Exercise 5 – One word answer

Q 1. Figstack?
Q 2. Cody by Sourcegraph?
Q 3. SpellBox?
Q 4. AskCodi?
Q 5. BlackBox?

Exercise 6 – Small answer

Q 1. What does GitHub Copilot specialize in providing for developers?
Q 2. How does aiXcoder contribute to a developer's workflow?
Q 3. What is TabNine known for in the realm of coding?
Q 4. What collaborative aspect does Figstack focus on for developers?
Q 5. What is the primary function of Cody by Sourcegraph?

Exercise 7 – Long answer

Q 1. How does GitHub Copilot utilize artificial intelligence to assist developers, and what types of code-related suggestions and completions does it generate?
Q 2. In what ways does TabNine utilize machine learning for context-aware code completions, and how does it adapt to a developer's coding style and preferences?

Answers

Exercise 1 – MCQ

Ans: 1 B, 2 C, 3 A, 4 C, 5 B, 6 A, 7 D, 8 B, 9 C, 10 D

Exercise 2 – True/ False

Ans: 1 True, 2 False, 3 True, 4 False, 5 True, 6 True, 7 False, 8 True, 9 False, 10 False

Exercise 3 – Fill in the blanks

Ans: 1 Code snippets and suggestions, 2 Productivity, 3 Machine Learning, 4 Designing, 5 Code search

Exercise 4 – Match case

Ans: 1 E, 2 D, 3 C, 4 B, 5 A

Exercise 5 – One word answer

Ans: 1 Collaboration, 2 Code-search, 3 Spelling, 4 Community, 5 Security

ONLINE RESOURCES

Practice Paper
Link
https://forms.office.com/r/BLFAfetTdP
QR Code

Video Content
Link

https://www.youtube.com/playlist?list=PLzlh_31VWEFqiIkmy_tBryzLuvz9y3ggp

QR Code

Chapter 7: Meeting Tools

7.1 Spinach

Spinach.ai is an innovative AI-powered meeting tool that's much more than just a note-taking app. Think of it as your own personal AI project manager that joins your meetings, captures key points, and helps you move your projects forward. Here's a quick rundown of its key features:

Smarter Note-taking:

1. Automatic recording and transcription: Ditch the manual note-taking! Spinach records your meetings and transcribes everything accurately, saving you tons of time and effort.
2. Action item and decision capture: Spinach intelligently identifies key decisions and action items from the discussion, making them easily searchable and actionable.
3. Meeting summaries in a flash: Get concise and comprehensive summaries of your meetings automatically generated, complete with speaker attribution and timestamps.

Enhanced Collaboration:

1. Shared agendas and follow-ups: Create and share meeting agendas beforehand, and easily track follow-up items after the meeting to ensure everyone's on the same page.
2. Integration with your existing tools: Spinach seamlessly connects with project management platforms like Jira and Asana, automatically suggesting tickets and updates based on discussion points.
3. Real-time collaboration on notes: Collaborate on meeting notes in real-time with your team, adding comments, clarifications, and edits as needed.

Boosting Meeting Efficiency:

1. Meeting templates for different types of sessions: From daily standups to retros and brainstorming sessions, Spinach offers pre-built templates to optimize your meeting flow and focus.
2. Actionable insights and trends: Gain valuable insights from your meeting history, identifying recurring themes, areas for improvement, and individual contributions.
3. Improved time management: By streamlining note-taking and action item tracking, Spinach frees up your time to focus on what truly matters - driving results.

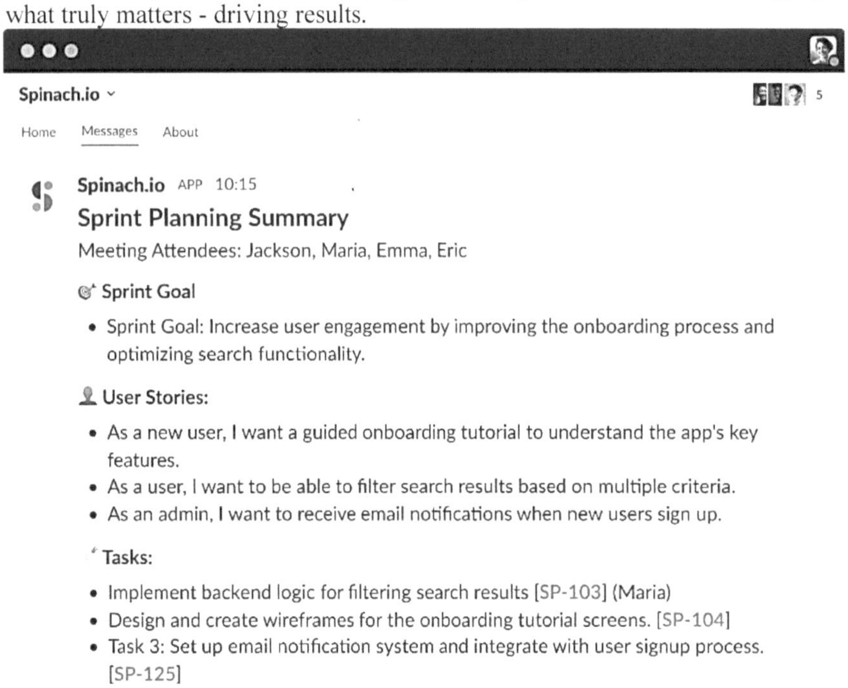

Spinach was designed with development teams in mind and packs a level of functionality that would leave other leafy greens shaking in their boots!

Like your own personal AI Scrum Master, Spinach can run your daily standups, create meeting summaries, and make ticket suggestions at the click of a mouse. This agile meeting tool runs on GPT-4 technology andzintegrates with a slew of other work tools (including ClickUp) for more efficient processes. Instead of meeting recordings or transcripts, Spinach generates organized summaries to document blockers and encourage your team to take action.

Spinach best features

1. Multiple integrations to assist in your sprint planning, daily standups, sprint retrospectives, and backlog grooming meetings
2. Handles all written updates and highlights made in any meeting, including minutes, taking notes, action items, and key decisions
3. Suggests bug or feature tickets directly into Slack
4. Supplies attendees with context from proper meetings and builds your agenda for you

Spinach limitations

1. Lacking several classic AI meeting features that other tools have to document discussions in additional ways

Spinach pricing

1. Free
2. **Pro**: $99 per month

Spinach.ai is an AI-powered meeting tool that can be used in a variety of ways to make your meetings more productive and efficient.

Here are some of the most common uses:

1. Taking notes and capturing action items:

Spinach.ai can automatically record your meetings and transcribe everything that is said. It then uses AI to identify key decisions and action items, which are added to a central list that can be easily shared with all participants. This saves you the time and hassle of taking notes yourself, and ensures that everyone is on the same page about what needs to be done.

2. Creating meeting summaries:

After your meeting, Spinach.ai will automatically generate a concise and comprehensive summary that includes the main points of discussion, the decisions that were made, and the action items that were assigned. This is a great way to quickly catch up on what happened if you missed the meeting, or to share the key takeaways with people who weren't there.

3. Keeping track of progress:

Spinach.ai can track the progress of your action items over time. It will remind you of upcoming deadlines and let you know when someone has completed a task. This helps to ensure that everyone is accountable for their commitments and that projects stay on track.

4. Improving meeting participation:

Spinach.ai can help to improve meeting participation by making it easier for everyone to contribute. Its real-time chat feature allows participants to share their thoughts and ideas easily, and its polls and surveys can be used to gather feedback quickly and efficiently.

5. Identifying trends and insights:

Over time, Spinach.ai can collect data on your meetings, such as the topics that are discussed most often, the people who participate the most, and the decisions that are made. This data can be used to identify trends and insights that can help you to improve your meetings in the future.

In addition to these general uses, Spinach.ai can also be used in a number of other ways, such as:

- Preparing for meetings: You can use Spinach.ai to create an agenda for your meeting and to share it with all participants beforehand.
- Following up on meetings: You can use Spinach.ai to send out a follow-up email after your meeting with the key takeaways and action items.

- Getting feedback on meetings: You can use Spinach.ai to collect feedback from participants on how your meetings could be improved.

1. Sembly
- Sembly is a cross-platform web and mobile app that accompanies users on Microsoft Teams, Zoom, and Google Meet meetings, making content available for review, search, and sharing, powered by its highly accurate, second generation proprietary transcription engine.
- Sembly AI is a cloud-based meeting assistant software designed for companies of all sizes. The platform is built on the foundation of data science capabilities blended with a deep understanding of various corporate processes.
- It is a smart meeting assistant that seamlessly records, analyzes, and transcribes your conversations to offer meeting summaries and take actionable insights.
- Users can easily join calls or meetings without having to install or download any applications.

Sembly AI Key Features

1. Meeting recording and transcription
Users can easily read, replay, and share the text content of their meetings with each other. This allows them to stay in sync with each other and make informed decisions based on their conversations.
2. Sentiment
Dive deep into understanding the highlights of your meeting and take the necessary steps.
3. Meeting sharing
Users can share the different moments of a meeting or give insight to colleagues once the meeting is over even if they were not part of it.
4. Meeting summary
Sembly AI's glance view feature helps users save time. It helps users understand the different topics that were discussed and the outcome of a meeting. In addition, you can share structured outcomes of the meeting with team members and clients who were not part of the meeting.
5. Workspace and collaboration
The collaboration feature enables users to modify meeting transcriptions and update key items.

Sembly AI isn't just another meeting recording tool. It's your personal AI assistant, transforming meetings from time-consuming slogs into productive action centers. Here's a peek into its superpowers:

1. Meeting Mastery:
- Automatic Attendance: Ditch manual joining or forgetting to record. Sembly joins your Zoom, Google Meet, or Microsoft Teams meetings automatically, capturing every word and nuance.
- Instant Transcripts & Notes: No more frantically scribbling. Sembly generates accurate transcripts and insightful notes in real-time, ready for review or sharing.
- AI-powered Insights: Forget sifting through hours of recordings. Sembly identifies key decisions, action items, risks, and notable figures, giving you an instant grasp of the meeting's essence.

2. Boosting Productivity:
- Actionable Tasks: Turn discussion points into actionable tasks with automatic integration with tools like Slack, Trello, and Asana. No more lost follow-ups!
- Meeting Summaries & Highlights: Share concise summaries with absent team members or revisit key points instantly, saving everyone valuable time.
- Automated Commitments: Track individual commitments made during the meeting, ensuring accountability and progress measurement.

3. Smarter Collaboration:
- Shared Meeting Library: Build a searchable library of past meetings, making knowledge readily accessible and accelerating future discussions.
- Live Collaboration on Notes: Take simultaneous notes with your team, adding edits and insights in real-time for a collaborative understanding.
- Integrations: Connect Sembly to your favorite tools to streamline workflows and keep information flowing seamlessly.

4. Beyond Meetings:
- Audio & Video Processing: Upload past recordings or transcripts for insights, edit speaker names, or even translate languages.
- Customizable Workflow: Tailor Sembly to your needs, from automatic topic labeling to adding custom keywords for deeper analysis.

- Seamless Scalability: Whether you're a small team or a large organization, Sembly adapts to your size and meeting styles.

How Sembly works
Sembly automatically joins your calls with no downloads or installs.
1. Before the meeting:
How to get started?
Sync Sembly with your Outlook or Google calendar. Sembly will automatically join all your calls with no downloads or installs.

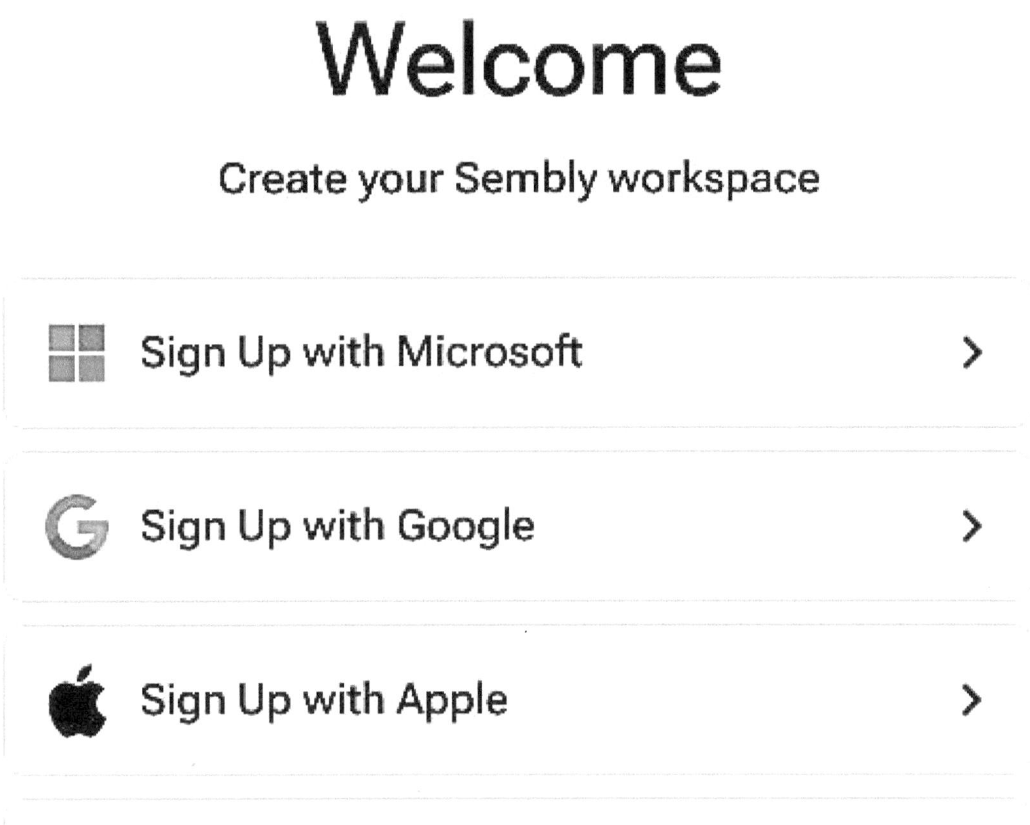

What if I don't want to sync my calendars?
No problem! You can invite Sembly to a future or an ongoing meeting or you can record an in-person meeting using your mobile phone.

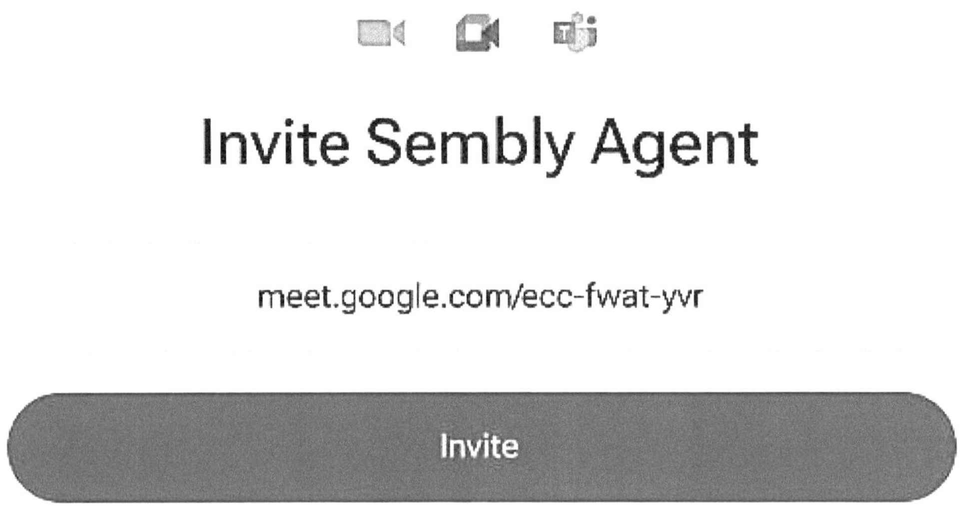

What platforms Sembly can join? Can I record in-person meetings?
Sembly works with Microsoft Teams, Google Meet, and Zoom.

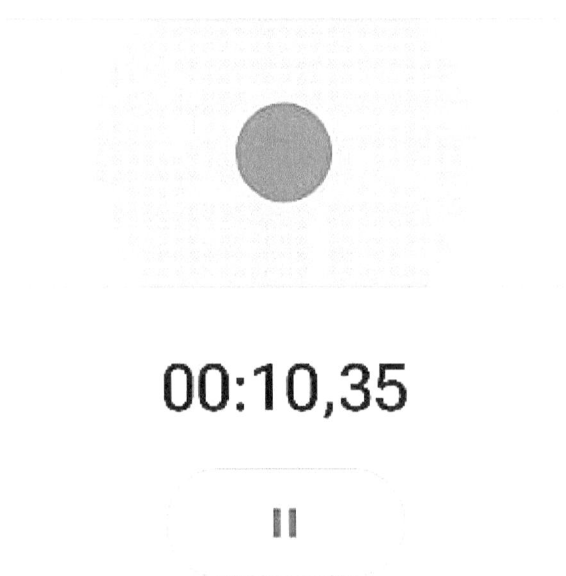

Can I upload my past recorded audio or video files?
Yes! Use the upload feature to upload a previously recorded audio or video file and Sembly will do the rest.

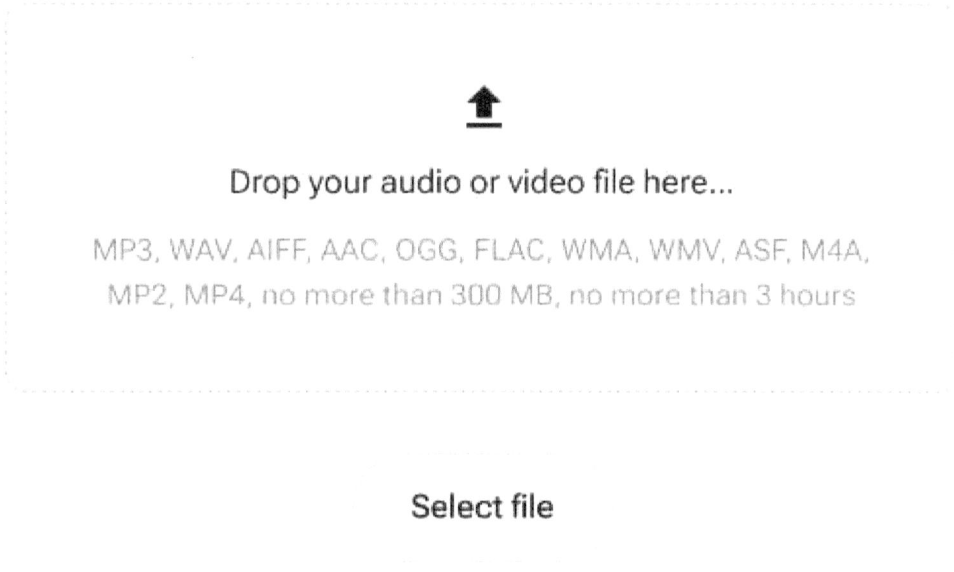

2. During the meeting
How would I know if Sembly joined my call?
Sembly shows up on your call as a regular participant — it will join any call it is invited to, introduce itself, and record the call. It can even attend a call when you're not there!

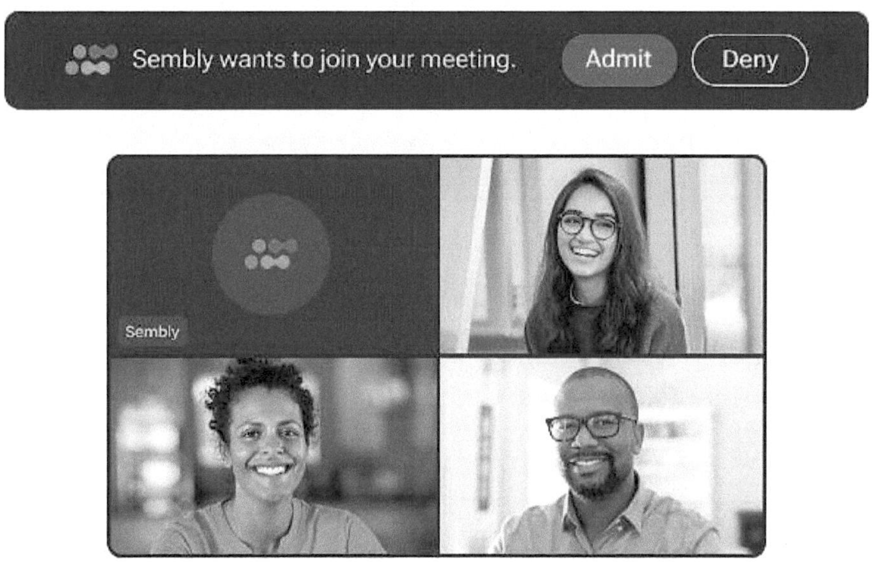

How can I pause/resume meeting recording?
Use the webapp, Chrome Extension, or mobile app to control Sembly during the call — you can pause/resume Sembly recording or stop it from attending the rest of the call.

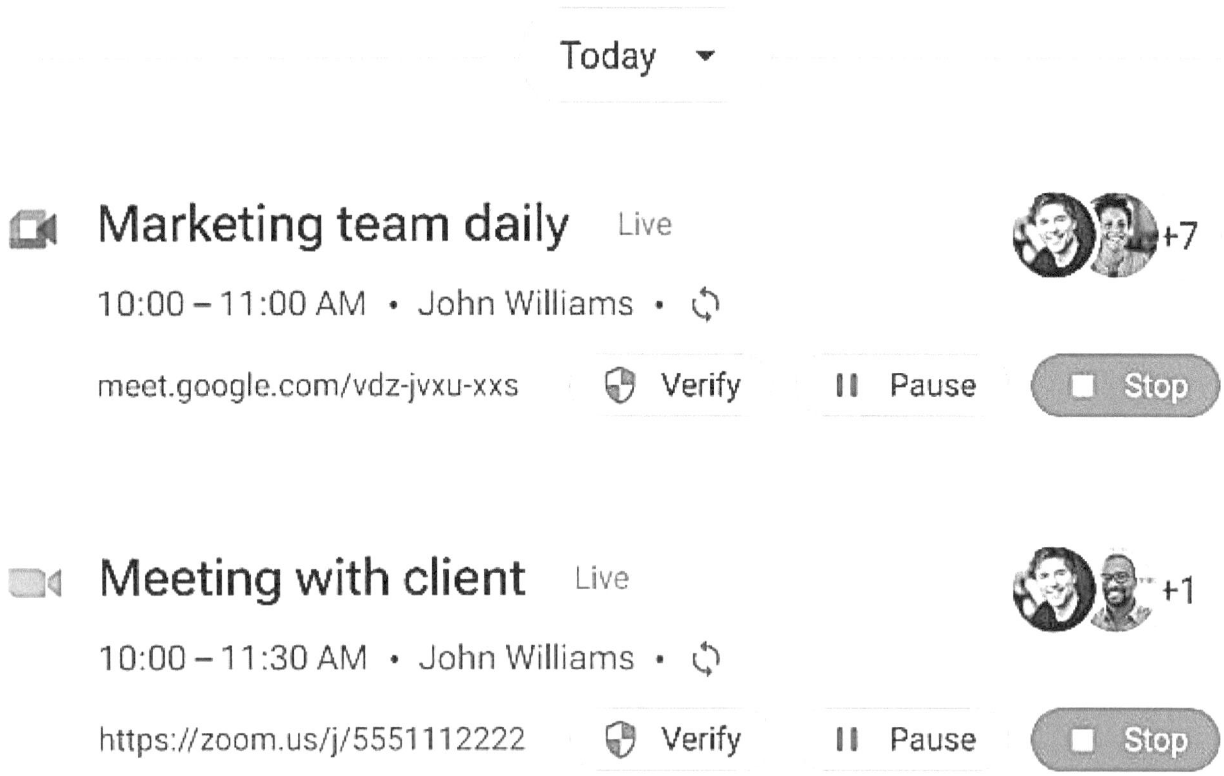

How can I remove Sembly from the call?

You can use the "stop" button in Sembly interfaces or simply remove the Sembly Agent participant from your conference call using your conference platform features.

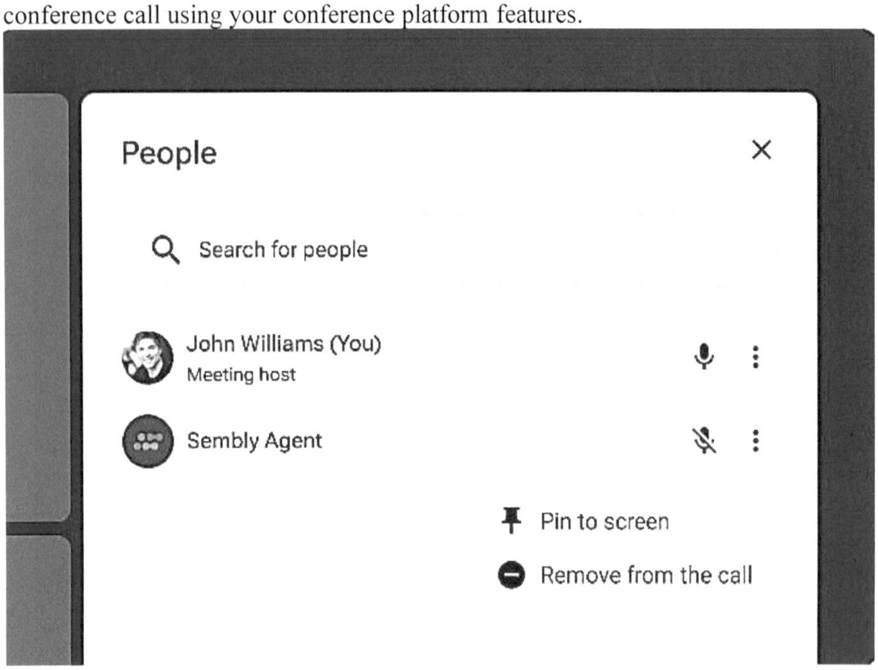

What I need to do when the meeting ends?

Nothing! Just hang tight while we process your meeting. It may take up to 50% the duration of the call to fully process the meeting. Results will be available in the Sembly webapp and on the Sembly mobile app.

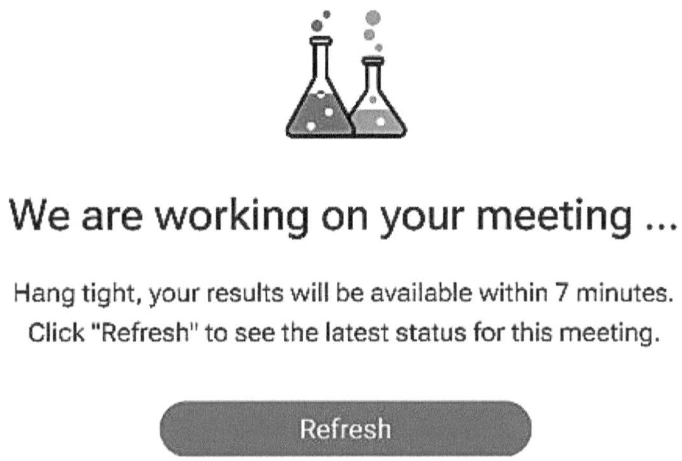

3. After the meeting
What will Sembly do after the meeting?
After the meeting, Sembly will present the Meeting Notes, the insights in Key Items, and the full transcript of the meeting. It will also execute any integration rules you setup to send content to other apps.

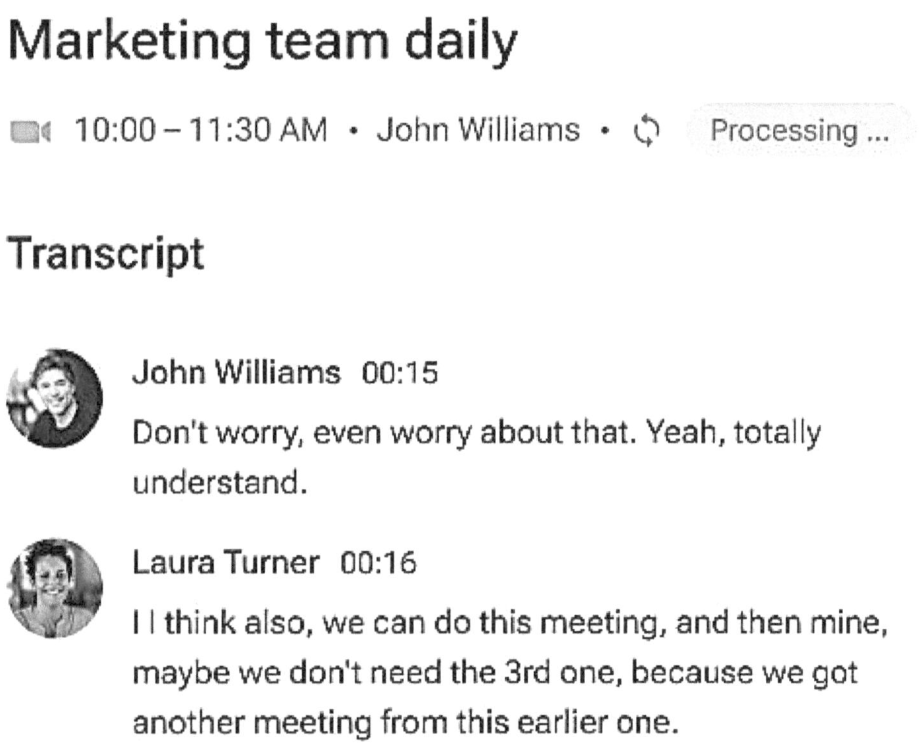

Where I can find my meeting recordings?
After it is processed, your meeting is available in the My Meetings tab.

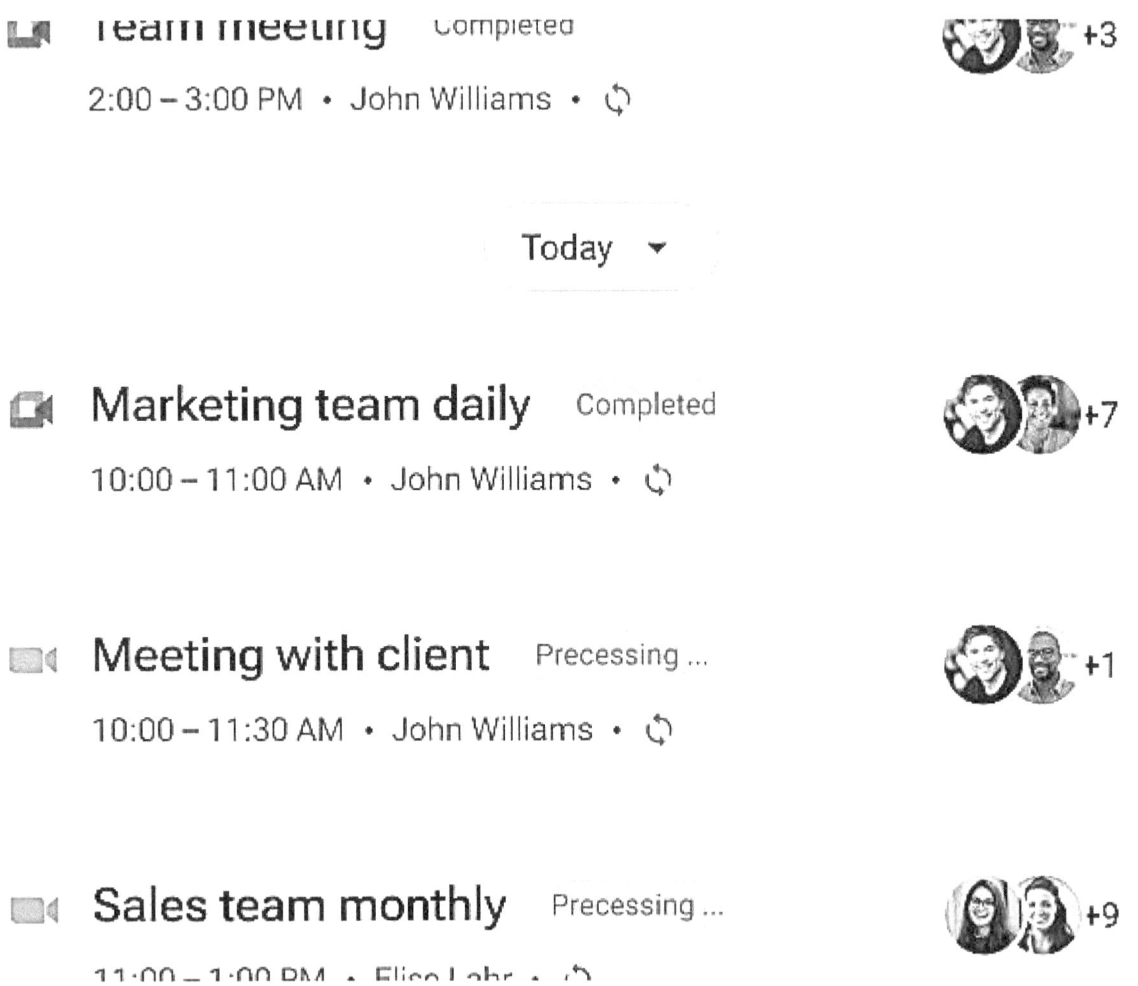

What is Sembly Meeting Notes?

Sembly's meeting notes view presents a focused digest of the meeting, including key topics discussed and insights under each of those topics. Meeting Notes will appear in the same language the meeting was conducted in. For mixed-language meetings, Sembly will pick the language most appropriate for that meeting.

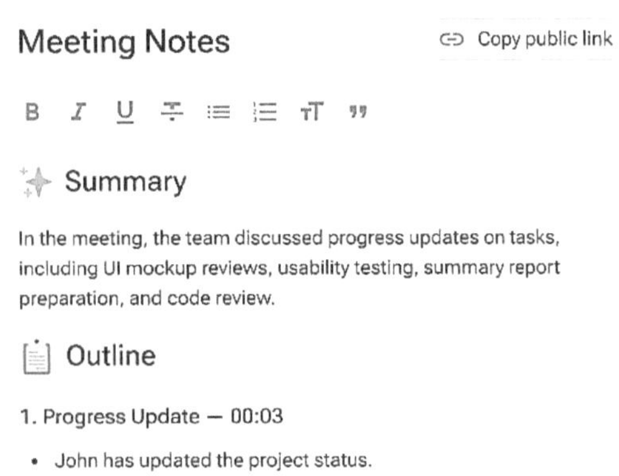

How can I share meeting notes with the team?

You can easily share Sembly Meeting Notes. These notes can be exported to PDF, markdown, shared directly with other Sembly users, or as a guest link for those who don't have a Sembly account.

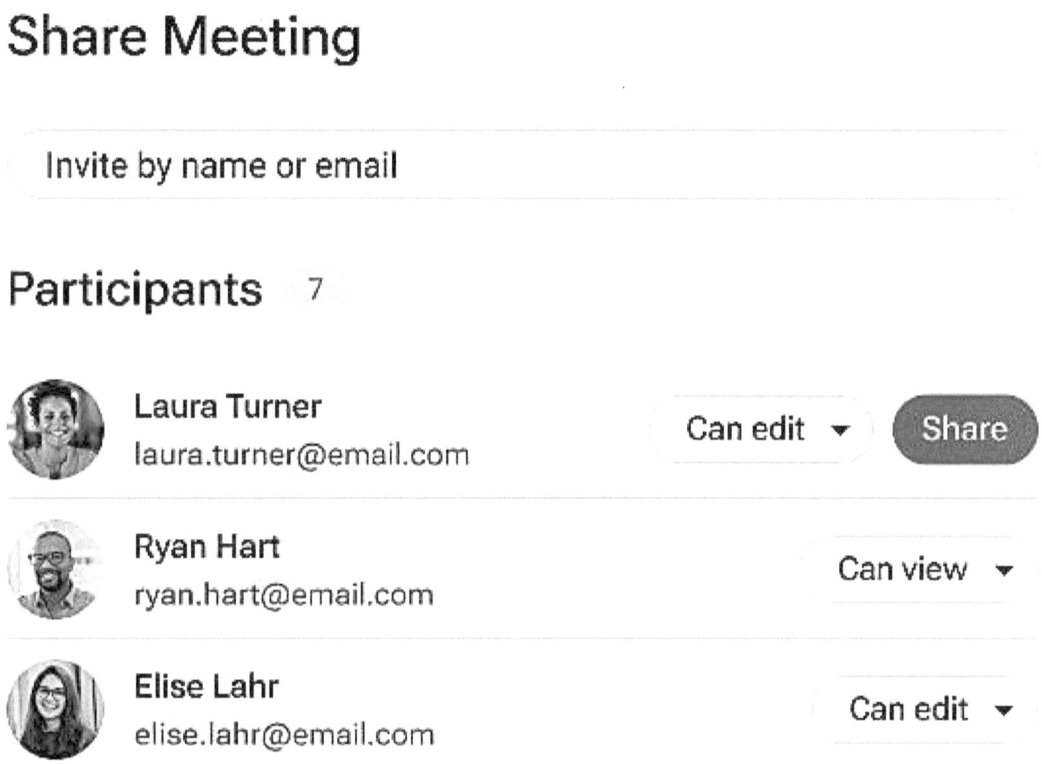

7.3 Fireflies

Fireflies.ai is an AI-powered platform that offers automated transcription of live meetings and audio files in minutes. Considered by many as an AI meeting assistant, it serves as a central hub for post-meeting collaborations and meeting recordings.

The platform is not just a transcription tool. It's a comprehensive meeting assistant that offers various time-saving features like Smart Search Filters and conversation analysis. These features help users quickly identify critical action items, tasks, and other key meeting insights.

This tool is designed to be user-friendly and intuitive, ensuring a smooth and hassle-free experience for its users. It integrates with your calendar and joins meetings automatically, records and transcribes your conversations, and even helps you analyze conversations to identify critical metrics.

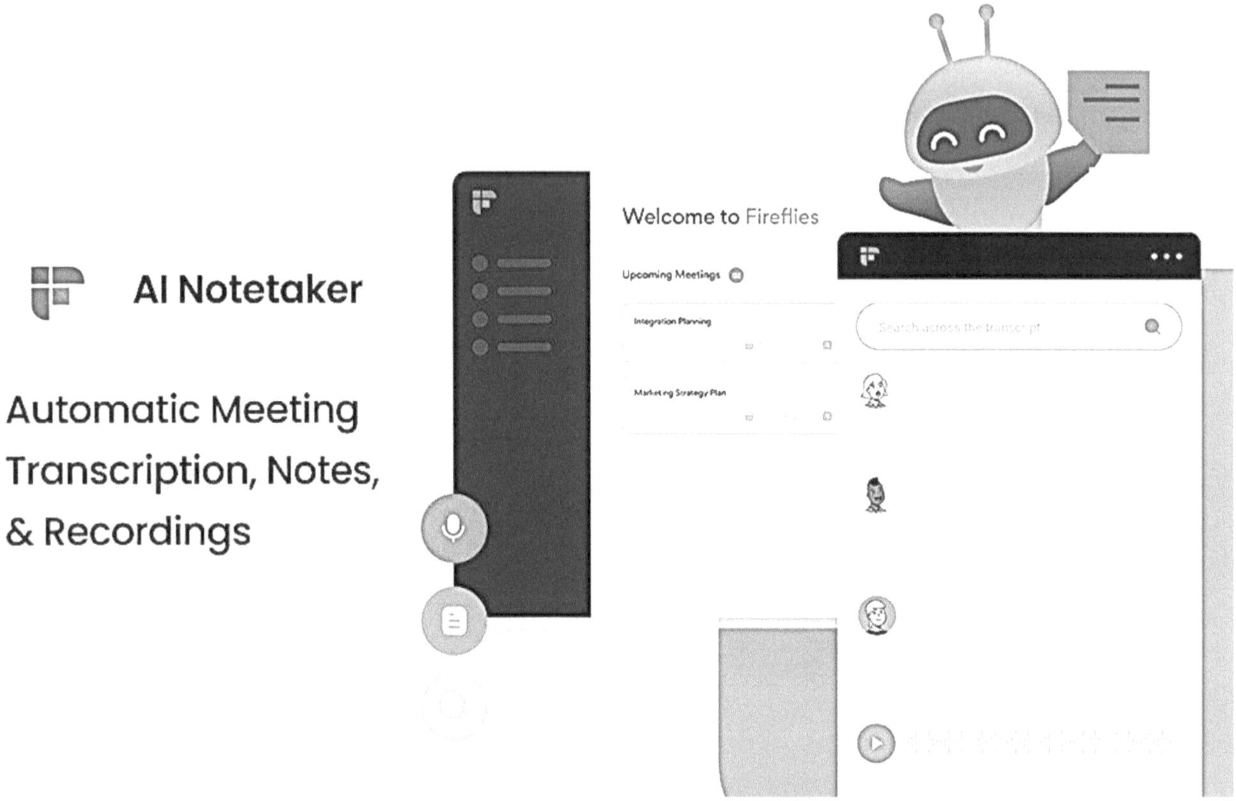

Some refer to Fireflies as a meeting transcription app. Others, an AI meeting assistant. And then there are those who say that Fireflies is an app that transcribes audio files to text.
All are correct. Fireflies can do all those.
To simplify things further, let's refer to Fireflies as your AI meeting assistant—an umbrella term that covers everything that Fireflies can do.

1. Records and transcribes your online and in-person meetings so that you can focus on your conversations.
2. Help teams achieve productive post-meeting collaborations.
3. Has a powerful, time-saving feature called Smart Search Filters. You can search across your automatically-generated transcript to identify critical action items, tasks, and other key meeting insights after your call. You can review hour-long meetings in minutes. And that's not even an exaggeration.
4. Automate your workflow through Fireflies' integrations.
5. Analyze conversations to identify critical metrics like sentiments and speaker's word per minute, silence duration, talk-to-listen ratio, etc.
6. Other notable features include Soundbites, Threads, and more. We're going to dissect these later.

For now, let's get started on how to use Fireflies.ai for your meetings, shall we?

Getting started with Fireflies

How to sign up for Fireflies.ai

Signing up for Fireflies.ai is a hassle-free process.
1. Open the Fireflies app.
2. You can sign up via Outlook Calendar or Google Calendar. We used Google Calendar for this guide.

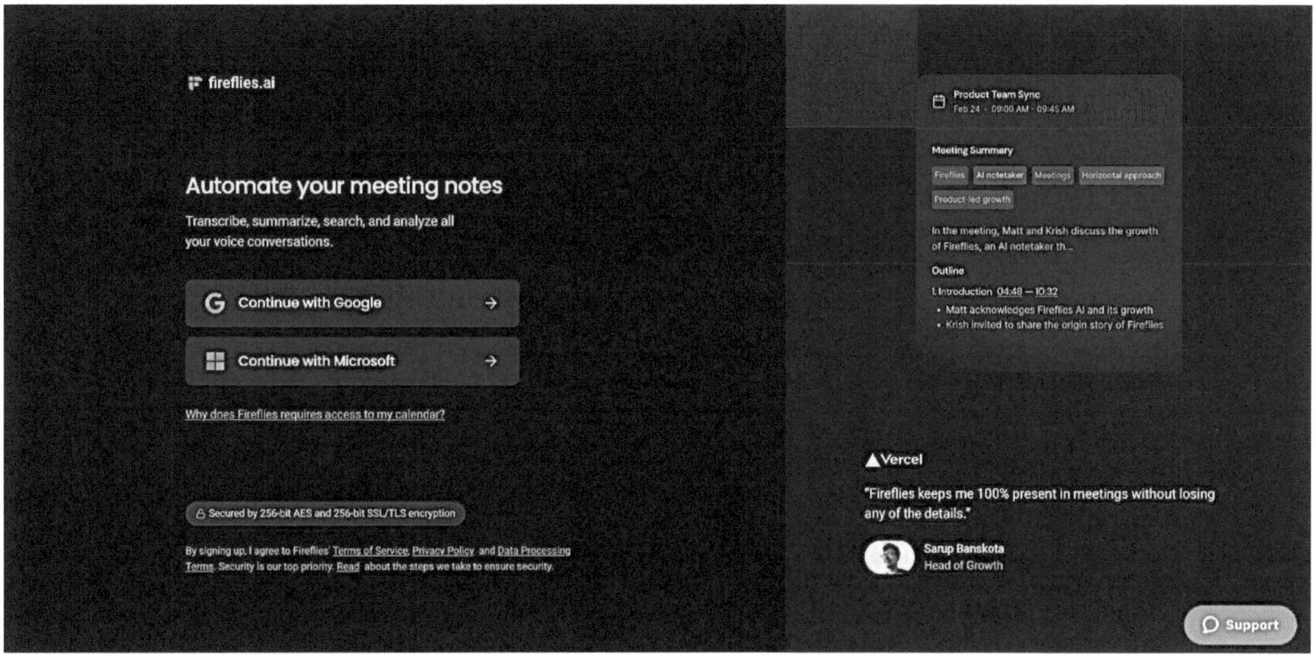

3. Sign in to your Google account

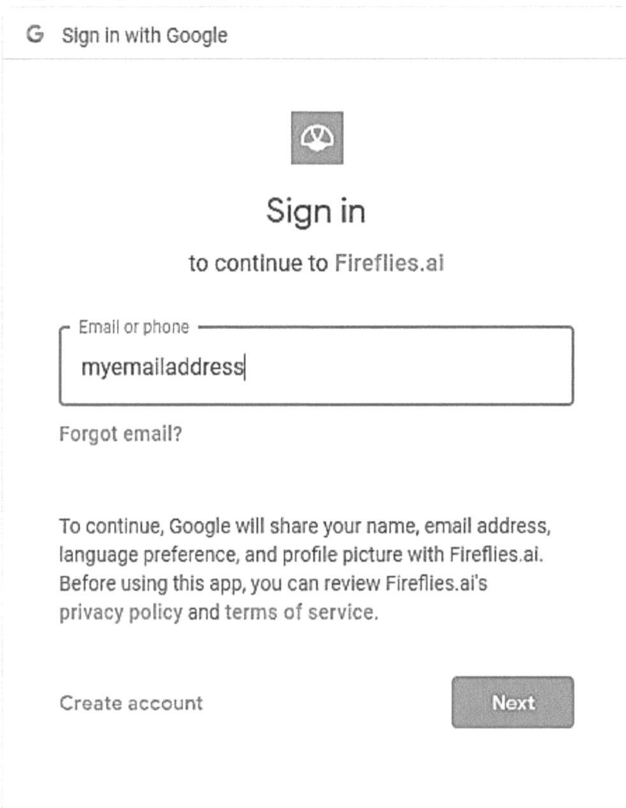

4. Click **Allow** to enable Fireflies

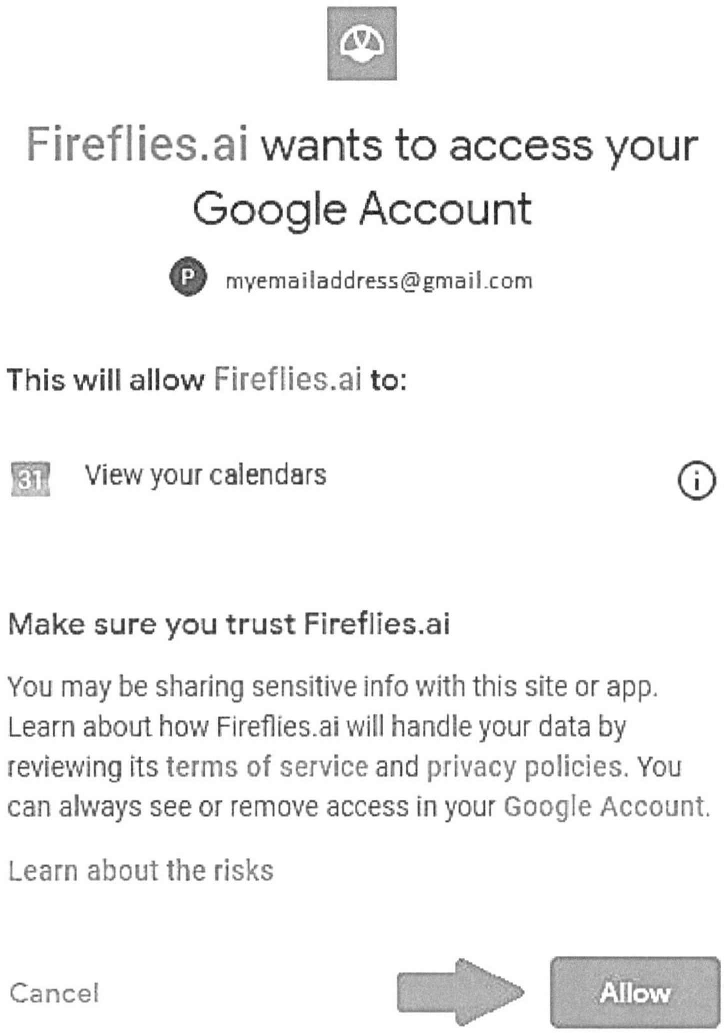

How to customize your Fireflies account
After signing up, Fireflies will give you the option to customize your account.
You can set the preferences, which includes meetings that Fred (Fireflies AI notetaker bot) will join, who receives the meeting recaps, and how to enable the meeting compliance feature to name a few.
You don't have to do this right away. You can opt to do this at a later time. We, however, highly suggest that you complete this process so that you'll get a better Fireflies experience.
Here's how to customize your account:

1. Go to app.fireflies.ai
2. Log in using Google or Outlook credentials
3. After you've successfully logged in, click Settings located on the left menu bar

On the Settings page, you can customize Fireflies according to your goals.
In the Auto-join Settings section, you can select how Fred will automatically join your meetings. Fred can join your meetings in three ways:

1. Fred will join **all** calendar events that have a meeting link
2. Fred will **only** join calendar events that you own
3. Fred will join specific calendar events that you invited **fred@fireflies.ai** to
4. Fred will join only your internal meetings, which has your company domain
5. Fred will join external events that don't have your company domain in the email

Once you've chosen your preferred way in which Fred will join, Fred will continue to use this method until you change it.
In addition, our system will automatically detect meetings with teammates and meetings with external participants based on the email domains of participants.

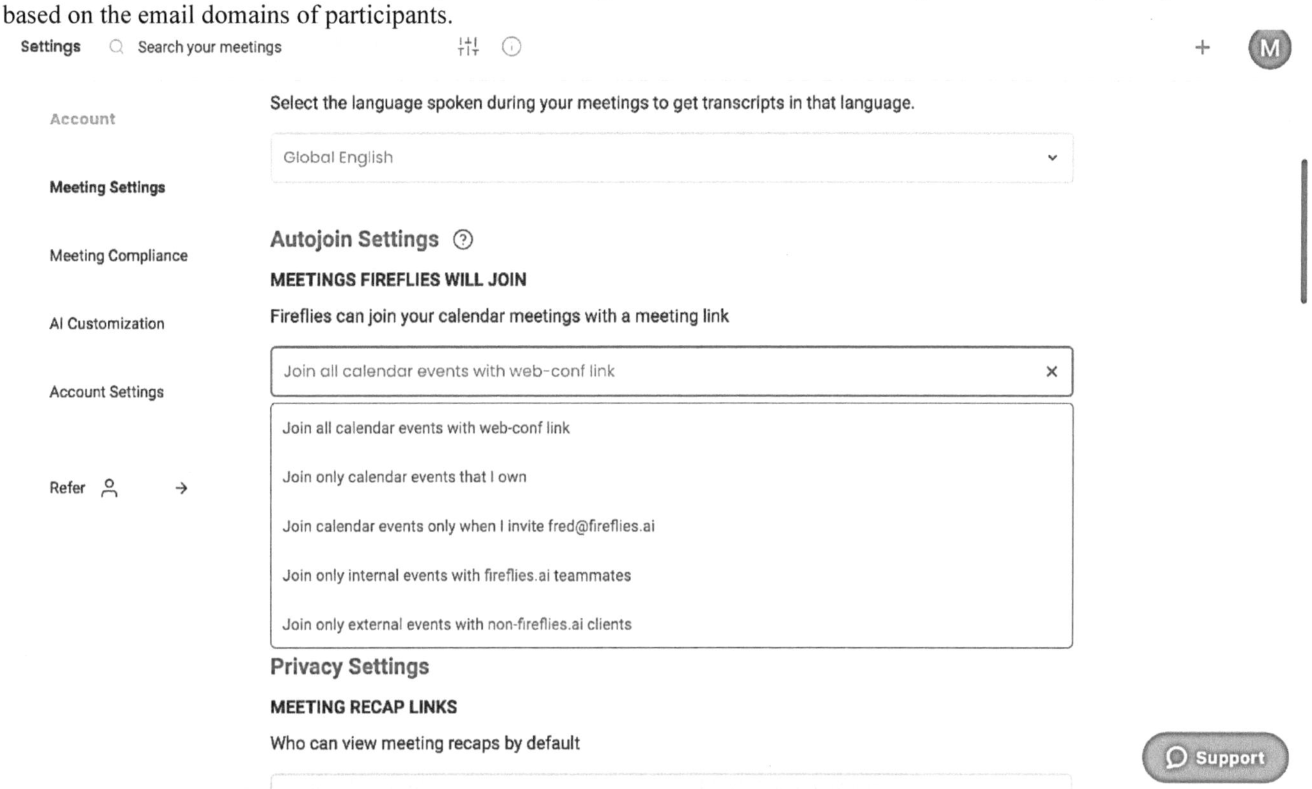

In the **Email Settings** section, you can select who will receive the transcripts and audio recaps after your meeting.
Note that if you choose *Send recaps to only me and my teammates*, "teammates" refers to the teammates you have invited or added to your Fireflies workspace.

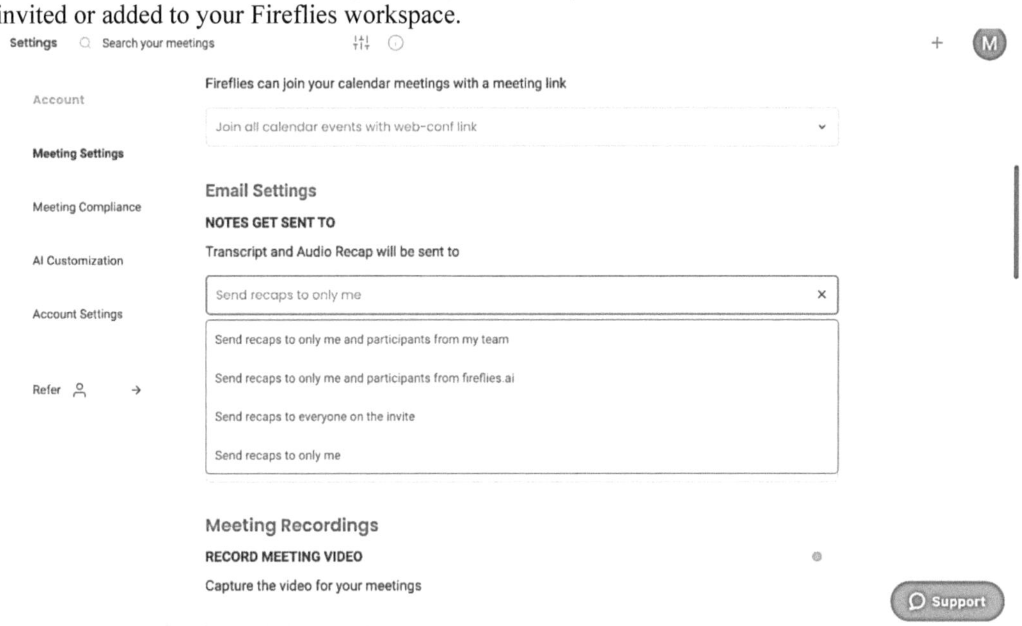

The **Privacy Settings** section is where you can select the participants who can view the meeting recaps.

Here's a cool setting that you should try: **Meeting Rules**. Through this setting, Fred will join meetings by detecting certain keywords.

In the Meeting Rules section, you can input keywords you want Fred to join. If the title of a meeting contains any of the pre-specified words, Fred will join it.

For example, if you want Fred to join meetings that have the words "voice" and "lessons" in them, Fred will automatically join those meetings.

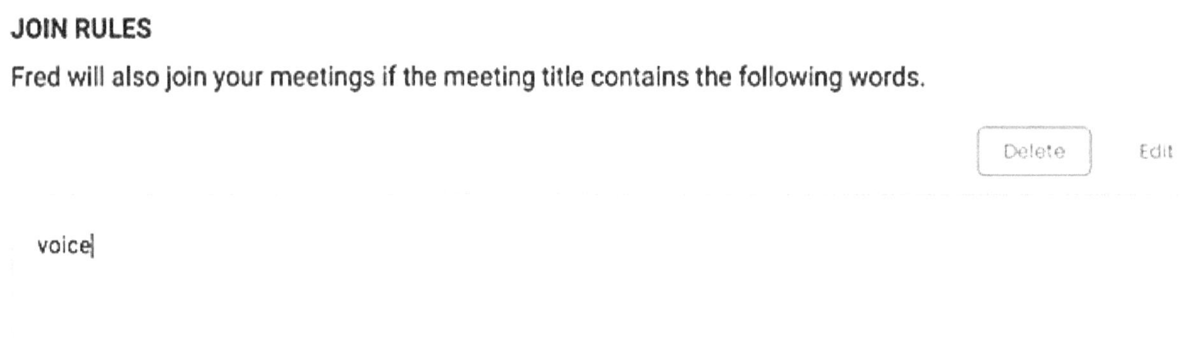

You can also include keywords of the meetings that you **don't** want Fred to join.

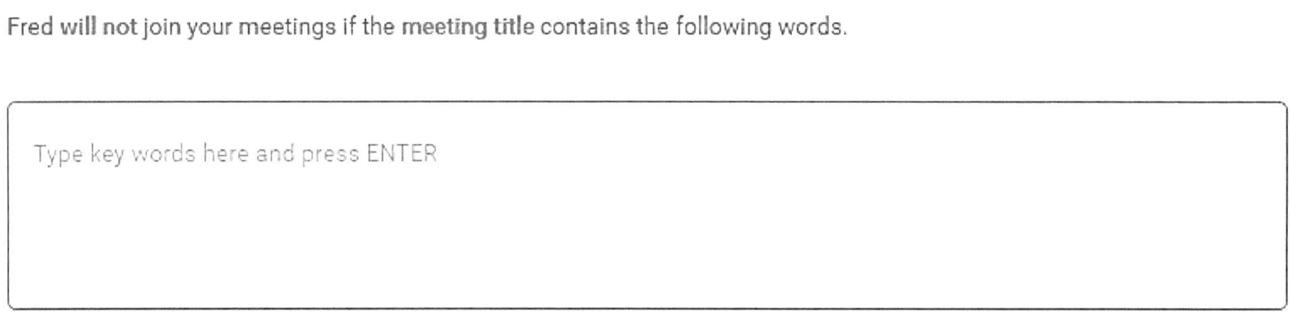

The **Meeting Compliance** section is where you can automatically enable a call disclaimer notification. This is an important part of every call.
We encourage you to use this feature to gain or revoke consent from the meeting attendees.
You can customize the message according to the call recording law in your geographical location or to your preference.
You can edit the notification by clicking the text. Don't forget to click **Save** once you're done.
Turn on **PARTICIPANTS ARE NOTIFIED WITH YOUR MESSAGE** to enable notifications.

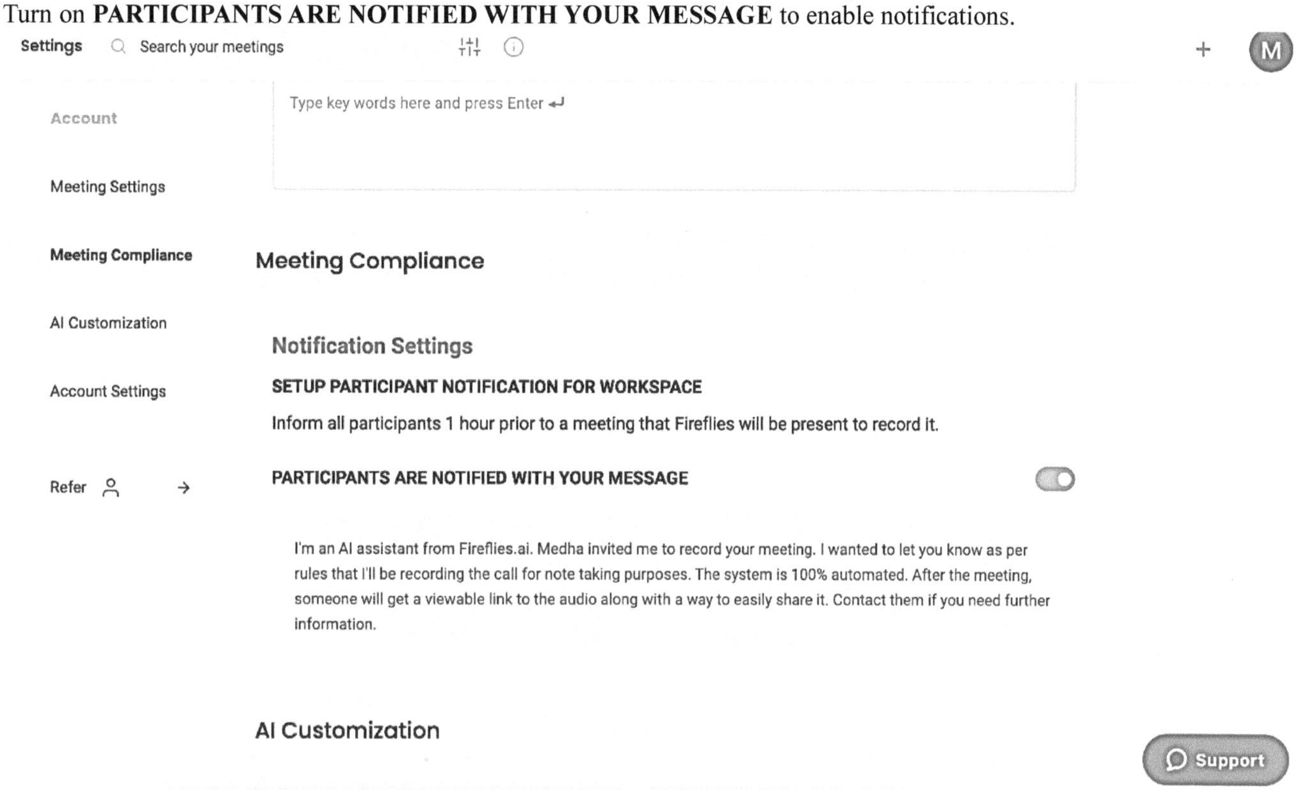

In the **Industry Settings** section, select the type of meeting you usually attend. This enables Fireflies to optimize the speech model according to the industry ensuring precise transcriptions.

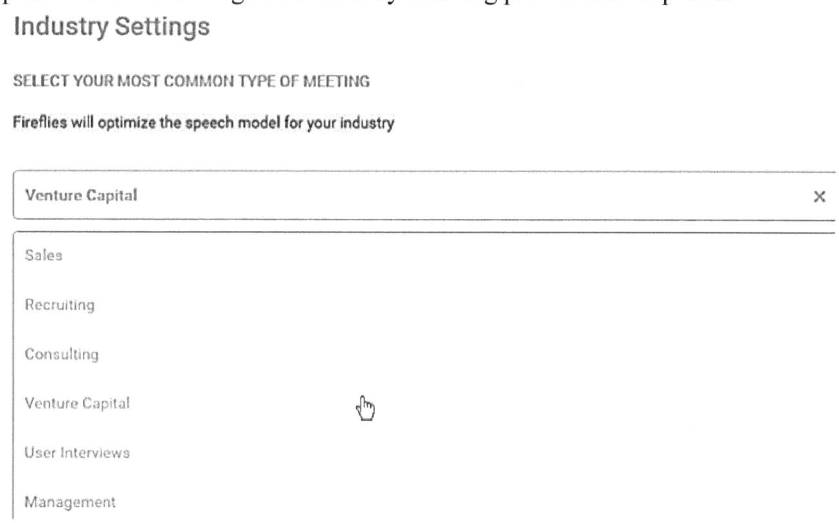

In the **Custom Vocabulary** section, you can add words or phrases that are unique to your business using Custom Vocabulary. This makes for better AI transcription.
Key Features that Make Meetings Shine:
1. Automatic Recording and Transcription: Ditch the pen and paper! Fireflies.ai seamlessly records your meetings across various platforms like Zoom, Google Meet, and Microsoft Teams. The AI then transcribes everything accurately, saving you valuable time and effort.

Fireflies.ai logo

1. Action Item and Decision Capture: No more struggling to remember who said what and what needs to be done. Fireflies intelligently identifies key decisions and action items from the discussion, presenting them in a clear and actionable list.
2. Meeting Summaries in a Flash: Get concise and comprehensive summaries of your meetings automatically generated, complete with speaker attribution and timestamps. No more scrambling to write up minutes – Fireflies has it covered.
3. Shared Agendas and Follow-ups: Create and share meeting agendas beforehand, ensuring everyone is aligned. Fireflies also helps track follow-up items after the meeting, keeping everyone accountable and moving forward.
4. Integration with Your Tools: Fireflies seamlessly connects with project management platforms like Asana and Jira, automatically suggesting tickets and updates based on discussion points. Streamline your workflow and avoid context switching.
5. Real-time Collaboration on Notes: Collaborate on meeting notes in real-time with your team. Add comments, clarifications, and edits, ensuring everyone has access to the latest information.
6. Meeting Templates for Different Types of Sessions: From daily standups to brainstorming sessions and retros, Fireflies offers pre-built templates to optimize your meeting flow and focus.
7. Actionable Insights and Trends: Gain valuable insights from your meeting history, identifying recurring themes, areas for improvement, and individual contributions. Use this data to continuously improve your meetings and team dynamics.
8. Improved Time Management: By streamlining note-taking, action item tracking, and follow-ups, Fireflies frees up your time to focus on what truly matters – driving results and making progress.

Who Benefits from Fireflies.ai?

Fireflies.ai is a game-changer for anyone who wants to make their meetings more productive and impactful. It's ideal for:

1. Individuals: Stay organized, remember key points, and improve your own meeting participation.
2. Teams: Enhance collaboration, ensure everyone is on the same page, and track progress effectively.
3. Project Managers: Streamline project management, track action items, and improve team communication.
4. Executives: Gain insights into meeting effectiveness, identify trends, and make data-driven decisions.

Getting Started with Fireflies.ai:

Creating an account with Fireflies.ai is simple and straightforward. Just head over to their website and sign up for a free trial. They offer different plans to suit your individual or team needs, with flexible pricing options.

Once you're set up, simply invite Fireflies.ai to your meetings, and let the AI magic unfold. You can focus on participating, engaging in discussions, and generating ideas, while Fireflies takes care of the rest.

7.4 Krisp

In the age of virtual meetings and remote work, background noise has become the uninvited guest we all dread. The dog's bark, the neighbor's lawnmower, even your own keyboard clicks – these unwanted sounds can disrupt calls, frustrate colleagues, and make you sound unprofessional. Enter Krisp, the AI-powered noise cancellation tool that puts the mute button on unwanted audio, leaving your voice crystal clear.

What is Krisp?

Krisp isn't just another noise reduction app. It's a sophisticated, real-time audio cleaner that leverages powerful AI algorithms to identify and remove unwanted background noise from your microphone feed. Think of it as a dedicated audio bodyguard, standing guard against any sounds that threaten to sabotage your calls.

Say Goodbye to Noise:

1. Eliminate Background Distractions: Whether it's keyboard clicks, traffic rumbles, or construction noise, Krisp effectively neutralizes a wide range of background sounds, ensuring your voice is the only star of the show.
2. Crystal-Clear Calls: Enjoy improved call quality and intelligibility. Your colleagues will hear every word you say, loud and clear, without any intrusive background distractions.
3. Focus on Content, Not Context: Eliminate the stress of worrying about background noise interfering with your message. With Krisp, you can fully focus on your content and deliver your ideas with confidence.

Beyond Noise Cancellation:

1. Echo Removal: Say goodbye to annoying echoes bouncing around your workspace. Krisp's intelligent algorithms effectively detect and eliminate echo, ensuring smooth and uninterrupted communication.
2. Automatic Gain Control: No more fiddling with volume controls! Krisp automatically adjusts your voice level to ensure consistent audio quality, even in dynamic environments.
3. Multiple Device Support: Whether you're using a headset, laptop speakers, or an external microphone, Krisp seamlessly integrates with your existing audio hardware.

Benefits for Everyone:

1. Individuals: Improve your professional presence in virtual meetings and presentations. Leave a lasting impression with clear, uninterrupted audio.
2. Teams: Enhance collaboration and communication within your team. Meetings become more productive and focused without background noise distractions.
3. Remote Workers: Create a quieter, more productive work environment at home. Eliminate noise interruptions and maintain focus throughout your workday.
4. Content Creators: Produce high-quality audio for podcasts, videos, and more. Capture crystal-clear voice recordings without any unwanted background noise.

Getting Started with Krisp:

Krisp offers a variety of plans to suit your individual or team needs. You can start with a free trial to experience the magic firsthand. Simply download the app, choose your audio source, and let Krisp take care of the rest.

How does Krisp work?

Krisp.ai works by using advanced machine learning techniques to identify and separate unwanted background noise from the audio in a call or recording. This allows users to communicate in a silent environment, regardless of their location or the level of background noise.

A combination of deep neural networks and machine learning algorithms is used to create a highly accurate and effective real-time noise cancellation system. The artificial intelligence engine is designed to learn from the environment and adapt to different types of background noise in a given environment, making it ideal for professionals who require high-quality audio communication in a variety of environments.

Features

1. Krisp offers a number of features that make it a powerful tool for improving communication. Some of the software's key features include:

1. Real-time Noise Reduction: Krisp.ai eliminates background noise in real time, providing users with clear, distraction-free communication.
2. Virtual Microphone and Speaker: The software is available as a virtual microphone and speaker that can be used with any communication software.
3. Deep Learning Algorithms: The technology behind this application is based on deep learning algorithms, allowing it to recognize and eliminate a wide range of sounds.
4. Easy to use: It is easy to use and requires no technical knowledge or special equipment.

Here's how to Set Krisp AI Up (Step by Step):

Step 1: Download Krisp.AI

To start using Krisp.AI, download the app for Mac or Windows from the official website. Once the installation is complete, open the app and log in with your account credentials.

Step 2: Select Krisp as your microphone and speaker

Open up your video conferencing app and head to the settings. Change the Speaker/Microphone setting to Krisp. You can also use Krisp as your microphone and speaker for other conferencing apps which Krisp didn't provide a tutorial for.

Step 3: Enable machine learning

By toggling on Krisp, the app uses machine learning to remove background noises that aren't human voices such as dogs barking, vacuums, and more. Krisp eliminates human and non-human noise near you and only lets your voice go through the microphone.

Step 4: Choose Krisp in the Zoom settings

Keep in mind, the Krisp speaker might filter out other types of audio, so it's best to keep it on "Original sound" when you're presenting. Select Krisp as your microphone and speaker in Zoom settings to enjoy noise-free communication.

Step 5: Use Krisp on different apps

Krisp is a standalone tool that lives in the menubar of your computer and is silently watching all microphone inputs and videoconference outputs and cancels out any noise there. You can use Krisp to mute any kind of noise source, including barking dogs, screaming children, the sound of appliances, street noises, and more. 96 other people are already using Krisp, so why not give it a try and join the club?

Step 6. Test Krisp

To make sure Krisp is working properly, you can test it by having someone talk while making noise in the background, such as turning on a blender or vacuum. You'll notice that Krisp mutes the background noise while keeping the person's voice clear.

Step 7. Enjoy noise-free communication

Now that Krisp is up and running, you can enjoy noise-free communication with your colleagues, friends, and family. Have a productive meeting, enjoy a virtual happy hour, or catch up with loved ones without any distracting background noise.

7.5 Otter.ai

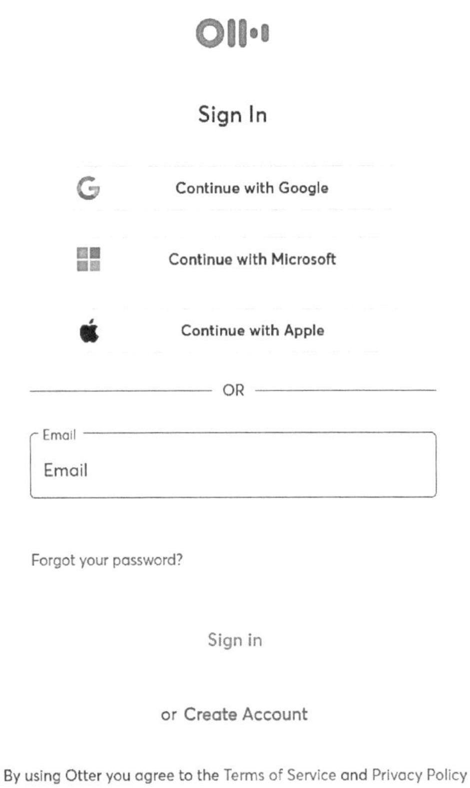

Otter.ai is an AI-powered software that provides automatic speech recognition and transcription for audio and video files. Transcribing meetings is not the only feature that Otter.ai offers. Otter.ai can help you capture, organize, and share your notes from meetings, interviews, lectures, podcasts, and more. Otter.ai uses artificial intelligence and natural language processing to generate accurate and searchable transcripts that you can edit, highlight, comment on,

and export. Otter.ai also integrates with popular platforms such as Zoom, Google Meet, Microsoft Teams, Dropbox, and YouTube to make your workflow easier and more efficient.
Otter.ai is more than just a transcription tool. It is a smart assistant that helps you turn your conversations into actionable insights and collaborative knowledge. For example:
1. The Otter app allows you to record your own ideas or conduct an interview with anybody, wherever.
2. You may submit voice-containing audio or video files to Otter, and it will begin transcribing the content into text.
3. When you have a lot of video conferences to attend, the Otter Bot may be programmed to join in on the calls and transcribe the conversations for you.
Ottter.ai is a transcription or speech-to-text app powered by artificial intelligence and machine learning that also serves as a meeting subscription or summary tool.

I've used Otter.ai extensively as a journalist and educator, and recommend it to the college students who I teach. While the transcriptions it generates are not perfect, these are searchable and easily editable, which makes it a huge timesaver for journalism, oral history projects, or anything that requires an interview.

Otter.ai's text-to-speech functionality can also be helpful for students who struggle with written language as it can generate lecture captions in real time. In addition, Otter.ai can serve as a meeting assistant through its OtterPilot feature, which allows users to generate an Otter.ai bot that can attend meetings virtually, then record, transcribe, take screenshots of slides, and even summarize the highlights of the meeting.

How does Otter AI work?
Before diving into the usage, it's vital to understand how this software works. The AI platform uses advanced natural language processing (NLP) algorithms to generate accurate and searchable transcripts that you can edit, highlight, comment, and export. This primary functionality is complemented by several other features that enhance the effectiveness of the software.
Furthermore, it integrates with popular platforms like Zoom, Google Meet, Microsoft Teams, Dropbox, and YouTube, thereby simplifying your workflow and boosting efficiency.
Using Otter AI: A step-by-step guide

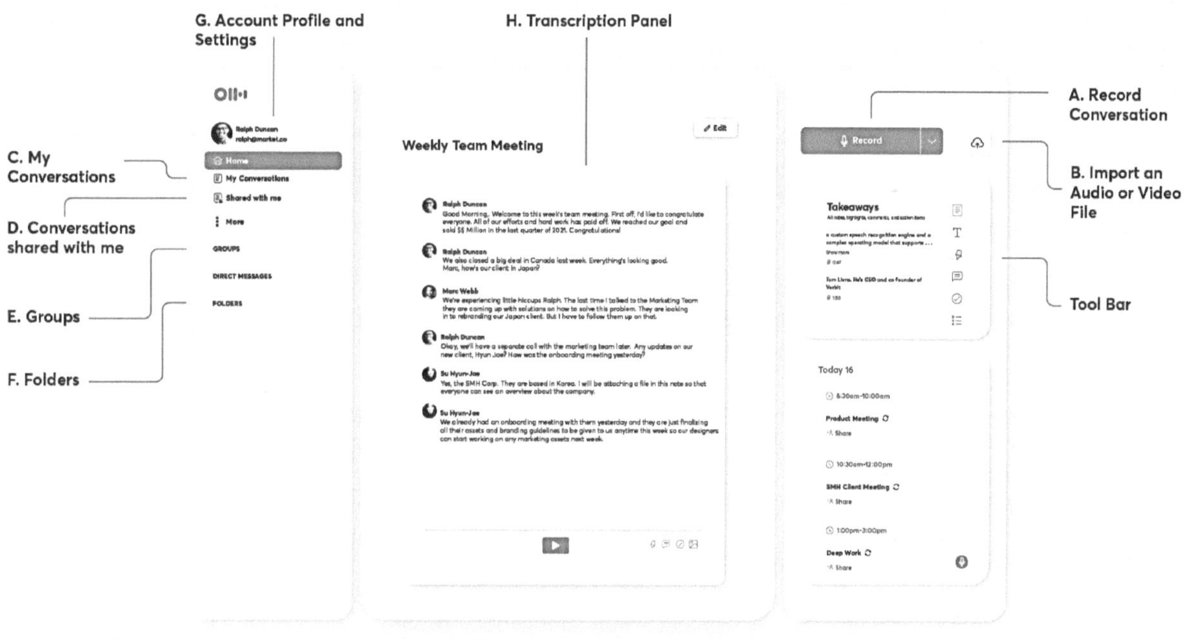

Now that we have an understanding of what Otter AI is let's walk through a step-by-step guide on how to use it.

Step 1: Registering for an Otter AI account

To begin using Otter AI, you need to first sign up for an account. The registration process is straightforward and requires basic information such as your name and email address.

Step 2: Downloading the Otter AI app
Once you've registered, the next step is to download the Otter AI app. It's readily available for your iOS, Android, or web browsers. The app empowers you to record audio and video straight from your device or import files from different sources.

Step 3: Recording or importing files
Having installed the app, tap the blue microphone icon at the bottom of the app to start recording audio or video. Feel free to pause, resume, or stop the recording whenever you need to.
To import a pre-existing file, tap the plus icon in the top right corner of the app and select "Import from." You can choose from various options, including Dropbox, Google Drive, Zoom, YouTube, and more.
Learn how to transcribe audio to text effortlessly with FreeSubtitles.Ai.

Step 4: Reviewing and editing transcripts
After recording or importing a file, Otter AI immediately generates a transcript for you. Access the transcript either through the app or a web browser.
You can also tap on any word in the transcript to edit it. Add speaker names, highlights, comments, photos, and keywords to make your transcript more comprehensive.

Step 5: Sharing transcripts
When you want to share your transcript, tap the share icon in the top right corner of the app. Choose your preferred method of sharing: email, text message, social media, or copy the link.

Key features:

1. Speech-to-Text Transcription:
1. Otter.ai specializes in providing accurate and real-time transcription of spoken language. Users can record meetings, interviews, lectures, or any other spoken content, and Otter.ai will transcribe the spoken words into text.

2. AI-Powered Features:
1. Otter.ai utilizes advanced AI and machine learning algorithms to enhance transcription quality. It can recognize different speakers, understand context, and improve accuracy over time.

3. Real-Time Collaboration:
1. One notable feature of Otter.ai is its ability to support real-time collaboration. Multiple users can access and contribute to a shared transcription, making it useful for collaborative note-taking during meetings or group discussions.

4. Integration with Popular Apps:
1. Otter.ai integrates with various productivity and communication tools, allowing users to sync their transcriptions with applications like Zoom, Microsoft Teams, Google Meet, and others.

5. Searchable and Organized Transcriptions:
1. Otter.ai organizes transcriptions in a searchable format. Users can search for specific keywords or phrases within the transcriptions, making it easier to find and review specific content.

6. Usage in Different Settings:
1. Otter.ai is used in a variety of settings, including business meetings, educational lectures, interviews, and personal note-taking. It can be valuable for professionals, students, journalists, and anyone who needs accurate and efficient transcription services.

7. Freemium Model:
1. Otter.ai offers a freemium model, allowing users to use the service for free up to a certain usage limit. Premium plans with additional features and higher usage limits are available for those with greater transcription needs.

8. Mobile and Web Applications:
1. Otter.ai is available as both a mobile app and a web application, providing users with flexibility in accessing and managing their transcriptions across different devices.

7.6 Fathom

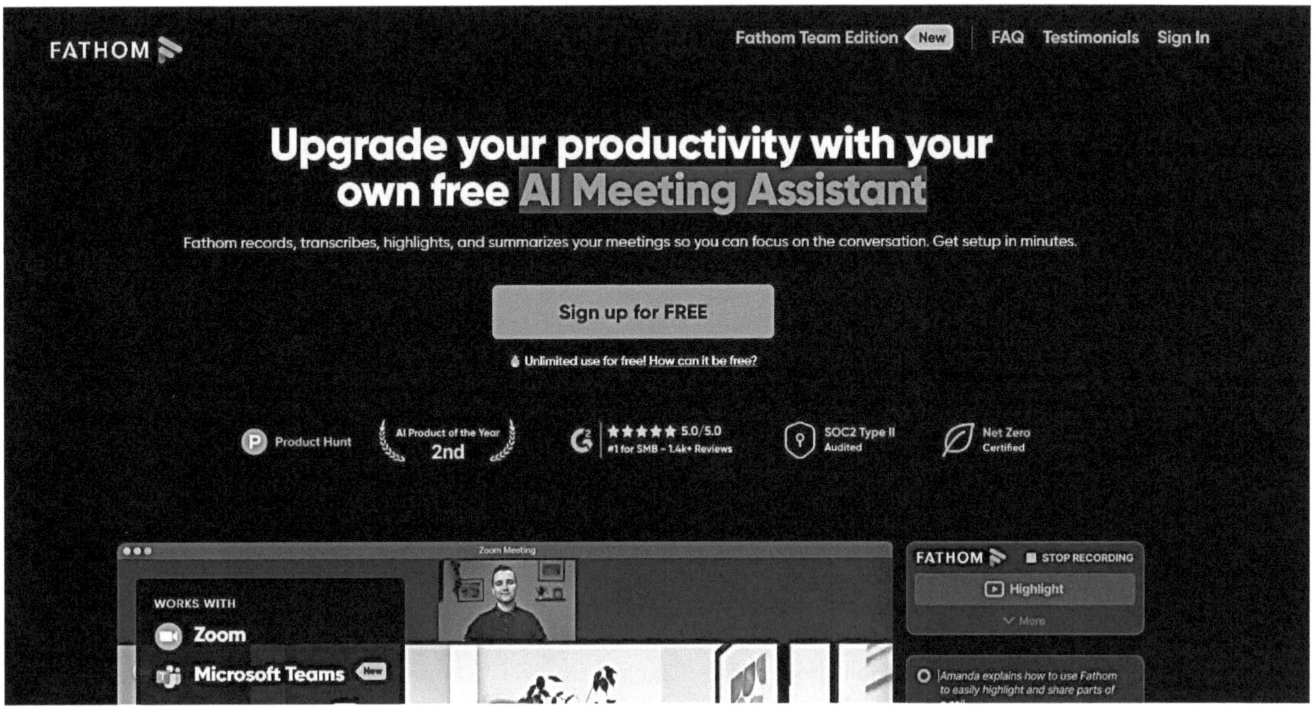

Exercise

Exercise 1 – MCQ

Q 1. What is the primary focus of Spinach in the realm of meetings?

A. Project management
B. Virtual collaboration
C. Audio enhancement
D. Augmented reality

Q 2. Sembly is known for its features related to:

A. Document collaboration
B. Scheduling and appointment coordination
C. Virtual backgrounds
D. Real-time transcription

Q 3. Krisp is designed to enhance meetings by:

A. Providing virtual reality integration
B. Removing background noise from audio
C. Offering augmented reality features
D. Facilitating real-time collaboration on documents

Q 4. What does tl;dv focus on in the context of meetings?

A. Live transcriptions
B. Augmented reality
C. Concise and summarized meeting recordings
D. Real-time collaboration on documents

Q 5. Otter.ai utilizes AI to provide:

A. Virtual backgrounds
B. Live transcriptions and summaries
C. Audio enhancement
D. Document collaboration

Q 6. Fathom is known for its features related to:

A. Virtual reality integration
B. Real-time collaboration on documents
C. Analyzing user engagement during meetings
D. Scheduling and appointment coordination

Q 7. Which tool is specifically focused on real-time collaboration on documents during meetings?

A. Fireflies
B. Sembly
C. Spinach
D. Krisp

Q 8. Fireflies is known for:

A. Analyzing user engagement during meetings
B. Scheduling and appointment coordination
C. Removing background noise from audio
D. Virtual collaboration

Q 9. What is the primary function of Spinach during meetings?
A. Project management
B. Real-time collaboration on documents
C. Augmented reality features
D. Virtual collaboration

Q 10. What does Krisp specialize in during meetings?
A. Scheduling and appointment coordination
B. Real-time collaboration on documents
C. Audio enhancement by removing background noise
D. Virtual reality integration

Exercise 2 – True/ False

Q 1. Spinach is a meeting tool designed for virtual collaboration and project management.
Q 2. Sembly is a meeting tool that focuses on simplifying scheduling and appointment coordination.
Q 3. Fireflies is primarily known for its capabilities in virtual backgrounds and augmented reality during meetings.
Q 4. Krisp is a meeting tool designed to enhance audio quality by removing background noise.
Q 5. tl;dv is a meeting tool focused on providing concise and summarized meeting recordings.
Q 6. Otter.ai is a meeting tool that utilizes artificial intelligence to generate live transcriptions and summaries.
Q 7. Fathom is known for its virtual reality integration, providing immersive meeting experiences.
Q 8. Spinach offers features for real-time collaboration on documents and notes during meetings.
Q 9. Sembly incorporates AI-driven insights to analyze meeting dynamics and optimize team collaboration.
Q 10. Fireflies focuses on providing tools for tracking and analyzing user engagement during virtual meetings.

Exercise 3 – Fill in the blanks

Q 1. Spinach is a meeting tool that focuses on enhancing ___________ during virtual meetings.
Q 2. Sembly is known for its features that streamline ___________ and coordination in meetings.
Q 3. Fireflies uses AI to assist in ___________ and transcribing meeting discussions.
Q 4. Krisp is a tool that specializes in eliminating ___________ during virtual meetings.
Q 5. What does tl;dv primarily offer in the context of meetings?

Exercise 4 – Match case

1. Match the meeting tool focused on enhancing engagement during virtual meetings	A. tl;dv
2. Connect the meeting tool known for streamlining planning and coordination in meetings	B. Krisp
3. Pair the meeting tool that utilizes AI for note-taking and transcribing meeting discussions	C. Fireflies
4. Match the tool specialized in eliminating background noise during virtual meetings	D. Spinach
5. Connect the meeting tool that primarily offers meeting summaries	E. Sembly

Exercise 5 – One word answer

Q 1. Spinach?
Q 2. Sembly?
Q 3. Fireflies?
Q 4. Krisp?
Q 5. tl;dv?

Exercise 6 – Small answer

Q 1. What is the primary focus of Spinach in virtual meetings?
Q2. How does Sembly contribute to meeting efficiency?
Q 3. What role does Fireflies play in meetings, and how does it utilize AI?
Q 4. What is Krisp known for in the context of virtual meetings?
Q 5. How does Otter.ai enhance meeting accessibility and documentation?

Exercise 7 – Long answer

Q 1. In what ways does Sembly streamline the planning and coordination of meetings, and how does it assist organizers and participants in managing various aspects of the meeting process?

Q 2. How does Fireflies leverage artificial intelligence for note-taking during meetings, and what benefits does its AI transcription feature provide to meeting participants?

Answers

Exercise 1 – MCQ

Ans: 1 B, 2 B, 3 B, 4 C, 5 B, 6 A, 7 B, 8 A, 9 D, 10 C

Exercise 2 – True/ False

Ans: 1 False, 2 True, 3 False, 4 True, 5 True, 6 True, 7 False, 8 True, 9 True, 10 False

Exercise 3 – Fill in the blanks

Ans: 1 Engagement, 2 Planning, 3 Note-taking, 4 Background noise, 5 Meeting summaries

Exercise 4 – Match case

Ans: 1 D, 2 E, 3 C, 4 B, 5 A

Exercise 5 – One word answer

Ans: 1 Engagement, 2 Planning, 3 Note-taking, 4 Noise-cancellation, 5 Summaries

ONLINE RESOURCES

Practice Paper

Link https://forms.office.com/r/CXHcgpLr1D

QR Code

Video Content

Link https://www.youtube.com/playlist?list=PLzlh_31VWEFpNgaoIFXZU9f0R5q1nnruZ

QR Code

Chapter 8: Image Design Tools

8.1 Midjourney

Midjourney, one of the most popular image-generating AI services, announced yesterday the launch of the "Alpha" version of its website, available to a select few users.

The San Francisco–based independent research lab announced they will be testing out the site, Midjourney.com. It is currently only available to users who have generated over 10,000 images on its predecessor, messaging app Discord. The tech company confirmed that the website will roll out to the rest of us soon, the announcement read: "Don't worry, we will be making it available to more people over the coming month!" This will be music to the ears of the 17.5 million plus users in its server on the Discord App.

Midjourney AI is a powerful text-to-image generator that allows you to turn your wildest imaginations into stunning visual creations. Think of it as a magic brush that paints according to your words! Here's the breakdown:

What it Does:

1. Generates Images: Midjourney takes your text prompts (descriptions of what you want) and uses its artificial intelligence to create unique and captivating images. From surreal landscapes to futuristic robots, the possibilities are endless.
2. Discord-Based: Unlike some AI art tools, Midjourney operates within the Discord chat platform. This means you can interact with the bot directly, experiment with different prompts in real-time, and share your creations with a vibrant community of artists and enthusiasts.
3. No Special Skills Needed: You don't need artistic skills to use Midjourney. The focus is on your imagination and how you craft your prompts. Even simple descriptions can yield surprising and beautiful results.

Key Features:

1. Prompt Engineering: The key to unlocking Midjourney's potential lies in writing effective prompts. You can use specific keywords, adjectives, art styles, and even references to other artists to guide the AI in generating the desired image.
2. Variations and Iterations: Midjourney allows you to generate multiple variations of your initial image, refining it until you achieve the perfect outcome. You can also upscale the resolution and add details to existing images.
3. Community-Driven: Midjourney boasts a strong and supportive community on Discord. You can get tips and inspiration from other users, participate in challenges, and even collaborate on projects.

Getting Started:

1. Beta Access: Currently, Midjourney is in open beta, and access requires a paid subscription. There are different tiers with varying amounts of "prompts" per month.
2. Discord Server: Once subscribed, you join the official Midjourney Discord server where you'll find the AI bot waiting for your creative prompts.
3. Tutorial Resources: Numerous tutorials and guides available online and within the Discord server can help you master the art of crafting effective prompts and navigating the platform.

Step-by-Step Guide to Using Midjourney

Create anything that you can imagine!

1. Join Midjourney's Discord

To get started, visit Midjourney.com and choose the "Join the Beta" option, or alternatively, you can directly navigate to the Midjourney Discord by clicking on this link: https://discord.gg/midjourney.

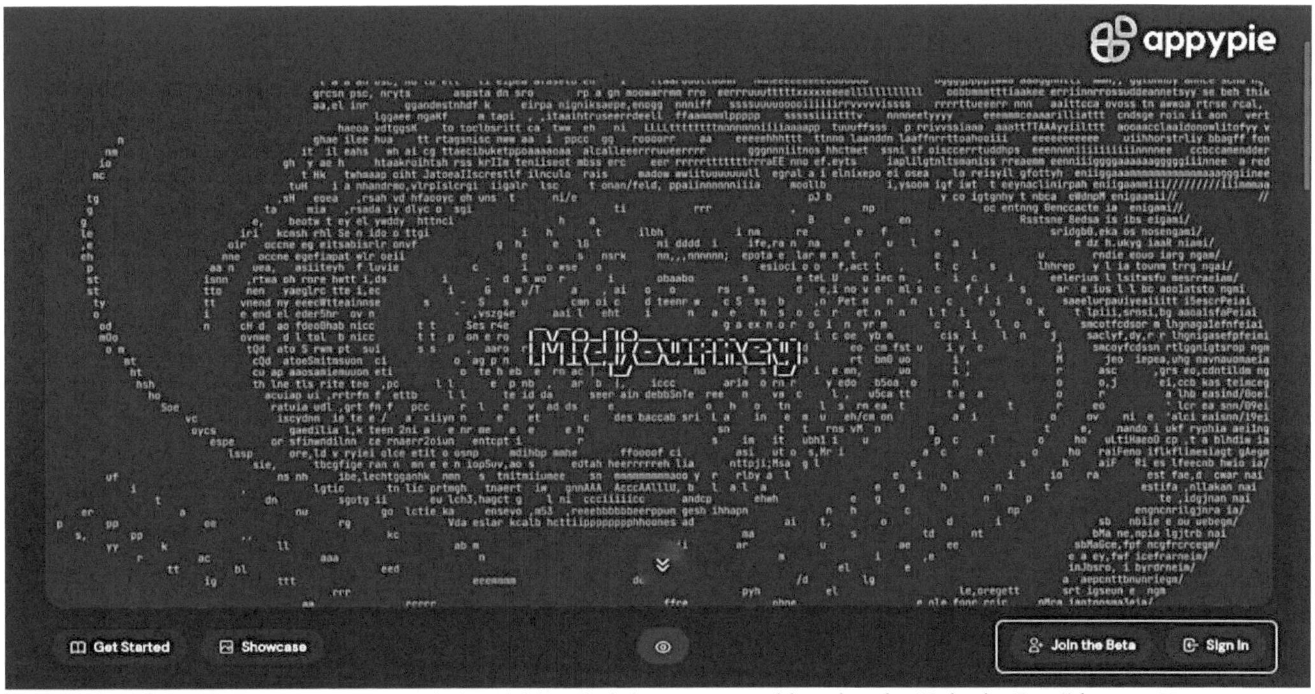

To initiate your Midjourney journey, begin by visiting their homepage and locating the "Join the Beta" button. Upon clicking it, you will be directed to a screen where you can seamlessly proceed to Discord and register for this remarkable service. After completing the registration process, you will gain access to the web-based Discord interface or have the option to download the desktop application, opening up a world of creative possibilities.

With Midjourney, you can enjoy a set number of complimentary images. However, once you reach this limit, a monthly subscription fee is required to unlock unlimited image creation. The pricing structure offers two options: $8 per month, granting access to 200 images, or a premium plan of $24 per month, providing unrestricted image generation capabilities.

1. Navigate a Newbies Channel
2. Midjourney's Official Server

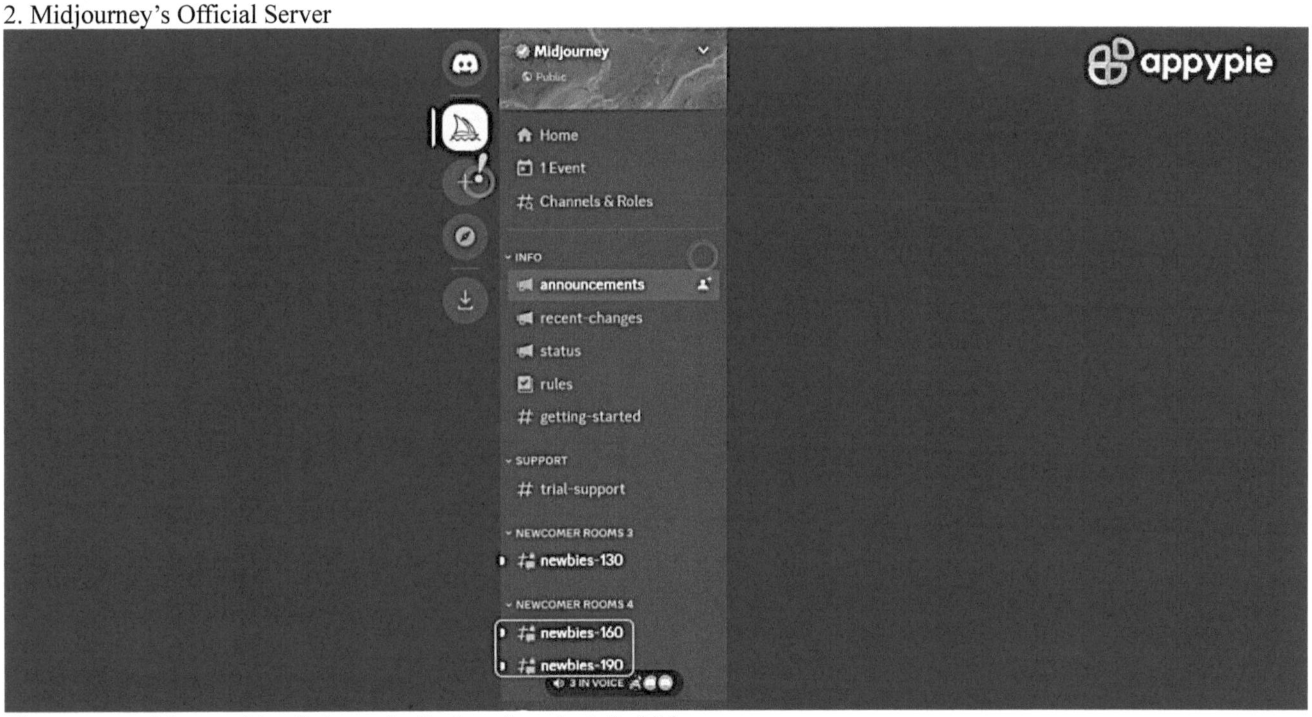

Choose any of the newbies-# channels displayed on the left sidebar.

1. Other Servers
With Midjourney Bot, you have the ability to generate images on any server that has invited the bot. Simply refer to the instructions provided on your server to find out where and how to utilize this powerful tool.
2. The Power of /imagine Command
In order to utilize the Midjourney Bot on Discord, you'll need to employ specific commands. These commands serve as a gateway to create images, customize default settings, track user details, and carry out other valuable functions. To generate an image, simply employ the /imagine command and provide a brief text description, referred to as a Prompt, to outline your desired image. The bot will then skillfully generate a one-of-a-kind image based on your input.

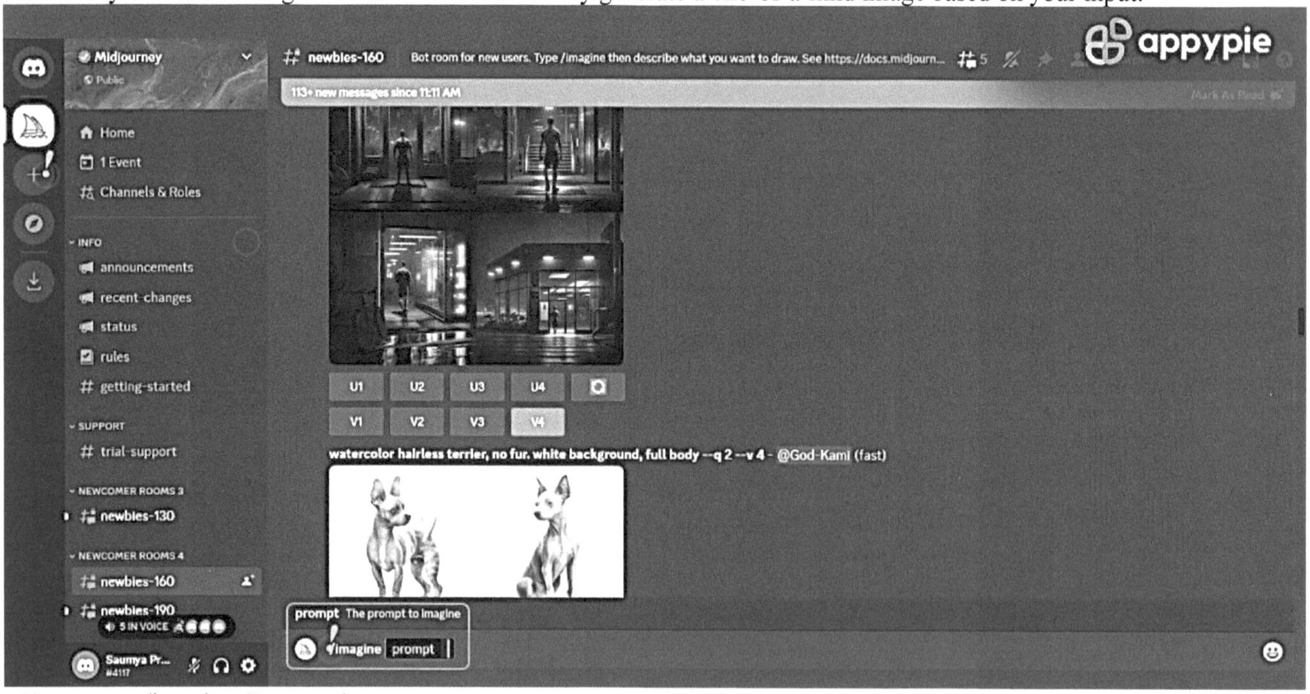

- How to use /imagine Command
1. To initiate the image generation process, either type "/imagine prompt:" directly in the conversation or select the "/imagine" command from the available slash commands pop-up menu.
2. Enter a descriptive text in the prompt field, outlining the image you wish to create.
3. Click the return key to send your message.
4. Processes your First Image
Allow Midjourney AI to Bring Your Descriptions to Life. The Midjourney Bot typically takes approximately one minute to generate four image options based on your provided description.

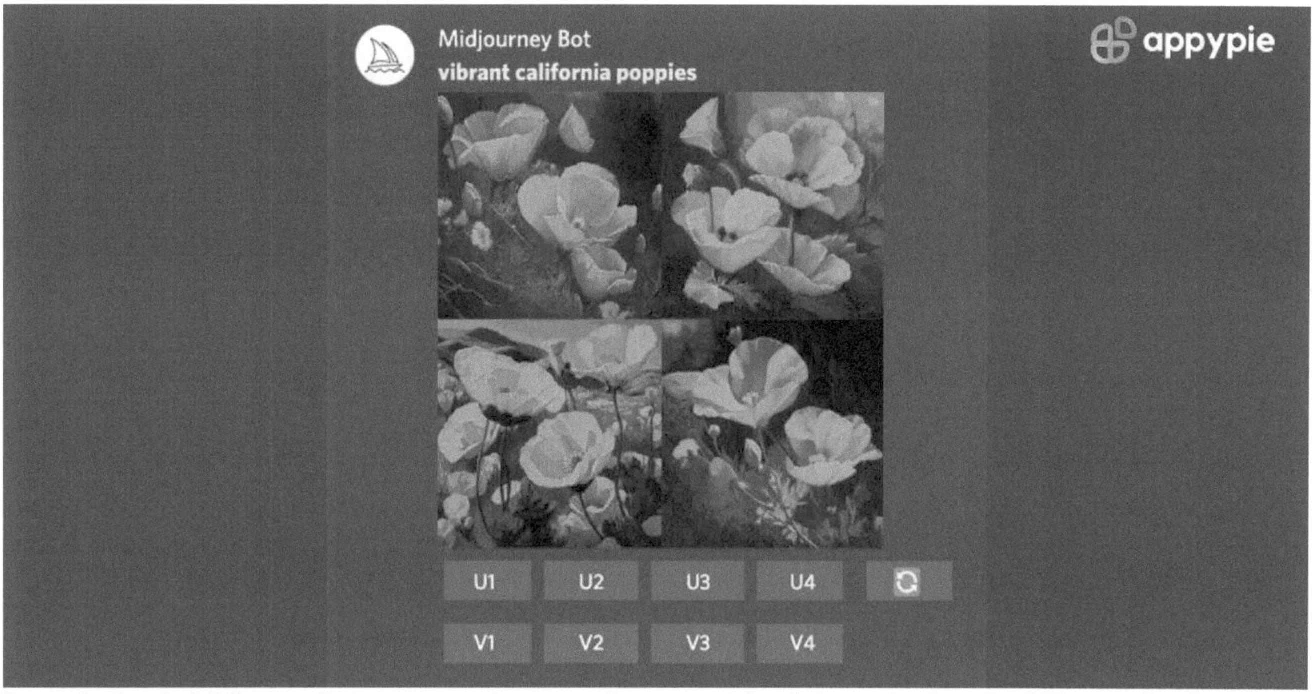

By employing the Midjourney Bot, users can enjoy a complimentary trial period, granting them the ability to undertake approximately 25 Jobs free of charge.

A Job refers to any activity that involves utilizing the Midjourney Bot, such as employing the /imagine command to generate image grids, upscale images, or create image variations. To keep track of the time remaining in your complimentary trial period, simply use the info command to access the Fast Time Remaining feature. This allows you to stay informed about your remaining free trial duration.

1. Explore and Enhance the Generated Images with Upscaling and Variations

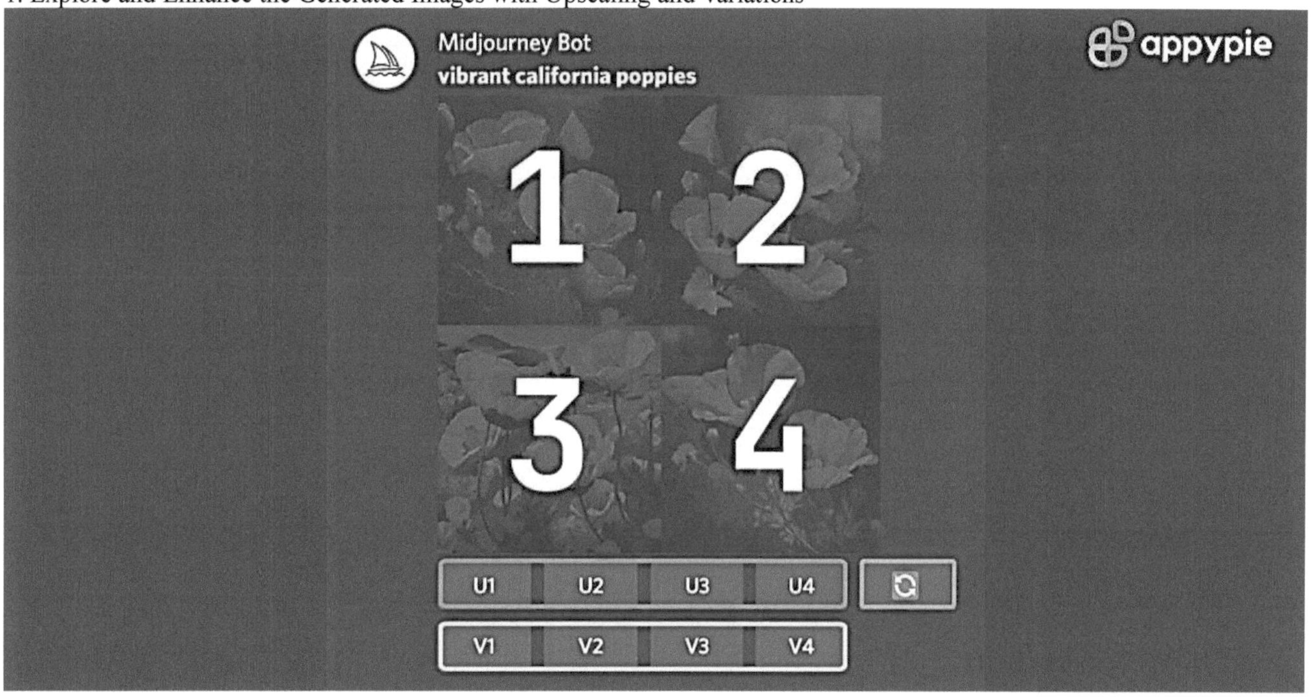

Once the initial image grid has completed its generation process, you'll notice the emergence of two rows of buttons.

1. U1 U2 U3 U4

By selecting the U button, you can upscale the chosen image, resulting in a larger version enriched with additional details.

1. V1 V2 V3 V4
Clicking on the "V" button triggers the generation of subtle variations of the selected image within the grid. This process creates a fresh grid of images that share a similar style and composition to the originally chosen image.

Explore Midjourney with Custom Images
1. Share your image on Discord by simply clicking the plus sign located beside the message input area, allowing you to upload your desired file.
2. Opt for "Upload a File" and select the image you wish to upload from your device.
3. Press the enter key to successfully upload your image to Discord.
4. To incorporate your uploaded image into a prompt on Midjourney, begin by typing "/imagine" as you typically would.
5. When the prompt box appears, you have two options for adding the image. You can either drag and drop the image file directly into the prompt box or copy the image link and paste it into the prompt box.
6. To copy the image link, simply right-click on the image and choose the "Copy Link" option. Afterward, you can paste the copied link into the prompt box.

8.2 DALL.E 2

DALL·E 2 is an AI system that can create realistic images and art from a text description. It is an extension of DALL·E, which was developed by OpenAI in 2021. DALL·E 2 has some improvements over DALL·E, such as:
1. It can generate images with 4x greater resolution (1024x1024 pixels).
2. It can expand images beyond what's in the original canvas, creating expansive new compositions.
3. It can make realistic edits to existing images from a natural language caption.
DALL·E 2 uses a large neural network called a transformer to encode both the text and the image as a sequence of tokens, and then generate new tokens that represent the desired image. It also uses another neural network called CLIP to guide the image generation process based on the text input. DALL·E 2 can combine concepts, attributes, and styles in novel and surprising ways, demonstrating a high level of creativity and imagination

Like GPT-3, DALL·E is a transformer language model. It receives both the text and the image as a single stream of data containing up to 1280 tokens, and is trained using maximum likelihood to generate all of the tokens, one after another. [A][A]
A token is any symbol from a discrete vocabulary; for humans, each English letter is a token from a 26-letter alphabet. DALL·E's vocabulary has tokens for both text and image concepts. Specifically, each image caption is represented using a maximum of 256 BPE-encoded tokens with a vocabulary size of 16384, and the image is represented using 1024 tokens with a vocabulary size of 8192.
The images are preprocessed to 256x256 resolution during training. Similar to VQVAE,[1,2] each image is compressed to a 32x32 grid of discrete latent codes using a discrete VAE[3,4] that we pretrained using a continuous relaxation.[5,6] We found that training using the relaxation obviates the need for an explicit codebook, EMA loss, or tricks like dead code revival, and can scale up to large vocabulary sizes.
This training procedure allows DALL·E to not only generate an image from scratch, but also to regenerate any rectangular region of an existing image that extends to the bottom-right corner, in a way that is consistent with the text prompt.

We recognize that work involving generative models has the potential for significant, broad societal impacts. In the future, we plan to analyze how models like DALL·E relate to societal issues like economic impact on certain work processes and professions, the potential for bias in the model outputs, and the longer term ethical challenges implied by this technology.
A powerful creative tool
DALL·E allows users to create quickly and easily, and artists and creative professionals are using DALL·E to inspire and accelerate their creative processes. We've already seen people use DALL·E to make music videos for young cancer patients, create magazine covers, and bring novel concepts to life.
Other features include:
1. Edit allows users to make realistic and context-aware edits to images they generate with DALL·E or images they upload using a natural language description.
2. Variations can take an image generated by DALL·E or an image uploaded by a user and create different variations of it inspired by the original.
3. My Collection allows users to save generations right in the DALL·E platform.

Capabilities:

1. Creating original, realistic images: DALL-E 2 can go beyond simply depicting objects; it can create entire scenes, apply different styles (painting, sculpture, etc.), and even combine seemingly unrelated concepts in a visually plausible way.
2. High resolution and accuracy: Compared to its predecessor, DALL-E 2 generates images with four times the resolution, leading to much sharper and more detailed results.
3. Text manipulation: Not only can you generate images from scratch, but you can also modify existing ones using DALL-E 2. You can add, remove, or change elements within an image based on your text prompts.

Limitations and Safety:

1. Limited availability: Currently, DALL-E 2 is in beta and only accessible to a limited number of users through waitlist applications.
2. Misuse potential: Like any powerful AI tool, DALL-E 2 has the potential to be misused for creating harmful or offensive content. OpenAI has implemented various safety measures, but it's important to be aware of these risks.
3. Text dependency: The quality of the generated images heavily depends on the clarity and specificity of your text prompts. Mastering "prompt engineering" is key to getting the most out of DALL-E 2.

Signing Up & Buying Credits

1. Go to DALL·E's website and click Try DALL·E. You'll find the AI image generator at https://openai.com/dall-e-2

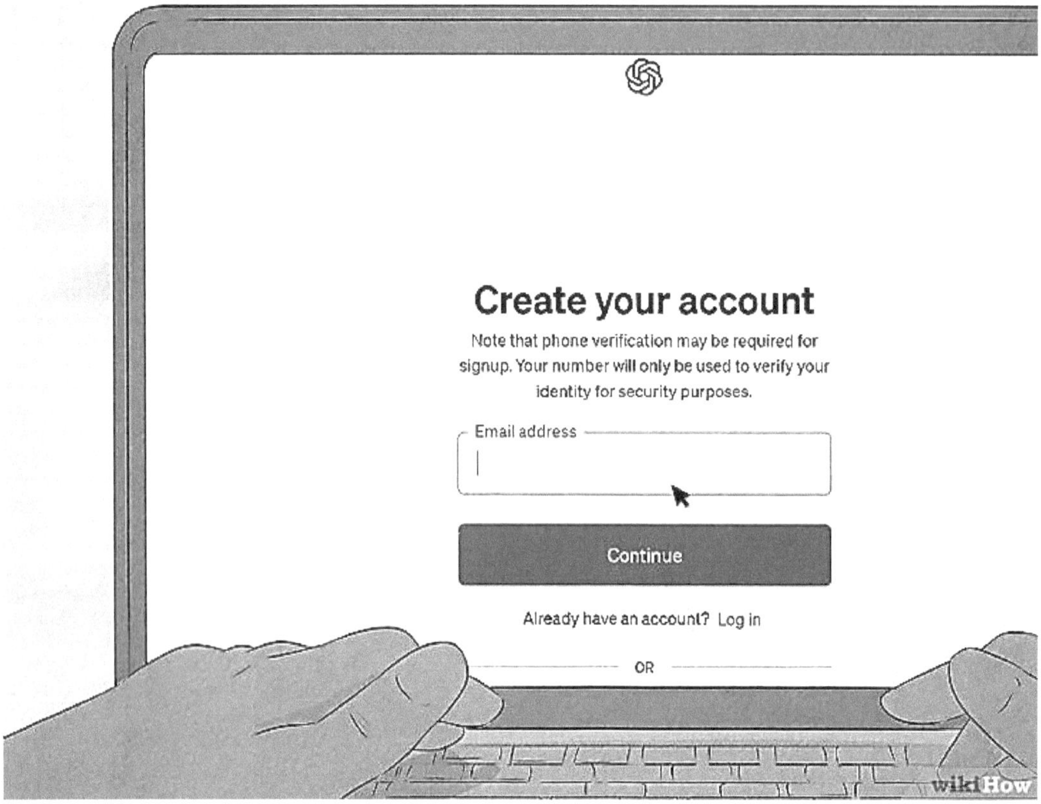

2. Create a new account by clicking the Sign up button. If you already have an OpenAI account, you can sign in and skip the rest of the steps in this section. Otherwise, follow the on-screen steps to set up your account, including mobile verification.

- You can also sign up using your existing Google, Microsoft, or Apple account.
- OpenAI requires a phone number for security reasons.

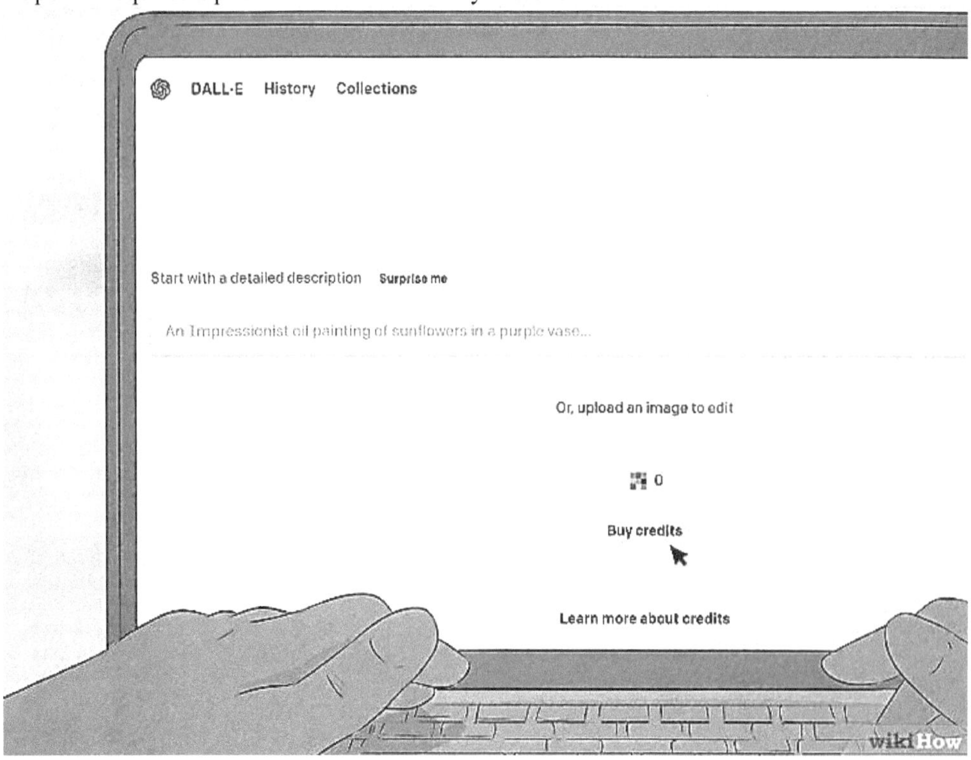

3. Click the Buy credits button on the DALL·E main page. It's directly under the prompt box.

4. Click the + or - buttons to decide how many credits you want.115 credits is $15, and there's no discount for buying credits in bulk. One credit is good for one prompt of four image variations, so 115 credits will get you 115 prompts generated.

- Note that your DALL·E credits expire 12 months after you buy them, so ensure you can use up all of your credits before they expire.

Creating Images

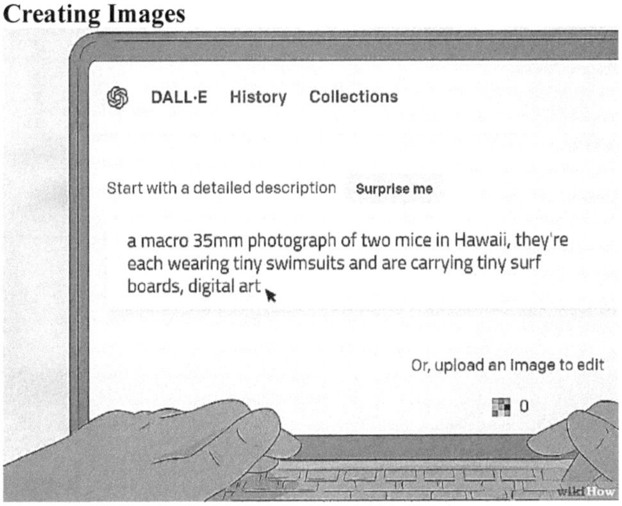

1. Enter a prompt in the text box on DALL·E's main page. After you've signed up or logged in, you'll be brought to the DALL·E homepage, which has a text box where you can enter prompts. The prompt box will have a placeholder

prompt in it, and it's next to a button that says **Generate**. You can write anything from a very simple prompt to a more detailed one, and DALL·E will generate your image based on that prompt.
- Be specific and detailed without going overboard.
- If you want the end image to have a certain art style, mood, or look, include that in the prompt. However, don't make your prompts too wordy; this can have the opposite effect and make your images harder to understand.

2. Adjust your prompt as needed. If your images didn't turn out how you wanted, you can adjust the prompt to tweak the end results.
For example, if your original prompt for DALL·E was "a skateboarding dog," you might adjust it to say "a brown skateboarding dog" or "a skateboarding dog wearing a baseball cap." This specificity will help DALL·E make an image that is closer to what you want.

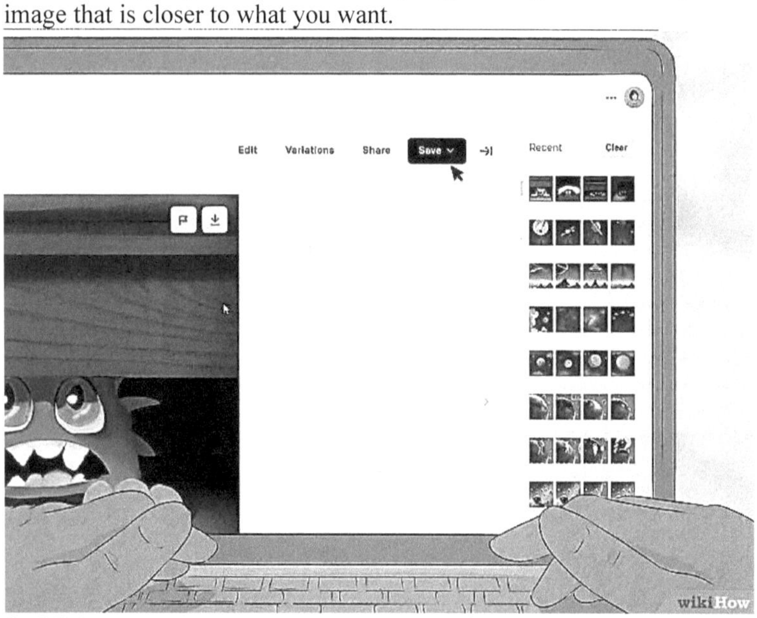

3. Click on the image for more options. When you click on any of your generated images, you can choose from several options in the upper-right corner.
- **Download:** Download the image to your computer.
- **Save:** Save the image to a collection.

- **Share:** Share the image to DALL·E 2's feed.
- **Edit:** Use advanced editing options
- **Variations:** Generate four alternative images of the same prompt (though this will use another credit)

Writing Great Prompts

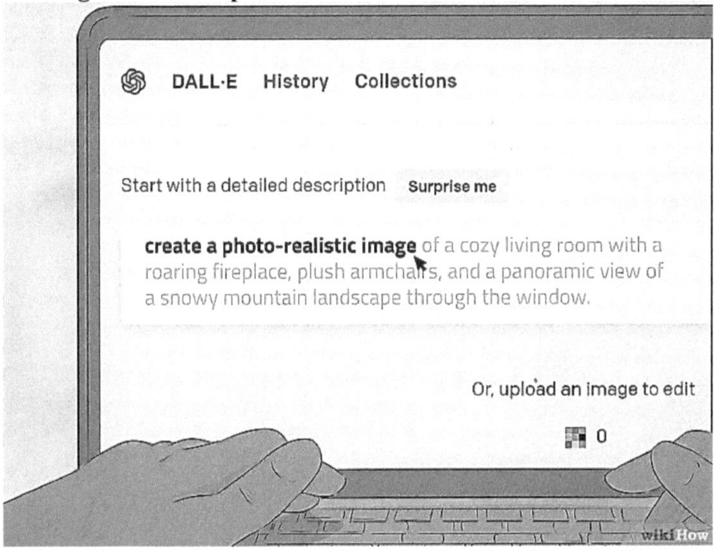

1. Include a specific art style if you're looking for one. If you want to create an image that looks like a painting, include the style of impressionism, cubism, or baroque. If you want to create a photo-realistic image, try including information such as camera type and focal distance.

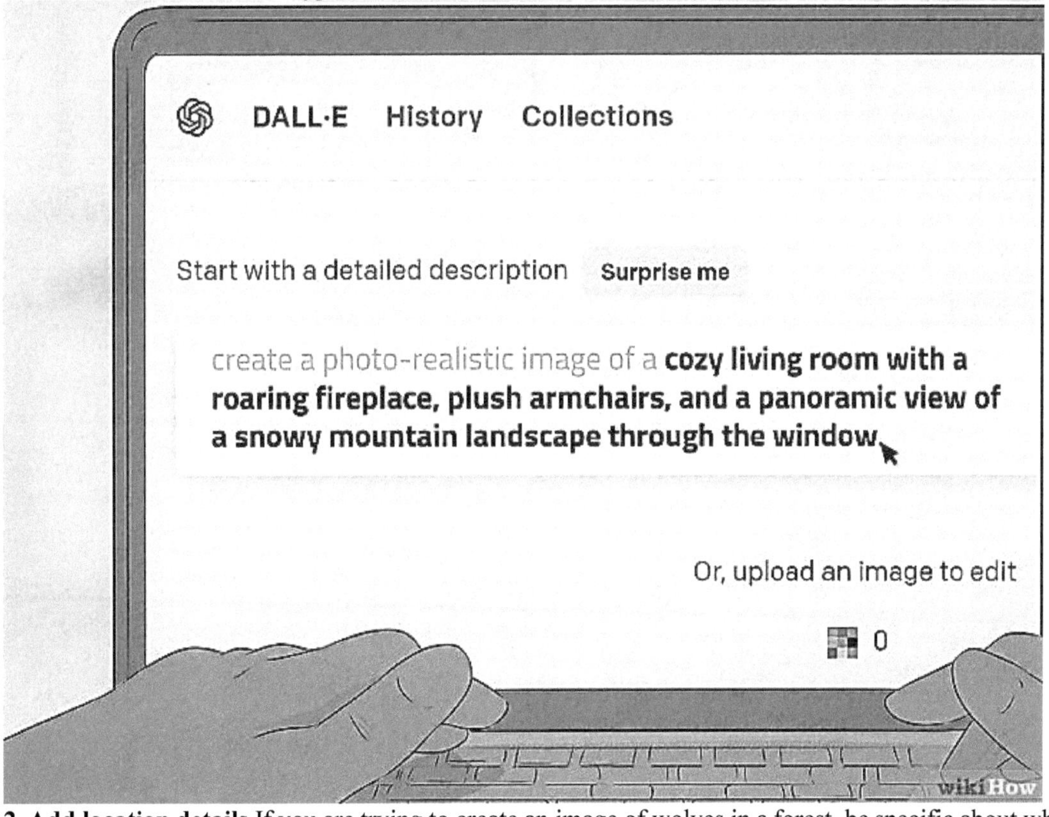

2. Add location details. If you are trying to create an image of wolves in a forest, be specific about what you want the forest to look like. Are there a lot of trees or are they in a clearing? What season is it? What time of day is it?

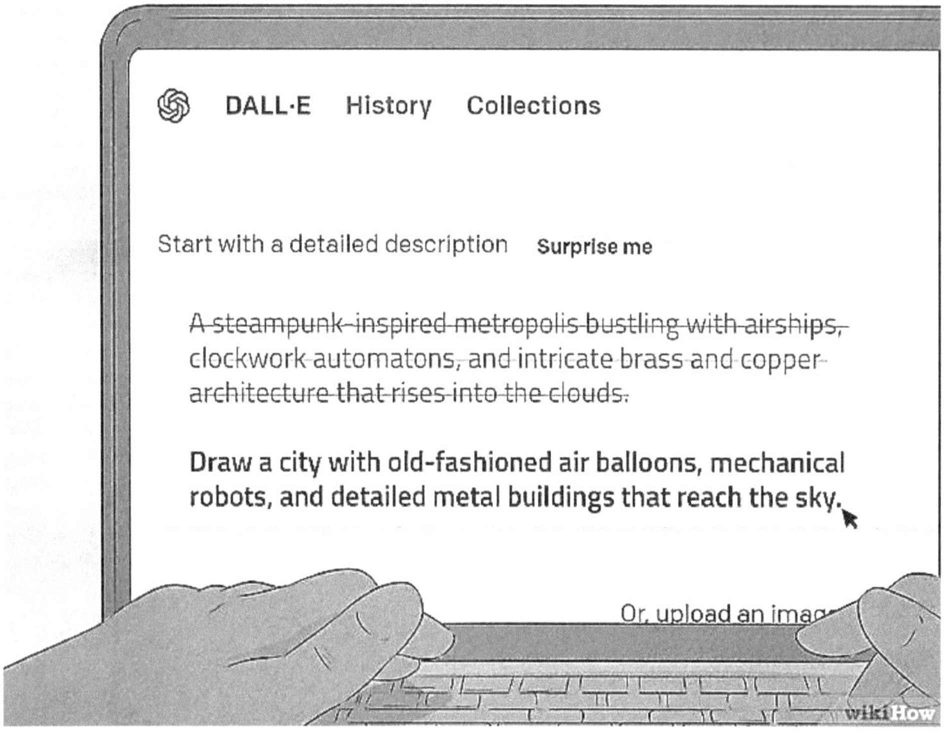

3. Avoid getting too detailed. Intricate details such as image orientation or object placement can actually have the opposite effect and can lead to your image not being readable.

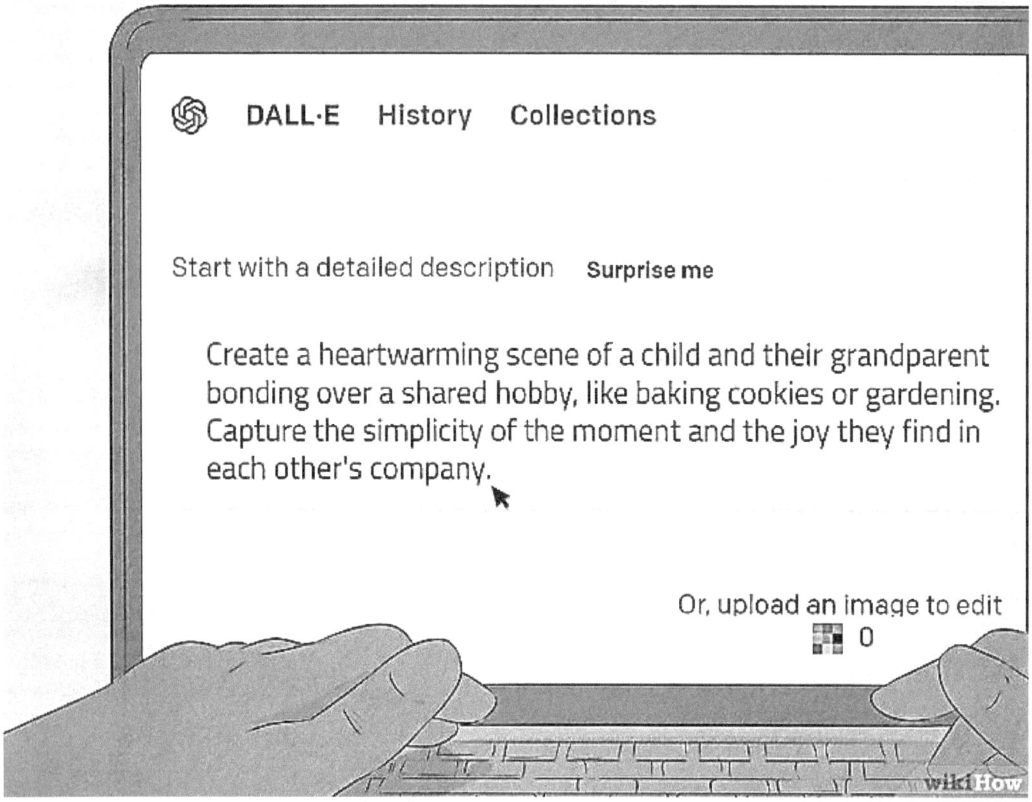

4. Start with a simple concept. After figuring out the concept, you can add more details to your prompt to tweak it further and bring it closer to the image you're trying to achieve.

5. Read prompts from other people. Try joining communities of people who like to use DALL·E 2 on Reddit or Discord and study how other people write prompts, especially those who get results like what you're looking for. Some people are protective over their prompts, but many are willing to share.

Advanced Features

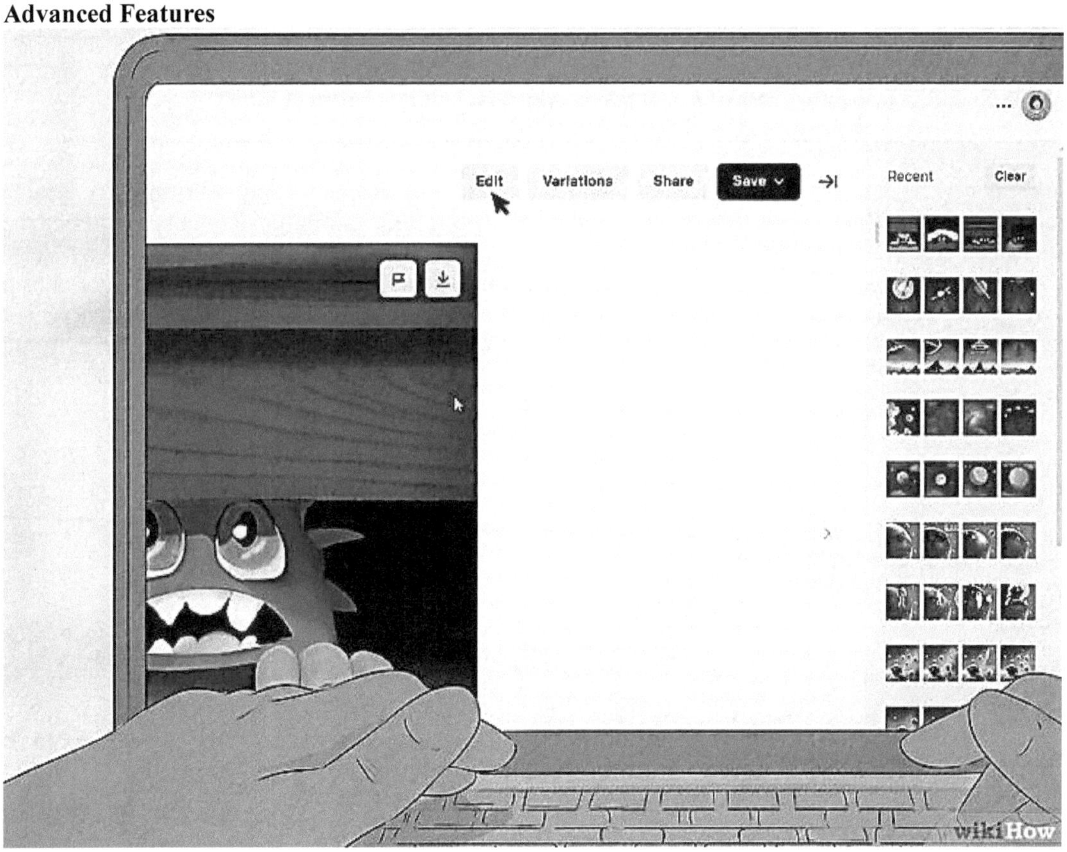

Click a photo and select the Edit button. There are two main advanced editing modes with DALL·E 2: inpainting (eraser) and outpainting (add generation frame).

1. To inpaint, select the **eraser** tool (keyboard shortcut E) with the image open in the editor. Paint over a spot in the image you want to replace, then use the prompt pop-up to describe the entire image, including what you want to fill in the spot you erased.
2. To outpaint, select the **Add generation frame** tool (keyboard shortcut F) and position it so your image expands in the direction you want. Use the prompt bar to describe what you want to fill the new part of the image.

8.3 NightCafe

NightCafe AI is an AI image generator developed by NightCafe Studio. It works pretty much the same way as any other popular text-to-image tool such as DALL-E 2.0 or Midjourney — you feed it a text prompt, and NightCafe generates original images based on that prompt.

Alternatively, if you have a photo you think could use some improvement, simply toss it into NightCafe and let the "neural-style transfer" add some AI-generated artistry to it. The control of the whole process is all yours, right from the style to the final touch.

Behind the curtain, NightCafe is a tag team of VQGAN and CLIP doing the heavy lifting. VQGAN sketches out your vision, and CLIP ensures it doesn't stray off-course. And with some serious GPU muscle, NightCafe speeds through the rendering like it's on a caffeine rush.

But there's more! NightCafe AI is an all-in-one AI art generator platform that encompasses several generative models, including:

1. Stable Diffusion
2. DALL-E 2
3. LIP-Guided Diffusion
4. Neural Style Transfer
5. And, of course, VQGAN+CLIP

The ultimate goal here is to ensure that you no longer have to hop between sites or apps; it's all under one digital roof. As for ease of use, it comes with a user-friendly interface that requires no technical proficiency beyond simple browsing. Meanwhile, for the professionals, there's room to tinker, refine, and upscale for that pixel-perfect finish.

NightCafe AI is an online tool that employs artificial intelligence to generate unique AI art, but that's not all. In addition to using the Night Cafe AI generator for your art creation, you can participate in art challenges and connect with fellow AI art lovers worldwide. This tool provides you with a community you'll hardly find on any other platform, making it truly outstanding. Let's unravel how AI NightCafe works, including its main features.

How Does NightCafe AI Actually Work?

The NightCafe creator AI requires no lengthy special training or artistic skills from you. Any user from any location in the world can create NightCafe AI art. If you have access to a laptop or mobile device and a good internet connection, you can explore creator NightCafe studio. All you need to do is visit their website, click "Create," select your preferred style and use their other features to generate your AI art. NightCafe AI uses different AI algorithms to process your text or image descriptions to generate AI art. You can also join the NightCafe community by sharing your art, engaging with others, and participating in daily challenges. AI art NightCafe generator encourages creativity and collaboration.

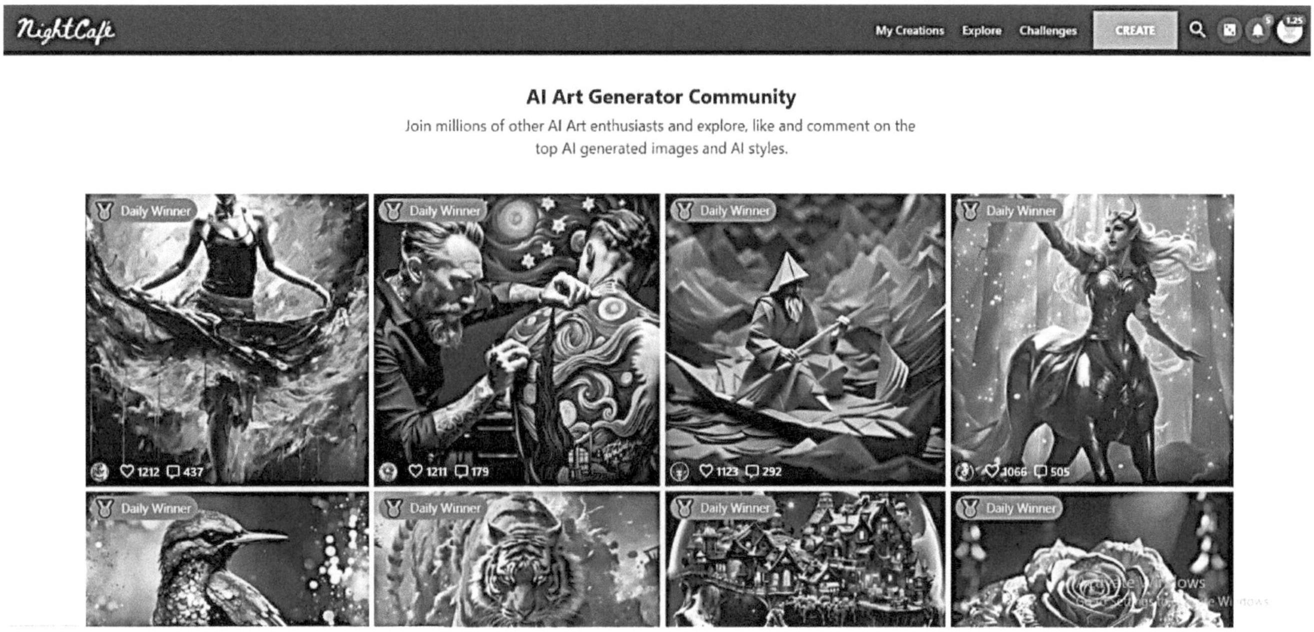

Main Features of the NightCafe Studio AI Art Generator

Being a part of the creator NightCafe community means enjoying some exciting features and benefits. The main features of the NightCafe Studio AI art generator include the following:

1. Text and image-to-image art generation: You can input text prompts describing the art or character you wish to generate. Select your model, style, and number of images to produce your NightCafe art. An example of a text prompt you can input is "a portrait of an old man wearing a hat fishing at sea." Users of NightCafe can also upload images and convert them to AI art following similar steps.

2. Multiple algorithms: Unlike most AI art generators, NightCafe uses various algorithms, such as Stable Diffusion, DALL-E 2, CLIP-Guided Diffusion, VQGAN+CLIP, and Neural Style Transfer. This variety ensures the generation of consistent and accurate NightCafe Art.

3. AI art community: By using AI NightCafe, you become part of the millions who use the online platform to generate, share, and chat about AI art. You don't only have access to NightCafe Studio's AI algorithms but a vibrant community that can further challenge and inspire you to enhance your AI art creation skills. The presence of chat rooms and AI art daily challenges makes the community of NightCafe active and exciting. You can follow artists you admire, like, and comment on their art and also receive the same treatment as part of the community.

4. Style variety: There are various character styles to choose from when generating your AI art on NightCafe, including vibrant, hyper-real, artistic portraits, anime, striking, and CGI character.

How to use NightCafe Studio's Online Artificial Intelligence art generator, step by step

1. Go to creator.nightcafe.studio **on the browser of your choice**

You will be taken to the basic create form on the NightCafe generator home page.

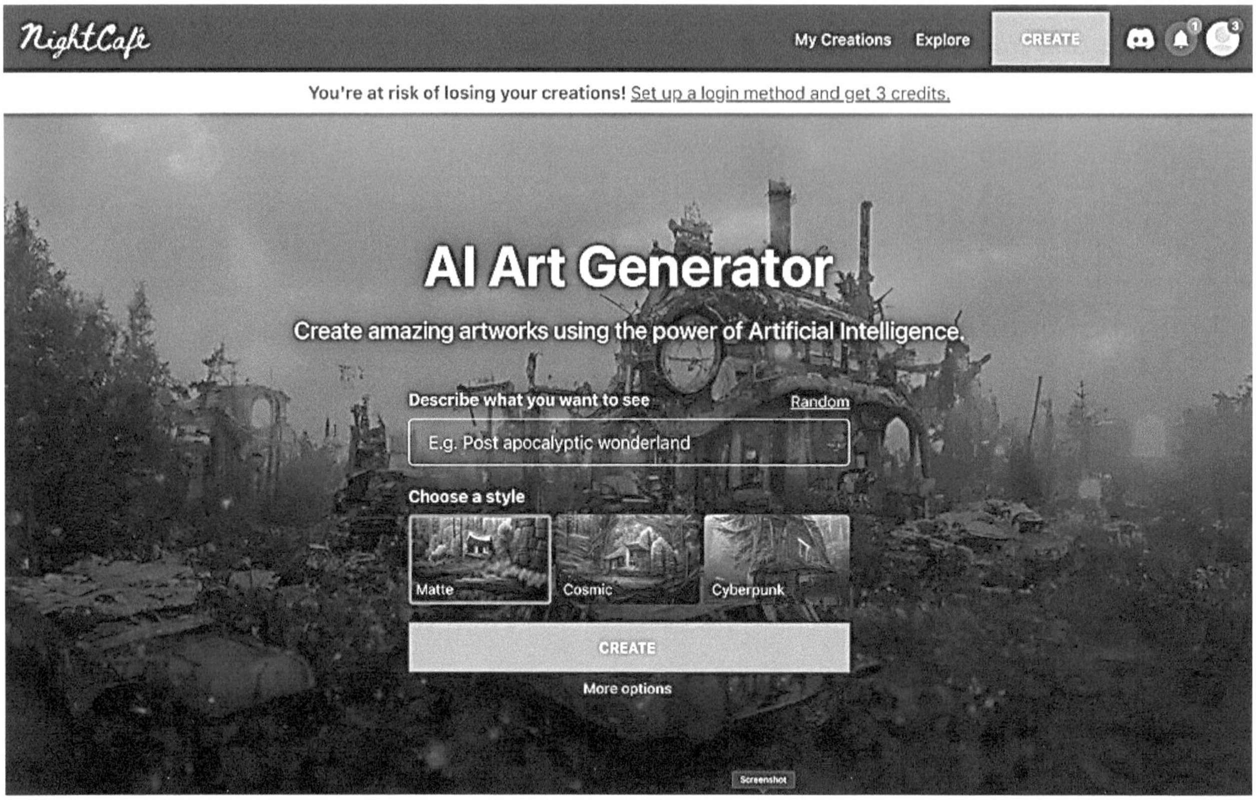

2. Type your prompt into the prompt box or generate a random one using the random button on the top right side of the prompt box

This is the fun part! Describe what you'd like the NightCafe AI to generate. Descriptive, to the point, direct prompts work best. Want some advice on how to write prompts that help generate beautiful images? Check out our Artist spotlights with top NightCafe AI artists on our blog, found here!

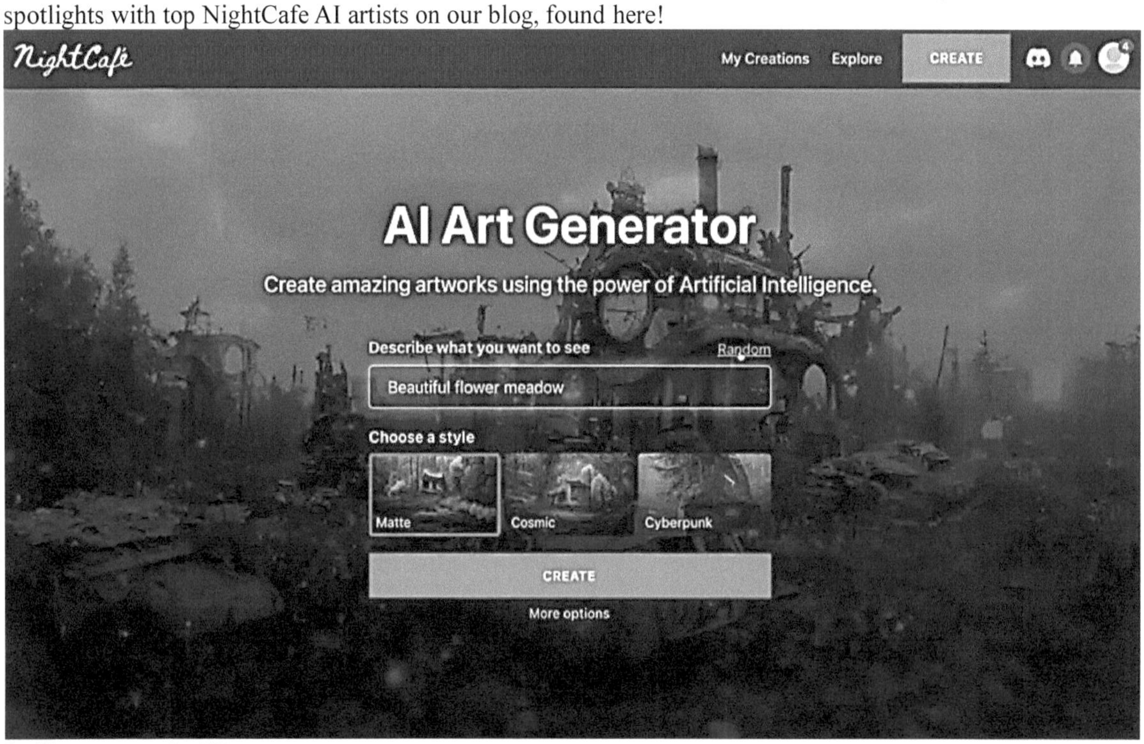

3. Choose a style. Hit create.

That's it! You've created your first AI art piece! The hardest part of it all is waiting for it to generate (which will only be a couple of minutes).

Setting up an account with NightCafe Studio

While you wait for your artificial intelligence art piece to generate, now would be a good time to set up a way to login to your account so you don't lose your work. (We even prompt for you to do so at the top of the "my creations" page!) You can connect your NightCafe account with Facebook or Google, or you can use a trusted email and password.

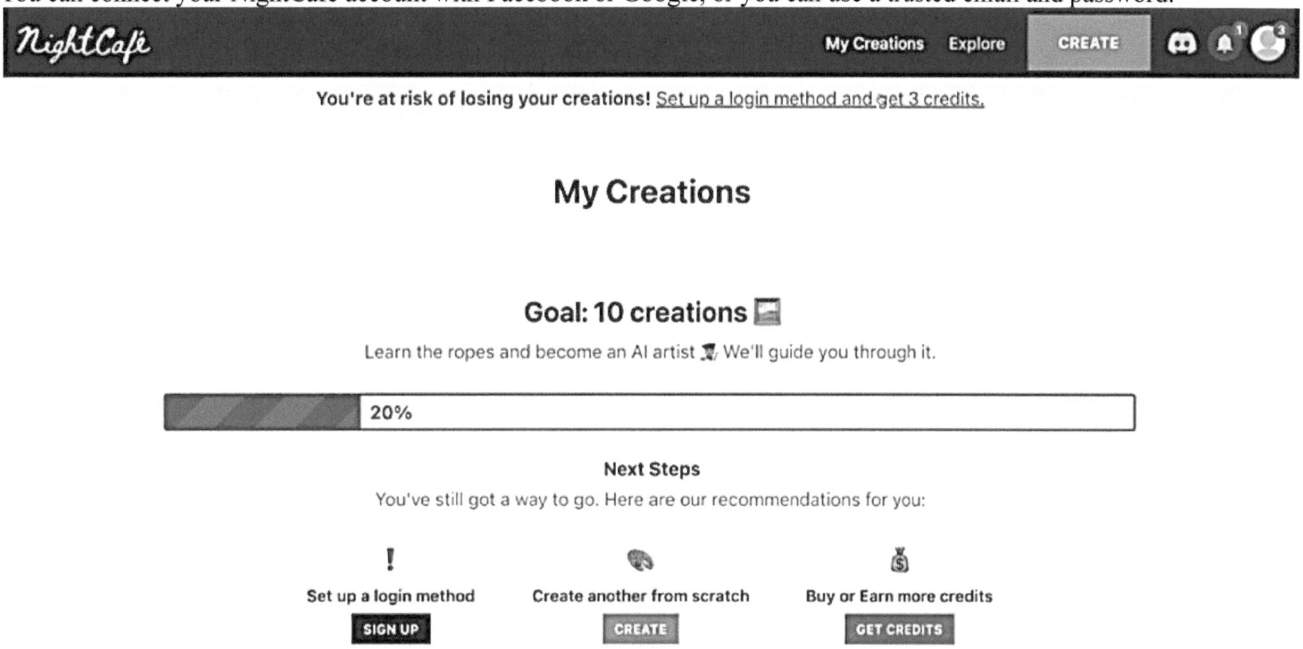

Generating art on the Create page with advanced settings *off*

When you are done setting up your login information, next thing to do is use the 'create' page.

1. Click the pink 'create' button in the top right-hand corner

Choose "Text to image/video" on the next page to be taken to the "create form". This create form is a little different than the one we were just on - it has more ways to control the art you're making. Here you can:

1. Choose a prompt from our pre-written prompt list
2. See all the one-of-a-kind artistic presets
3. Switch from the Artistic (VQGAN+CLIP) algorithm to the Coherent (CLIP-Guided Diffusion) creation method

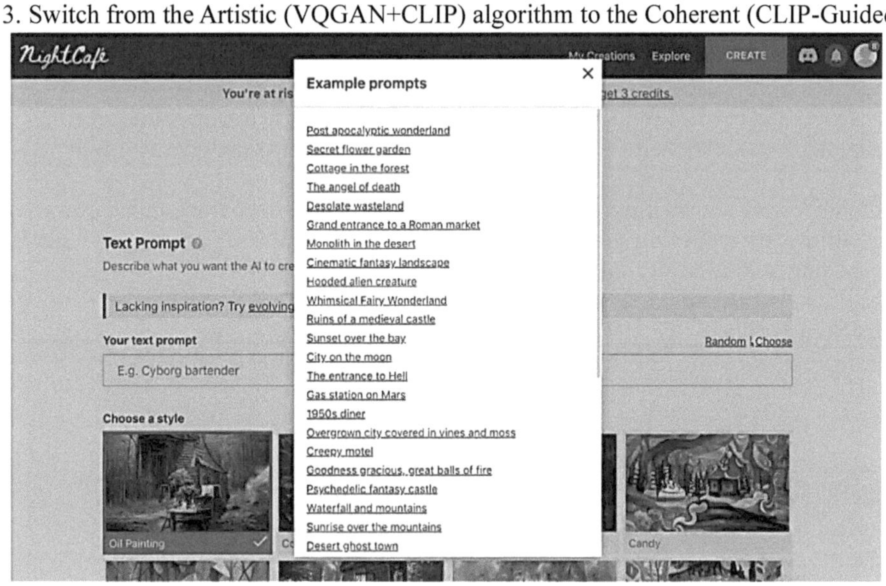

8.4 BlueWillow

BlueWillow is a free AI art generator that creates AI-generated images and digital artwork through the use of written text prompts. It is an aggregator of multiple AI models, including Stable Diffusion, and chooses to use the model that is able to create the best image for users.

Key Features

AI Artwork Generator: BlueWillow allows you to create stunning images for any project effortlessly.

Logos: BlueWillow enables users to create their own logos, making it a valuable tool for brand identity development and customization.

Photo-realistic Images: The platform allows users to generate photo-realistic images, creating lifelike graphics with a high level of detail and realism.

Graphics: BlueWillow can generate a wide assortment of images based on user prompts, offering versatility in the types of visuals it can create.

Quick Image Generation: With its AI technology, generating images is simple and easy to do. Generation is quick, you can have a new image in just a matter of seconds.

Wide Range of Image Styles: A wide range of image styles are available, giving you the ability to create anything from logos to artwork.

Instant Sharing: You can share your creations instantly and engage with other users to share ideas.

Customization: Users can customize backgrounds, font types, and colors, or add filters and 3D models.

How to use BlueWillow?

1. **Dashboard**: After logging in, you'll be taken to your dashboard. Here, you can see an overview of your account, including any ongoing projects or tasks.
2. **Create a Project**: To start using the AI, you'll need to create a new project. Click on the 'New Project' button and fill in the details such as the project name and description.
3. **Define Parameters**: Define the parameters for your image generation task. This could include things like the style of image, resolution, color scheme etc.
4. **Generate Image**: Click on 'Generate' to start the image generation process. BlueWillow AI will start creating your image based on the parameters you've set.
5. **Review the Image**: Once the image has been generated, review it. If you're not satisfied with the result, you can adjust the parameters and generate a new image.
6. **Save & Download**: If you're happy with the generated image, save it to your project and download it to your device.
7. **Get Support**: If you encounter any issues or have s while using BlueWillow AI, reach out to their support team through the 'Help' or 'Support' option in your dashboard.

BlueWillow Use Cases

1. **Graphic Design:** Graphic designers can use BlueWillow for logo and graphic creation. It can help in generating unique and creative designs, saving time and effort.
2. **Digital Art:** Digital artists can use this tool to explore new ideas and generate artwork with AI technology. It can be used to create a variety of art styles, from abstract to realistic.
3. **Marketing:** Marketing professionals can use BlueWillow for creating quick and diverse image options for campaigns. It can help in producing high-quality images for social media posts, marketing materials, and web designs.
4. **High-Fidelity Visual Assets:** BlueWillow allows users to create high-fidelity visual assets, from anime characters to life-like photographs. This can effectively reduce the gaps between physical and virtual realities, making it useful for a variety of applications like gaming, virtual reality, and more.

How to use BlueWillow Step By Step Tutorial

Step 1 - Join Community

Get invited to their group with almost 1M subscribers, for free.

Step 2 - Create User

Choose a username to become a member.

Step 3 - Connect Email

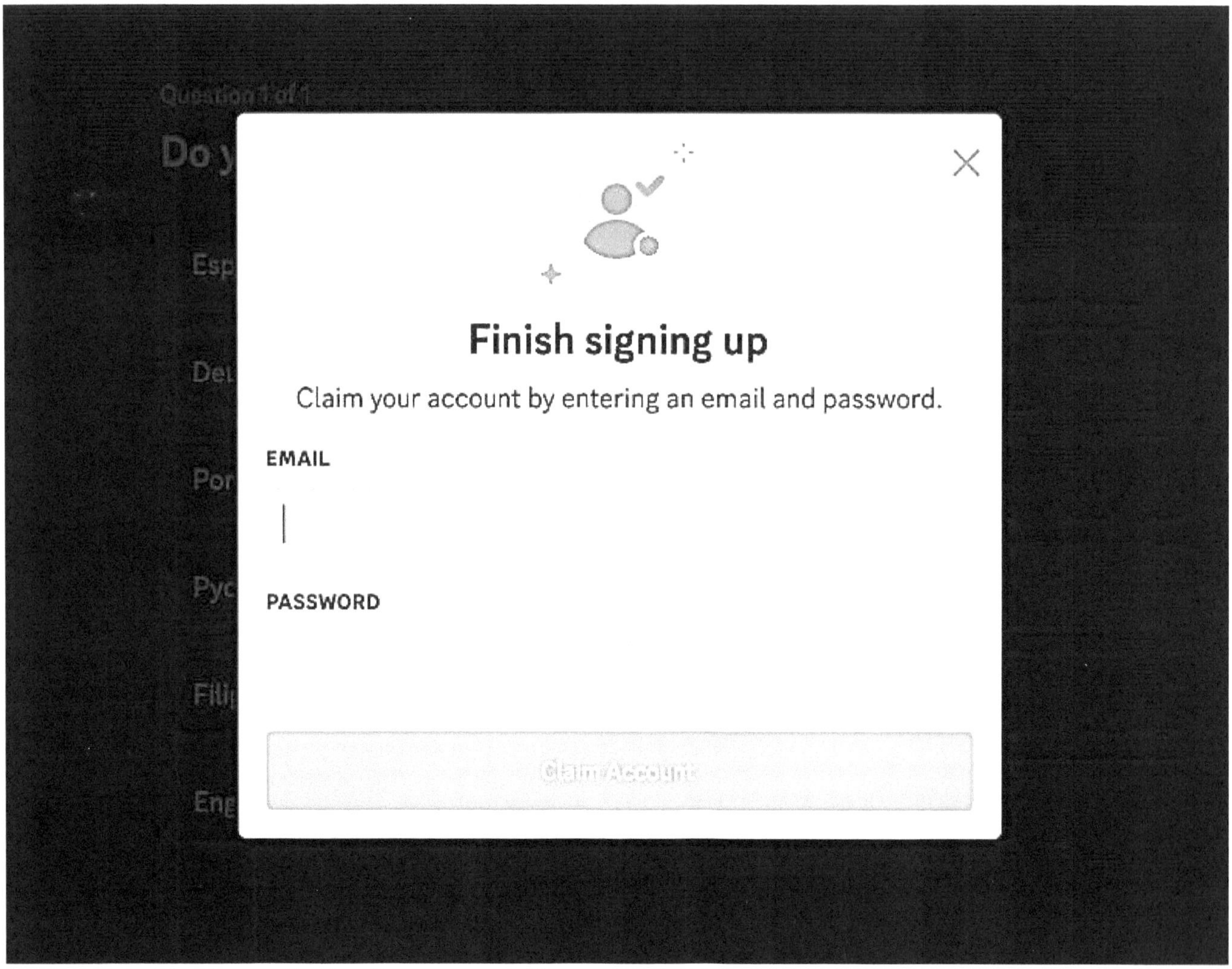

Claim your account by confirming the username with any email address.
Step 4 - Create Image

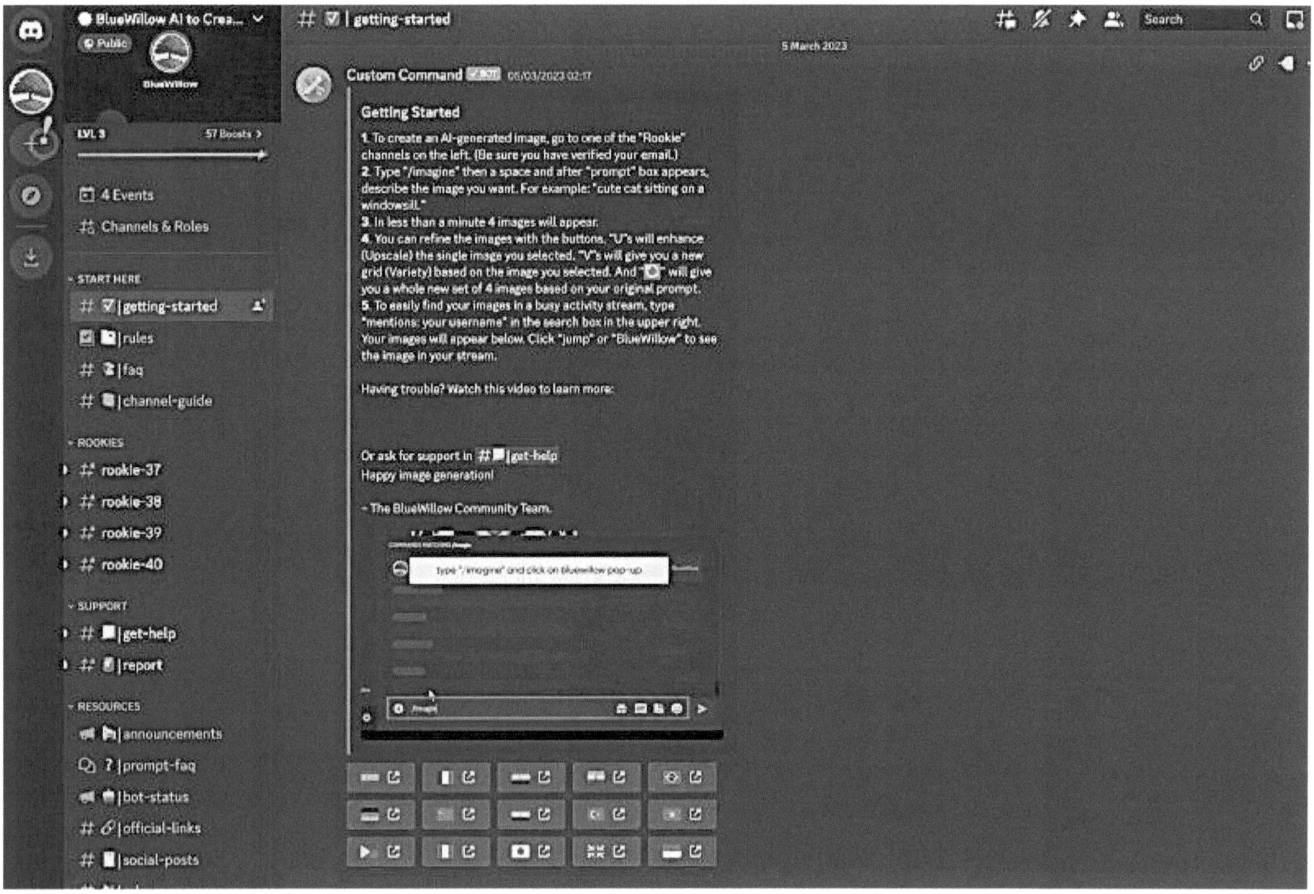

Follow simple instructions to generate images in seconds.

Step 5 - Receive Content

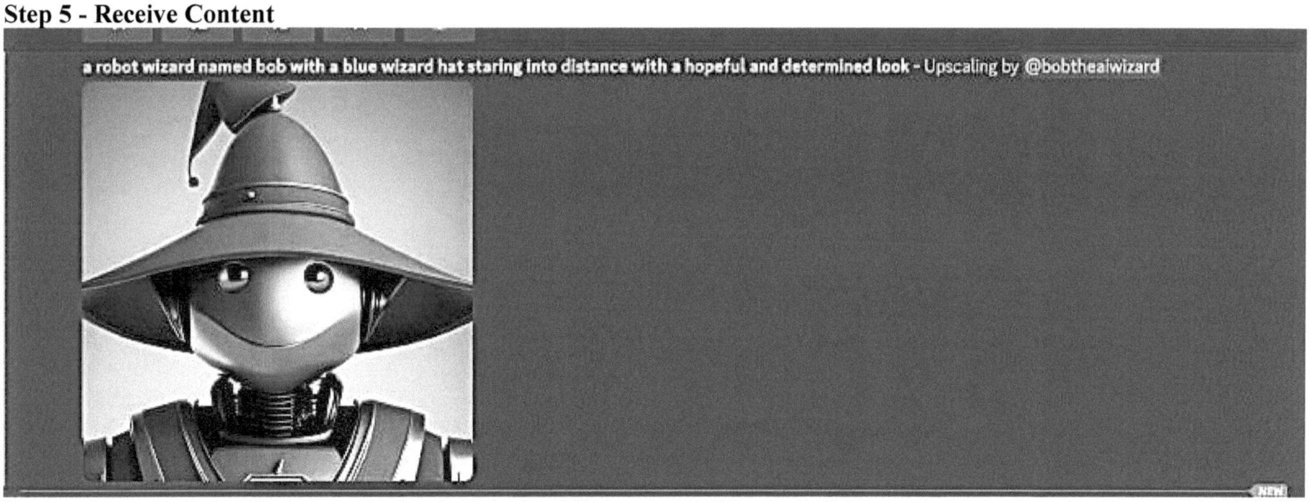

Once you're satisfied with the result, simply download the content with a few clicks.

8.5 Bria

Bria AI, an Israeli-based AI image generator, enters the scene with a groundbreaking approach to address copyright issues in generative AI. By licensing visual content ethically and compensating creators, Bria AI aims to redefine the AI image generation market.

The AI image generation landscape welcomes a disruptor as Bria AI launches its innovative platform. Hailing from Israel, Bria AI takes a revolutionary approach to tackle copyright challenges, setting new standards for responsible AI. Bria AI stands out by licensing visual content from renowned sources like Getty Images, Alamy, and Envato. This commitment to ethical content acquisition aims to resolve the copyright issues plaguing generative AI.

Bria AI's foundation model introduces a compensation system akin to Spotify's micropayments for musicians based on streams. This model ensures that creators and artists receive their fair share, fostering a sustainable AI ecosystem.
Getty Images, entangled in a lawsuit with the makers of Stable Diffusion, became a minority investor in Bria AI. Their partnership aided in securing licensing agreements and demonstrates a collective commitment to ethical AI practices.
Bria AI's strategy revolves around using only permissible content. This ensures that creators' rights are upheld and copyright issues are averted, promoting responsible AI practices.
Bria AI's compensation model functions as an agent for content creators. This innovative approach guarantees fair compensation, aligning the interests of creators and the AI model.
Bria AI's platform draws inspiration from Stable Diffusion's DreamStudio and OpenAI's DALL-E. Users can explore and remix stock photos, adding different backgrounds and elements to create unique compositions.
While Bria AI's early text-to-image diffusion models may lag behind frontrunners like Midjourney, DALL-E, and Stable Diffusion, the rapid pace of AI development suggests imminent improvements in image quality.
Bria AI's ethical approach addresses critical copyright concerns that have shadowed competitors in the AI image generation market. By prioritizing ethics and legality, Bria AI sets a new industry standard.
Edward Klaris, a managing partner at Klaris Law, emphasizes that Bria AI's solution aligns with ethical, legal, and international perspectives. This innovative approach not only stands on ethical grounds but also makes sense from a business standpoint.
Bria AI's entrance into the AI image generation arena marks a significant shift towards ethics and legality. By licensing content responsibly, compensating creators, and collaborating with industry leaders, Bria AI sets a new benchmark for responsible AI. As AI image generation continues to evolve, Bria AI's commitment to ethics and innovation is poised to shape the industry's future.

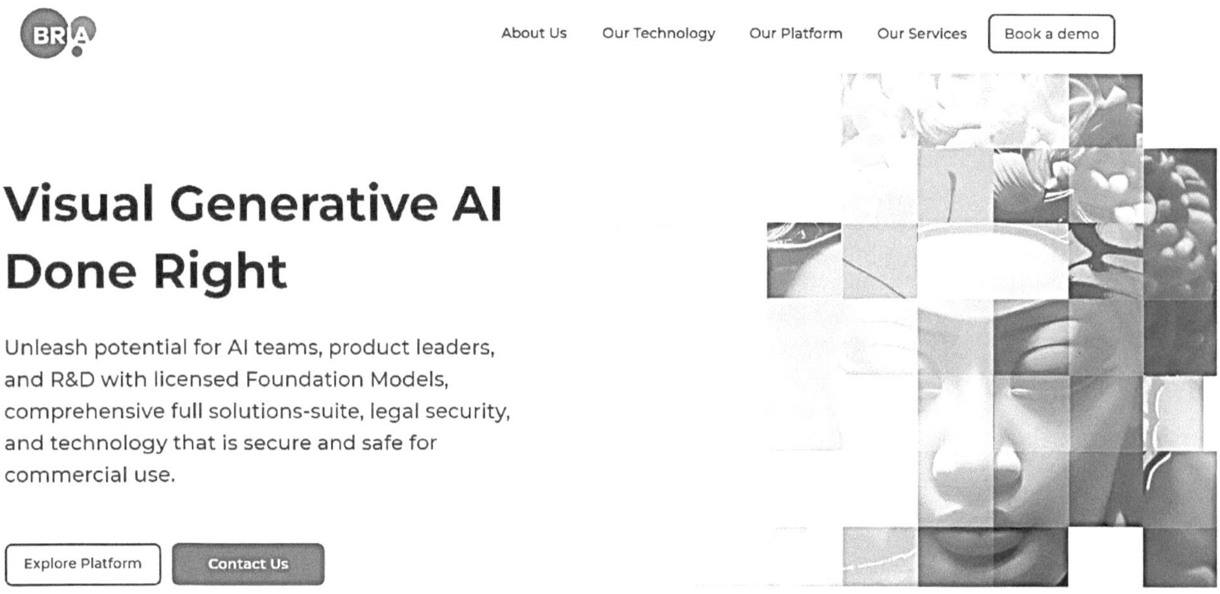

How Bria AI Works

Bria AI is a cutting-edge tool that uses artificial intelligence (AI) to generate unique and attention-grabbing visuals based on text input. Whether you're a part of an AI team, a product leader, or an R&D professional, Bria AI provides licensed Foundation Models and a comprehensive suite of solutions to meet your needs. Here's how it works:

1. Enter a textual description of the visual you want to create. You can use natural language or keywords to describe the visual.
2. Bria AI's AI algorithm analyzes the text and generates a visual that matches the description. You can see the visual on your screen in seconds.
3. You can customize the visual further by adjusting the size, color, layout, and other parameters. You can also add text or logos to the visual.
4. You can download the visual in high-resolution formats and use it for your personal or commercial purposes.

How to use Bria Step By Step Tutorial

Step 1 - Sign Up

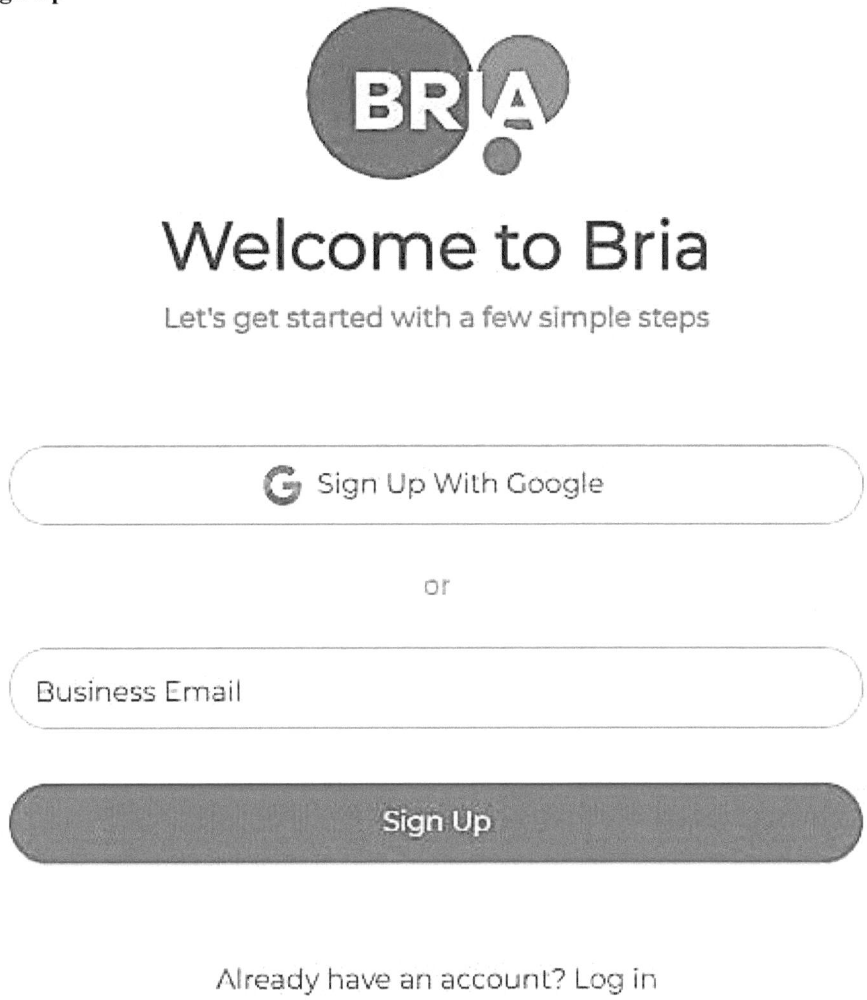

You can sign up with a Google account or with a business email.

Step 2 - Provide Description

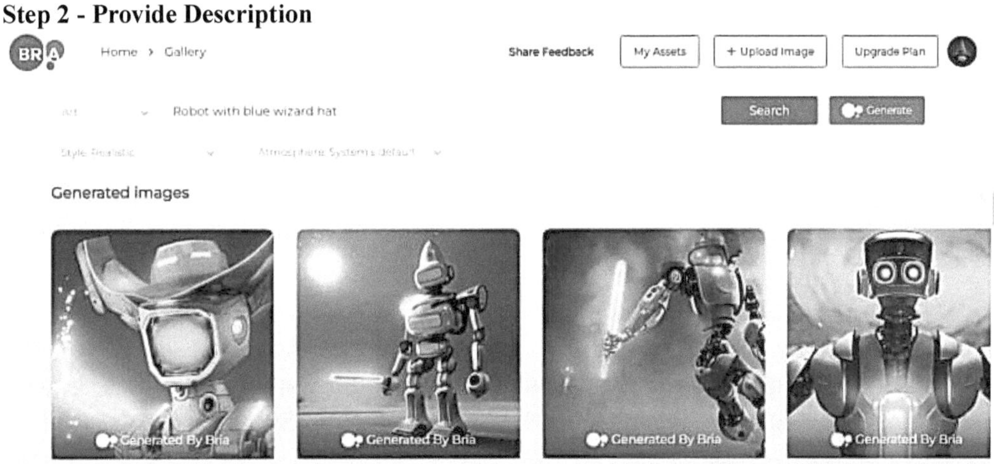

Provide the Bria AI tool detailed description of the image you would like it to generate. There are 3 different selections of styles and filters to choose from. It will generate several images for you to choose from.

Step 3 - Stock Images

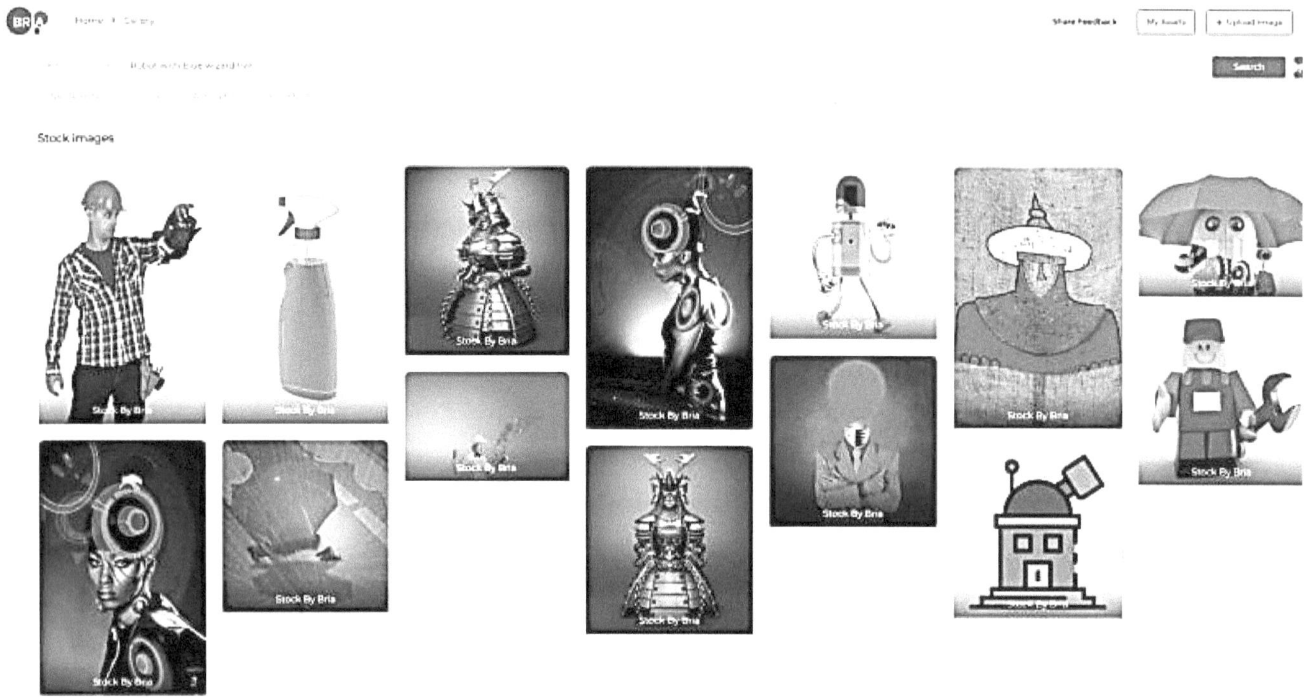

If the generated images are not exactly what you were looking for, then you can check out the stock images that match your description by scrolling down.

Step 4 – Background

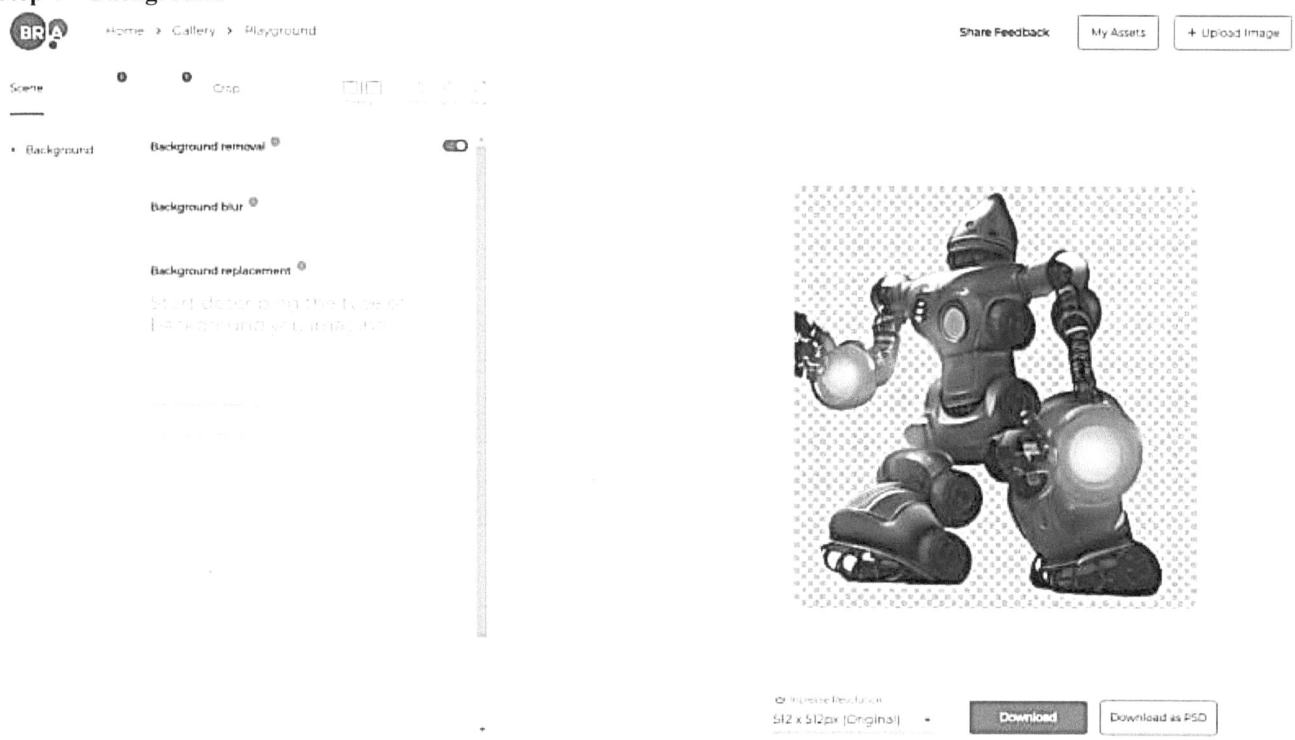

You can edit all the details of the background, you can make the background transparent, blur it, or generate new background. The paid plans allow you to also add or remove images from the background.

Step 5 – Crop

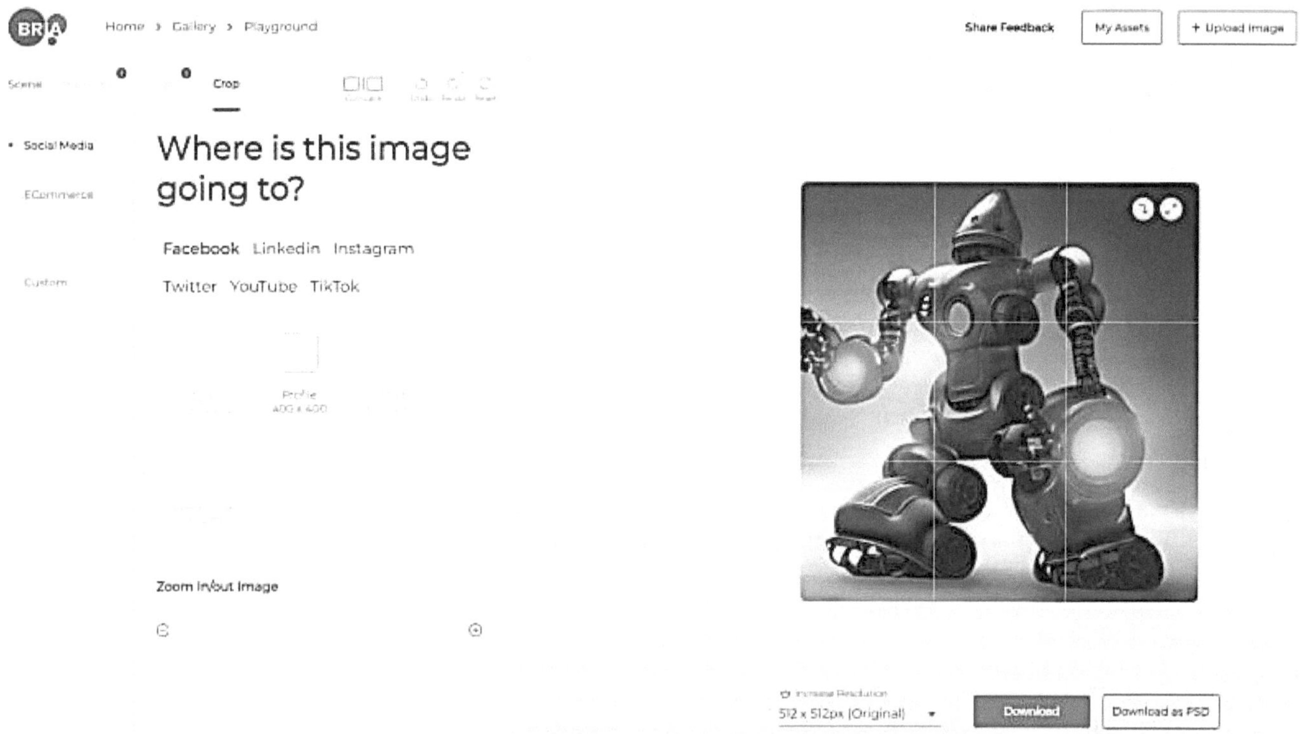

You can crop the image depending on where this image is going. For Instagram, Facebook, and other social media platforms, the tool will provide an exact size image for each platform.

Step 6 – Download

You can download the image with 512 x 512px resolution as a free user, paying users can download the images with higher resolution and also as a PSD file.

Key features:
Image Generation:
1. Create new visuals from scratch: Describe the image you want in text, and Bria AI will generate photorealistic representations based on your prompts.
2. Generate multiple variations: Get several options for the same prompt, exploring different compositions, styles, and lighting.
3. Text-to-video conversion: Create short video clips from textual descriptions, bringing your ideas to life with motion.

Image Editing and Enhancement:
1. Edit existing images: Modify objects, backgrounds, and other elements within your uploaded images.
2. Expand images: Take a small image and enlarge it while maintaining quality, saving you time and effort.
3. Enhance resolution: Improve the clarity and detail of your images, giving them a sharper appearance.
4. Visual expression enrichment: Apply styles, effects, and color palettes to amplify the emotional impact of your visuals.

Brand Consistency and Customization:
1. Fine-tuning for brand specific content: Train Bria AI on your brand assets (logos, colors, etc.) to generate visuals that match your style guide and maintain brand consistency.
2. Remove unwanted elements: Eliminate distractions and unwanted objects from your visuals for a cleaner and more focused message.
3. Streamline PSD transfer: Generate images directly in specific PSD formats, speeding up your design workflow.

Technical Features and Ease of Use:
1. Multiple access points: Bria AI offers a web interface (Bria AI Studio), API integration, SDKs, and widgets for seamless integration into existing workflows.
2. Full legal compliance: Bria AI works with trusted data sources and ensures copyright and privacy protection for generated content.
3. Responsible AI practices: Bria AI implements measures to prevent bias, ensure fairness, and safeguard against harmful content generation.
4. Scalability: Cloud-based processing allows you to handle large volumes of images and videos efficiently.

8.6 Stockimg

Stockimg AI is an AI-powered design service that can generate logos, images, posters, book covers, and more. It uses artificial intelligence to create high-quality and unique designs based on text input. You can choose from a wide range of categories and styles, and customize the results to your liking. Stockimg AI is a fast and easy way to create professional images for various purposes, such as branding, marketing, publishing, or personal projects. You can try it for free at Stockimg AI or learn more about it from Paxi AI, Medium, or Trending AI Tools.

StockImg AI is a progressive image-era tool that harnesses the power of artificial intelligence to streamline design techniques. It caters to an extensive range of design needs, together with trademarks, e-book covers, posters, illustrations, QR codes, textual content effects, and more. Let’s delve deeper into what makes StockImg.AI stand out.

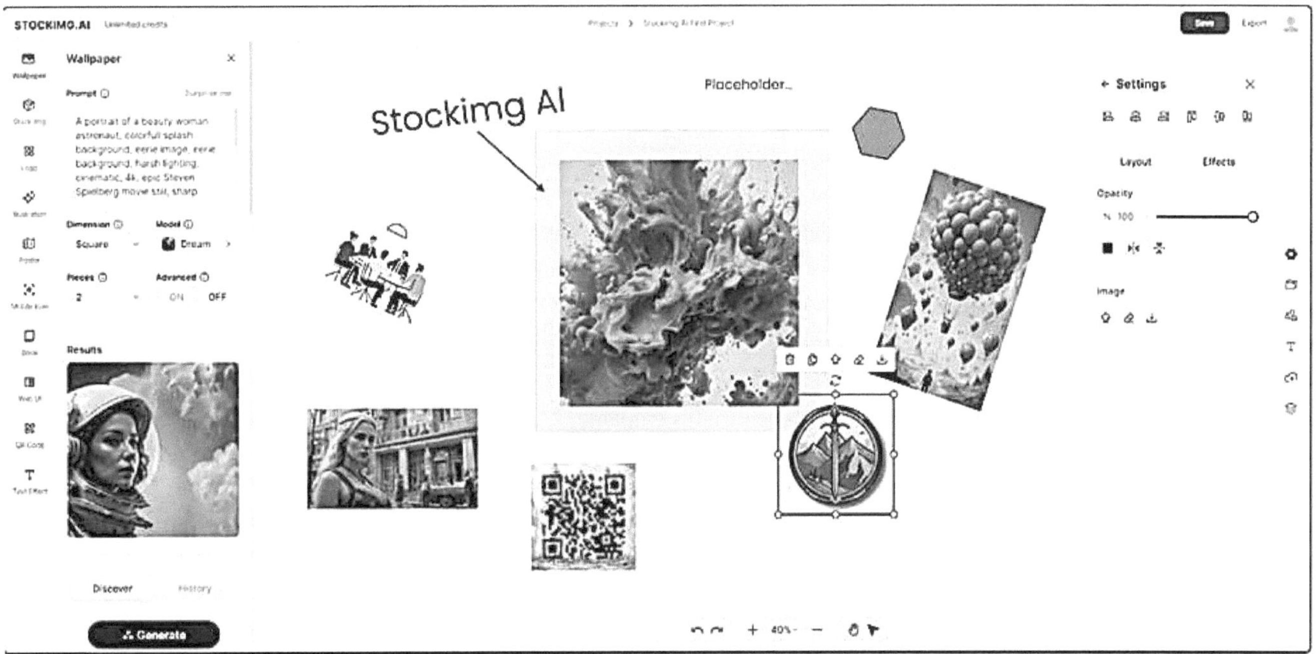

StockImg-AI-Image-Generator

Key Features of StockImg AI Image Generation Tool
Stockimg.AI boasts a variety of features that make it a valuable addition to any designer's toolkit:

1. Wide Range of Design Categories
StockImg AI provides access to an extensive selection of design categories, making it suitable for diverse design projects. whether or not you're operating on branding, advertising, or personal creative endeavors, you will find the right class to suit your desires.

2. User-Friendly Interface
One of the standout functions of StockImg AI is its person-friendly interface. Even in case you're no longer a seasoned fashion designer, you can generate expert-great pics fast and easily. The intuitive platform ensures a smooth design process.

3. Free Trial and AI-Made Images Section
Curious to see what StockImg AI can do for you? You can explore its capabilities with a free trial. Additionally, Stockimg.AI provides a section dedicated to AI-generated images, allowing you to preview and gather inspiration before you start your own project.

4. Social Media Presence
StockImg AI doesn't just stop at providing a tool; it also offers a sense of community and support. Stay updated on the latest news, tips, and tricks through Stockimg.AI's active presence on social media platforms like Twitter, Instagram, and TikTok.

Use of StockIMG AI
Now, let's take a closer look at how Stockimg.AI can be a game-changer for various design needs:

– **Create Eye-Catching Logos**
For businesses and individuals looking to establish a strong brand identity, StockImg AI can help you create eye-catching logos that leave a lasting impression.

– **Design Engaging Book Covers**
Authors and publishers can benefit from Stockimg.AI by designing captivating book covers that attract readers and stand out in a crowded market.

– **Generate Visually Appealing Posters**
Event organizers, marketers, and promoters can leverage StockImg AI to craft visually appealing posters that draw attention and effectively convey their messages.

– **Craft Unique Wallpapers, Illustrations, and Icons**
Whether you're working on digital or print projects, StockImg AI empowers you to create unique wallpapers, illustrations, and icons that align with your creative vision.

– **Develop Web and Mobile UI Designs**

Web and mobile designers can enhance their projects with AI-generated imagery, making it easier to create captivating user interfaces.

StockImg AI: Pros and Cons

Now, let's weigh the pros and cons of using Stockimg.AI:

Pros:

1. **Time-Saving**: StockImg AI accelerates the design process, allowing you to create high-quality images in seconds, saving you valuable time.
2. **User-Friendly**: Its intuitive interface makes it accessible even to those with limited design experience.
3. **Wide Design Categories**: With an extensive selection of design categories, it caters to diverse creative needs.
4. **Inspiration**: The AI-made images section provides inspiration for your projects.
5. **Community and Support**: Stockimg.AI's active presence on social media offers a supportive community and updates on the latest developments.

Cons:

1. **Limited Free Trial**: While the unfastened trial is valuable, it is able to have barriers to the quantity of pix or features available.
2. **Subscription Costs**: Depending on your needs, the subscription expenses may also upload up, especially for superior functions

StockImg AI Pricing

Let's talk about the pricing options for StockImg AI:

1. **Free**: $0/monthly
2. **Starter**: $19/month
3. **Premium**: $29/month
4. **Enterprises**: Custom (Contact us for a tailored plan)

StockImg AI is aware that extraordinary customers have distinct wishes, which is why they provide a variety of pricing options. whether or not you are simply starting or require extra advanced features, there's a plan that suits your price range.

Benefits of Using Stockimg.ai

There are many benefits to using Stockimg.ai, including:

1. High-quality images: Stockimg.ai uses advanced AI technology to generate high-quality images that are perfect for any project.
2. Variety of image types: Stockimg.ai can generate a variety of different image types, so you can find the perfect image for your needs.
3. Easy to use: Stockimg.ai is easy to use, even if you're not familiar with AI image generation.
4. Affordable: Stockimg.ai offers a variety of pricing plans to fit your budget.

Use Cases for Stockimg.ai

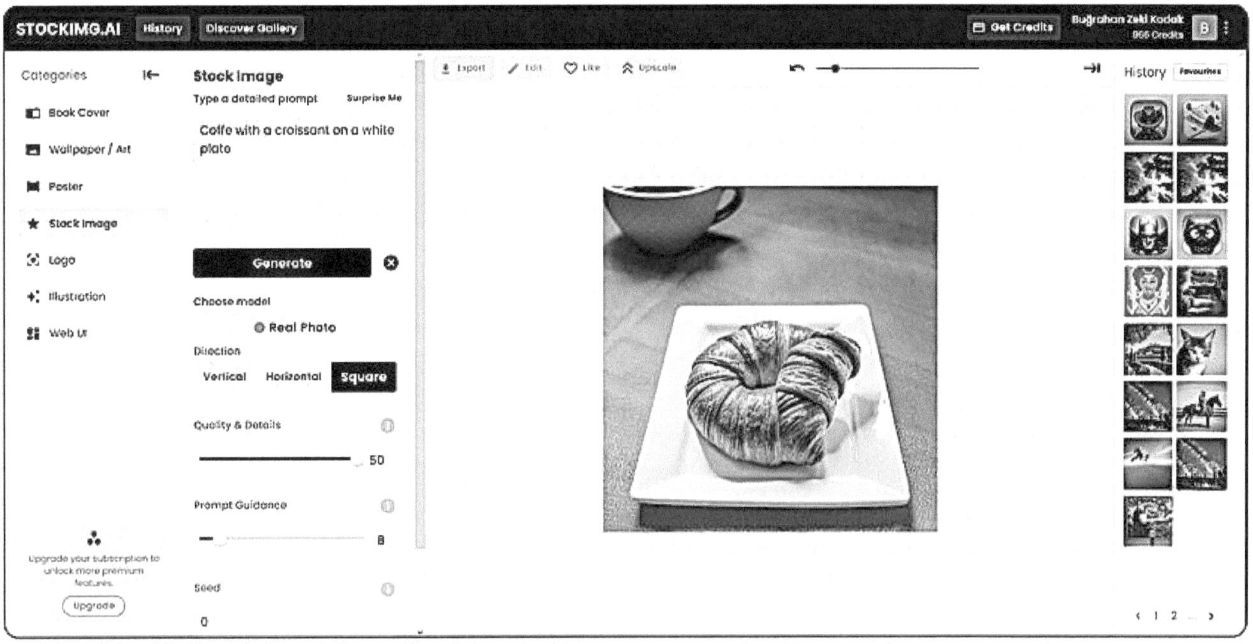

Stockimg.ai can be used for a variety of purposes, including:

1. Creating book covers: Stockimg.ai can help you create professional-looking book covers for your self-published books.
2. Designing posters: Stockimg.ai can help you create eye-catching posters for your events or promotions.
3. Generating logos: Stockimg.ai can help you create unique and memorable logos for your business.
4. Illustrating stories: Stockimg.ai can help you bring your stories to life with beautiful illustrations.
5. Creating web and mobile UIs: Stockimg.ai can help you create user-friendly and visually appealing web and mobile UIs.

To use Stockimg.ai, simply follow these steps:

1. Go to the Stockimg.ai website.
2. Select the type of image you want to generate.
3. Enter a few keywords that describe the image you want.
4. Click the "Generate" button.
5. Select the image you like the best.

Exercise

Exercise 1 – MCQ

Q 1. What is the primary focus of Midjourney in image design?

A. Graphic design
B. Stock photography
C. Image editing and manipulation
D. AI-driven image generation

Q 2. Which tool is associated with the name "DALL.E 2" in the realm of image design?

A. Graphic design
B. AI-driven image generation
C. Stock photography
D. Image editing and manipulation

Q 3. NightCafe is known for its features related to:

A. Stock photography
B. Image editing and manipulation
C. AI-driven image generation
D. Graphic design

Q 4. BlueWillow is primarily focused on:

A. Image editing and manipulation
B. Graphic design
C. AI-driven image generation
D. Stock photography

Q 5. What does the tool Bria specialize in within the context of image design?

A. AI-driven image generation
B. Graphic design
C. Image editing and manipulation
D. Stock photography

Q 6. Stockimg is primarily associated with:
A. Graphic design
B. AI-driven image generation
C. Stock photography
D. Image editing and manipulation

Q 7. Which tool is specifically known for its AI-driven image generation capabilities?
A. NightCafe
B. Stockimg
C. Midjourney
D. BlueWillow

Q 8. DALL.E 2 is a tool focused on:
A. Image editing and manipulation
B. Graphic design
C. AI-driven image generation
D. Stock photography

Q 9. BlueWillow primarily deals with:
A. Stock photography
B. Graphic design
C. AI-driven image generation
D. Image editing and manipulation

Q 10. What is the main feature of Bria in the context of image design?
A. Stock photography
B. Image editing and manipulation
C. AI-driven image generation
D. Graphic design

Exercise 2 – True/ False

Q 1. Midjourney is an Image Design Tool primarily focused on traditional graphic design techniques.
Q 2. DALL.E 2 is an Image Design Tool known for its AI-driven image generation capabilities.
Q 3. NightCafe is primarily associated with stock photography rather than AI-driven image generation.
Q 4. BlueWillow is an Image Design Tool specialized in graphic design and visual arts.
Q 5. Bria is an Image Design Tool focused on AI-driven image generation rather than traditional graphic design.
Q 6. Stockimg is specifically designed for image editing and manipulation.
Q 7. DALL.E 2 utilizes advanced algorithms for creating realistic images based on textual prompts.
Q 8. BlueWillow integrates features for stock photography within its image design capabilities.
Q 9. Midjourney employs machine learning techniques for image editing and manipulation.
Q 10. Stockimg primarily focuses on providing a diverse collection of stock photography.

Exercise 3 – Fill in the blanks

Q 1. Midjourney is an image design tool that specializes in ___________ and visual storytelling.
Q 2. DALL.E 2 is known for its advanced capabilities in ___________ generation using artificial intelligence.
Q 3. NightCafe is an image design tool that focuses on creating visually appealing ___________.
Q 4. BlueWillow is recognized for its features in ___________ and manipulating visual elements in images.
Q 5. Stockimg is a tool designed for easily finding and utilizing ___________ in image design projects.

Exercise 4 – Match case

1. Match the image design tool specializing in illustration and visual storytelling	A. Bria
2. Connect the image design tool known for advanced image generation using artificial intelligence	B. BlueWillow
3. Pair the image design tool focusing on creating visually appealing artwork	C. NightCafe
4. Match the tool recognized for its features in editing and manipulating visual elements in images	D. DALL.E 2
5. Connect the image design tool catering to the needs of graphic creators with its creative features	E. Midjourney

Exercise 5 – One word answer

Q 1. Midjourney?
Q 2. DALL.E 2?

Q 3. NightCafe?
Q 4. BlueWillow?
Q 5. Bria?

Exercise 6 – Small answer
Q 1. What is the primary focus of Midjourney in image design?
Q 2. How does DALL.E 2 contribute to image design, and what does it specialize in generating?
Q 3. What is the main emphasis of NightCafe in the realm of image design?
Q 4. What features does BlueWillow offer for image design, particularly in terms of visual elements?
Q 5. How does Bria cater to image design, and who are its primary users?

Exercise 7 – Long answer
Q 1. How does Midjourney contribute to the field of image design, and what specific aspects of visual creation and storytelling does it specialize in, making it a distinctive tool for illustrators and designers?
Q 2. In what ways does NightCafe focus on image design, and what artistic elements does it emphasize to create visually appealing artwork, making it a valuable tool for artists and designers?

Answers

Exercise 1 – MCQ
Ans: 1 D, 2 B, 3 C, 4 A, 5 B, 6 C, 7 A, 8 C, 9 D, 10 D
Exercise 2 – True/ False
Ans: 1 False, 2 True, 3 False, 4 True, 5 False, 6 False, 7 True, 8 False, 9 False, 10 True
Exercise 3 – Fill in the blanks
Ans: 1 Illustration, 2 Image, 3 Artwork, 4 Editing, 5 Stock photos
Exercise 4 – Match case
Ans: 1 E, 2 D, 3 C, 4 B, 5 A
Exercise 5 – One word answer
Ans: 1 Illustration, 2 Generation, 3 Artwork, 4 Editing, 5 Graphic

Online Resources

Online test form is available here:
Practice Paper
Link: https://forms.office.com/r/RcdLKgWwdA

QR Code:

Link: https://www.youtube.com/playlist?list=PLzlh_31VWEFrapCfywmMKzhPPvZlnoEf5

QR Code:

Chapter 9: Video Tools

9.1 Fliki

Fliki.ai is a web-based platform that utilizes artificial intelligence (AI) technology to convert text into lifelike speech and video. It offers a user-friendly interface and a range of features to create engaging and professional videos for various purposes such as YouTube, social media, marketing, education, and more.
Fliki.ai allows users to customize their videos by choosing themes, voices, and adjusting parameters like speed, pitch, and emotion. It also provides the option to add personalized media, music, subtitles, transitions, and effects. The platform offers high-quality AI voices, voice cloning, podcast, and ebook creation features, making it a versatile tool for content creators.
Fliki.ai offers a range of features that make it a powerful and versatile platform for AI video generation. Here are some key features of Fliki.ai:

1. **Text-to-Video Conversion:** Fliki.ai uses advanced AI technology to convert text into lifelike speech and video. It allows you to transform your written content into engaging and professional videos effortlessly.
2. **Customizable Video Content**: Fliki.ai gives you full control over your video content. You can customize various aspects of your videos such as background, font, color, size, position, and animation of the text. This enables you to create videos that align with your brand or specific requirements.
3. **Extensive AI Voice Library:** Fliki.ai offers an extensive library of AI voices. With over 850 AI voices available in more than 50 languages and accents, you can choose the perfect voice to bring your text to life. You can also adjust the speed, pitch, and emotion of the voice to suit your needs.
4. **Voice Cloning:** Fliki.ai allows you to clone any voice from an audio sample. This feature enables you to create videos with your own voice or replicate the voice of a celebrity or influencer, adding a personalized touch to your content.
5. **Media and Effects Library:** Fliki.ai provides a media library with a wide selection of images and videos to enhance your videos. You can also add your own media, music, subtitles, transitions, and effects to make your videos more dynamic and engaging.
6. **Podcast and Ebook Creation:** In addition to video generation, Fliki.ai supports the creation of podcasts and ebooks. You can export your audio as MP3 or WAV files for podcasting purposes, or generate an ebook in PDF format, expanding the reach of your content.

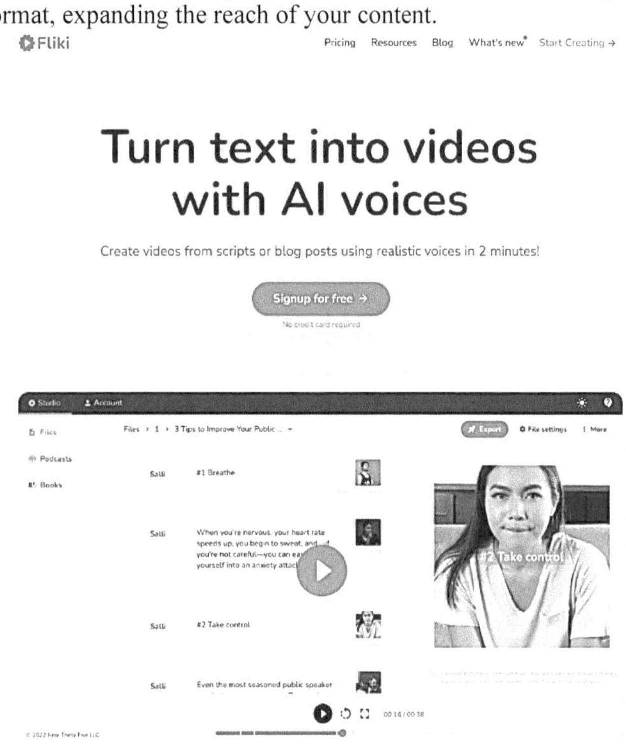

Here step by step guide explanation:

Step 1 - Record your steps
Use any screen recording tool to record the steps in your demo.
If you are using MacOS, we recommend using the built-in QuickTime screen recorder. This can be activated by pressing Command + Shift + 5 key.
Make sure to record each step as a separate clip; this will help you easily update your video in the future.
You will not have to re-record the entire video if any step changes.
It's recommended to keep each step small, about 10-15 seconds long.

Step 2 - Create a video file
Once you have all the video snippets ready, head over to Fliki.
Select "**+New file**", enter the file name, choose Video type, and hit "**Create**".

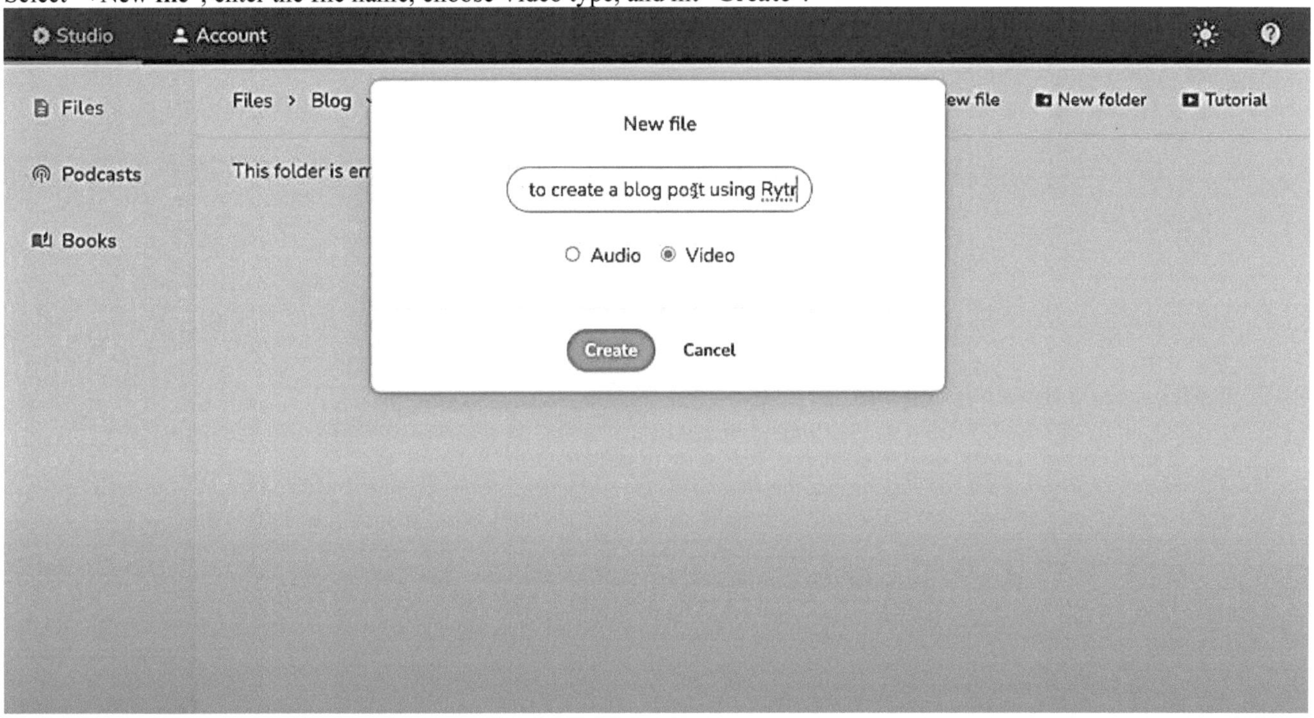

Step 3 - Upload recorded media
Click on the thumbnail icon in the section to bring up the Media selection menu, and select the "**My Library**" tab and hit "**Choose File**", select your recorded files one by one and add them to the library.
Once in the library, you can assign each clip/step in a different scene/section.

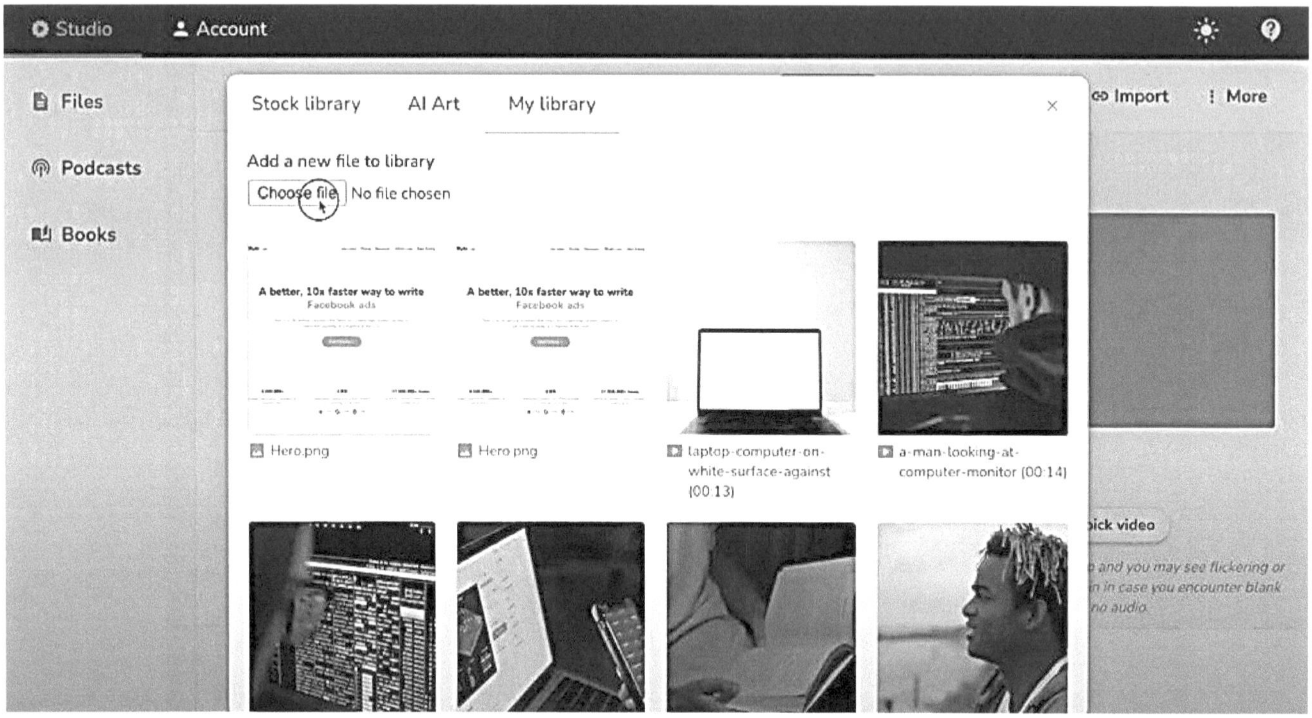

Step 4 - Add script and customize
Once all the scenes have been created, you can add the voiceover script describing the step in each scene.
Click on the voice name on the left part of the scene to change the voice.
You can change the video size, disable the transition, and customize the subtitle by clicking on "**Video settings**",
Select "**More**" and choose "**Background music**" to search for or upload a music to go along with your presentation.

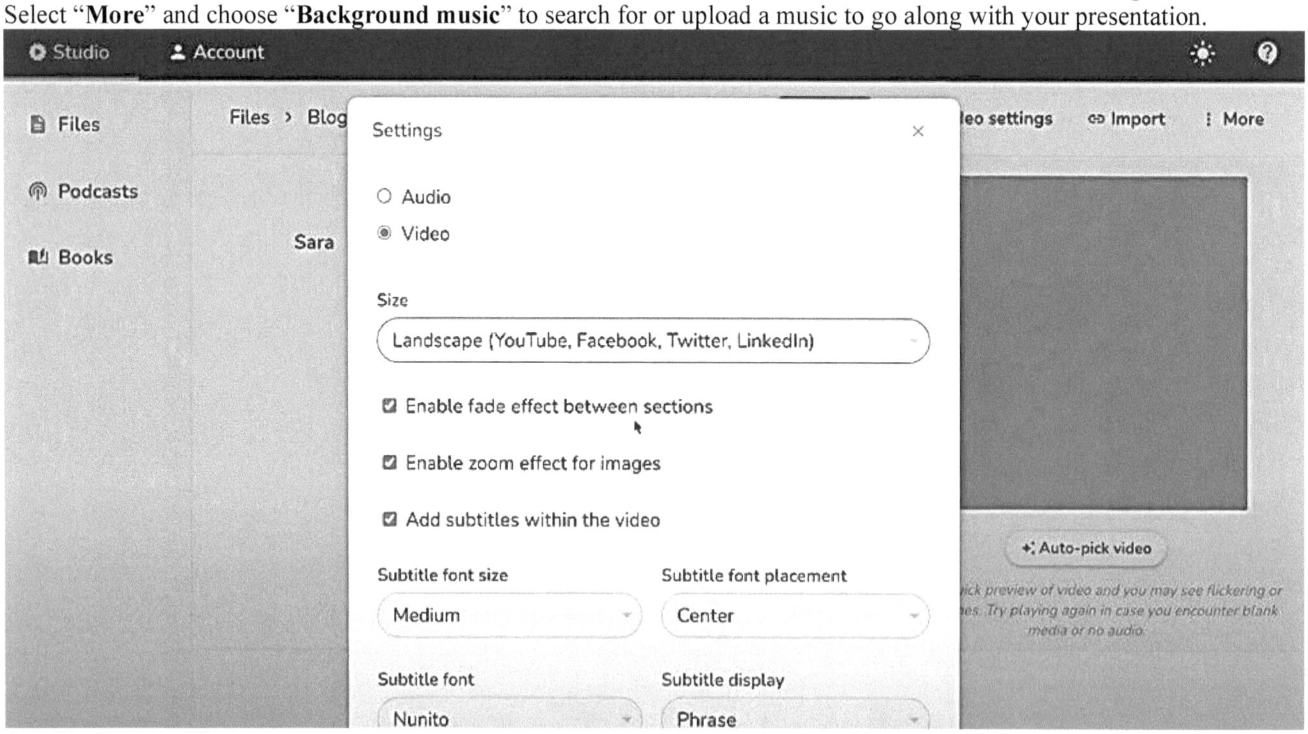

Step 5 - Preview & Export
Finally, you can preview the video and hit **"Export"** to process and download the video.

9.2 Lumen5

Lumen5 is an exceptional AI-driven video creation platform, simplifying the complex process of converting text into engaging visual content. Its user-friendly drag-and-drop interface and automatic text transformation capabilities make video creation a breeze, saving precious time and effort.
Lumen5 comes with a vast library of music, images, and themes, allowing users to craft unique, attention-grabbing content. Its variety of video formats caters to different platforms, offering the flexibility businesses need in the digital age.
Brand consistency is vital, and Lumen5 AI knows this. They include a branding kit feature that lets businesses easily incorporate their logos, colors, and fonts into videos. Plus, with the instant video creation feature, you can quickly turn written content into professional-grade videos, ensuring clear communication and high viewer engagement.

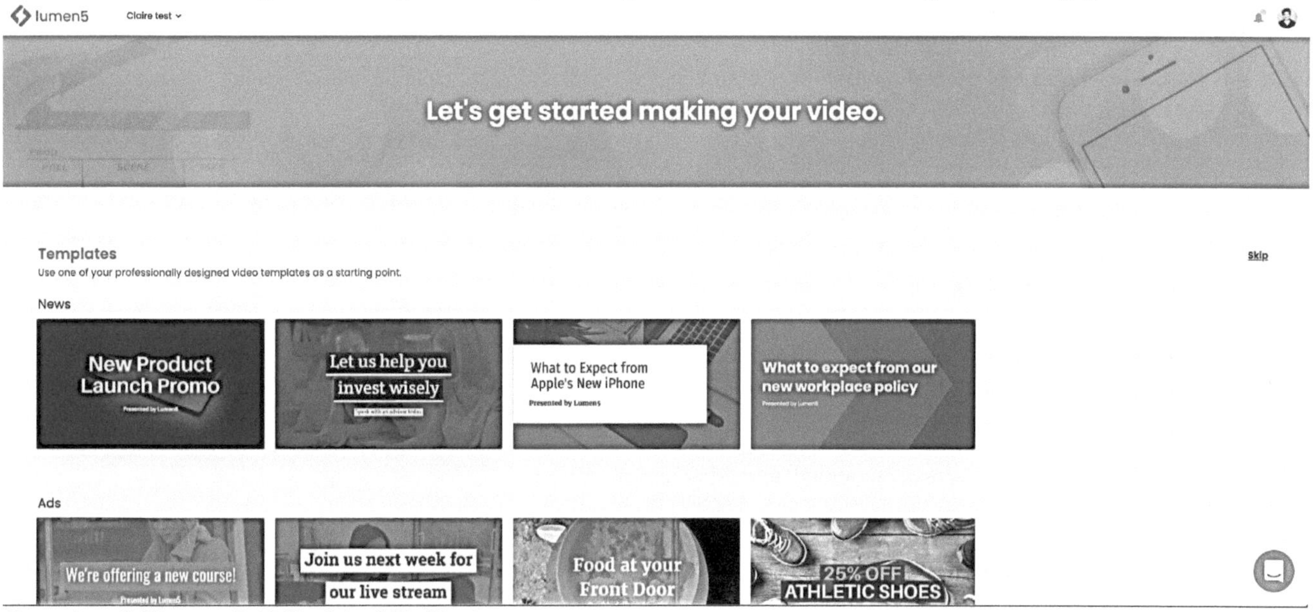

Overview Of Lumen5 AI Tool And Its Features

Lumen5 is an AI-powered video creation platform that allows users to convert text into engaging videos with its intuitive drag-and-drop interface.

Video Creation From Text

Lumen5's innovative approach to video creation from text sets it apart in AI-powered tools. You simply input your blog post, article, or script into the platform, and the artificial intelligence gets to work, analyzing your content and identifying key points.
It then uses these nuggets of information to draft a storyboard for your video. More than just a basic transformation tool, Lumen5 creates engaging visual narratives that capture the essence of your written words.
This unique feature allows brands and businesses to repurpose their existing content and reach wider audiences with compelling video formats. Dynamic online video creation has never been so efficient and convenient!

AI-based Workflow

Lumen5 is a top-tier content conversion tool mainly due to its revolutionary AI-based workflow. This feature simplifies video creation by automatically transforming written content into dynamic videos.
Imagine turning your blog posts into engaging clips within minutes – that's the streamlined efficiency Lumen5 offers. The platform leverages intelligent algorithms to pick key points from your text and match them with relevant visuals from an extensive image and video library. It's like having your own AI-powered video editing software that intuitively understands your brand language, saving you time while maintaining quality output.
The result? Quick, custom-made business video production right at your fingertips!

Extensive Library Of Music, Images, And Themes

Lumen5's feature-packed platform boasts an extensive library of music, images, and themes that can be used to enhance any video content.
1. A comprehensive library of audio, visuals, and design elements: This vast collection helps create engaging videos that resonate with your target audience. With a diverse mix of soundtracks and visually appealing themes, you're guaranteed to find something to suit every type of video content.

2. Abundant resources of soundtracks, visuals, and artistic designs: Marketers can use these options to create captivating social media posts or explainer videos.
3. A wide array of soundtracks, visuals, and artistic templates: These resources are perfect for businesses looking to save on production costs without sacrificing quality or appeal.
4. The varied assortment of music, images, and visually appealing themes: This robust library allows users to craft unique videos in 10-15 minutes—a time-efficient solution for busy content creators.
5. Extensive range of music, visuals, and customizable templates: With the added bonus of customizing these elements according to brand guidelines, this library ensures consistency throughout all video content produced on the platform.
6. Vast selection of music, images, and design options: Regardless of the project or desired aesthetic, Lumen5 has a wealth of resources at your disposal.
7. The extensive repertoire of audio, visuals, and design choices: Creatives will find endless inspiration in Lumen5's broad collection.
8. Diverse options of audio, visuals, and creative themes: Use these plentiful assets for everything from storyboard creation to generating engaging ads.
9. Ample variety of music, images, and customizable visual elements: Whatever your business needs—ad generation or social media post creation—this library provides ample choice for all users.

Multiple Video Formats

Lumen5 offers various video formats to cater to different needs and preferences. Whether you're looking to create square videos for social media, landscape videos for YouTube, or vertical videos for mobile devices, Lumen5 has got you covered.

With its versatile platform, users can easily customize their videos to fit various platforms and engage their target audience effectively. So whether it's Instagram stories, Facebook ads, or YouTube tutorials, Lumen5 provides the flexibility needed to create captivating content in the right format.

Branding Kit

Lumen5's branding kit is a powerful feature that allows businesses to maintain brand consistency in their videos. With customizable designs, users can easily add logos, colors, and fonts to create professional-looking videos that align with their brand identity.

This ensures that every video created with Lumen5 reflects the unique style and personality of the business. Whether you're creating social media posts or marketing videos, the branding kit feature is a valuable tool for marketers who want to make a lasting impression on their audience.

Instant Video Creation

Lumen5's instant video creation feature allows users to transform written content into engaging videos in minutes. With just a few clicks, you can convert blog posts, articles, or text-based content into visually appealing videos that captivate your audience.

The AI-powered platform utilizes automation technology to analyze the text, identify key points and relevant visuals, and then seamlessly generate a professional-looking video. This saves both time and effort compared to traditional video production methods.

A high-quality video effectively communicates your message and keeps viewers engaged from start to finish.

Use Cases Of Lumen5 AI Tool

THE Lumen5 AI tool can be used for content creation on social media, explainer videos, generating ads, video marketing, storyboarding, and video editing.

1. Content Creation For Social Media

Lumen5 is the perfect tool for easy and effective content creation for social media. With its AI-powered video creation platform, you can convert your blog posts and Zoom recordings into captivating videos that will engage your audience. The intuitive drag-and-drop interface allows you to customize designs, ensuring brand consistency and appeal. Lumen5's extensive library of music, images, and themes gives you plenty of options to create engaging content that stands out on social media platforms.

Whether you're a marketer looking to promote your brand or a business owner wanting to share valuable information with your followers, Lumen5 has covered you when creating high-quality videos for social media posts.

2. Creating Explainer Videos

Lumen5 AI Tool provides an excellent platform for creating explainer videos. With its drag-and-drop interface and AI-powered automation, users can easily transform their written content into engaging videos that simplify complex topics.

The extensive resource library of images, video footage, and music enhances the visual appeal of these explainer videos, making them more captivating for the audience. Whether you want to educate your customers about your products or services or provide step-by-step tutorials, Lumen5 offers advanced features that enable you to create professional-looking explainer videos effortlessly.

3. Generating Ads

Lumen5's AI Tool is an excellent solution for generating ads that capture attention and drive conversions. With its powerful video creation capabilities, marketers can transform text-based content into engaging videos perfect for advertising campaigns.

By utilizing Lumen5's intuitive drag-and-drop interface and customizable designs, businesses can create visually stunning ads that align with their brand identity and resonate with their target audience.

The platform's AI automation also allows marketers to efficiently convert blog posts into videos or Zoom recordings into captivating clips, making it easier than ever to produce high-quality ad content.

Whether for social media platforms or other marketing channels, Lumen5 provides the tools to create impactful ads that grab viewers' attention and boost engagement.

4. Video Marketing

Lumen5 AI Tool is a game-changer for video marketing. With its AI-powered automation, creating compelling videos for your brand has never been easier. By converting blog posts and Zoom recordings into engaging clips, Lumen5 helps you repurpose existing content to attract and engage a wider audience.

The intuitive drag-and-drop interface makes the video creation process user-friendly, even for beginners. Plus, with access to an extensive resource library of images, video footage, and music, you can enhance your video content and make it more visually appealing.

Whether you're looking to promote your business on social media or create eye-catching ads, Lumen5 has covered all aspects of video marketing.

5. Storyboarding

Storyboarding is one of the key use cases of the Lumen5 AI tool, allowing users to visually plan out their videos and ensure a smooth flow of content. With Lumen5's drag-and-drop video editor, you can easily arrange your images, text, and video clips logically.

This feature enables you to create an organized visual narrative that captivates your audience from start to finish. Whether creating a promotional video or an educational clip, storyboarding with Lumen5 helps you bring your ideas to life with precision and creativity.

6. Video Editing

Video editing is a crucial aspect of Lumen5's AI-powered video creation platform. With its intuitive drag-and-drop interface and AI automation, users can easily edit their videos to perfection.

Whether trimming, cropping, or adding transitions, Lumen5 provides all the tools for effective video editing. The platform also offers a resource library filled with images, video footage, and music that users can use to enhance their video content.

So whether you're an experienced videographer or a beginner looking to create professional-looking videos, Lumen5's video editing capabilities have covered you. Start creating stunning videos today with ease and efficiency using Lumen5.

How To Use Lumen5

Creating compelling videos for your business can be a time-consuming and expensive endeavor. But what if there was a way to create stunning videos in just minutes, without any technical skills or a huge budget? Enter Lumen5, the ultimate video creation tool. In this blog post, we'll take a deep dive into Lumen5 – an AI Video Generator and show you step-by-step how to use Lumen5 to create professional videos that will captivate your audience

How To Use Lumen5:

Choose a Format

When you select Create Video, you'll be offered the choice of using a social media format or a custom format. You may also skip this step.

Remember that you may alter it at any moment. The following alternatives are available: Facebook, Instagram, Twitter, Snapchat, YouTube, LinkedIn, and Pinterest. Custom (Landscape, Square, Vertical, and Letterbox).

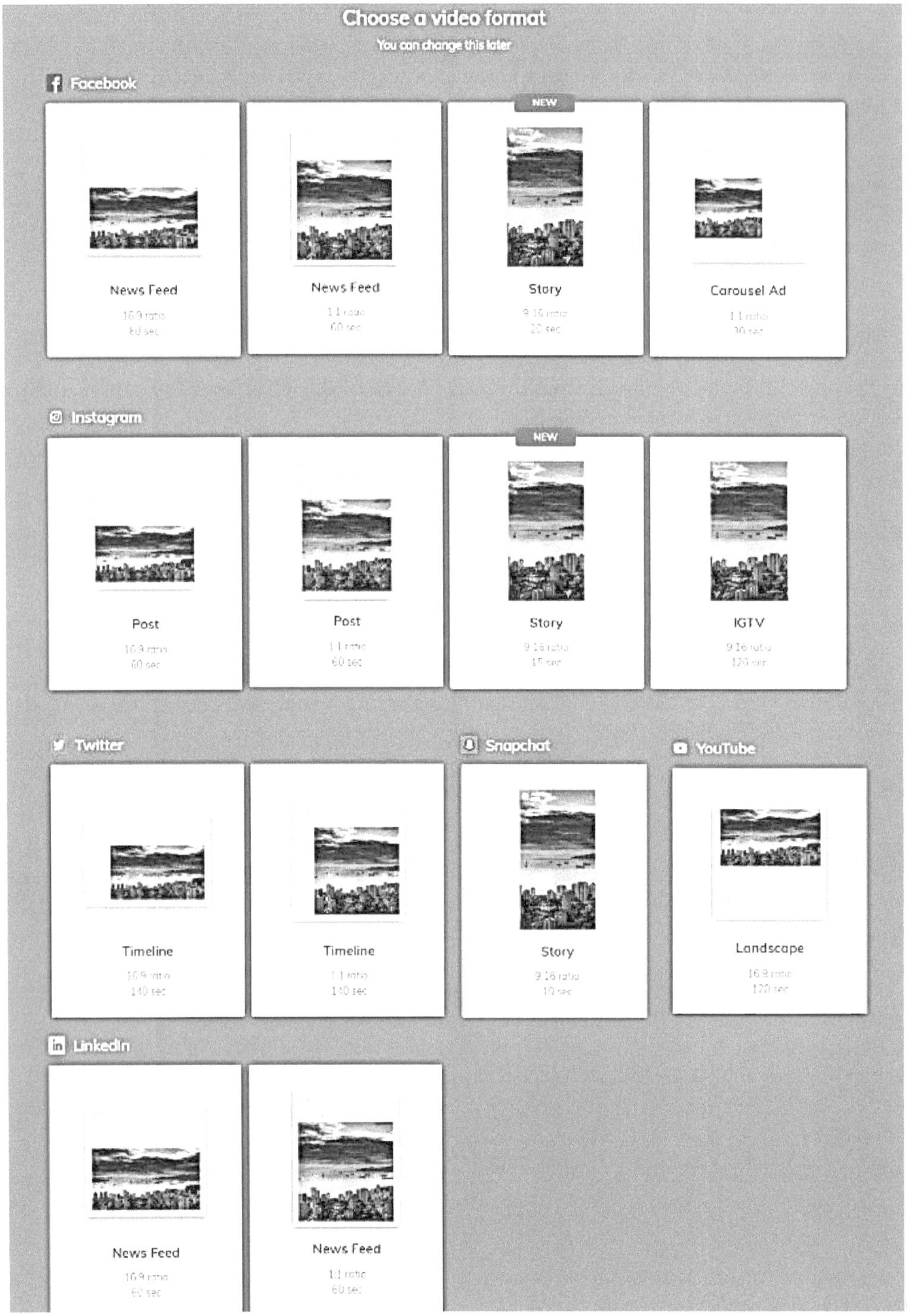

Choose a Format

Choose a Theme

After Lumen5 login, you'll be sent to the video creation page. This is your starting place. Choose the design that best fits your video concept.

Choose a Theme

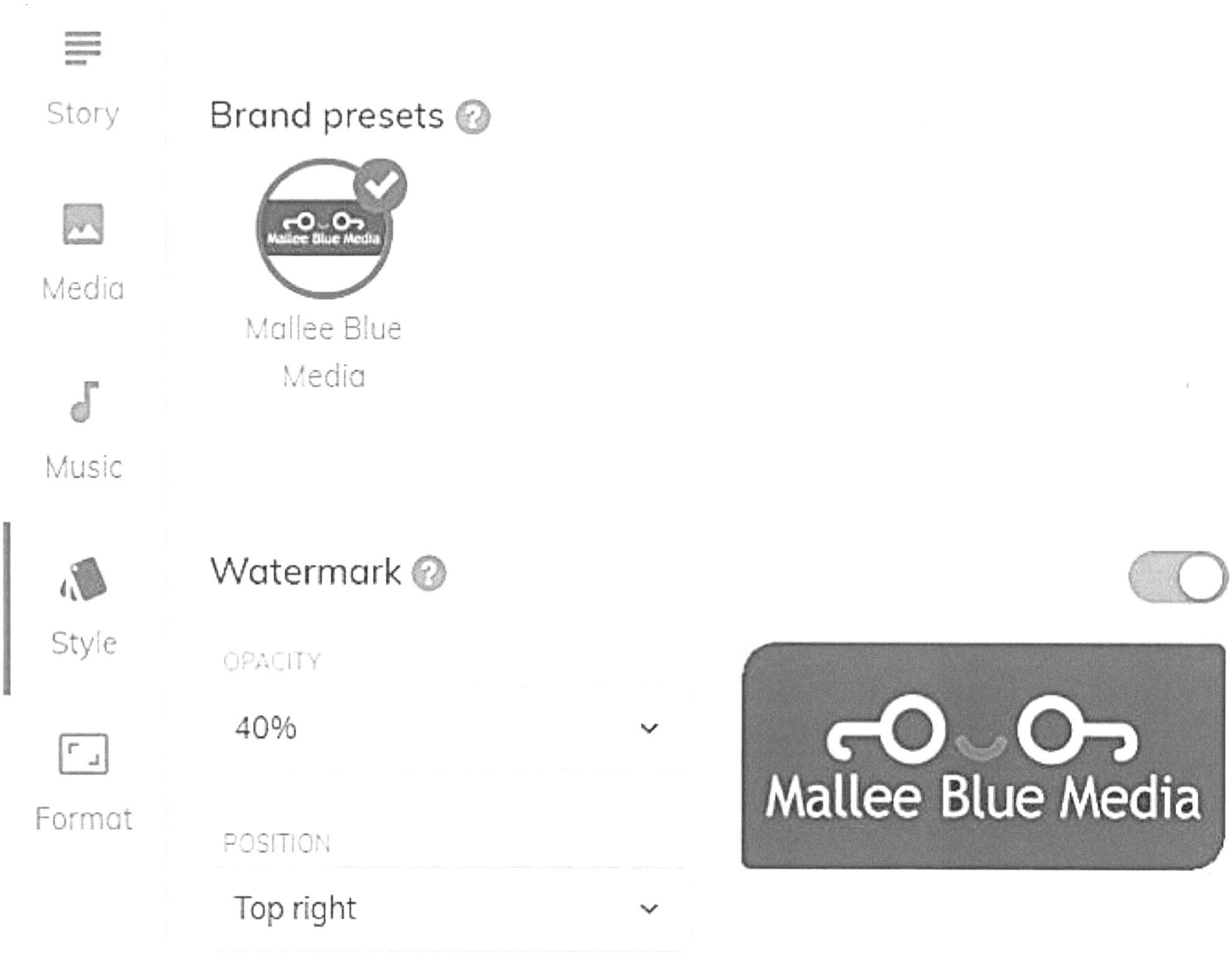

Add Your Logo

By toggling the button next to Watermark, you can select whether or not to incorporate your logo. When it's green, your uploaded logo will be shown in your film.

You may also change the opacity and location of your logo. To view your choices, click the drop-down menu next to each and choose one.

Choose Your Colors

You may match the text and background colors to your brand identification by using the Style menu option. By clicking the Change theme button, you may change the theme.

Click the drop-down button next to each choice to pick the color you want to use for the text, subtitle, highlighted region, and accent color. Use the same steps to choose your chosen font or upload your own.

How To Convert Text To Video

How to turn blog posts into videos with Lumen5! To begin the video making process, you have a few alternatives to pick from. You have two options:

1. Import material from an existing URL, such as a blog post or news item, into the program.
2. Copy and paste your written text into the left-hand Story Tab.
3. Your work will be shown in the Story Tab on the left side of the screen. Feel free to alter this and eliminate any unnecessary stuff from your video.

When you click the "Convert to Video" button, Lumen5 creates a stable foundation for you to build your video on. You just need to storyboard and modify the material.

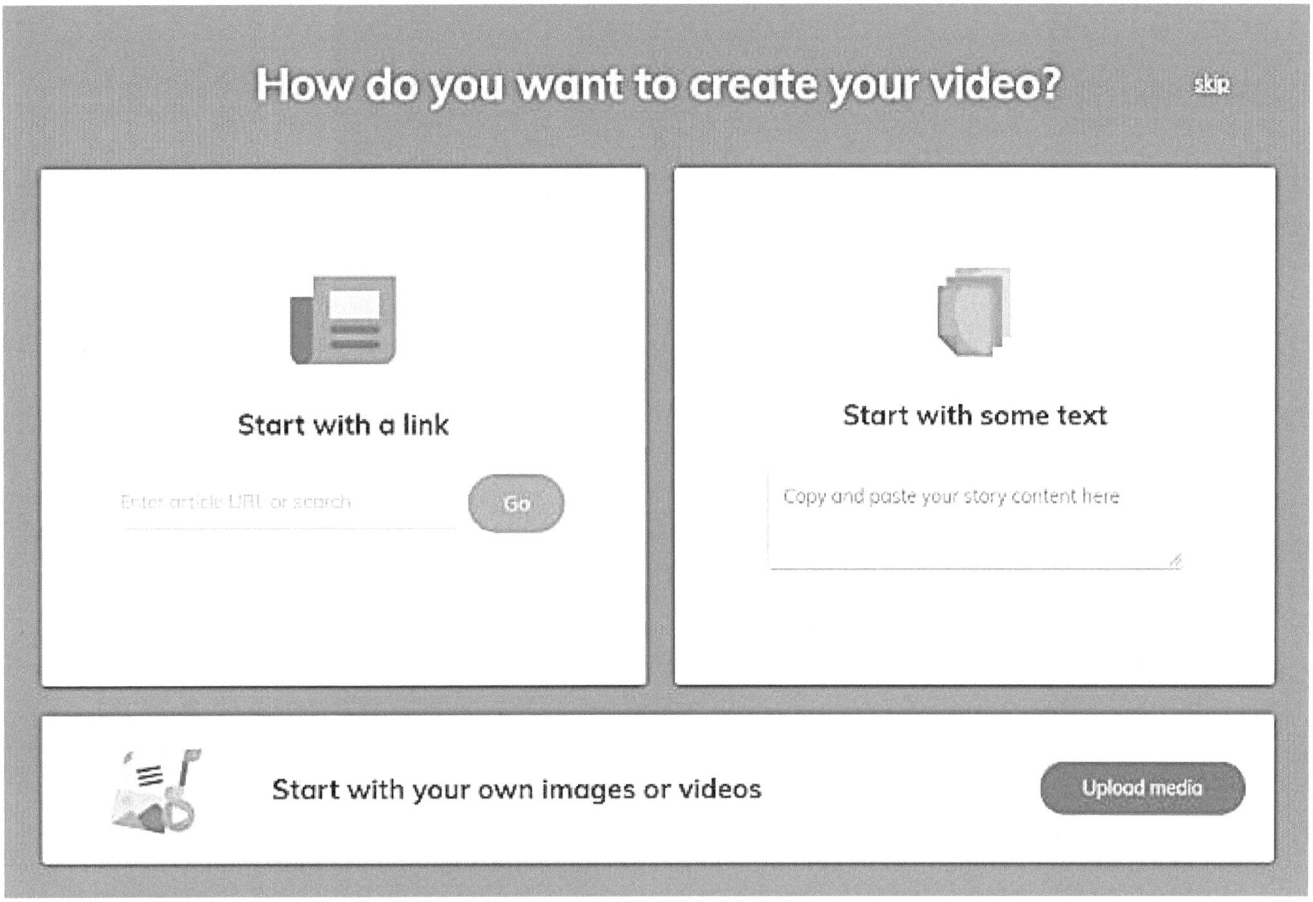

Convert Your Existing Content

How To Use Lumen5: Customize Your Storyboard
Best features of Lumen5 text to video free. When you enter a URL or paste anything into the text field, a foundation for your video is instantly constructed. The text will show on the left side of the screen on your editing dashboard. The storyboard will show on the right side of the screen.
Lumen5 utilizes artificial intelligence (AI) to handpick phrases (see highlighted text) and pictures for you when you input a URL. You may either retain their recommendations or clean the board.

Your Storyboard

You may still make changes if you want to accept the AI recommendations. As an example, suppose you wish to include the opening paragraph. When you click on it, it will be added to the storyboard.

If your text is too lengthy, the system will construct a sub-scene (an extra slide with the same picture or video). If you opt to ignore the AI recommendations, the method remains the same.

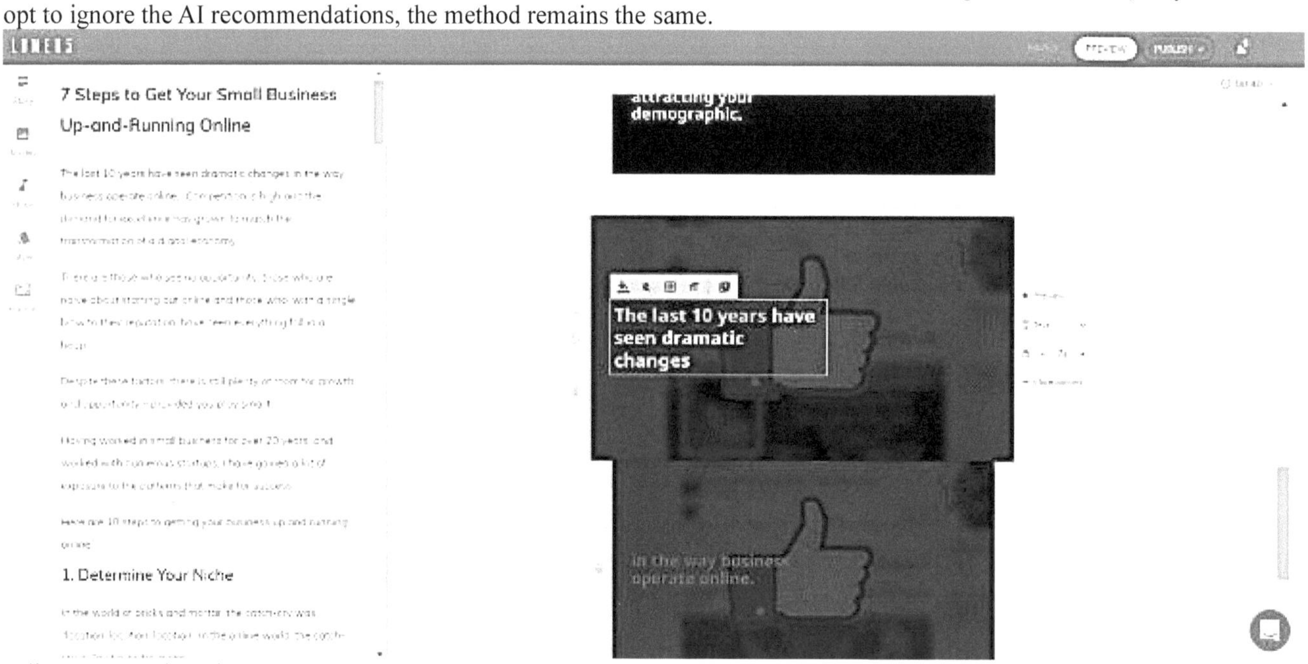

Edit your Storyboard

Edit Text

Click within the box to update your storyboard wording. Edit, add, or remove text. AI calculates Lumen5:

1. Text placement.
2. Slide length.
3. Highlighting text.

You may ignore the advice and alter anything. Rendering will animate the media backdrop. Click Preview to preview slide animations.

Edit Text

You have the option of selecting the kind of text (if any). You have the following options:

1. Title.
2. Simple text.
3. Quote.
4. There is no text.

If you want your text to be Title text, for example, click Title and it will change.

Change The Position Of The Text

If you click inside the slide near the text, it will open some more editing features, including Text position. This is the function you want to use.

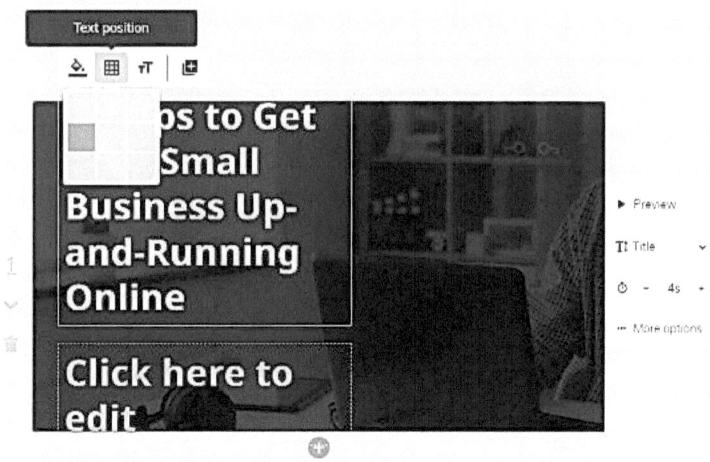

Change The Position Of The Text

If you center the text, it will not cut off a word. It does still however cut off the hyphenated words. It's better than before, but still not ideal.

Choose Your Media

You have complete control over each slide, including selecting a backdrop from the media library or uploading your own (maximum file size is 15MB). To search, choose material from the left-side menu and select material from the Library, GIFs, and Uploads.

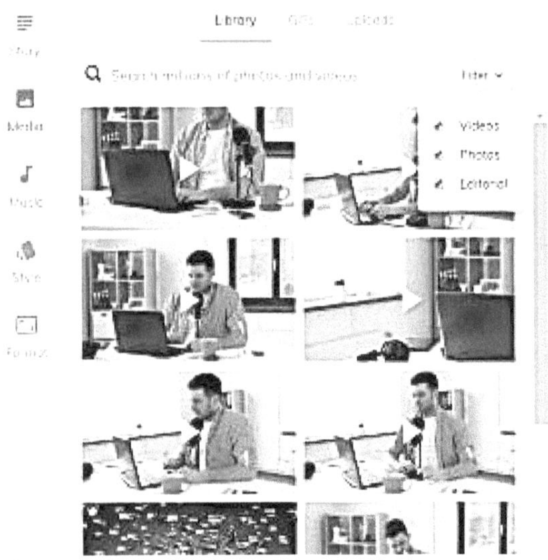

Choose Your Media

Also, there is a filter that enables you to pick between Videos, Photos, and Editorial. When you've found a media file you want to utilize in your storyboard, drag it from the media area to the slide where you want it to appear.

More Editing Options

Although Lumen5 allocates the amount of time each slide plays automatically, you may adjust it. Look for the time indicator and modify the length of the slide by clicking the plus or negative sign.

Length of time each slide plays

Trim a Video Or Change The Layout

As seen in the picture below, choose More choices. A pop-up window will appear, allowing you to adjust the layout or the brightness level. Trim from the same pop-up window allows you to change the length of a video backdrop.

Trim a Video

Add Or Delete a Scene Or Subscene

In the picture below, notice the green bar at the bottom of the slide. When you click the + symbol, you will be able to create a scene or a sub-scene. The down arrow on the slide's left side will shift the slide down in your storyboard. Because this is the initial slide, there is simply a down arrow.

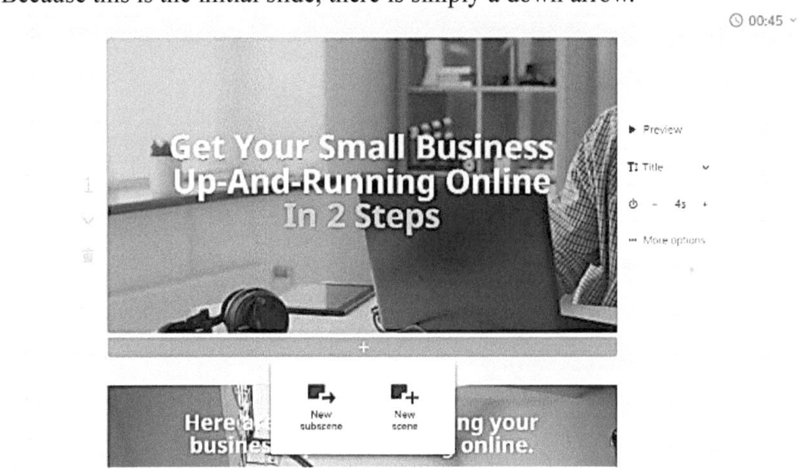

Add Or Delete a Scene Or Subscene

Other slides will feature an up and down arrow to help you move the slide to the desired location. The trash can symbol is precisely what it seems to be. Click it to remove any slides from your video that you don't want to appear.

How To Use Lumen5: Add Music

Lumen5 provides access to a collection of royalty-free audio recordings. You may also submit your own. Choose Music from the left-hand navigation menu. You'll notice that you can arrange the library by mood, making it simpler to locate a music that fits the vibe of your film.

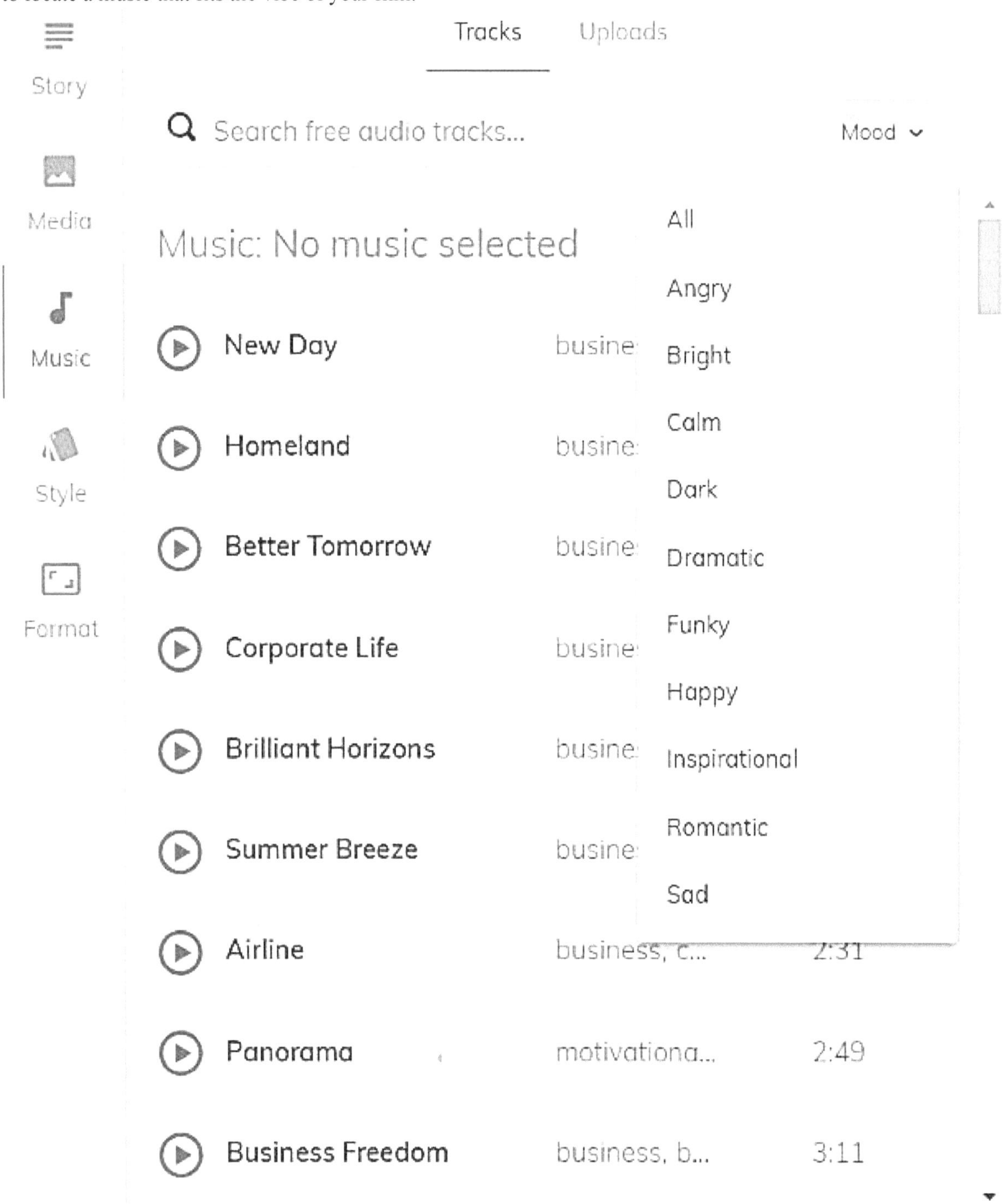

Add Music

Click the Play icon on the left to listen to a track. When you've found (or uploaded) the music you want, click on it to add it to the video. Leave that box blank if you do not wish to incorporate music.

Preview & Publish Your Video

Preview the video after all your slides are ready. You may then modify or publish your video. Your storyboard's upper right corner shows the video's duration. You may choose Fast or Slow from the drop-down next to the time. Normal defaults.

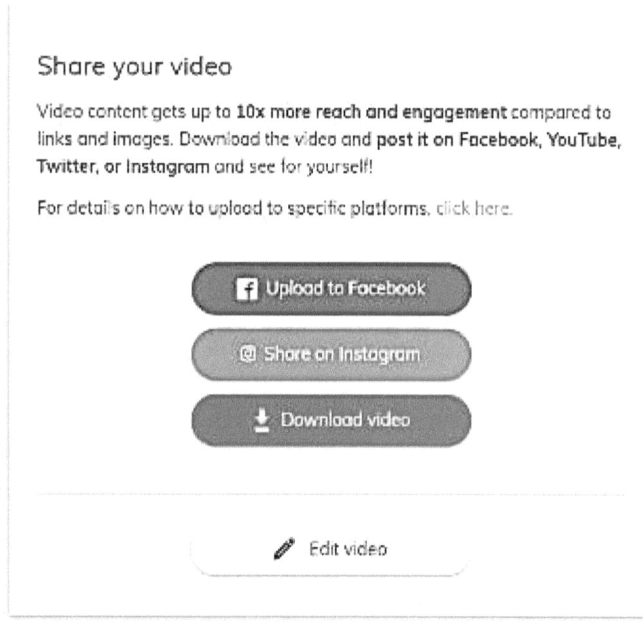

Preview & Publish Your Video
Lumen5 works best when you press Publish. Your video renders in minutes. Finishing will trigger an email. Click your finished video on your dashboard. Upload it to Facebook, Instagram, your PC, or modify it.

9.3 Synthesia

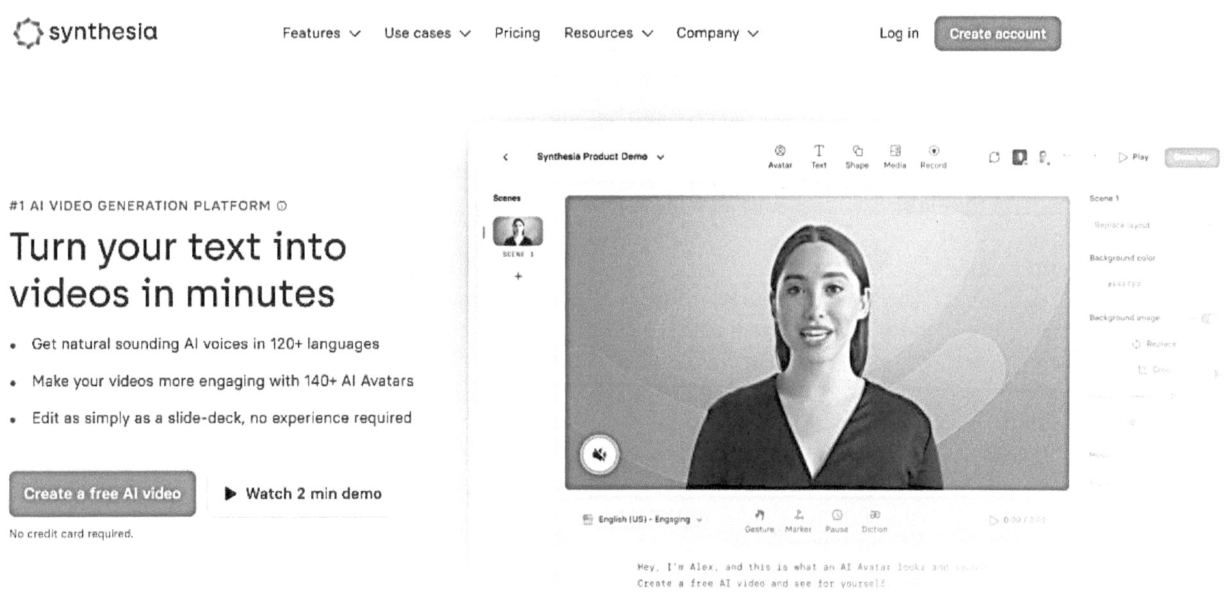

Synthesia AI, founded in 2017 by Victor Riparbelli and a group of AI researchers and entrepreneurs from prestigious institutions, enables individuals to create professional-quality video content without needing cameras, microphones, or studios.

Synthesia combines generative AI, voiceover, and editing to create high-quality training videos. It offers a range of features, like AI avatars and voices, text-to-speech, and an AI script assistant to streamline the video creation process. You can also customize an AI avatar to look and sound like you and access a vast library of over 65 professional video templates.

Its ability to quickly generate AI avatar videos sets Synthesia apart from traditional video creation methods. With over 150 AI avatars to choose from speaking over 120 languages, content creators can customize their videos to match their branding and messaging.

Who is Synthesia Best For?

Anyone interested in AI video generation should use Synthesia, but there are a few specific types of people who would benefit the most:

1. Educators looking for efficient video content creation tools, particularly for instructional videos, tutorials, or e-learning content.
2. Content creators and social media YouTube influencers looking to leverage artificial intelligence for video content production, enhancing their video creation workflow and increasing their content output.
3. Businesses aiming to enhance their video content strategy and webinars, utilizing AI video generation to produce engaging, professional, and visually appealing content.
4. Individuals and organizations interested in avatar-based video creation, personalizing video content, and adding a human touch to their messaging or branding.
5. Professionals, content creators, and businesses seeking innovative AI video production tools, streamlining video editing, voiceover, and video creation processes.
6. Marketers who want to create compelling how-to and product videos that stand out from the competition and resonate with their target audience.
7. Customer service teams who want to provide personalized and visually appealing product releases and how-to videos for their customers.
8. Bloggers looking to compliment their written articles with engaging videos and lower website bounce rates.
9. Sales rep trainers looking to create interactive and engaging training videos for their sales team.

Synthesia Key Features

I will start things off by going over all of Synthesia's standout features for producing professional and engaging video content with AI.

AI Avatars & Voices

1. AI Avatars: Select from a wide range of over 150 AI Avatars with various ethnic backgrounds.
2. 120+ Languages & Accents: Produce videos in over 120 languages, including various accents and voice tones.
3. Text-to-Speech: Type your text to transform it into high-quality voiceovers in minutes.
4. Custom AI Avatars: Design a personalized AI Avatar.
5. Gestures: Add nuanced gestures to your AI avatars, such as a nodding head or raised eyebrows.
6. Voice Cloning: Create an identical copy of your voice and combine it with a customized AI Avatar.

Media & Integrations

1. AI Script Assistant: Generate video scripts effortlessly using prompts similar to ChatGPT.
2. Screen Recorder: Capture videos of your screen using the integrated screen recording feature.
3. Media Library: Get unlimited access to a vast collection of copyright-free images, videos, icons, shapes, and other resources.
4. Music Library: Access a vast selection of royalty-free soundtracks for your video.
5. Upload Soundtrack: Add your own music or soundtrack to your video.
6. Upload Font: Upload your own font family to maintain brand consistency.
7. Auto-Generated Closed Captions: Make your videos more accessible by automatically including closed captions.
8. Import PowerPoints: Import PowerPoint presentations and add expertly recorded voiceovers to take them to the next level!
9. Commenting: Receive feedback, add comments, and edit your videos in one place.
10. Preview Video: Before generating your video, preview it to ensure you like it.
11. 65+ Video Templates: Choose from over 65 expertly crafted video templates.
12. Upload Media Elements: Share your images, videos, infographics, and other files.

13. Add Animations: Animate elements in your video by using a marker.

haring & Exports
1. Video Embeds: Easily embed your videos and have them automatically updated with new versions.
2. MP4 Downloads: Download your videos in Full HD, with a resolution of 1920 x 1080.
3. Branded Share Page: To brand your Synthesia share page, upload your logo.
4. CTA on Share Page: Include a call-to-action button on your share page.

Security
1. SOC2 & GDPR Compliant: Synthesia systems and processes have undergone independent audits and certifications.
2. SAML/SSO: Get a fast and secure log-in for your entire company.
3. Content Moderation: To ensure the ethical use of Artificial Intelligence, Synthesia employs content moderation on videos produced using Synthesia.

Here's a step-by-step breakdown of how to make Synthesia videos.

Step 1: Write a video script
A good video script in an essential foundation for both AI videos and traditional videos. So before you log in to Synthesia, take the time to plan out what you want your video to say and show.
How you write your script will depend on a lot of factors, like:
Your audience and goal
The type of video you want to make
The visuals you want to include
We won't go into details on how to write a video script in this particular blog post, but we've covered the topic in depth here:
How to Write a Video Script (+5 Expert Tips)
A script can make all the difference in the end product. Here's our step-by-step guide to writing a video script.

Step 2: Choose a video template of start from scratch
One your video script is ready, it's finally time to log in to Synthesia.
In the dashboard, you have a few different ways to start making a video:
1. Click on 'New video' in the top right corner.Then, choose to either start a video form a blank slate or from one of the 55+ pre-designed video templates.

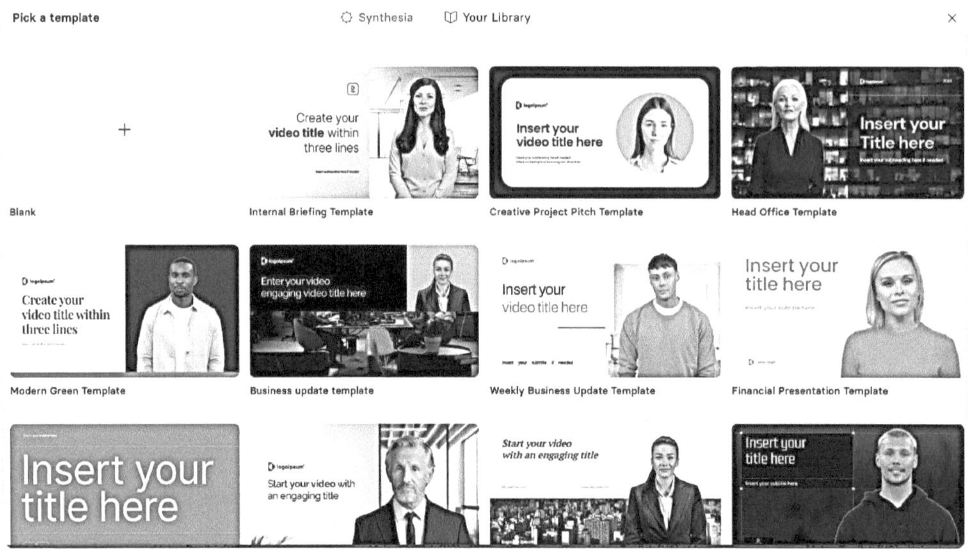

2. You can also go to 'Templates' on the left-hand side and start a video with a pre-designed video template.
3. Or, click on 'Import PowerPoint' to use your presentation slides as background in the video.

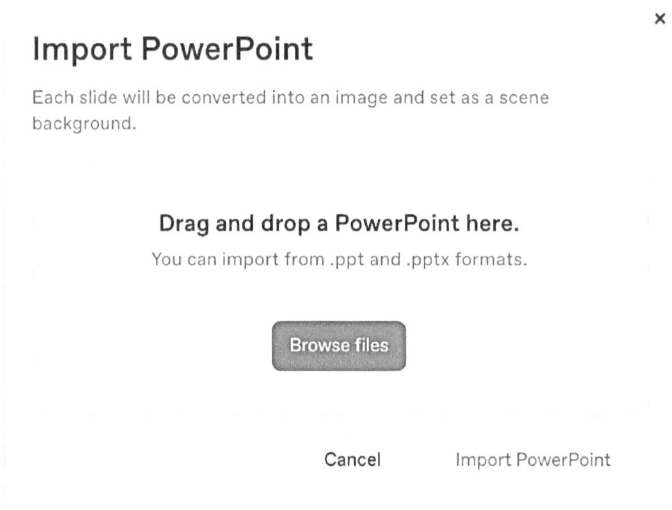

You can design your own video template and use that to create videos. This feature is particularly useful if you need your videos to look on-brand.

See how to do that in this guide:

How to Make Video Templates (2 Easy Ways)
With the help of templates, you can finally create more video content in less time — why not start today?
Learn more
If you're using a pre-designed template, you can add more scenes from the template by going clicking on + on the right-hand side of the video canvas.

There, you will see all the different video scenes that were designed to fit the template.

Choose as many scenes as needed.

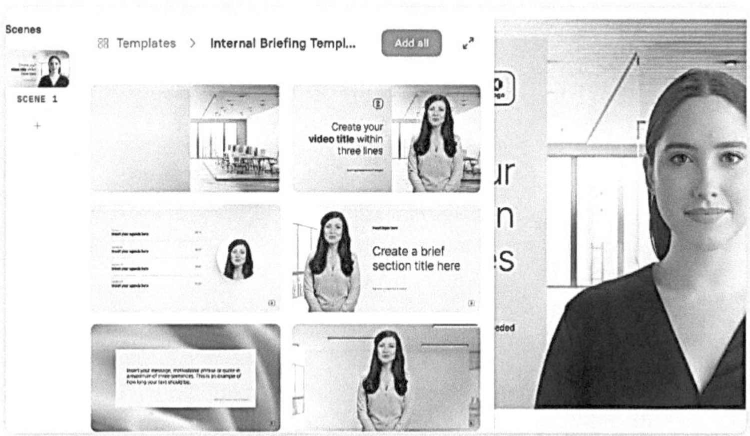

Step 3: Choose an AI avatar
Now it's time to choose which avatar(s) you want to use in your video.

To do that, simply click on 'Avatar' on top of the video canvas and choose one that will fit your video.

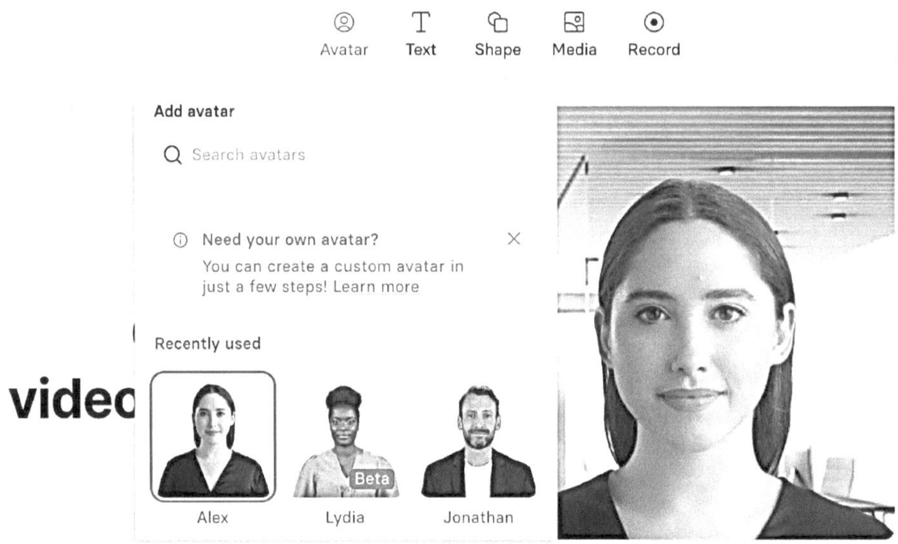

You will notice that most avatars come in multiple framings: waist-up and chest-up.
You can use the same avatar framing on all slides, or mix and match the framings in the different scenes to add visual interest to the video.
When you click on the avatar in the video canvas, an avatar layout window will pop up on the right-hand side.
In there, you can switch between displaying the full body avatar, a circle view, or no avatar (and only keep the voiceover).

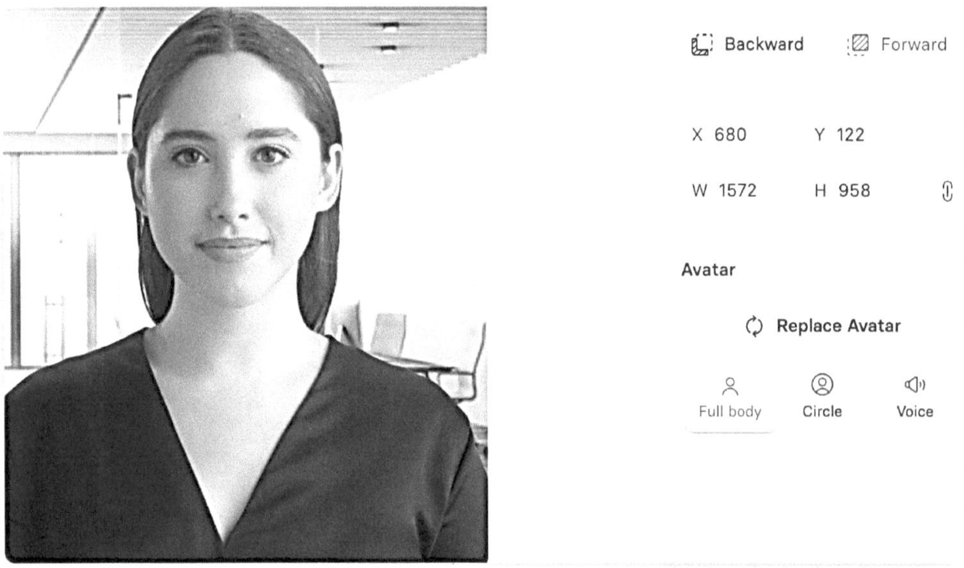

9.4 DeepBrain AI

DeepBrain Ai is an advanced artificial intelligence tool that revolutionizes video creation, allowing users to generate high-quality videos quickly and efficiently. The platform offers a user-friendly interface, powerful customization options, and cost-effective pricing plans, making it accessible to beginners and professionals.

Deepbrain.io versatile use cases include content creators and marketers, small and medium-sized businesses, e-commerce platforms, and social media influencers. The pros of using DeepBrain include timesaving and efficient video creation, high-quality professional results, versatile customization options tailored to specific needs, and affordable pricing plans.

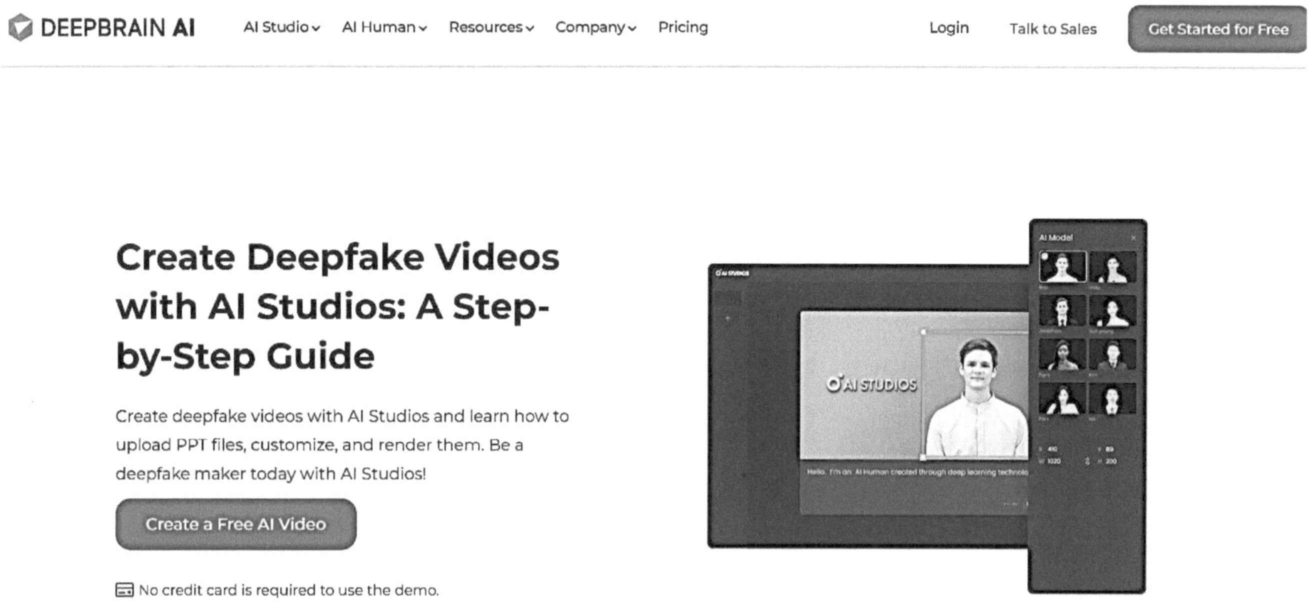

DeepBrain AI: Overview and Key Features

DeepBrain AI revolutionizes video creation with its advanced AI technology, offering a user-friendly interface, powerful customization options, and cost-effective pricing.

How DeepBrain AI video creation with AI works

- Thriving in the digital era requires compelling content that catches attention; this is where DeepBrain AI steps in. This cutting-edge platform uses artificial intelligence to revolutionize video creation, generating hyper-realistic AI Avatar videos from basic text inputs in as little as 5 minutes.
- With tools like text-to-speech conversion and a diverse library of lifelike avatars, content creation has never been handier or more efficient. Moreover, multilingual video production capabilities add another dimension of versatility to cater to global audiences.
- The customizable scenes ensure each output is unique and perfectly suits the user's needs. These features make video creation swift and bring professional results within reach for everyone – businesses, educators, tech enthusiasts or content creators- at an affordable price point.

Advanced video generation capabilities

- DeepBrain AI revolutionizes digital content creation with its advanced video generation capabilities. Touted as the number one AI video generator, this powerful tool utilizes cutting-edge technology to transform simple scripts into captivating videos in minutes.
- Its seamless video creation process is bolstered by AI-driven editing tools that foster efficiency and creativity.

- The platform's ultra-modern tech allows it to produce photorealistic AI avatars for use in videos, adding another layer of dynamism and realism to your content. With DeepBrain AI's rapid video content generation, users can leverage the power of automated video creation while maintaining high-quality results and professional standards.
- This makes DeepBrain AI not only efficient but also a versatile solution for all kinds of businesses seeking impactful visual communication tools.

Intuitive and user-friendly interface

Stepping into the arena of artificial intelligence solutions, DeepBrain AI sets an impressive standard with its intuitive and user-friendly interface. The platform is designed to simplify the complex video generation process by offering a seamless user experience that caters to beginners and professionals alike.

It's all about streamlining operations – crafting photorealistic avatars, perfecting industry-specific applications, or rapidly producing high-quality videos. It can all be handled in just a few clicks on this platform.

With such ease of use and advanced AI-powered content creation abilities, DeepBrain AI stands as a convenience pillar in today's fast-paced digital world.

Powerful customization options

- DeepBrain AI provides powerful customization options allowing users to tailor their AI-generated videos to meet their needs. With a wide range of templates and extensive customization capabilities, users can easily personalize every aspect of their videos, from the visuals to the voiceover.
- Whether adjusting color schemes, adding logos or text overlays, or choosing different video styles, DeepBrain AI offers unparalleled flexibility in creating unique and professional-looking videos.
- Users can also select from various languages and accents for their voiceovers, ensuring their message resonates with worldwide audiences. With DeepBrain AI's customizable AI solutions and versatile pricing options, businesses of all sizes can create high-quality videos that perfectly align with their brand identity and marketing goals.

Cost-effective pricing options

- DeepBrain AI offers cost-effective pricing options that make it accessible to many users. With their Starter Plan starting at just $30/month, beginners and professionals can take advantage of this powerful AI tool without breaking the bank.
- This plan includes 10 minutes per month, up to 10 minutes per video, 6 scenes per video, 100+ AI Avatars, 80+ Languages & Voices, and no watermark. The Pro Plan provides even more value at $79/month for those with more extensive needs.
- This plan offers 90 minutes per month, up to 20 minutes per video, up to 25 scenes per video, priority video processing, API access, and all the other features included in the Starter Plan. DeepBrain AI's flexible pricing options ensure you can choose the plan that best fits your requirements and budget while enjoying high-quality results from their advanced AI technology.

DeepBrain AI: Use Cases

DeepBrain AI's advanced video generation capabilities make it a valuable tool for content creators, marketers, small and medium-sized businesses, e-commerce platforms, and social media influencers.

1. Content creators and marketers

DeepBrain AI offers a game-changing solution for content creators and marketers, revolutionizing how videos are created. Its advanced AI technology, DeepBrain AI, enables users to generate high-quality videos quickly and efficiently.

Whether you're looking to create engaging marketing campaigns or captivating promotional videos, DeepBrain AI's powerful customization options allow you to tailor your content to suit your needs.

Additionally, its intuitive interface makes it easy for experienced professionals and industry newcomers to navigate through the platform seamlessly. By harnessing the power of artificial intelligence, DeepBrain AI empowers content creators and marketers with a cost-effective tool that delivers professional results every time.

2. Small and medium-sized businesses

Small and medium-sized businesses can benefit greatly from DeepBrain AI's advanced video creation tools. With its powerful customization options and intuitive interface, businesses can streamline their video production process while maintaining high quality.

By leveraging artificial intelligence applications offered by DeepBrain AI, small and medium-sized businesses can optimize their video editing efficiency and reduce costs by up to 80%. The company's industry-specific AI solutions also cater to various sectors such as financial services, retail & commerce, education, and media.

DeepBrain AI is a valuable resource for SMBs looking to enhance their marketing efforts through engaging videos that resonate with their target audience.

3. E-commerce platforms

For e-commerce platforms, DeepBrain AI offers a range of invaluable features. With its advanced video generation capabilities, businesses can create compelling product videos that drive sales and engagement.

The intuitive interface makes it easy for non-technical users to navigate and utilize the platform effectively. DeepBrain AI also provides powerful customization options, allowing e-commerce brands to tailor their videos to match their unique branding and style.

And with cost-effective pricing options available, businesses of all sizes can leverage the power of AI to enhance their online presence and boost conversions.

4. Social media influencers

Social media influencers can greatly benefit from using DeepBrain AI for their video content creation. With its advanced artificial intelligence capabilities, DeepBrain AI offers a range of tools and features that enable influencers to produce high-quality videos effortlessly.

DeepBrain AI allows influencers to engage their audience with visually appealing and informative content, from concept-explaining content to skill-sharing videos.

One key feature that makes DeepBrain AI ideal for social media influencers is its virtual avatars. These licensed digital characters provide a unique and personalized touch to videos, making them more relatable and engaging for viewers. Additionally, the intuitive interface and versatile customization options offered by DeepBrain AI allow influencers to create professional-looking videos without any prior technical expertise.

By leveraging the power of DeepBrain AI's video creation tools, social media influencers can save time and effort while maintaining the quality of their content. This timesaving technology enables them to focus on creating captivating stories and connecting with their audience rather than spending hours editing footage or learning complex software.

Step 1: Choose a topic for your video

The first step is to choose a topic for your video. What do you want to talk about? What are you passionate about? Once you have a topic, you can start brainstorming ideas for your video.

Step 2: Write a script or a set of instructions

Once you have your topic, you need to write a script or a set of instructions for your video. This will help DeepBrain AI understand what you want your video to look like.

Step 3: Choose the settings for your video

DeepBrain AI allows you to choose the settings for your video. You can choose the length, the style, and the background of your video.

Step 4: Generate your video

Once you have your script or set of instructions, you can generate your video. DeepBrain AI will create a video that follows your instructions.

Step 5: Edit your video

Once your video is generated, you can edit it to make sure it's perfect. You can add text, images, and music to your video.

Step 6: Upload your video to YouTube

Once you're happy with your video, you can upload it to YouTube. And that's it! You've now created an AI YouTube video with DeepBrain AI.

9.5 Runway

In the dynamic world of video editing, where creativity meets technology, a groundbreaking software has emerged to redefine the way we craft and manipulate visual content. Meet Runway, the ingenious AI-powered video editing software that is reshaping the landscape of content creation. With over 30 AI Magic Tools and a real-time collaborative approach, Runway is the creative companion you've been waiting for.

Runway is not just another video editing software; it's a transformational tool that empowers creators to bring their visions to life without the complexities of coding or intricate editing techniques. Launched in January 2019 by the visionary Cristal Valenzuela, Runway marries the prowess of machine learning with intuitive design, delivering an unparalleled video editing experience.

Simplifying Editing with AI Magic Tools

Runway eliminates the barriers that often deter individuals from venturing into video editing. Its user-friendly interface boasts a myriad of features, including masks, color correction, compositing, VFX, and more. An extraordinary feature is the dynamic keying, which swiftly transforms your video into a green screen canvas, expediting the editing process.

Elevating Realism with Depth Maps and Optical Flow

To achieve a heightened sense of realism, Runway provides accurate and distinctive depth maps that add depth and dimension to your footage. The optical flow feature, which comprehends object movement through relative motion analysis, adds a layer of sophistication to your creations.

Seamless Object Removal and Multi-Stream Video Format

Runway understands the nuances of editing, and that's why it incorporates an automatic repair function that effortlessly erases undesired elements from your video. Furthermore, creators can harness the power of the multi-stream video format, enhancing the visual appeal of their content while gaining access to advanced AI-generated analytics and metadata.

Key Features and Tools

Runway AI includes dozens of tools powered by AI models like DALL-E 2, Stable Diffusion and others. Here are some of the most popular features:

Text to Image

This tool allows you to generate unique images simply by providing text descriptions. Want a picture of a "cherry blossom tree on Mars"? No problem. The AI will create it from scratch.

You can specify the size, artistic style and other parameters to customize the type of image generated. The results are surprisingly high quality and creative.

Image to Image

Starting with any image, this tool can transform and edit it into new designs just through text prompts. Easily change the style, add or remove elements, combine images and more.

For example, you could take a photo of a person and make it look like a Renaissance painting or pencil sketch art. The possibilities are endless.

Infinite Zoom

With the infinite zoom tool, you can take any image and infinitely zoom into it by providing text prompts to generate additional details and content. This makes it easy to create mesmerizing zooming videos or giant wallpaper images.

Text to 3D

Instead of needing complex 3D modeling software, this tool allows you to generate 3D objects, textures, materials simply by describing what you want in text form.

For example, generate a 3D model of a "retro tv with gold trim" without having to build it vertex by vertex. You can then export the 3D objects to use elsewhere.

Text to Video

One of Runway's newest tools, this uses AI to generate stunning HD video from text descriptions in just seconds. Bring your wildest video ideas to life easily.

You can specify a length, style, background, music and other parameters to have full control over the video generated.

Video Editing

Beyond video generation, Runway also includes a full suite of video editing features:

1. Trim, crop, resize videos
2. Add music, voiceovers and sound effects
3. Include animated text, graphics and transitions
4. Adjust speed, add color grading and filters
5. Automatically remove backgrounds

Step#1 – Access Runway Website

Open your web browser and type https://app.runwayml.com/. It'll take you to the Runway account sign-up page. Create your account or choose "Login with Google."

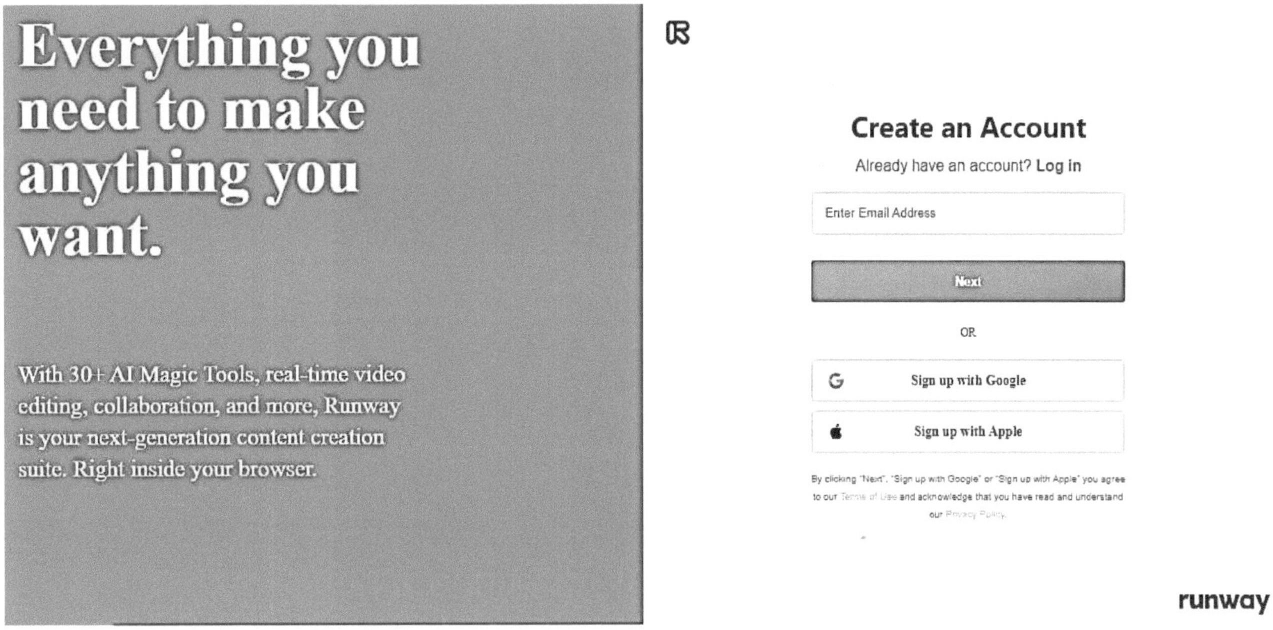

Step#2 – Understand the Interface

Just after logging in, you'll land on the RunwayML software's interface. Here you need to click on the "Gen-2 – image/text to videos". It'll redirect you to a new page containing a prompt box. Here you'll see 2 options for input, image, and text, so choose the one that suits your preferences.

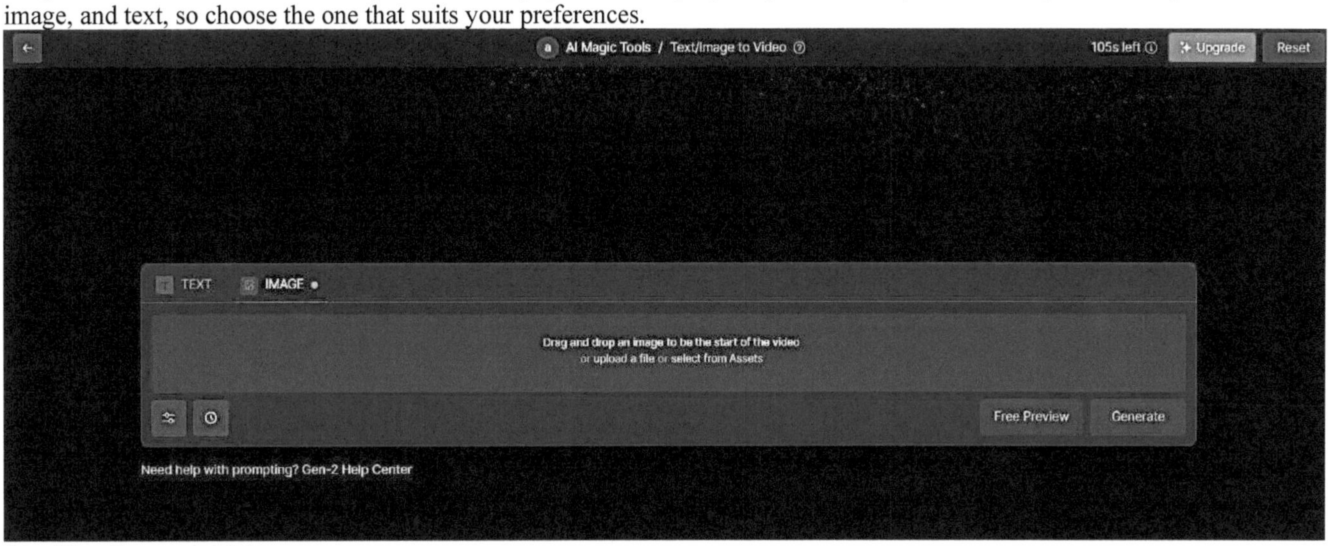

Step#3 – Generate Video

If you want to generate a video from a text prompt, then in the prompt box, precisely describe the scenario and then click "Generate." In case you want to turn an image into a video, then first dig into your photos gallery to find an image or generate a customized image using Midjourney. For best results, try to set the image ratio as 16:9.

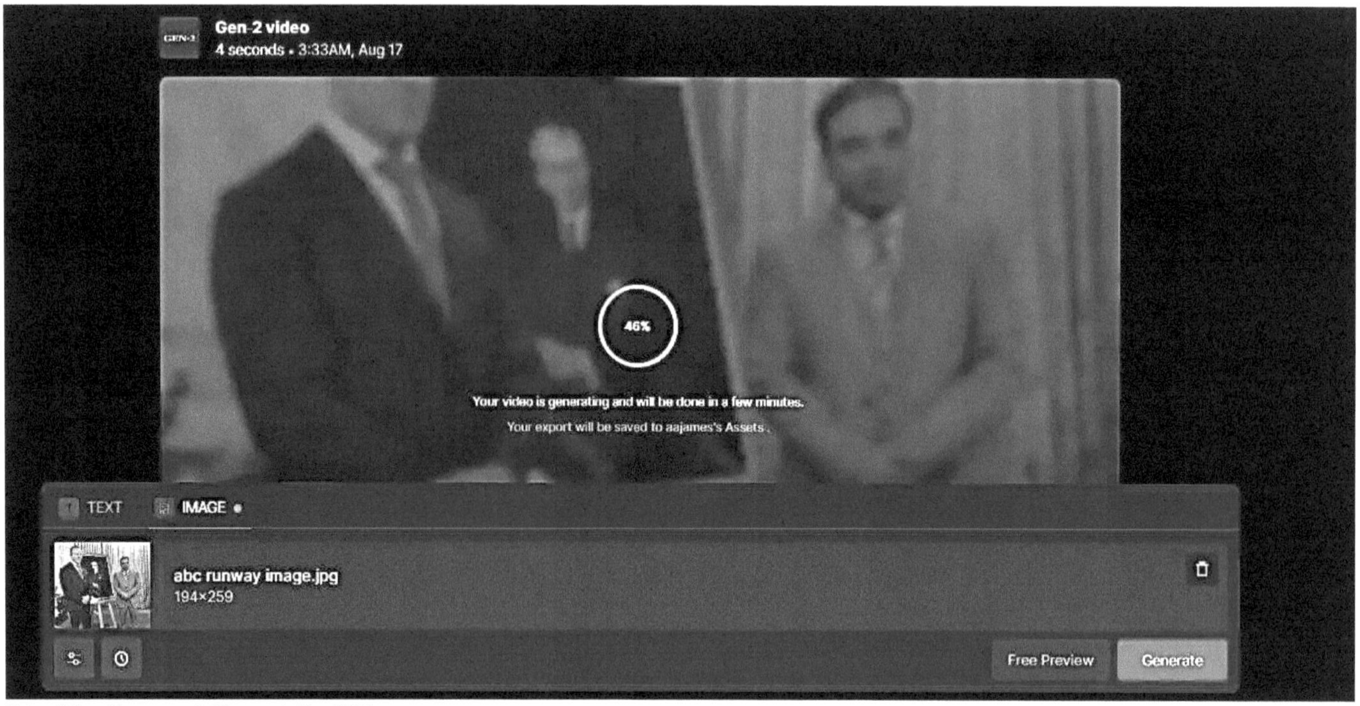

Step#4 – Save and Export the Video

Once done, you can preview the final video, and if you're satisfied with the results, then simply save or export the video. You can also share the video directly on your social media platforms.

9.6 Pictory

Pictory is an AI-driven software designed to help you make YouTube videos by utilizing stock footage videos and images. The videos and images are sourced from Storyblocks, a renowned provider of high-quality stock media. Pictory is a cost-effective alternative to having a separate account with Storyblocks, which can cost around $30 per month. The integration with Storyblocks gives Pictory an edge over other free video footage platforms, which often offer low-quality and limited videos.

How to Use Pictory

1. Script Writing
The first step in creating a video with Pictory is to write a script. This script outlines the content of your video. It's important to separate your text into chunks or lines to avoid having too much text in one scene.
2. Script to Video
Once your script is ready, go to Pictory and select the 'Script to Video' option. Here, you can paste your script and adjust the scene settings. You can choose to create new scenes based on line breaks, which means the scene will split based on each line break in your script.
3. Choose a Template
Pictory offers a wide range of templates to choose from. These templates can help you create a visually appealing video that aligns with your content. You can also choose the aspect ratio of your video, whether it's 16:9 for a standard video, 9:16 for a vertical video, or 1:1 for a square video.
4. Visuals and Audio
Pictory will scan your text and find videos related to it from Storyblocks. You can customize each scene by changing the visuals to match your script.
In addition to visuals, Pictory also provides a vast library of over 15,000 music tracks that you can use as background music in your videos. You can adjust the volume of the background music to ensure it doesn't overpower your voiceover.
5. Voiceover
Pictory offers an auto text-to-speech voiceover feature. However, the quality of this voiceover may not be as high as a human voice. For a more natural-sounding voiceover, you can use a second software like Murf. After generating your voiceover, you can upload it to Pictory and apply it to your entire video.
6. Final Adjustments
Once your voiceover is in place, you can make final adjustments to your video. You can change the text directly in Pictory, and customize the font, size, color, alignment, and more. You can also add an intro, outro, and branding to your video.
7. Generate and Download
Finally, you can generate your video. The time it takes to generate the video will depend on the length of your script. Once the video is generated, you can download it to your PC.
8. Final Thoughts
Pictory is an excellent tool for creating high-quality YouTube videos. It's user-friendly, customizable, and cost-effective. Whether you're a seasoned YouTuber or a beginner, Pictory can help you create engaging content that resonates with your audience.

Key Features of Pictory
Pictory is packed with a host of features that make video creation a breeze. Here are some of the key features:
1. Create Short Branded Video Snippets From Long Form Videos: Pictory's advanced AI extracts key points from your long-form content, such as Zoom, Teams, and Webinar recordings, and turns them into short, shareable video snippets.
2. Turn Scripts Into Sales Videos: Pictory can transform your scripts into high-conversion Video Sales Letters, complete with stock footage, music, and voiceovers, in just minutes.
3. Transform Blog Posts Into Videos: You can repurpose your blog content into engaging videos with Pictory. This can help boost your search engine rankings and increase your readership.
4. Automatic Caption Addition: Pictory automatically adds captions to your videos, which is crucial as 85% of social media videos are watched on mute. This feature eliminates the need for expensive outsourcing or spending hours trying to add captions yourself.
5. Partnership with Storyblocks: Pictory is in partnership with Storyblocks, a leading provider of high-quality stock media. This means you have access to a vast library of stock footage videos and images to use in your videos.

Getting Started with Pictory
Begin by signing up for our AI video creator or logging into your Pictory account. You can try Pictory without entering a credit card, so go ahead and grab a AI video creator free trial if you don't have an account yet.

Signing up or logging in brings you to the AI video creation platform. It's clean, simple, and intuitive to use. There's a menu at the top showing "My Projects", "Help", notifications, and an account menu.
Use this menu to navigate to existing projects, find resources, and change your profile settings.

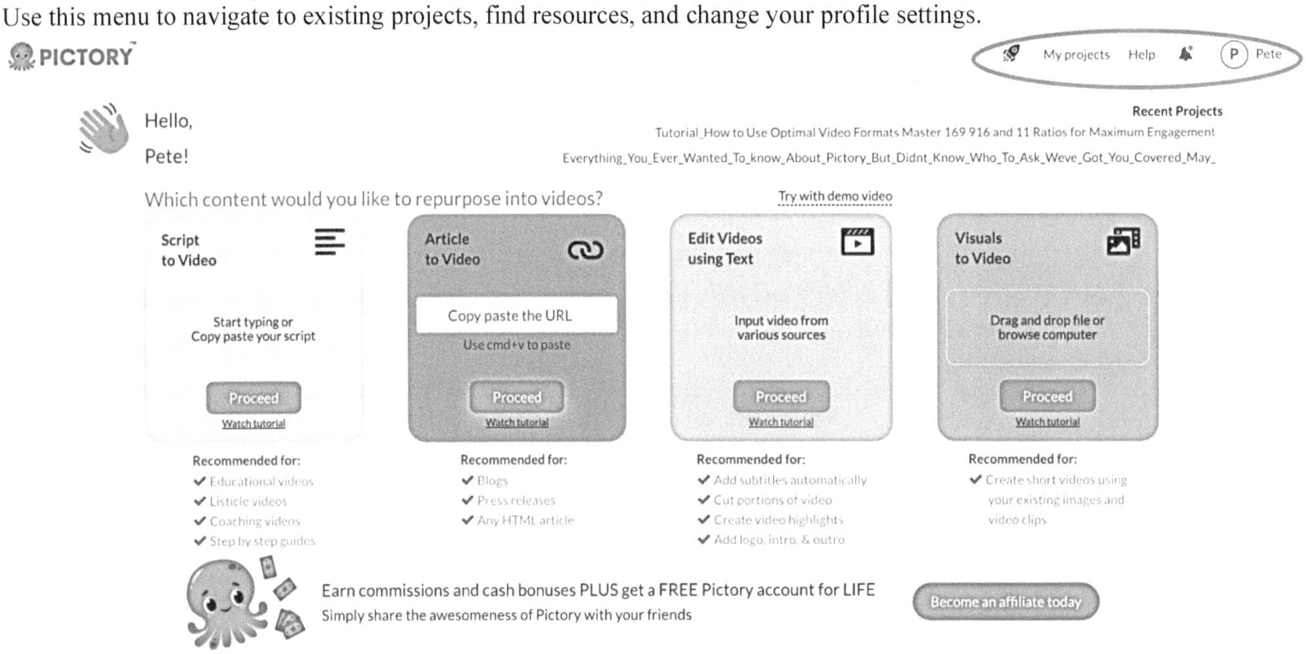

You can get back to the main dashboard by clicking the Pictory logo.
The main dashboard shows Pictory's four video creation methods: script to video, article to video, edit videos using text, or visuals to video.
Click any one of these to generate a new video.

Script to Video Generation

Script to Video lets you generate videos from the text you enter.

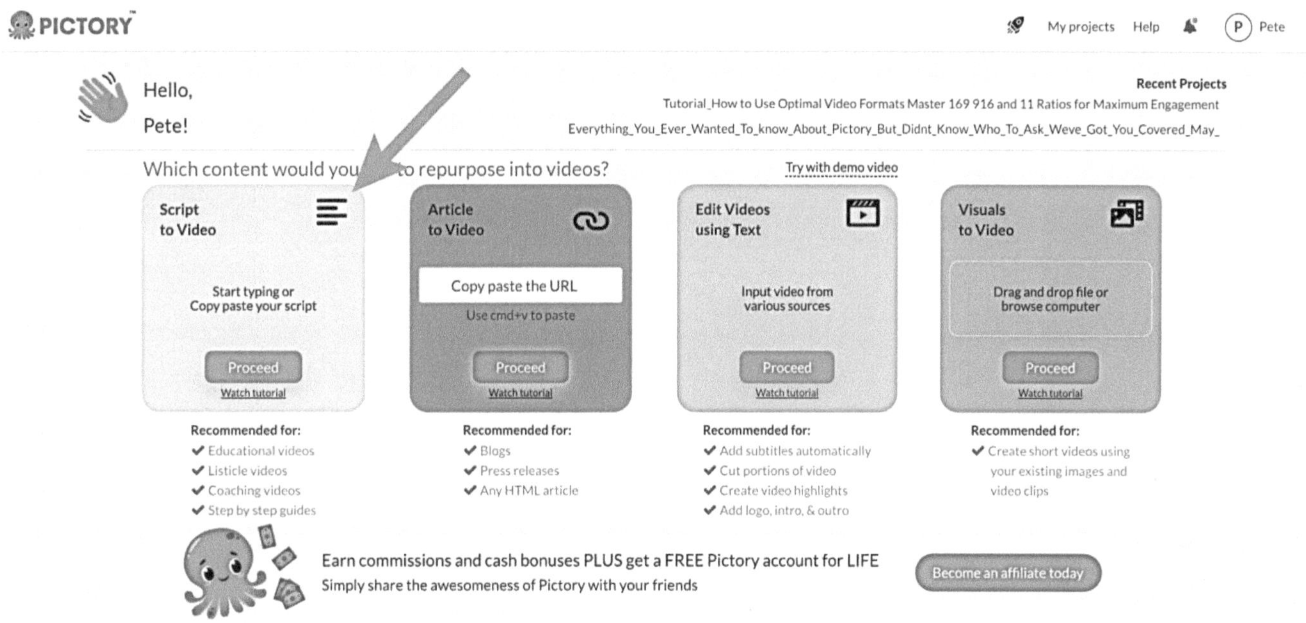

You can copy-and-paste some text in or type right into Pictory.

You can choose the scene settings here, such as to auto-highlighting keywords, automatically selecting visuals, and where to create new scenes.

Pictory lets you create new scenes on sentence breaks, line breaks, or both.
Pick the setting you prefer.
Once you enter the text and select the scene settings, click "Proceed" to continue.
Pictory then lets you select a template to style the video.

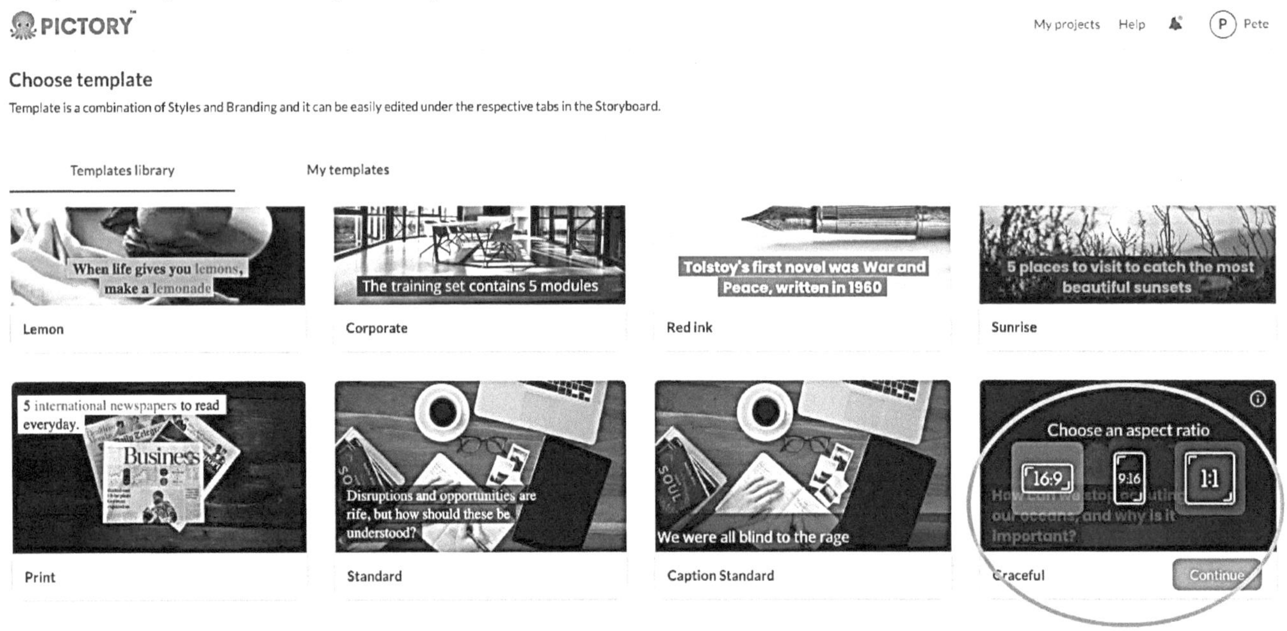

There are multiple templates available, and you can create your own. After you select the template, it's time to choose an aspect ratio: 16:9, 9:16, or 1:1.
Pictory will create a video storyboard once the text is entered and a template is selected.
Pictory automatically styles videos, but you can also manually edit videos scene-by-scene.

Article To Video
Article to Video lets you create videos from published blog posts, articles, press releases, or other text-based HTML pages. Simply copy and paste the article's URL into Pictory.

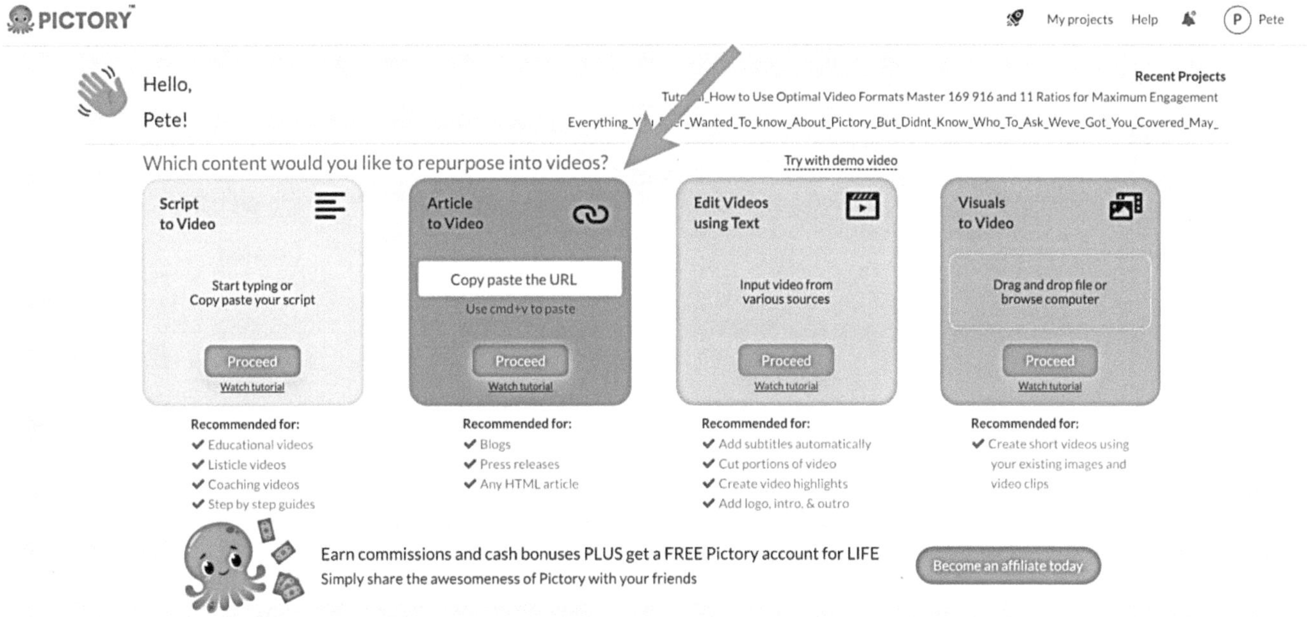

Pictory's AI will then extract key messages and turn the summary into a series of scenes.

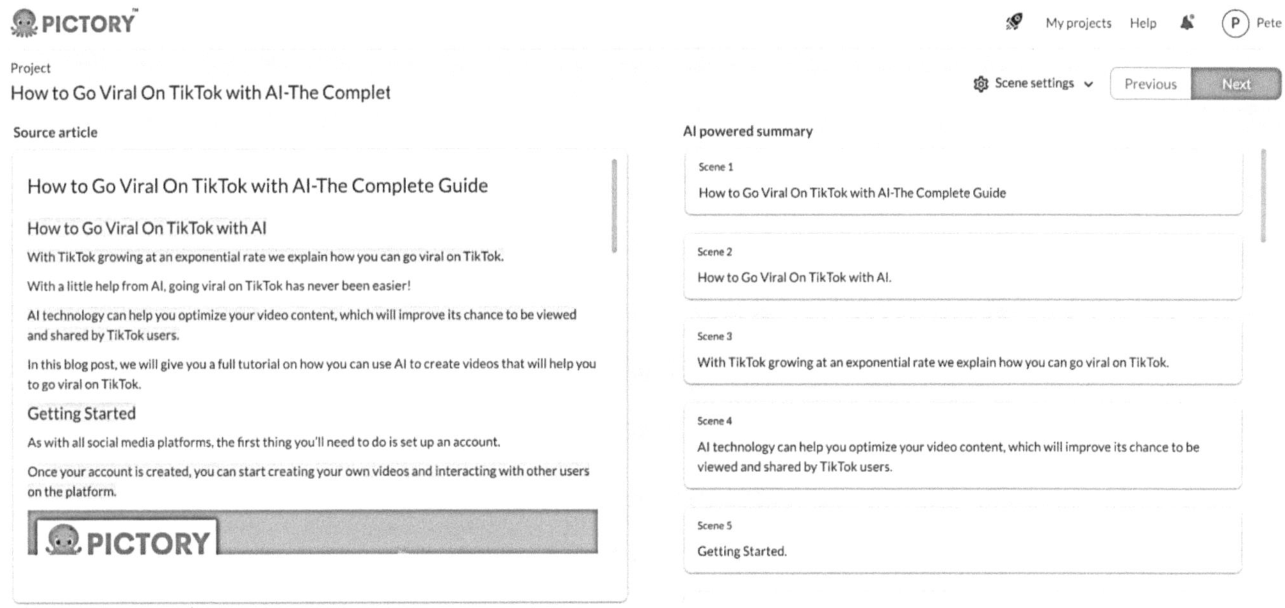

After that, you can pick a template to style and brand the video, along with the screen settings you want.

Pictory will then create a storyboard.

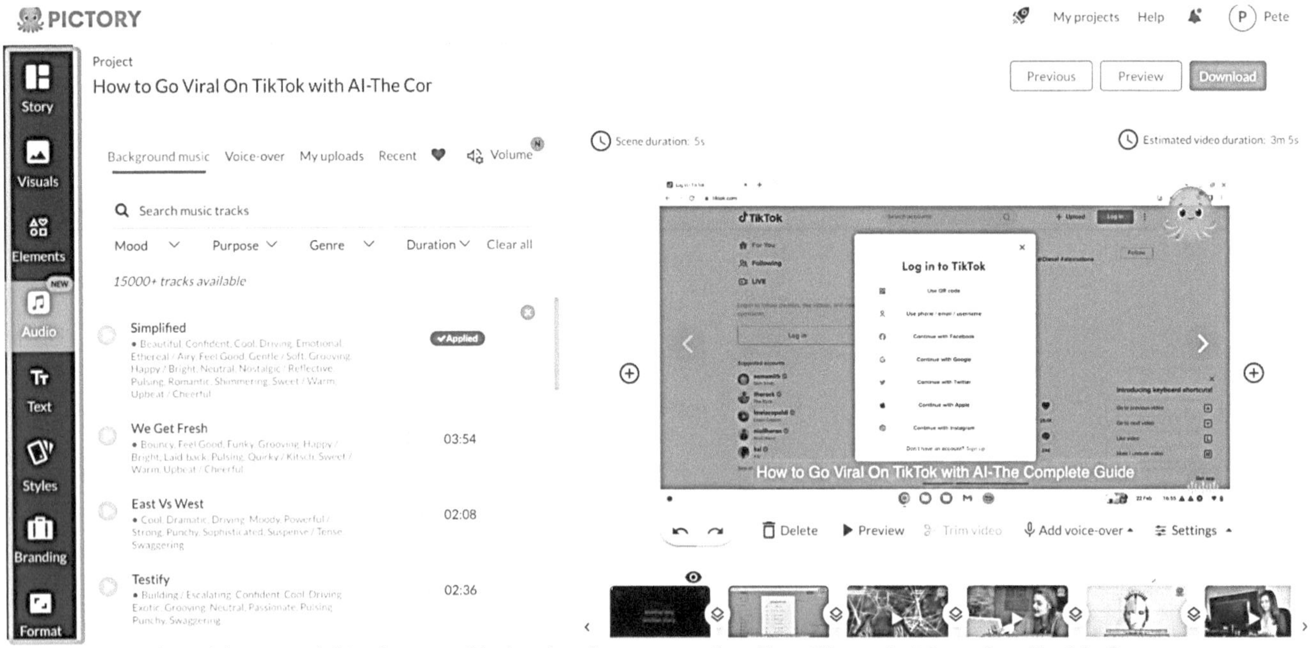

Once the storyboard is created, it's time to add visuals, elements, and styling. Pictory's AI can handle this for you, or you can do it yourself.

Edit Videos Using Text

The Edit Videos Using Text option is used to edit an existing video.

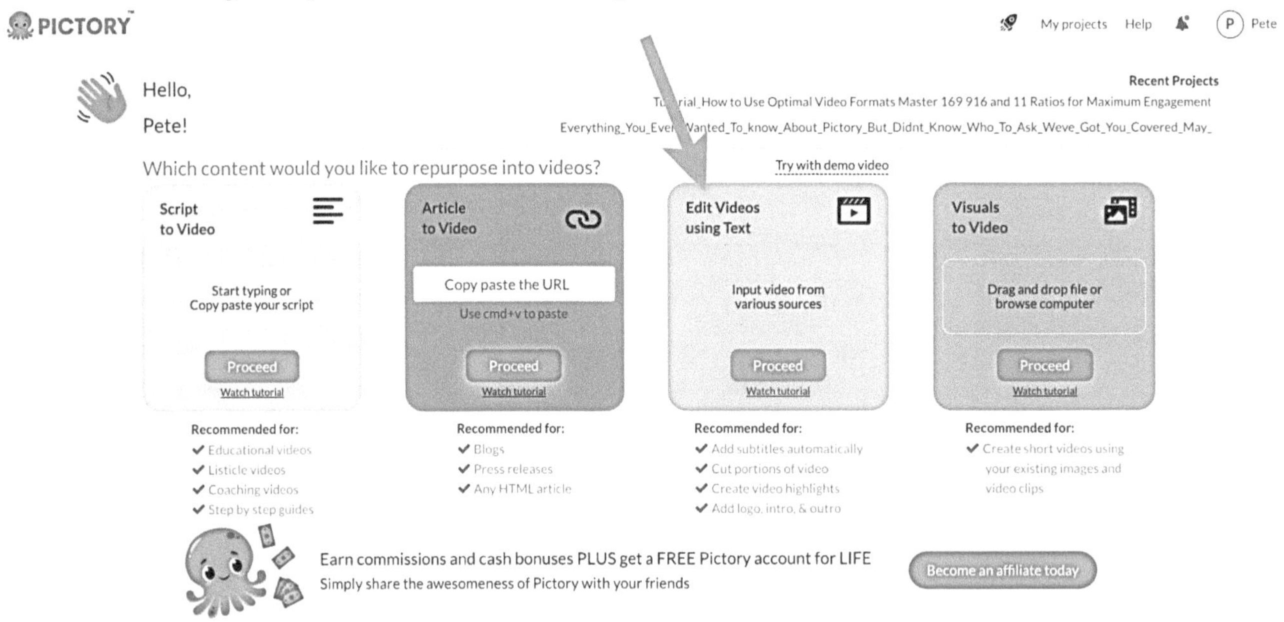

You can add the video from a YouTube link or an audio/video file upload.

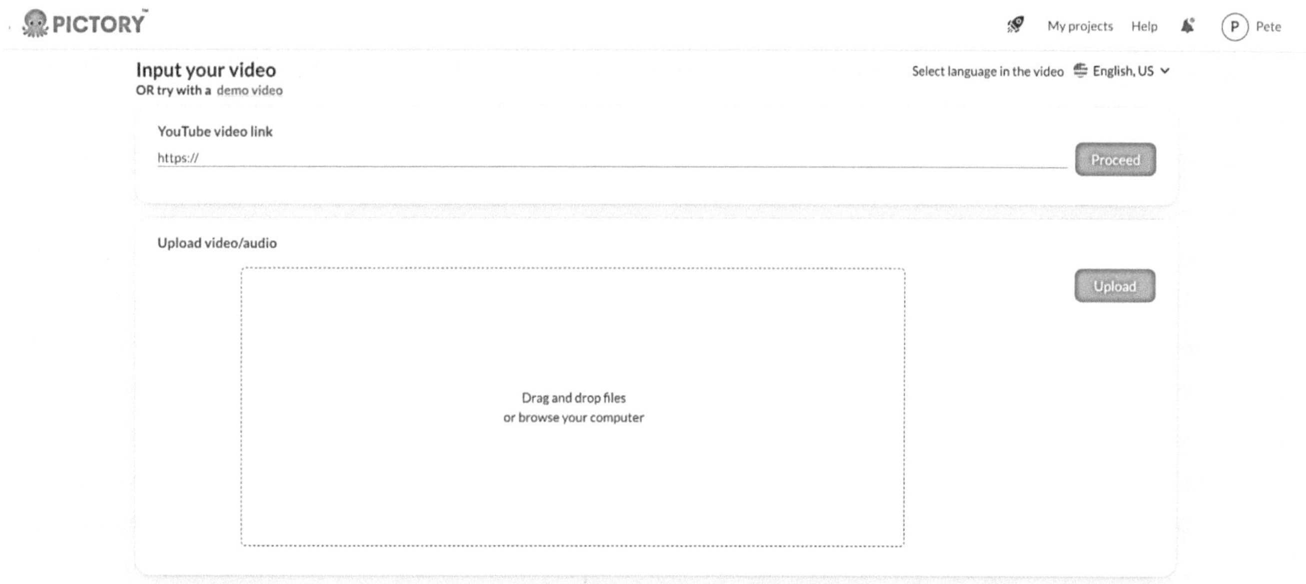

Pictory will ask for the number of speakers in the video. This helps Pictory AI make an accurate transcription and produce a high-quality video.

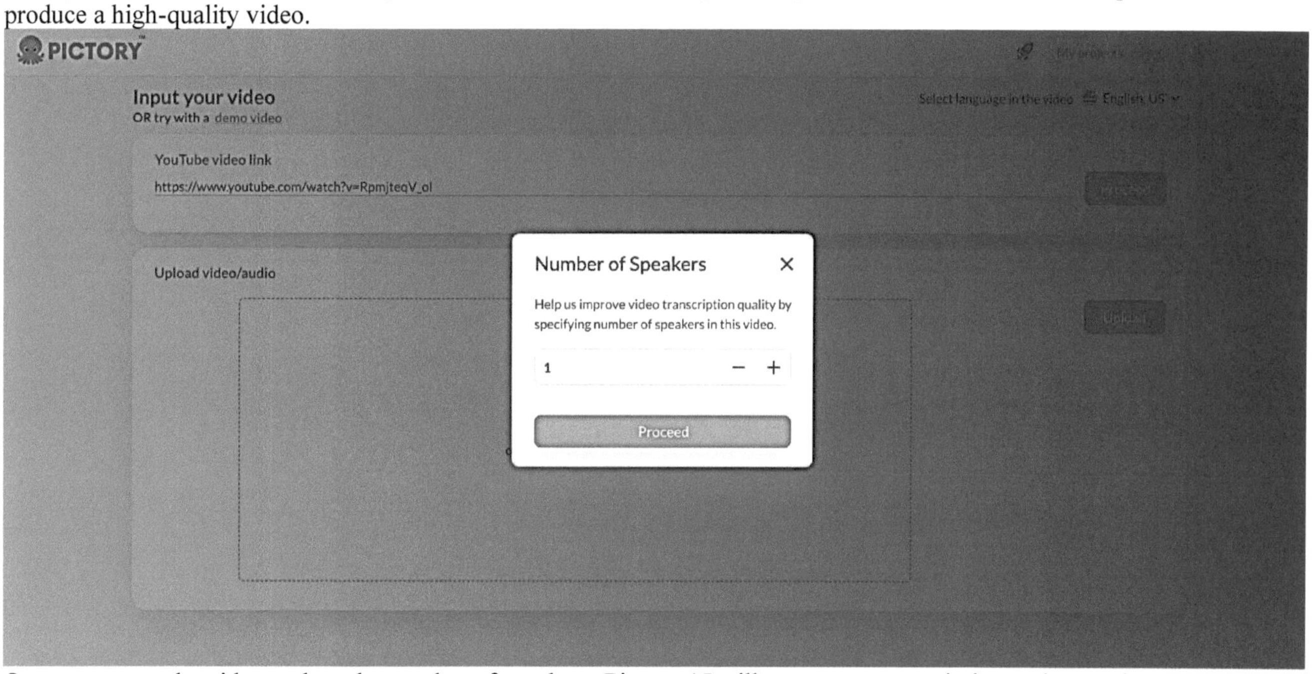

Once you enter the video and set the number of speakers, Pictory AI will generate a transcription and scene-by-scene storyboard.

You can now edit and style the video.

Visuals to Video

Visuals to Video lets you generate videos from images and video clips.

So if you want to make a product or art showcase, or edit together clips recorded on your mobile phone, this feature is perfect.

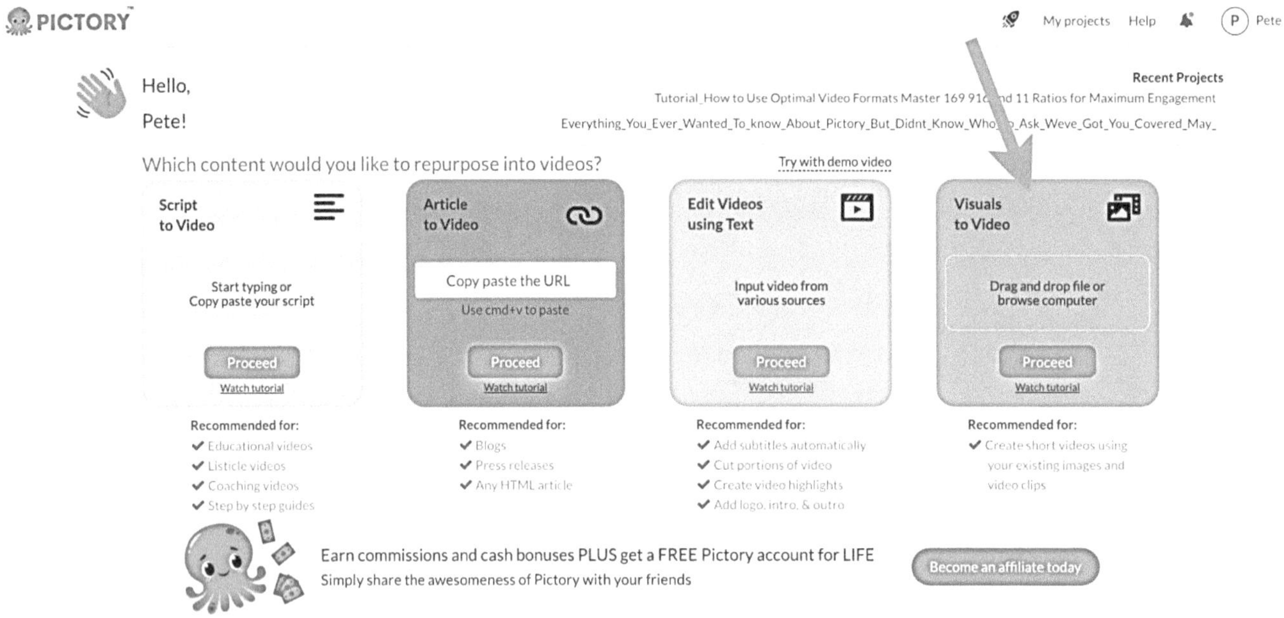

Add files from your computer, then arrange them into the sequence you'd like.

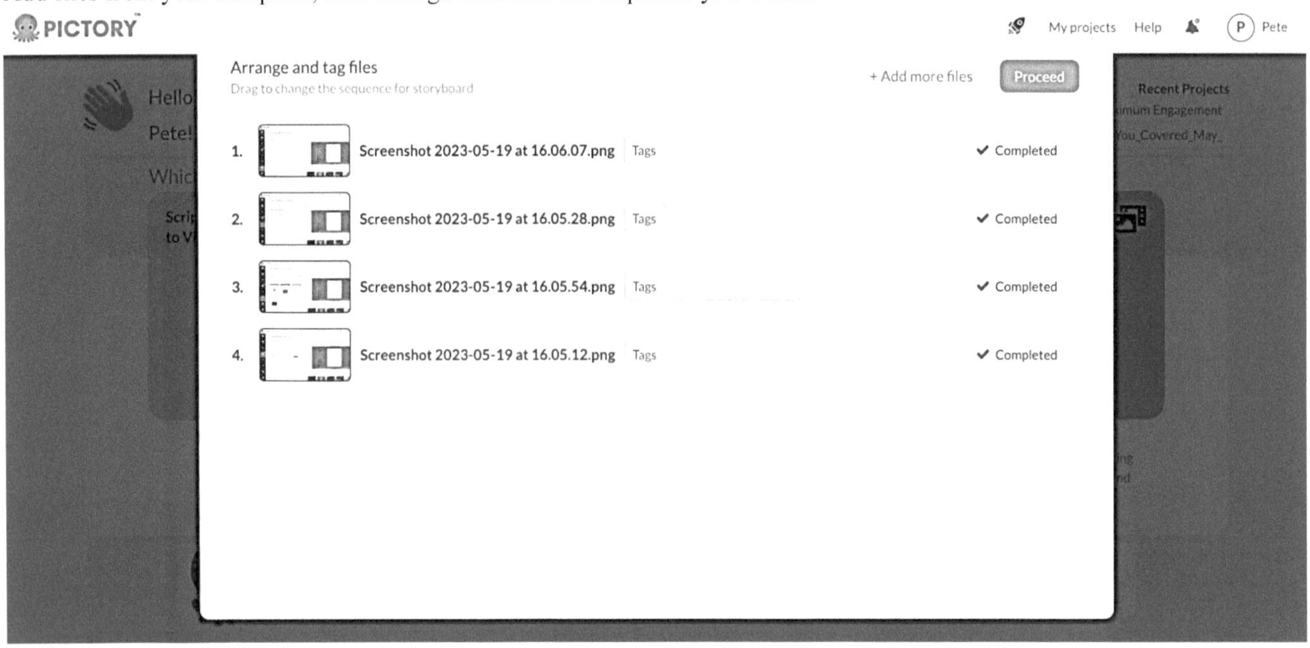

This creates a storyboard.

Exercise

Exercise 1 – MCQ

Q 1. What is the primary focus of Fliki in the realm of video tools?

A. Virtual reality experiences
B. Image editing and graphic design
C. AI-driven video synthesis
D. Real-time video editing

Q 2. Lumen5 is known for its capabilities in:

A. Virtual reality experiences
B. AI-driven video synthesis and creation
C. Deep learning for video quality enhancement
D. Real-time video editing

Q 3. What is the primary focus of Synthesia in the context of video tools?
A. Real-time video editing
B. Deep learning techniques for video quality
C. AI-driven video synthesis
D. Virtual reality experiences

Q 4. DeepBrain AI specializes in:
A. Real-time video editing
B. Virtual reality experiences
C. Video content creation using advanced AI algorithms
D. Deep learning for image editing

Q 5. Runway is specifically designed for:
A. Virtual reality experiences
B. AI-driven video synthesis and creation
C. Traditional video editing
D. Image editing and graphic design

Q 6. Pictory integrates AI-driven features to automatically generate:
A. Virtual reality experiences
B. Video scripts
C. Image captions
D. Deep learning algorithms

Q 7. What does Fliki primarily utilize machine learning for?
A. Image editing
B. Real-time video editing
C. Video synthesis
D. Virtual reality experiences

Q 8. Synthesia incorporates natural language processing techniques to generate:
A. Virtual reality experiences
B. Image captions
C. Video scripts
D. Deep learning algorithms

Q 9. Runway is designed for which creative professionals?
A. Graphic designers
B. Video content creators and filmmakers
C. Architects
D. Writers

Q 10. Pictory primarily focuses on:
A. Image editing
B. Real-time video editing
C. Virtual reality experiences
D. AI-driven video synthesis

Exercise 2 – True/ False

Q 1. Fliki is a Video Tool specializing in image editing and graphic design.
Q 2. Lumen5 is known for its capabilities in AI-driven video synthesis and creation.
Q 3. Synthesia is primarily focused on deep learning techniques for enhancing video quality.
Q 4. DeepBrain AI is a Video Tool specialized in video content creation using advanced AI algorithms.
Q 5. Runway is a Video Tool that focuses on providing virtual reality experiences rather than traditional video editing.
Q 6. Pictory integrates AI-driven features to automatically generate captions for videos.
Q 7. Fliki utilizes machine learning for real-time video editing and manipulation.
Q 8. Synthesia incorporates natural language processing techniques to generate video scripts.
Q 9. Runway is specifically designed for video content creators and filmmakers.
Q 10. Pictory focuses on image editing and manipulation rather than video-related features.

Exercise 3 – Fill in the blanks

Q 1. Fliki simplifies the process of creating ____________ videos for various purposes.
Q 2. Lumen5 is particularly useful for creating ____________ videos for social media and online platforms.
Q 3. With Synthesia, users can generate personalized video messages using ____________ characters.
Q 4. This tool is capable of recognizing and understanding ____________ elements in videos.
Q 5. With Runway, users can experiment with various creative techniques, making it a valuable tool for ____________ projects.

Exercise 4 – Match case

1. Fliki	A. Empowers users to create interactive and responsive videos.
2. Lumen5	B. Utilizes AI to create realistic videos with virtual avatars.
3. Synthesia	C. An AI-powered tool transforming text into engaging video content.
4. DeepBrain AI	D. A video editing tool with a focus on dynamic content enhancement.
5. Runway	E. Recognizes and understands contextual elements in videos.

Exercise 5 – One word answer
Q 1. What is Edit in Fliki?
Q 2. In Lumen5 Transform is?
Q 3. What is Analyze in DeepBrain AI?
Q 4. What is Create in Runway?
Q 5. What is Design in Pictory?

Exercise 6 – Small answer
Q 1. What type of content does Fliki focus on enhancing?
Q 2. What does Lumen5 transform text into?
Q 3. How does Synthesia create videos?
Q 4. What is DeepBrain AI specialized in analyzing?
Q 5. What does Runway empower users to create?

Exercise 7 – Long answer
Q 1. What distinguishes Fliki as a video editing tool, and how does it contribute to enhancing visual content through its features?
Q 2. How does Lumen5 leverage AI, and what role does it play in transforming text into engaging video content?

Answers

Exercise 1 – MCQ
Ans: 1 B, 2 B, 3 C, 4 C, 5 B, 6 C, 7 A, 8 C, 9 B, 10 A

Exercise 2 – True/ False
Ans: 1 False, 2 True, 3 False, 4 True, 5 False, 6 True, 7 False, 8 True, 9 True, 10 False

Exercise 3 – Fill in the blanks
Ans: 1 Dynamic, Shareable, Virtual, Contextual, Multimedia

Exercise 4 – Match case
Ans: 1 D, 2 C, 3 B, 4 A, 5 E

Exercise 5 – One word answer
Ans: 1 Visual, 2 Transformative, 3 Contextual, 4 Responsive, 5 Dynamic

ONLINE RESOURCES

Practice Paper
Link https://forms.office.com/r/6NTij8Vy8A
QR Code

Video Content
Link https://www.youtube.com/playlist?list=PLzlh_31VWEFoiNJsDyhE2BAmPoSI5RCMs
QR Code

Chapter 10: Customer Support and Sales Tools

10.1 SecondBrain (previously MagicChat)

In today's fast-paced digital landscape, businesses are constantly seeking innovative ways to engage customers and streamline knowledge sharing. SecondBrain.fyi, is revolutionizing website interactions.

By leveraging advanced AI technology, SecondBrain.fyi empowers businesses to provide personalized and instantaneous responses.

Besides, it ultimately transforms customer engagement and knowledge sharing customer support.

AI-powered writing companion that will help you write better articles, emails, messages and more.

Do you want to write better posts, tweets or messages? With the help of AI this extension will help you to generate amazing texts.

Second Brain is an AI-powered writing companion that helps users write better articles, emails, messages and more. It offers a variety of features such as text generation based on a prompt, rephrasing existing text, and creating custom AI tasks.

The tool works by generating text based on a given prompt, and it can also rephrase existing text for users who want to test out multiple options for their copy.

The AI behind Second Brain is Davinci-003, the most advanced text model from OpenAI. This tool is easy to use, and it can help users write better content without spending too much time and effort.

FEATURES

- Text generation based on prompt (You start the text, AI will complete it)
- Rephrasing existing text/sentences. Useful to test multiple options of your text
- Creating custom AI tasks (summarize the article, write professional email, etc..)

To use this tool you can do the following:

Step 1: Go to the website and select "***Create Free SecondBrain Bot***".

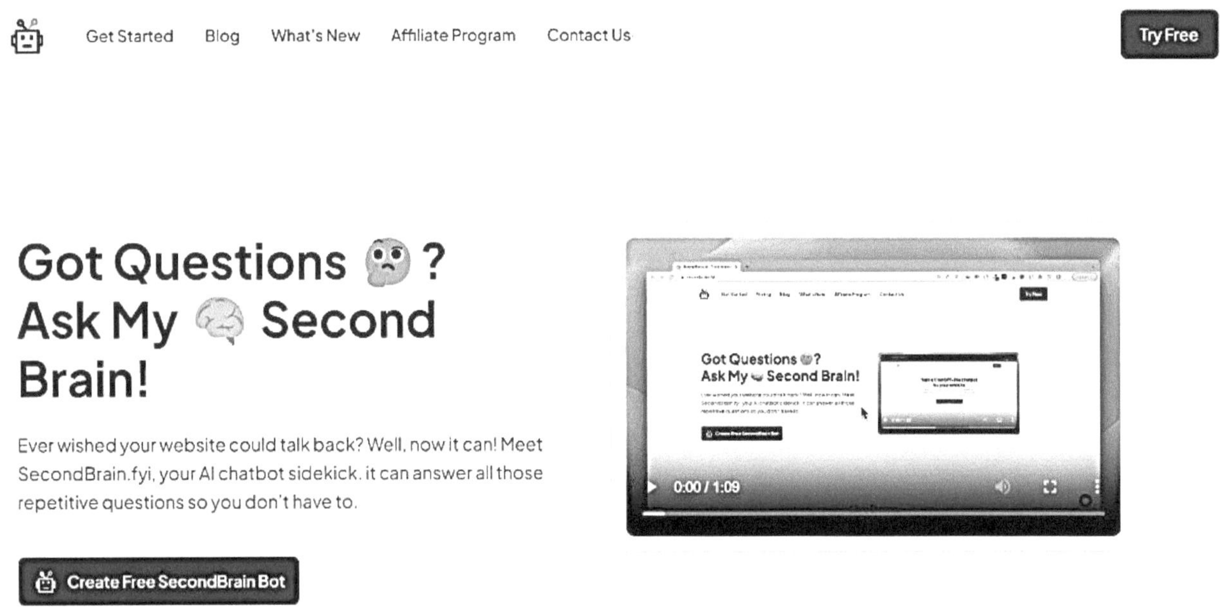

Step 2: Go to the main interface and select "***View all bots***". There, you create a "***New SecondBrain Bot***" and answer the s asked.

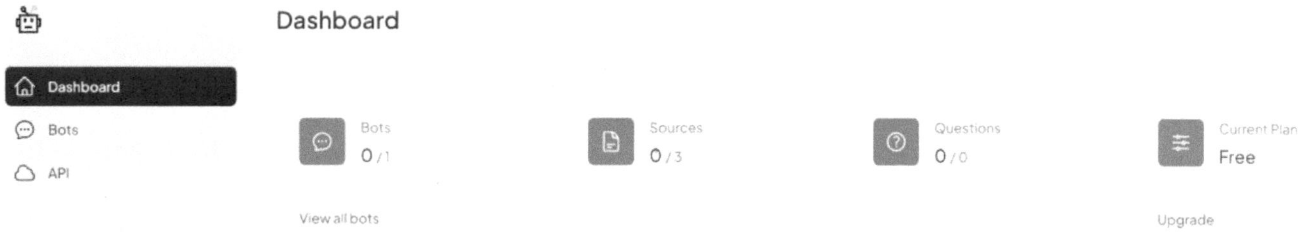
Dashboard
Dashboard
Bots
API
Bots
0 / 1
Sources
0 / 3
Questions
0 / 0
Current Plan
Free
View all bots
Upgrade

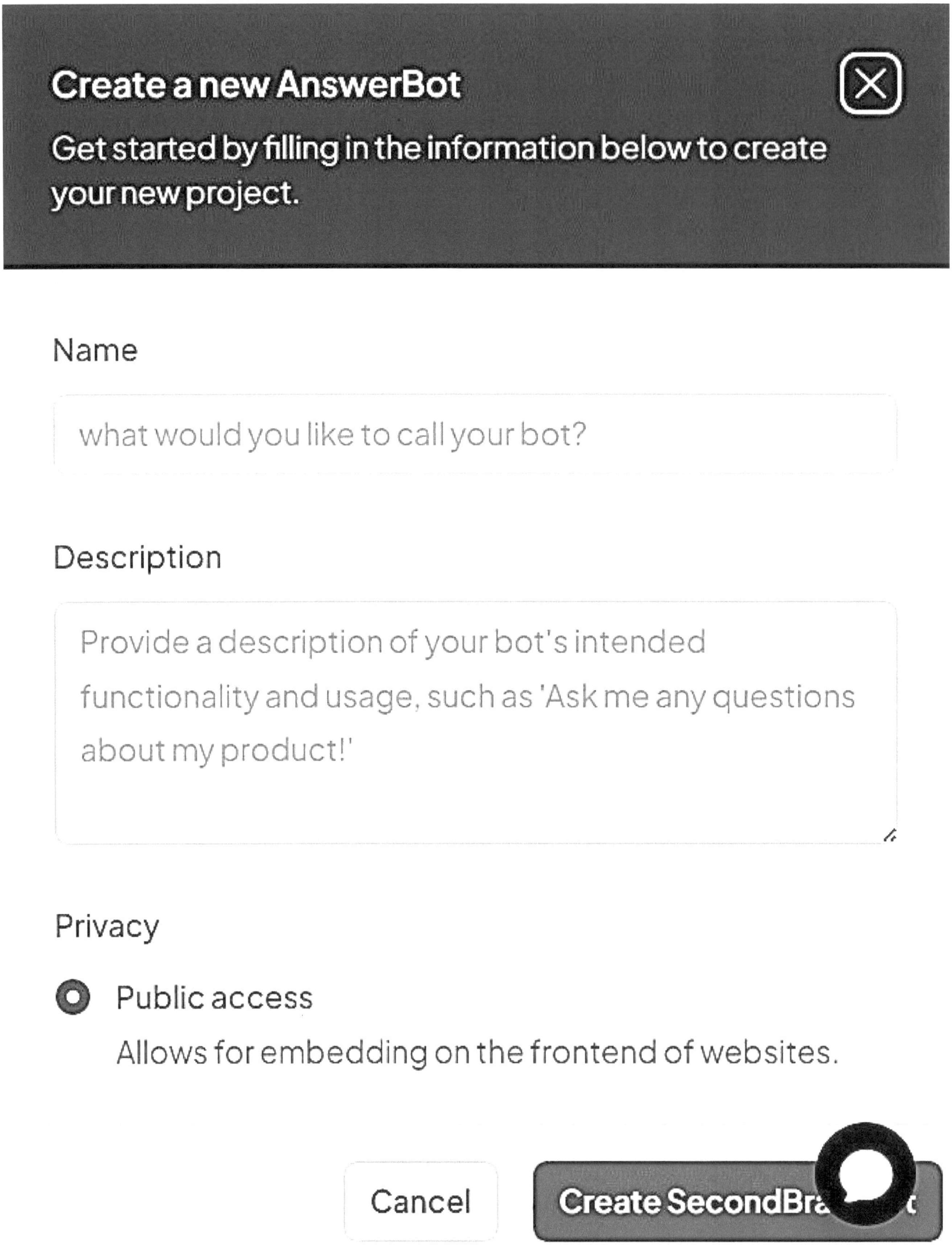
Create a new AnswerBot
Get started by filling in the information below to create your new project.
Name
what would you like to call your bot?
Description
Provide a description of your bot's intended functionality and usage, such as 'Ask me any questions about my product!'
Privacy
Public access
Allows for embedding on the frontend of websites.
Cancel

Step 3: Wait for a moment for the bot to be created. You can add several information sources and select "***Setting***" to set up some basic information.

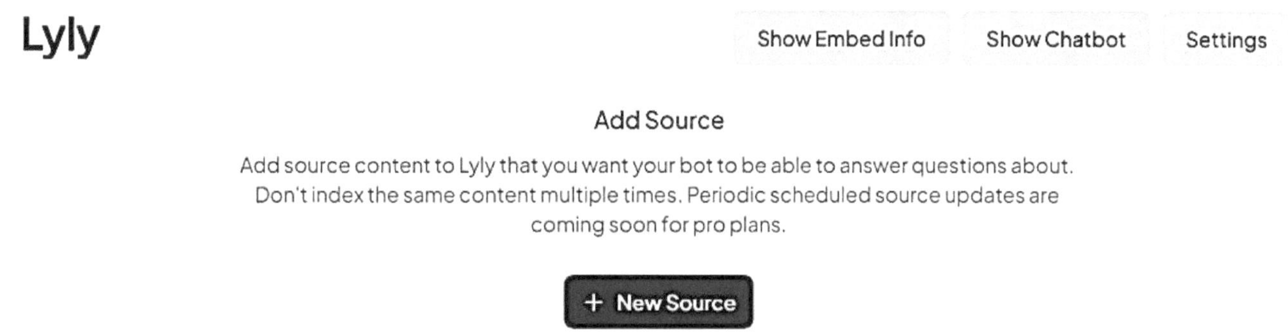

Step 4: Select "***Show Embed Info***" to get the code to paste into your website. Alternatively, select "***Show Chatbot***" to preview.

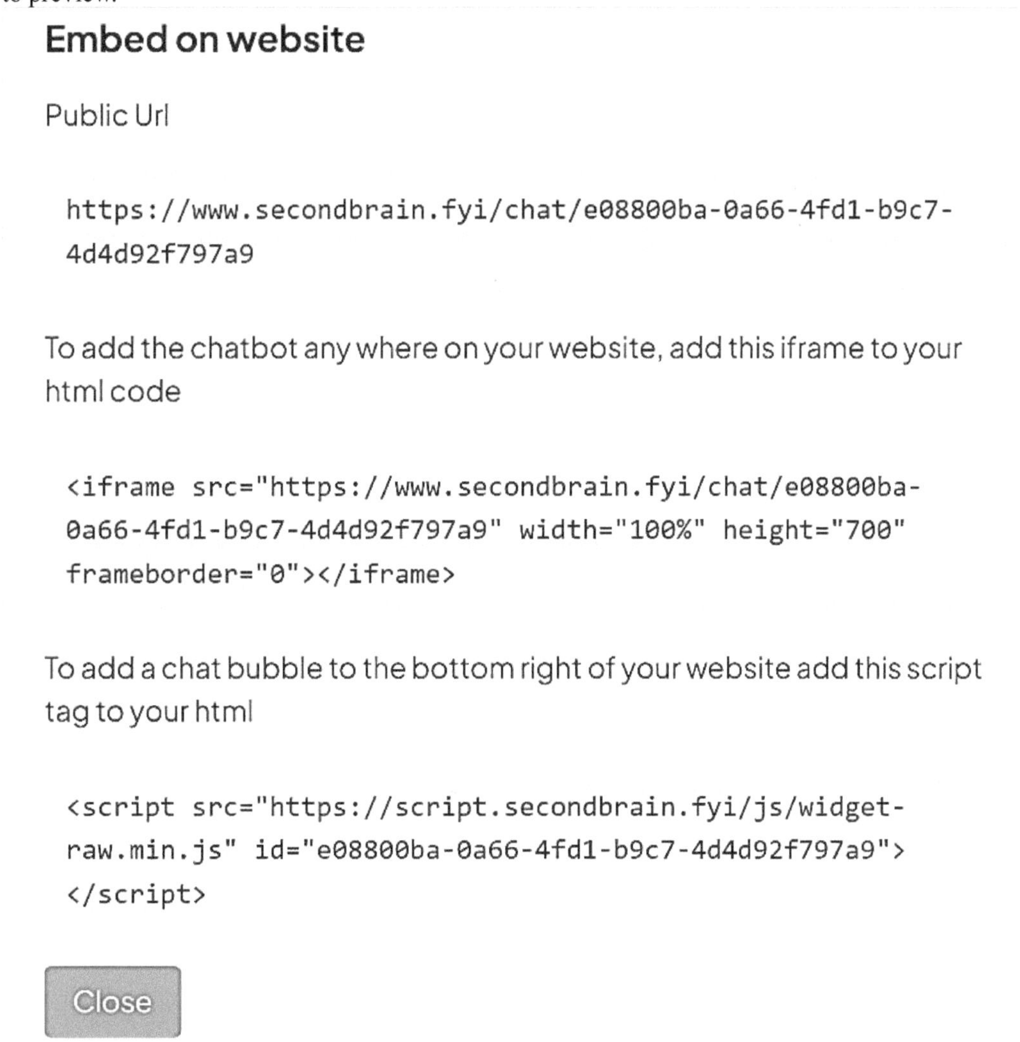

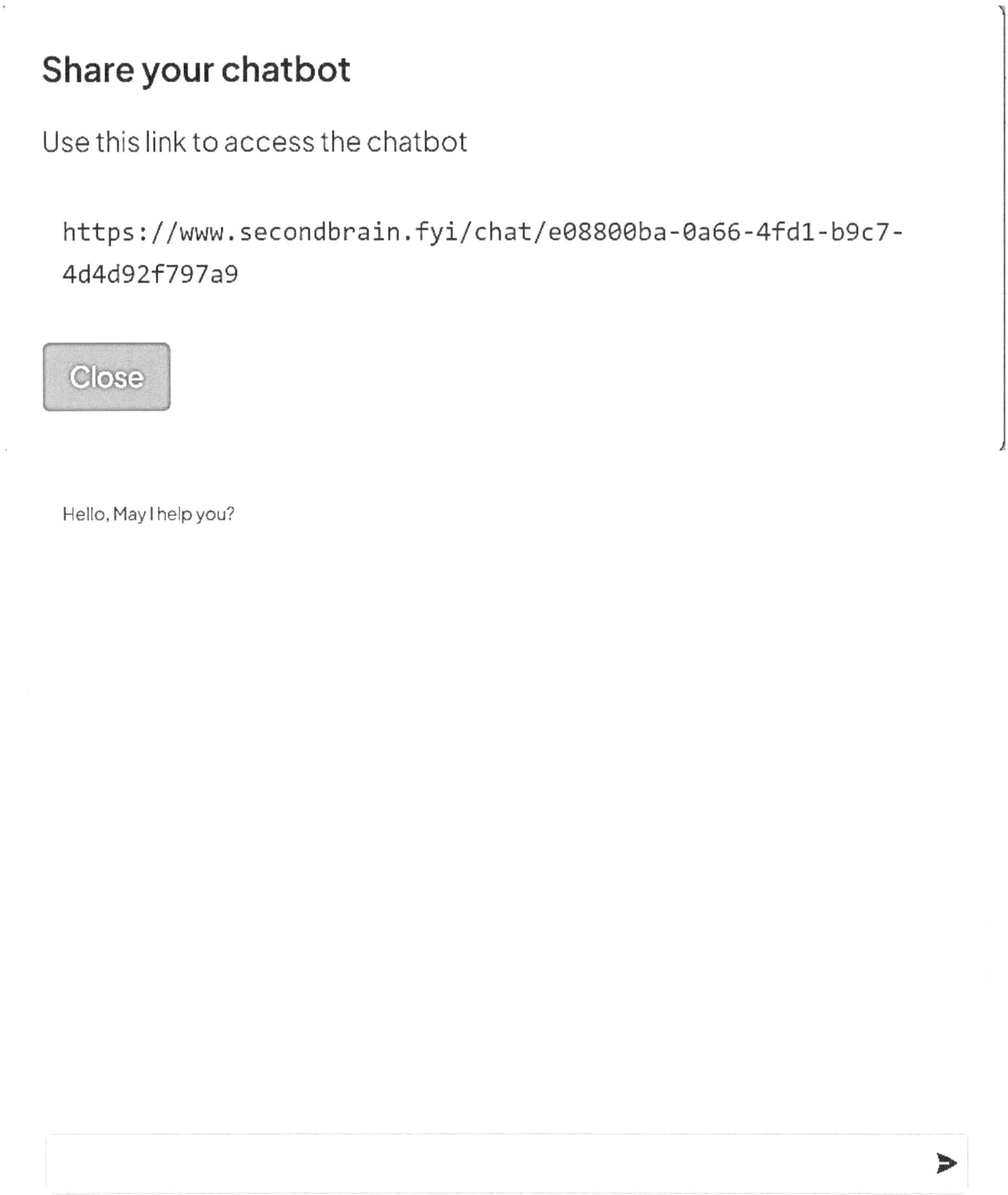

Finally, you can see how to use the tool in the first interface when you select "***Create Free SecondBrain Bot***" to better understand how to use it.

10.2 Chatfuel AI

Chatfuel is a leading chatbot building platform that enables businesses to create and deploy custom chatbots on Facebook Messenger and other platforms. With its easy-to-use interface and advanced features, Chatfuel has become a go-to tool for businesses looking to enhance their customer support and engagement.

One of the primary benefits of Chatfuel is its user-friendly interface, which enables even non-technical users to quickly create and launch a chatbot with its drag-and-drop interface. Additionally, Chatfuel offers a range of pre-built templates and plugins that make it easy to add advanced features, such as product listings, appointment scheduling, and more.

Aside from its ease of use, Chatfuel provides advanced features that help businesses personalize and optimize their chatbots. For instance, Chatfuel's natural language processing (NLP) capabilities enable chatbots to comprehend and respond to customer inquiries more effectively, resulting in a better overall customer experience. The platform also provides analytics and reporting tools that offer insights into chatbot performance, enabling businesses to make data-driven improvements to their chatbots over time.

Another significant benefit of Chatfuel is its integration capabilities. The platform can be easily integrated with a range of third-party services, such as CRM systems, marketing automation tools, and more. This enables businesses to create a seamless customer experience across multiple channels.

How does Chatfuel work?

First and foremost, Chatfuel is a potent chatbot builder emphasizing automation and adaptability.

Its main goal is to build all-purpose bots to perform various tasks, such as answering s and gathering emails.

This is how Chatfuel works:

1. It attracts customers:

Avoid losing out on potential customers amid a sea of activity by developing inventive ways to engage them.

2. X3 conversion rate using chatbot marketing

Organic sales increased by **10 times.**

3. It interacts with potential leads:

- Assist automatically throughout the entire customer journey.
- Chatbots handle **98%** of customer inquiries.
- Organic **sales increased** by 10 times.

Features

Multichannel Messaging: Allows users to manage their business communication across Facebook, WhatsApp, Instagram, and Websites.

Real-time Analytics: Allows users to track and analyze metrics in real-time.

Integration with CRM: Helps streamline the messaging process by instantly identifying and tracking user behavior.

Message Testing: Allows users to test different text, images, call-to-actions, and more to find the most effective ones.

Here are the main steps to use Chatfuel AI Customer Support and Sales Tools:

1. Choose a platform for your chatbot. Chatfuel supports WhatsApp, Facebook Messenger, Instagram, and Telegram. You can also create a web chatbot that can be embedded on your website or app.

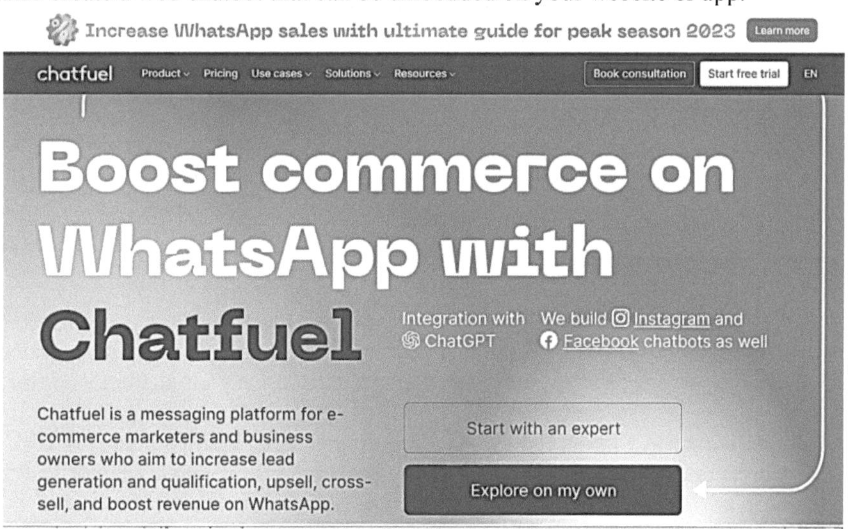

2. Create a WhatsApp business number or connect your existing one. Chatfuel is an official provider of the WhatsApp API, which means you can get the verified green badge and allow multiple agents to handle messages within a single number.

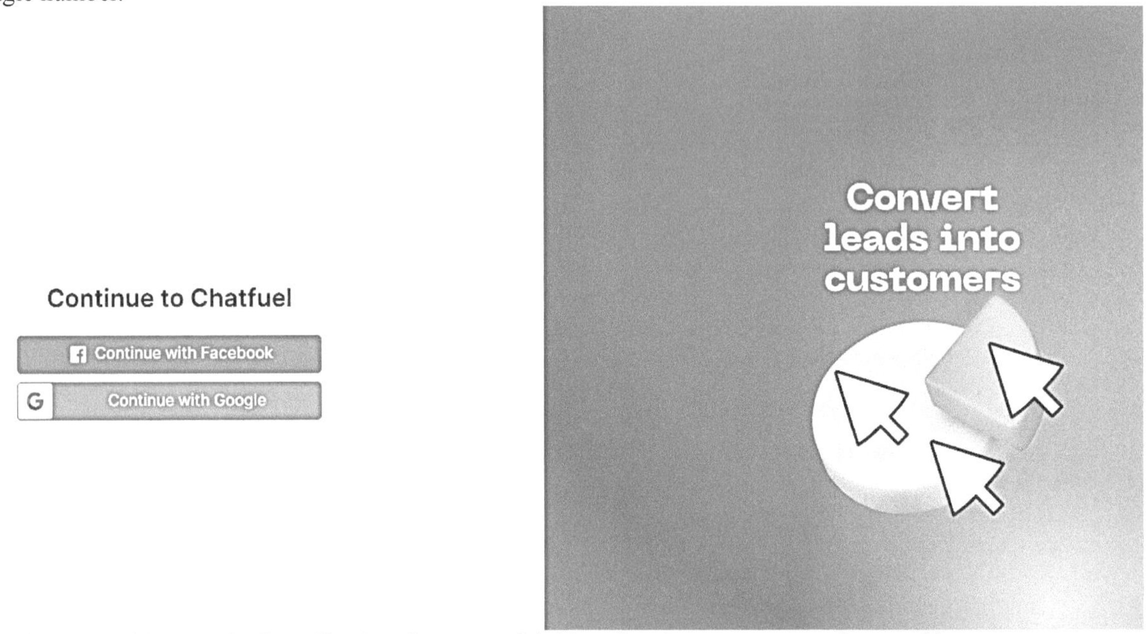

3. Integrate ChatGPT with your chatbot. ChatGPT is a powerful AI engine that can generate human-like responses and conversations. You can use ChatGPT to enhance your chatbot's capabilities and provide a more personalized and engaging experience for your customers.

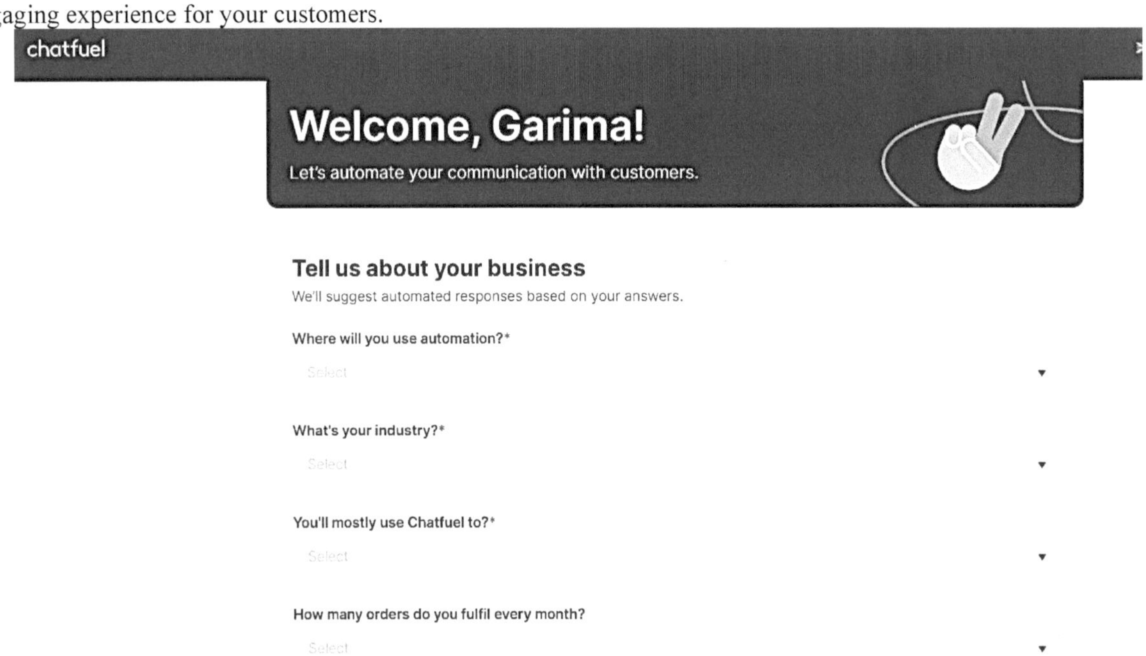

4. Build your chatbot's conversation flow. You can use Chatfuel's user-friendly interface, templates, guides, and resources to create a chatbot that suits your needs and goals. You can also customize your chatbot's appearance, language, and personality.
5. Add integrations and tools to your chatbot. Chatfuel allows you to integrate data from your store, CRM, or CDP with its API. You can also use segmentation, analysis, and A/B testing tools to optimize your chatbot's performance and effectiveness.

6. Launch your chatbot and monitor its results. You can publish your chatbot on your chosen platform and start interacting with your customers. You can also track and measure your chatbot's impact on your sales, customer support, and marketing metrics.

10.3 Second Nature

Second Nature AI is a cutting-edge sales training software that leverages conversational AI to create lifelike role-play scenarios. This assists them in refining their skills to excel in every sales interaction.

This AI tool aims to significantly improve the performance of sales representatives by providing them with a "virtual pitch partner."

This AI-driven partner engages in actual discussions with the reps, scores their performance, and offers actionable insights for improvement.

The software is versatile, catering to various industries such as insurance, technology, banking, and education.

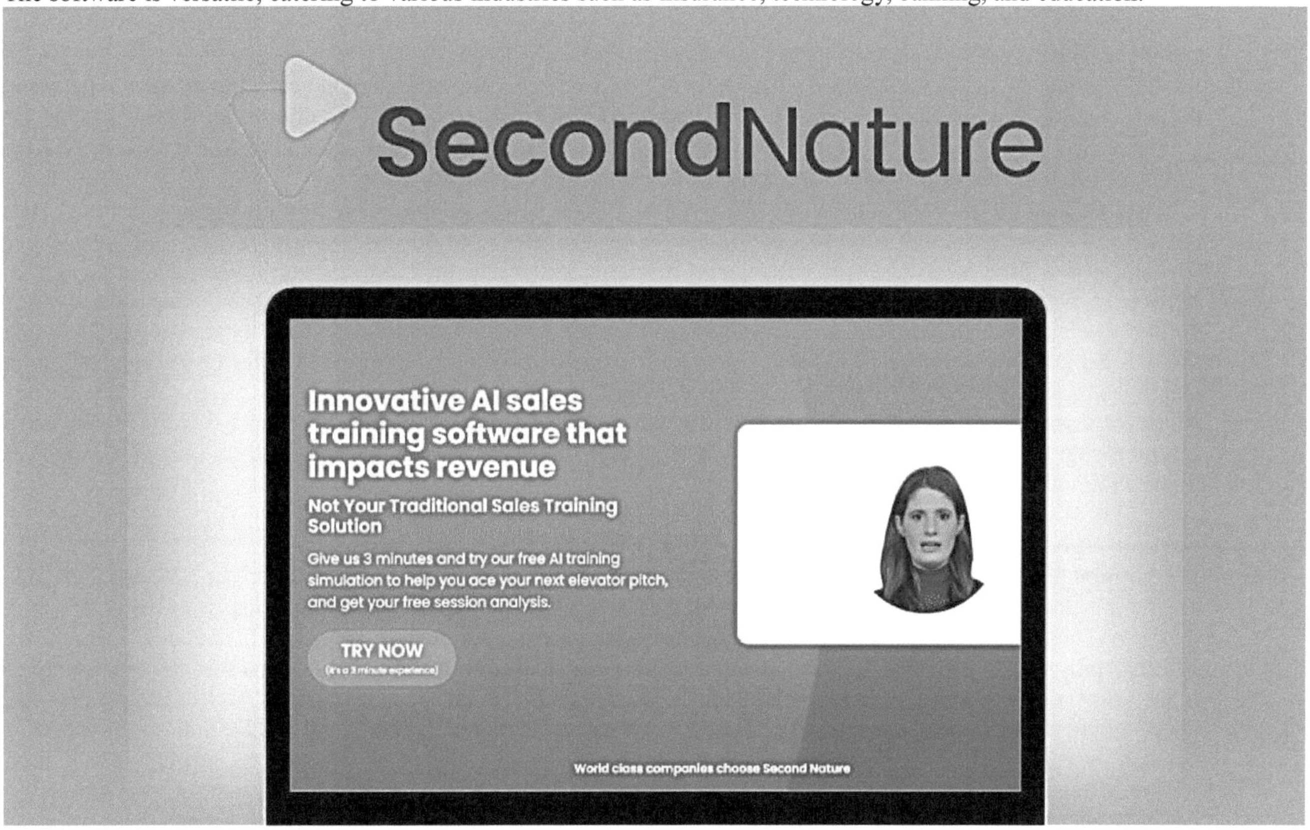

Second Nature AI Features

Second Nature AI is a sales training software that offers a plethora of features designed to enhance the skills of sales reps. Some of the features include:

1. Lifelike AI-Powered Role Plays: Simulate real-world sales scenarios.
2. Virtual Pitch Partner: Engages in actual discussions with sales reps.
3. Performance Scoring: Provides immediate feedback and scoring.
4. Industry-Specific Training: Customizable for insurance, technology, banking, etc.
5. On-Demand Training: Accessible anytime, anywhere.
6. Sales Proficiency Metrics: Measures improvement in sales skills.
7. Custom Avatars: Choose or create your training avatars.
8. Resource Library: Access to case studies, eBooks, and webinars for further learning.

Second Nature AI Use Case – Real-World Applications

Second Nature AI is an ideal tool for sales teams looking to upskill quickly and efficiently. It can be used for the following purposes:

1. Sales Onboarding: Reduce the time it takes to onboard new sales reps.

2. Skill Enhancement: Improve negotiation and pitching skills.
3. Industry-Specific Training: Tailor the training to specific industries like insurance or technology.
4. Remote Training: Ideal for remote teams to train from anywhere.
5. HR Training: This can also be used for HR professionals to improve their communication skills.

10.4 Kustomer

In the dynamic landscape of customer service, Kustomer stands at the forefront, offering a comprehensive suite of AI-driven tools designed to revolutionize how businesses engage with their customers. With a focus on the technology sector, the platform specializes in crafting innovative solutions that cater to emerging tech startups, providing them with a competitive edge in delivering exceptional customer experiences.

The commitment to excellence is exemplified by the dedication to creating engaging, informative content that translates complex tech terms into relatable language. As a copywriter specializing in the technology sector, you'll appreciate this approach, as it ensures that the technology-focused content is accessible to both tech-savvy audiences and those who may not be deeply immersed in the tech world.

Kustomer understands the transformative power of AI and machine learning in the finance industry, and has harnessed these technologies to develop a suite of cutting-edge AI tools tailored for the finance sector. From chatbots that automate 24/7 service without the need for a large support team to CRM-powered automation that scales personalized resolutions, the solutions are designed to drive efficiency and customer satisfaction.

The intent detection capabilities eliminate the need for manual triage, automatically routing bot conversations based on customer input. Plus, the code-free configuration ensures that even non-technical users can build and deploy sophisticated chatbot workflows with ease, thanks to the intuitive visual interface and pre-built templates.

In the ever-evolving world of customer service, Kustomer's AI solutions are here to stay, providing instant answers by deflecting common inquiries, assisting agents with AI-driven recommendations, and personalizing global support through language detection. This AI tool empowers businesses to deliver personalized, effortless customer service, thereby enhancing their brand image and customer loyalty.

In the vast sea of tech startups, Kustomer shines as a beacon of innovation and excellence, offering AI-powered solutions that set new standards in customer service. Join in the journey of transforming traditional banking and finance through the application of AI and machine learning.

Features of Kustomer

1. Chatbots for 24/7 automated service: The advanced chatbots are like having a dedicated support team available around the clock. They handle repetitive service requests effortlessly, providing instant responses to customer inquiries. These chatbots are highly customizable, allowing you to tailor them to your specific business needs.

2. CRM-powered automation for personalized resolutions: Kustomer's CRM integration takes customer service to the next level. It automates routine agent interactions and scales personalized resolutions. By connecting real-time CRM data to chatbot workflows, you can offer customers a more tailored and efficient service, making them feel valued.

3. Intent Detection: The AI-driven intent detection feature automatically identifies and routes bot conversations based on customer input. This ensures that each customer is directed to the right resources or agents, reducing response times and improving overall satisfaction.

4. Code-Free Configuration: Building and deploying sophisticated chatbot workflows has never been easier. The user-friendly visual interface and pre-built templates allow even non-technical users to create and customize chatbots to suit their unique requirements. No coding skills are required, making it accessible to all.

5. Sentiment Analysis: Understanding customer emotions is crucial for providing empathetic support. Kustomer's sentiment analysis feature identifies exactly how customers are feeling without requiring agents to sift through large volumes of text. This allows you to prioritize and address conversations that require immediate attention, ensuring customer frustrations are calmed effectively.

Kustomer Use Cases

1. Deflect Common Inquiries: Use the AI tools to deflect common customer inquiries by surfacing your Knowledge Base content. When customers reach out via forms, email, or chat, the system can instantly provide them with relevant information, reducing the need for manual responses.

2. Assist Agents with AI-Driven Recommendations: Encourage your support agents with AI models that continuously learn from historical conversation data. These models recommend the best responses and actions, eliminating guesswork and enhancing the efficiency of your customer support team.

3. Personalize Global Support: In a globalized world, language can be a barrier. Kustomer's AI can instantly identify a customer's origin language and route them to a native-speaking agent or auto-translate messages for fast resolution. This personalization ensures that language is no longer a barrier to providing exceptional customer support.

AI Text Enhancement – Agents will get a toolkit of one-click actions including the ability to expand short messages to more formal or friendlier responses; and tidying up spelling and grammar.

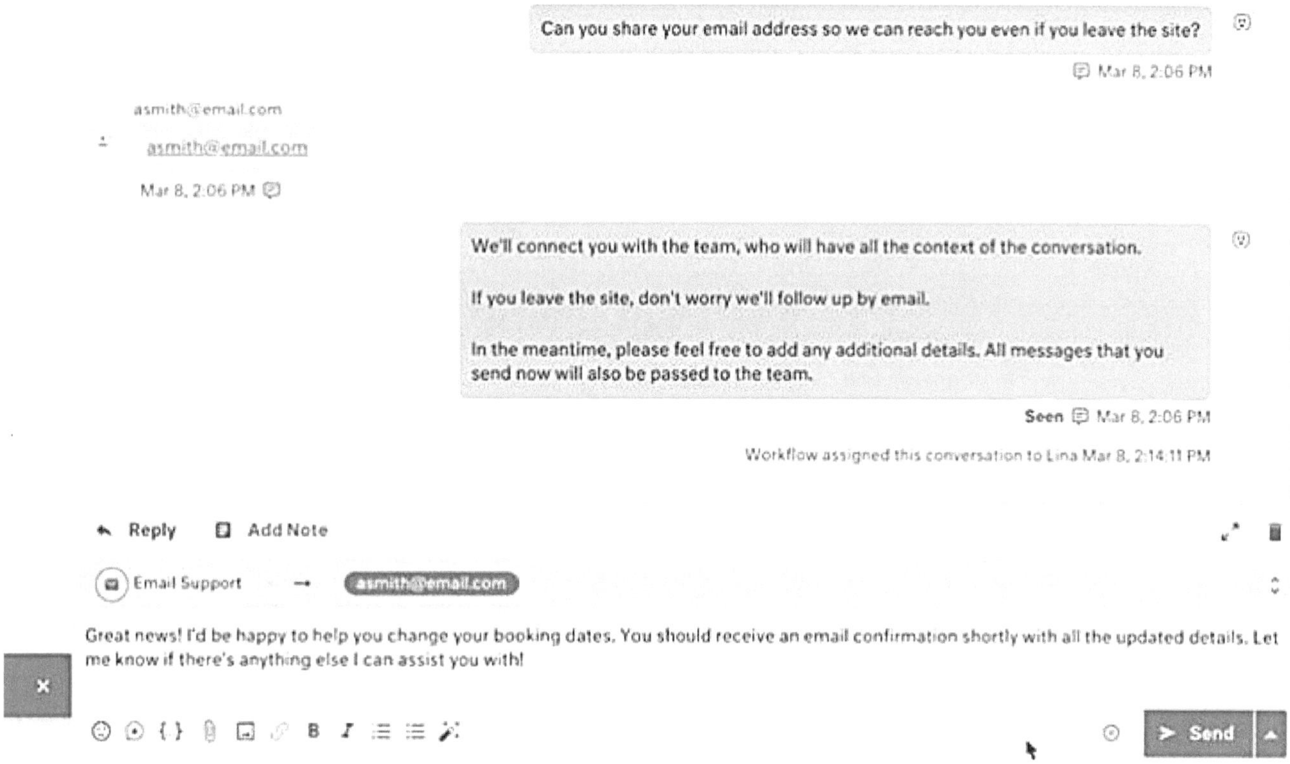

Conversation Summaries – We've regularly heard from customers about the friction that occurs when customer handoffs are made, whether from chatbot to agent, or agent to another agent. The receiving party has to start from scratch, combing through long chat threads to catch up. We've added new features to make those transitions easier, leveraging OpenAI to summarize the information, whether it's in a paragraph or a pithy sentence.

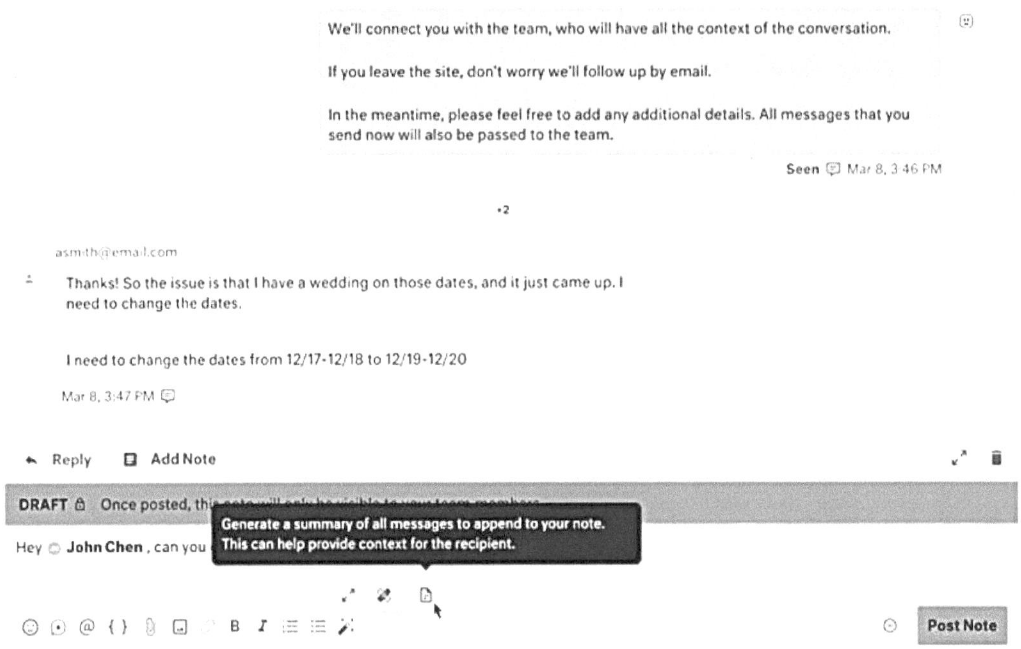

10.5 AutoResponder

1. Autoresponder.ai is a powerful chatbot tool that allows users to automate replies on popular messaging platforms such as WhatsApp, Facebook Messenger, Instagram, Telegram, Signal, and Viber. This innovative tool is designed to reduce workload and provide instant replies, while also offering highly customizable features to meet the specific needs of businesses and individuals alike.
2. Gone are the days of manual responses and delayed replies. With Autoresponder.ai, you can streamline your messaging efforts and ensure that no inquiry goes unanswered. By automating replies, you can save time and effort, allowing you to focus on more important tasks.
3. One of the standout features of Autoresponder.ai is its ability to customize rules for different messages on different messaging platforms. This means that you can set specific guidelines and responses for each platform based on your preferences and requirements. For example, you can set different rules for customer support inquiries on WhatsApp compared to sales inquiries on Facebook Messenger. This level of customization ensures that your replies are tailored to each platform and audience.
4. Autoresponder.ai also offers seamless integration with AI technologies, such as GPT/GPT-4 and Dialogflow AI. This integration allows you to trigger custom actions based on specific keywords or phrases. For example, you can set up an automated response that directs customers to a particular webpage or provides them with a discount code when they mention a specific product. This advanced functionality adds a layer of intelligence to your automated responses and enhances the overall user experience.
5. Using Autoresponder.ai comes with a myriad of benefits. Firstly, it significantly reduces the workload associated with responding to messages on multiple platforms. With automated replies, you can ensure that every inquiry receives an immediate response, even outside of business hours. This not only improves customer satisfaction but also reinforces your brand's reputation for prompt communication and excellent customer service.

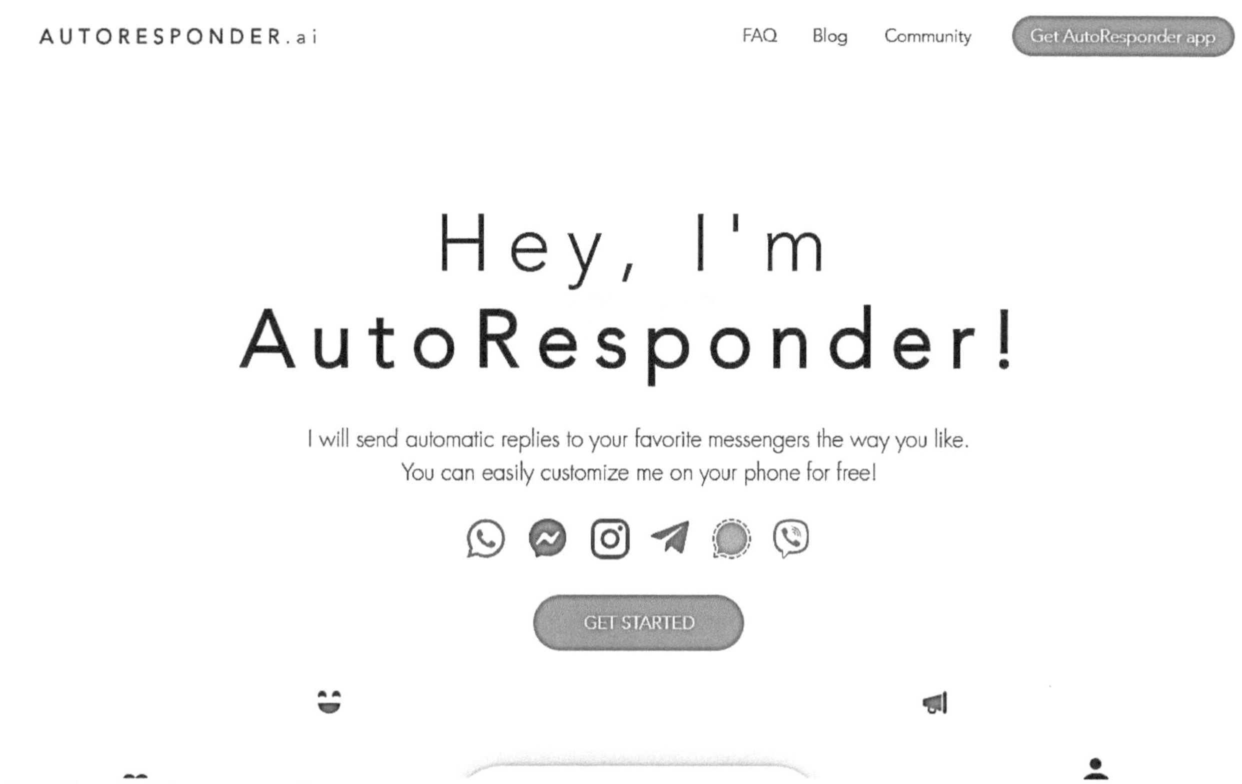

Benefits of AI Autoresponders

1. Efficiency Beyond Compare: Think about the number of customer queries and leads that come in daily. An AI autoresponder doesn't just send out a bland, generic message. It's capable of crafting responses tailored to each query, ensuring that the initial contact with a customer is both personal and instant.

2. Round-The-Clock Service: The digital world doesn't sleep, but humans need to. With an AI autoresponder, your business remains responsive 24/7. This means no customer is left waiting, and queries from different time zones are addressed promptly.

3. Scalability: As your business grows, the number of emails or messages will increase. AI autoresponders can handle thousands of messages concurrently without any dip in performance or quality.

4. Cost-Efficient: Hiring staff for customer support can get costly. With AI autoresponders, you can save cost on manpower while ensuring top-notch service.

5. Analytics and Insights: Modern AI autoresponders come packed with data analytics. This means you gain insights into customer behavior, preferences, and more, aiding in refining your marketing strategies.

Here's a breakdown of some key features, categorized by their target area:

Customer Support:

1. Smart Chatbot: Build and deploy AI-powered chatbots that automatically answer FAQs, collect information, and route complex inquiries to agents.
2. Live Chat Agent Assist: Equip agents with real-time AI suggestions for responses, resolutions, and next best actions based on the conversation context.
3. Email Ticketing Automation: Auto-respond to emails, categorize requests, and assign tickets to the appropriate agents based on pre-defined rules.
4. Self-Service Knowledge Base: Build a searchable knowledge base of FAQs, solutions, and guides for customers to find answers independently.
5. Sentiment Analysis: Analyze customer conversations to identify negative sentiment and proactively offer support or escalate issues.

Sales:

1. Lead Gen Bots: Deploy chatbots on your website or social media to qualify leads, schedule demos, and nurture existing leads 24/7.

2. Personalized Product Recommendations: Recommend relevant products or services to website visitors and existing customers based on their profile and browsing behavior.
3. Abandoned Cart Recovery: Automate email campaigns to recover abandoned carts and convert lost sales into completed purchases.
4. Dynamic Web Forms: Use AI to personalize website forms and landing pages based on visitor data, increasing conversion rates.
5. Sales Pipeline Management: Automate repetitive tasks like lead scoring, follow-up reminders, and reporting to streamline the sales process.

General Features:

1. Omnichannel Support: Manage all customer interactions across channels like email, chat, phone, and social media from a single platform.
2. Analytics and Reporting: Gain insights into customer behavior, agent performance, and campaign effectiveness through detailed reports and dashboards.
3. Integration with CRM and Marketing Tools: Connect AutoResponder to your existing CRM and marketing automation systems for a seamless workflow.
4. Easy-to-Use Interface: Build chatbots, workflows, and campaigns using a drag-and-drop interface without coding knowledge.
5. Customizable Automation: Set up triggers and rules to automate repetitive tasks and personalize customer interactions.

AutoResponder AI is a tool that helps you send automatic replies to your favorite messengers with the help of AI. It can be used for customer support, sales, or personal purposes. Here are the steps to use it:

1. Download and install the app from the Google Play Store or the [App Store].
2. Grant the app the necessary permissions to access your notifications and contacts.
3. Choose the messenger app you want to use with AutoResponder, such as WhatsApp, Telegram, or Facebook Messenger.
4. Create a new rule by tapping on the plus icon at the bottom right corner of the screen.
5. Enter the keywords or phrases that will trigger the rule, such as "hello", "thank you", or "order status".
6. Choose the type of response you want to send, such as a custom text, an AI-generated text, a web server response, a Dialogflow response, or a Tasker action.
7. Optionally, you can adjust the settings of the rule, such as the delay time, the reply frequency, the contact groups, or the reply mode.
8. Save the rule and test it by sending a message that matches the keywords or phrases to yourself or a friend.
9. Repeat the steps for creating more rules as needed.

10.6 MagicForm

MagicForm AI is an innovative tool designed to transform the customer experience by leveraging the power of artificial intelligence. This AI tool instantly learns everything about your company, ensuring it can effectively engage with your customers.

MagicForm uses AI to boost engagement and conversions with website visitors. Using GPT-3 technology, it offers personalized, lifelike responses to any user queries.

Unlike traditional chatbots, MagicForm AI continuously learns from each conversation, ensuring that it remains updated and relevant. With the help of AI technology, MagicForm makes a significant difference in how businesses interact with their customers.

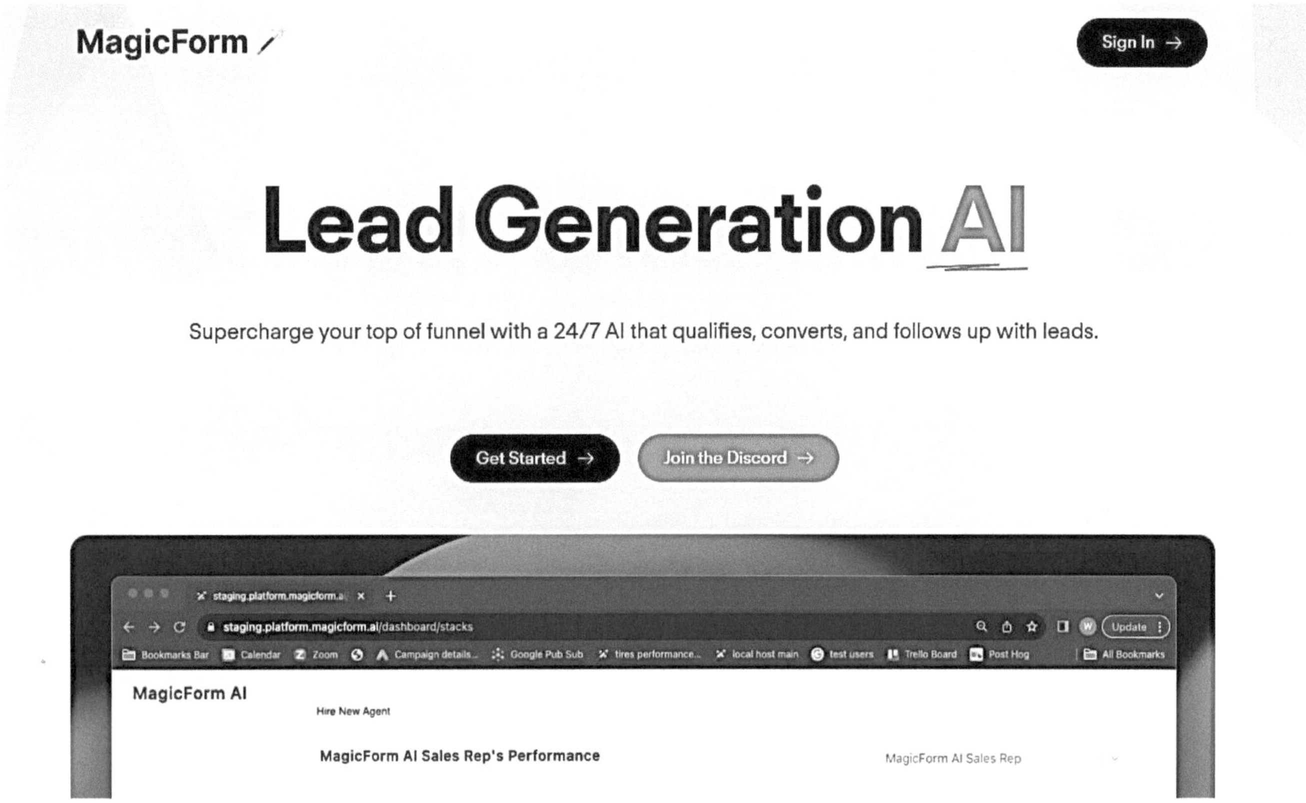

MagicForm AI Features

MagicForm AI is an AI sales rep tool that offers a wide variety of features designed to enhance customer interactions and boost conversions. Some of the standout features include:

1. Innovation: Instantly learn about your company to provide relevant interactions.
2. Continuous Learning: Unlike other chatbots, MagicForm AI learns from each conversation, ensuring it remains updated.
3. Keeping You In Control: Built on a robust AI framework, it's designed to be seamlessly integrated into your website.
4. Increase Conversions: Designed to effectively answer customer queries and drive conversions.
5. An Employee Like No Other: A reliable AI sales rep who's always available and never calls in sick.

MagicForm AI Use Case – Real-World Applications

MagicForm AI is not just another chatbot; it's a game-changer for businesses looking to enhance their customer interactions. It can be utilized for:

1. Customer Support: Answer queries in real-time, ensuring customers get the information they need.
2. Sales Assistance: Assist potential customers in making purchasing decisions.
3. Feedback Collection: Gather valuable feedback from customers to improve products/services.
4. Multilingual Support: Engage with customers across different languages and regions.
5. Lead Generation: Engage with website visitors and convert them into potential leads.

Unlocking the Benefits: How MagicForm Can Transform Your Business

The advantages of using MagicForm are truly magical. Here's how it can benefit your business:

1. Enhance Customer Engagement

MagicForm's personalized responses can significantly improve customer engagement, fostering stronger connections with your audience.

2. Increase Conversion Rates

By offering accurate and valuable information to customers, MagicForm helps boost conversion rates, ultimately driving more sales and business growth.

3. Reduce Costs

With its automation capabilities, MagicForm streamlines customer service tasks, allowing you to allocate resources elsewhere and reduce operational costs.

How to use MagicForm Step By Step Tutorial

Step 1 - Sign up

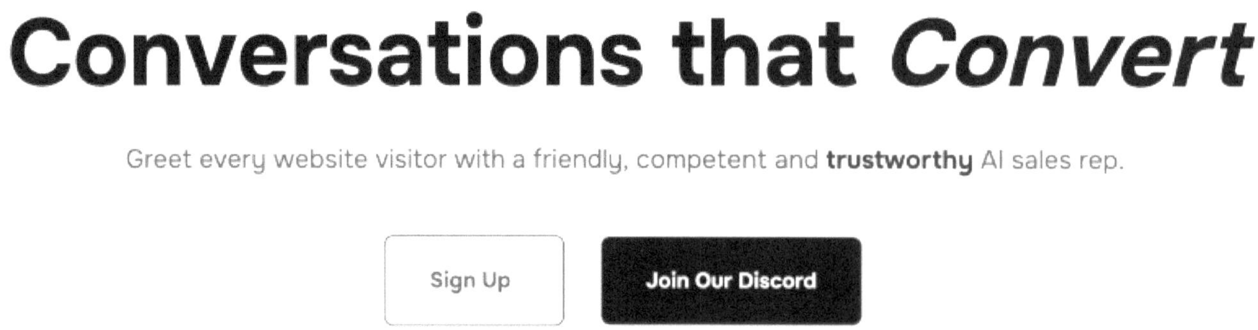

Sign up to MagicForm using your e-mail address

Step 2 - Fill out form

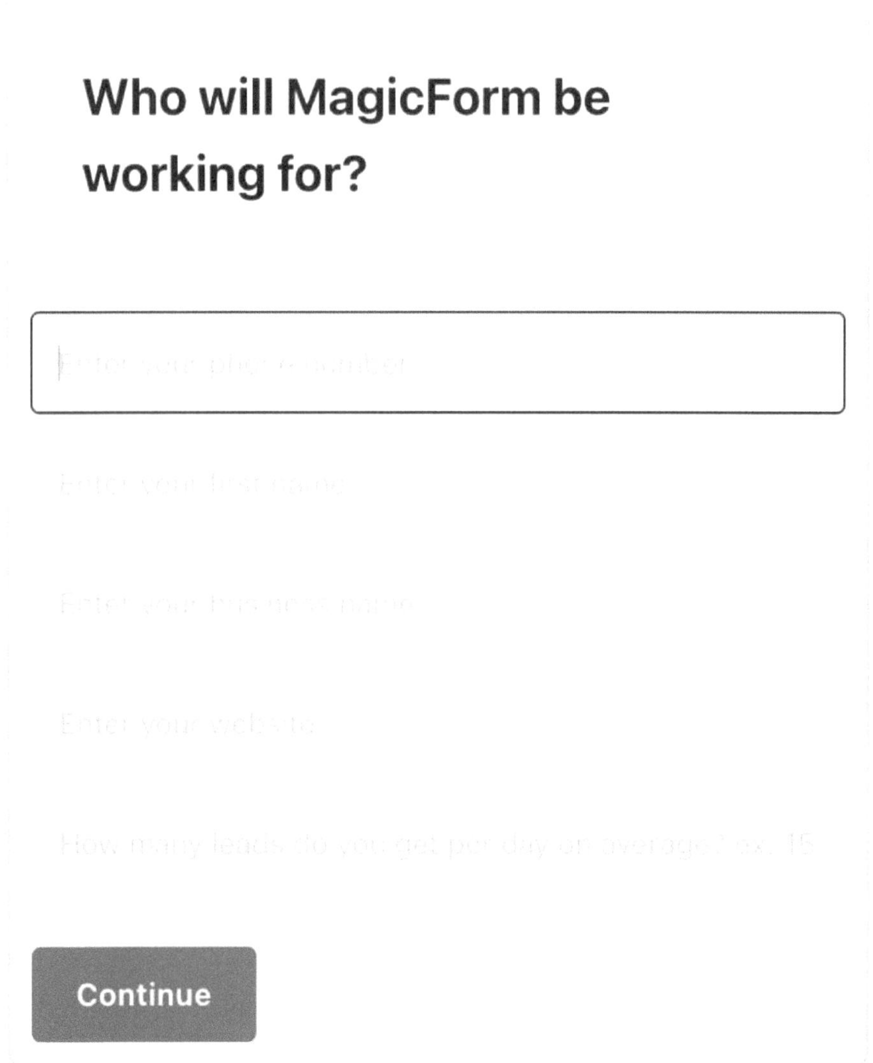

Fill out the form after signing up. Give MagicForm your phone number, first name, business name, website URL, and how many leads you currently collect per day on average.

Step 3 - Create new agent

The first thing to do after your setup is to create a new agent. Just hit the "Create New Agent" button and let's go!

Step 4 - Upload data

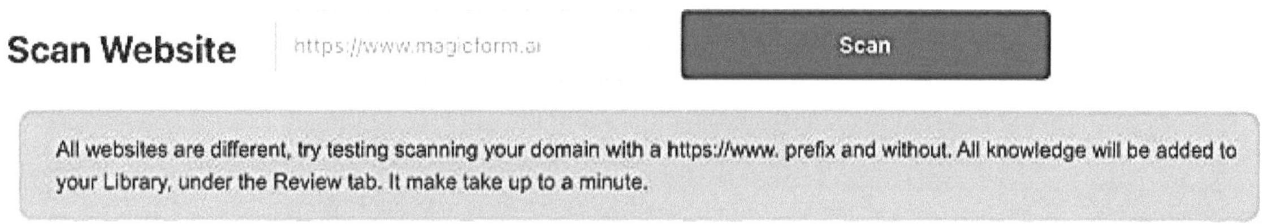

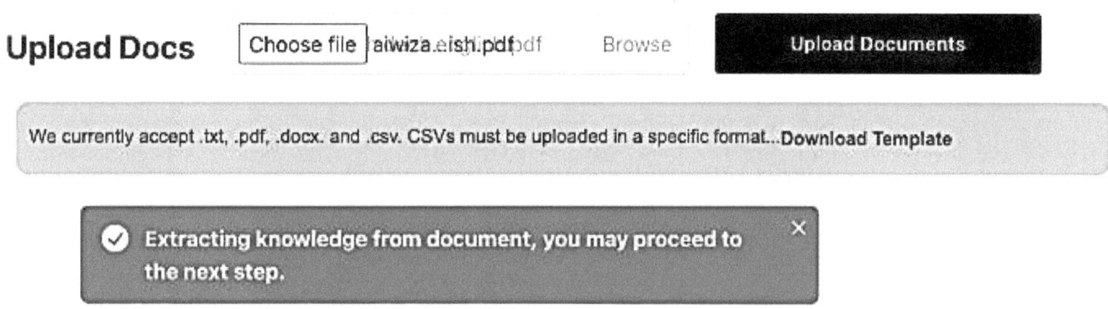

Hit the "Upload tab" in the top navbar and either enter the website URL to scan or upload txt, pdf, docx, or CSV documents. This step is needed to give the agent data for context. If you skip this part the agent will have no info about your site/product. I'm uploading a pdf about aiwizard.

Step 5 - Configure your agent

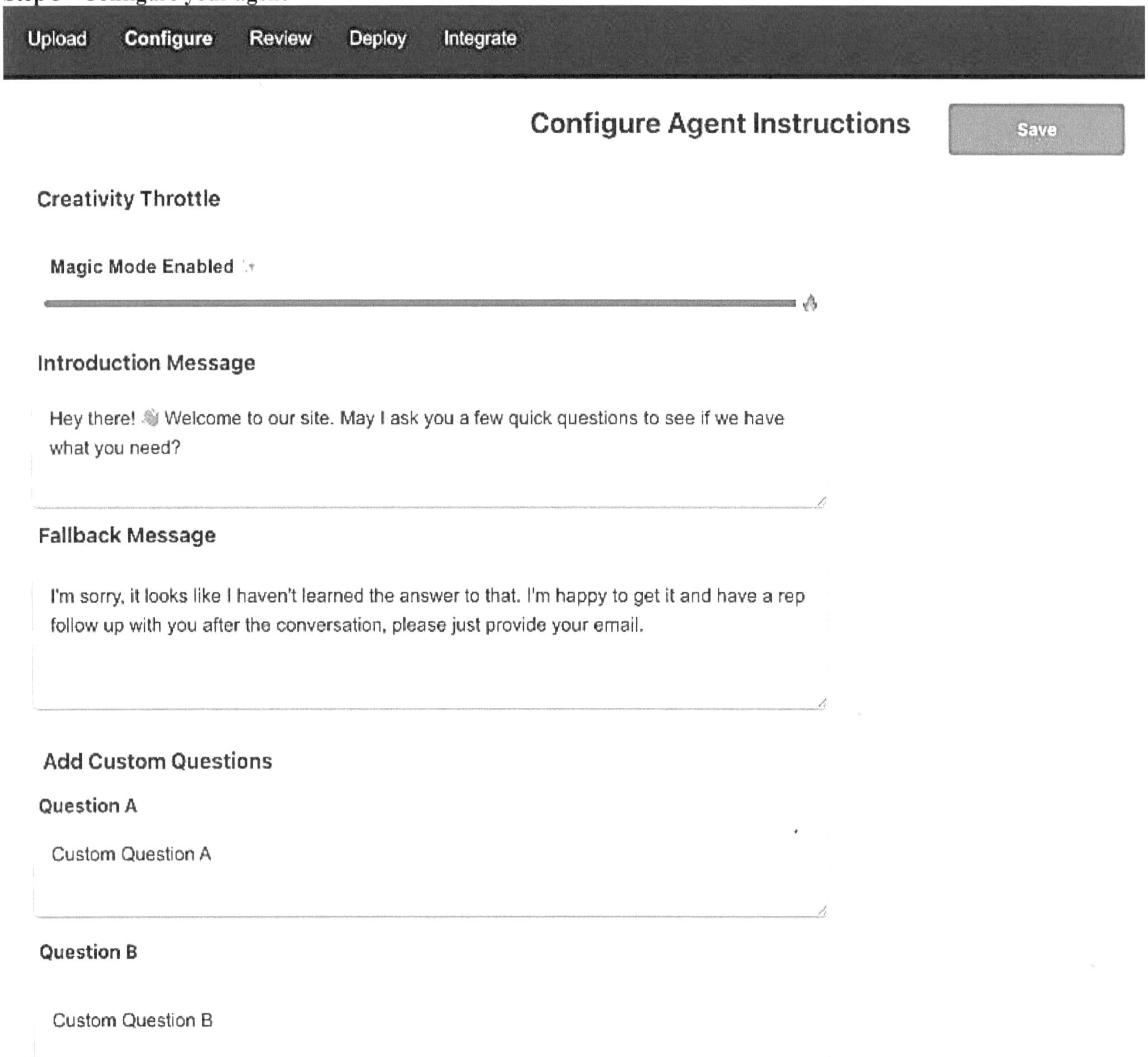

Now it's time to configure the agent. Hit "Configure" in the top navbar. First slide the creativity throttle. You can go from "Restricted to knowledge base only" to "Magic Mode", which gives the agent much more creativity. Then set your intro message, and fallback message, and ask a few custom s. Then you can set the agent's personality & purpose. We will leave it to the default friendly customer experience AI personality. The purpose is to gather information and steer the user toward the Call To Action. You can also enter a custom Call To Action and add additional instructions.

Step 6 - Review agent

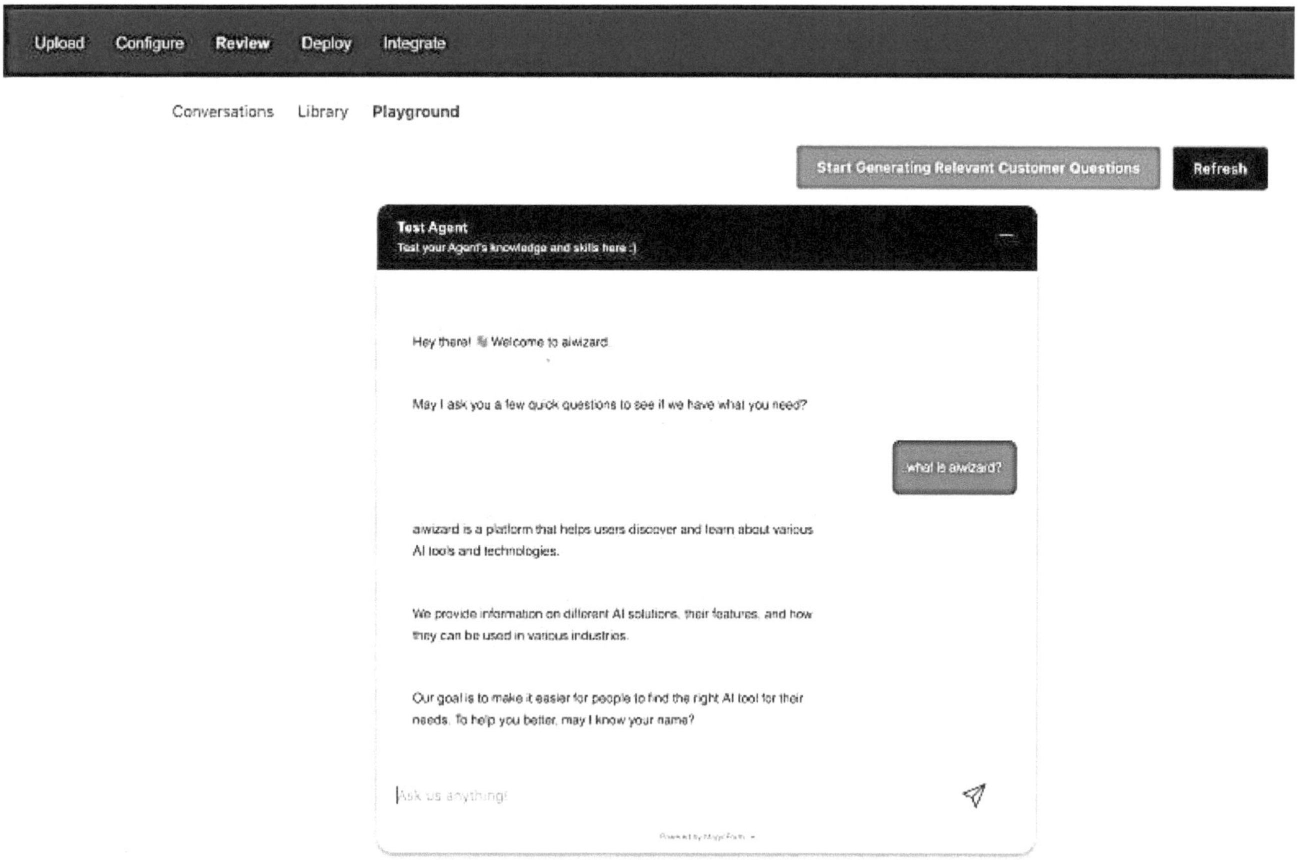

Time to test out the agent! In the "Review" tab you can check out the conversations the agent has already had, see the library of your MagicForm account and test the agent out in the playground. Here you see me having a quick chat with the agent about what aiwizard is.

Step 7 - Deploy

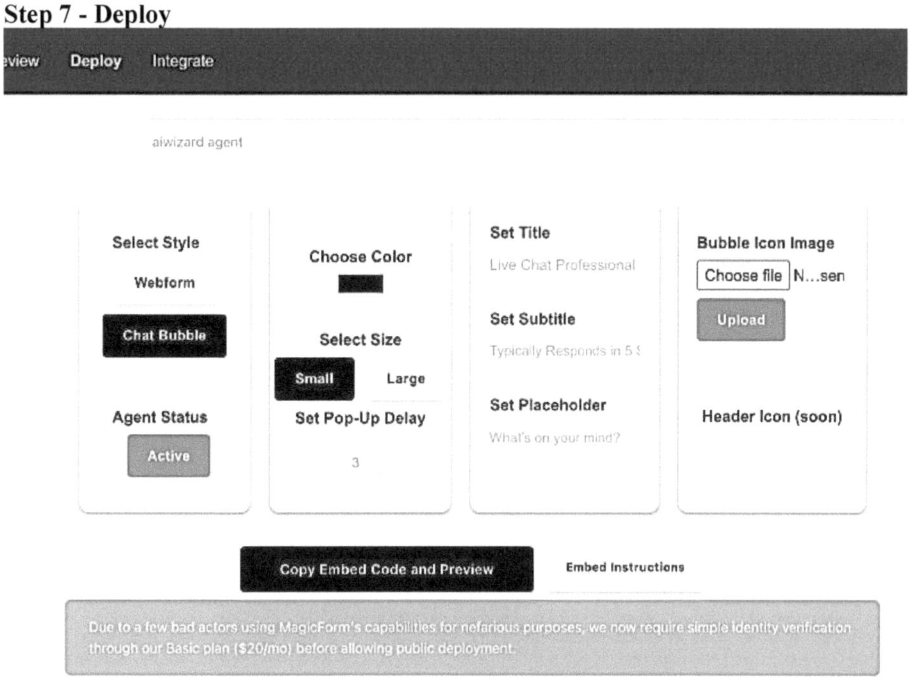

10.7 Conversica

1. Conversica is an AI-powered conversational tool designed to enhance revenue generation throughout the lifecycle for revenue teams. The tool functions as a Revenue Digital Assistant, capable of initiating and continuing conversations with potential customers through multiple channels, including email, SMS, and chat.
2. The conversational AI technology is intended to reduce the workload for sales teams and serves as a virtual assistant that converses and qualifies leads, manages appointment setting, and re-engages with previous contacts.
3. Conversica also integrates with leading CRM platforms such as Salesforce, that makes it simple for sales teams to track progress and act upon conversations.
4. The conversational AI technology uses natural language processing and machine learning to understand user inputs and tailor responses to produce a human-like conversation.
5. Conversica AI's dashboard also provides insights on the success of the virtual assistant's conversations with prospects, including response rates, conversions, and best-performing conversations.
6. The tool aims to optimize revenue generation by allowing sales teams to focus on more personalized and valuable interactions with interested prospects, while also ensuring continuous conversation with leads to enhance customer acquisition and engagement.
7. In summary, Conversica is an AI-powered conversational solution that serves as a Revenue Digital Assistant to manage and qualify leads, while also acting as a virtual assistant that can engage in conversations throughout the buyer's lifecycle.
8. With user-friendly functionality, customizable responses, and integrated reporting, Conversica aims to streamline the lead generation and engagement process for revenue teams, optimizing sales efforts and ultimately increasing revenue.

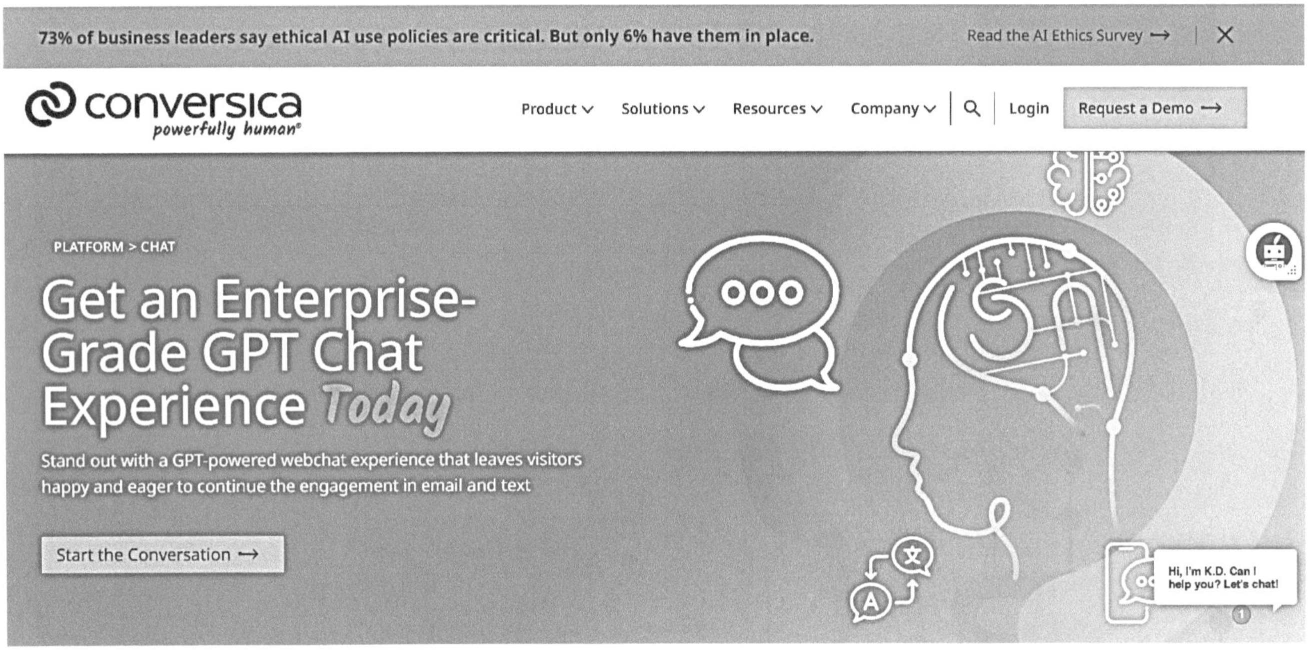

Real-Life Applications of ConversicaConversica has been successfully implemented by businesses across various industries to improve customer engagement and sales processes. Some notable examples include:

1. Automotive Dealership: A leading automotive dealership utilized Conversica's AI-powered bots to engage with leads and schedule test drives. The dealership experienced a significant increase in appointment numbers and a decrease in scheduling time. Conversica's bots also helped prioritize leads and boost conversion rates.
2. Financial Services Company: A financial services firm employed Conversica to engage with leads and streamline its sales process. By prioritizing leads and enhancing conversion rates, the company achieved a considerable increase in revenue.
3. Educational Institution: An educational institution employed Conversica's bots to engage with prospective students and address their inquiries. The institution witnessed a substantial increase in enrollment rates, as the bots provided timely and accurate responses to prospective students.

Key Benefits of ConversicaConversica offers numerous advantages to businesses, including:
1. Increased Efficiency: The AI-powered bots handle repetitive and time-consuming tasks, such as lead qualification and appointment scheduling, freeing businesses to focus on more strategic tasks.
2. Enhanced Customer Engagement: The bots deliver personalized and engaging conversations with customers, resulting in improved customer satisfaction and loyalty.
3. Improved Lead Generation and Conversion Rates: By engaging with leads across various channels and qualifying them based on specific criteria, Conversica's bots yield higher conversion rates.
4. Seamless Integration: Conversica integrates effortlessly with existing CRM and marketing automation platforms, enabling businesses to automate their lead generation and sales processes across multiple channels.

There are several methods for training Conversica's bots:
1. Data Feeds: The bots can be trained using data feeds from CRM and marketing automation systems, which may include customer behavior, preferences, and historical interactions. Analyzing this data enables the bots to better comprehend customer needs and respond with increasingly personalized messages.
2. Manual Feedback: Business users can provide manual feedback to train the bots. For example, if a bot misinterprets a customer's intent, a business user can offer feedback to correct the response. Consequently, the bot learns from this feedback and improves its accuracy over time.
3. A/B Testing: The bots can also be trained using A/B testing, where different versions of a message are tested to determine which one performs better. By analyzing the results of the A/B test, the bot can learn and adapt to provide more effective messages in future interactions.

Here is a step by step guide on how to use Conversica's AI Customer Support and Sales Tools:
1. Choose a Revenue Digital Assistant (RDA) for your specific use case, such as marketing, sales, or customer success. An RDA is a digital team member that can communicate with your prospects and customers via email, SMS, web chat, or voice, using natural language processing and conversation management skills.
2. Customize your RDA's name, persona, tone, and style to match your brand and audience. You can also tailor the RDA's conversations to fit your goals, such as generating more leads, booking more meetings, closing more deals, or increasing customer satisfaction and loyalty.
3. Integrate your RDA with your existing tech stack, such as CRM, marketing automation, or customer service platforms. This way, your RDA can access and update relevant data, trigger workflows, and sync with your human team members.
4. Launch your RDA and let it start engaging with your prospects and customers. Your RDA can initiate, respond, and follow up on conversations, as well as handle objections, qualify interest, and schedule appointments. Your RDA can also alert you when a lead or customer is ready to talk to a human, and hand over the conversation seamlessly.
5. Monitor, measure, and improve your RDA's performance using reports and analytics. You can track key metrics, such as conversation volume, response rate, conversion rate, revenue impact, and customer feedback. You can also use insights and best practices to optimize your RDA's conversations and outcomes.

10.8 Candide

Candide AI Tool is a platform that allows users to create and manage AI virtual assistants. It offers a variety of features that make it easy to create and deploy powerful AI chatbots including effortless document management unlimited pages and docs efficient workflows and custom bots and integrations with favorite tools.

Features of Candide :
1. Effortless document management: Candide sorts and manages Notion and PDF documents, allowing users to instantly retrieve information from their team's knowledge base.
2. Unlimited pages and docs: It allows users to empower their bot with unlimited pages and documents, ensuring that they have access to all of their team's knowledge and data.
3. Efficient workflows and custom bots: It allows users to create efficient workflows and custom bots without any development skills.
4. Integrations with favorite tools: It integrates with users' favorite tools, such as Slack, Notion, and Google Calendar, making it easy to use their AI virtual assistant in their everyday workflow.

Benefits:

1. Improved customer support: Candide AI virtual assistants can provide 24/7 customer support, answering customer s and resolving issues quickly and efficiently.
2. Increased productivity: It AI virtual assistants can help users to increase their productivity by automating tasks and providing them with the information they need quickly and easily.
3. Improved team collaboration: This AI virtual assistants can help teams to collaborate more effectively by providing them with a central place to share information and ask s.
4. Reduced costs: This AI virtual assistants can help businesses to reduce their costs by automating tasks and reducing the need for human support agents.

Use cases:
1. Customer support: Candide AI virtual assistants can be used to provide customer support for a variety of products and services, including e-commerce, software, and travel.
2. Lead generation: It is virtual assistants can be used to generate leads by qualifying prospects and scheduling demos.
3. Marketing and sales: It is virtual assistants can be used to promote products and services, answer customer s, and even book appointments.
4. Internal documentation chatbot: It can be used to create an internal documentation chatbot that can provide employees with access to company knowledge and resources.
5. Project management chatbot: It can be used to create a project management chatbot that can track tasks, deadlines, and progress.
6. Human resources chatbot: It can be used to create a human resources chatbot that can answer employee s about benefits, policies, and procedures.
Overall Candide AI Tool is a powerful and versatile platform that can be used to create and manage AI virtual assistants for a variety of use cases.

10.9 wARMER.ai

Here explanation step by step :

1

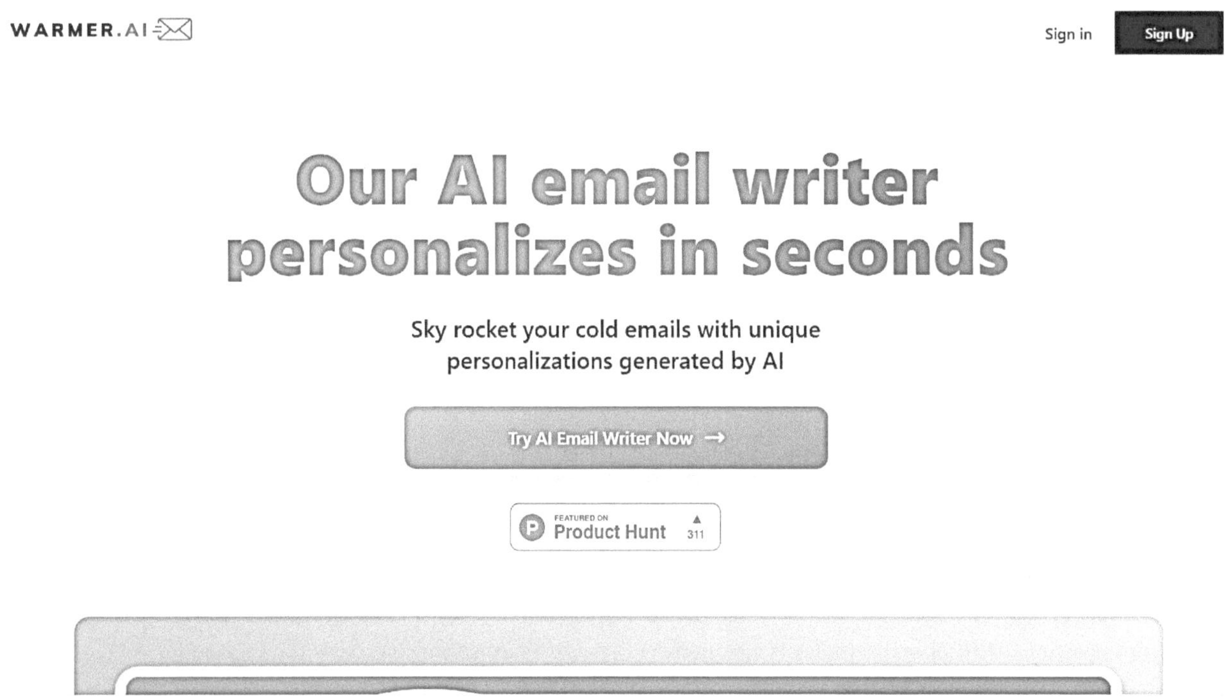

2. Click on the signup button, and to create an account.

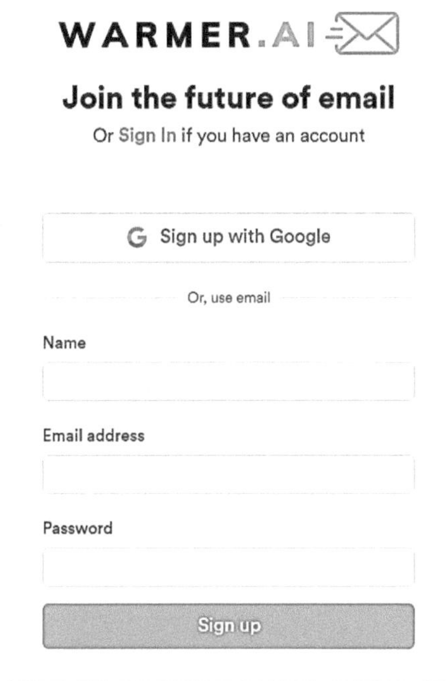

3. To check the verification, your email id to verify it.

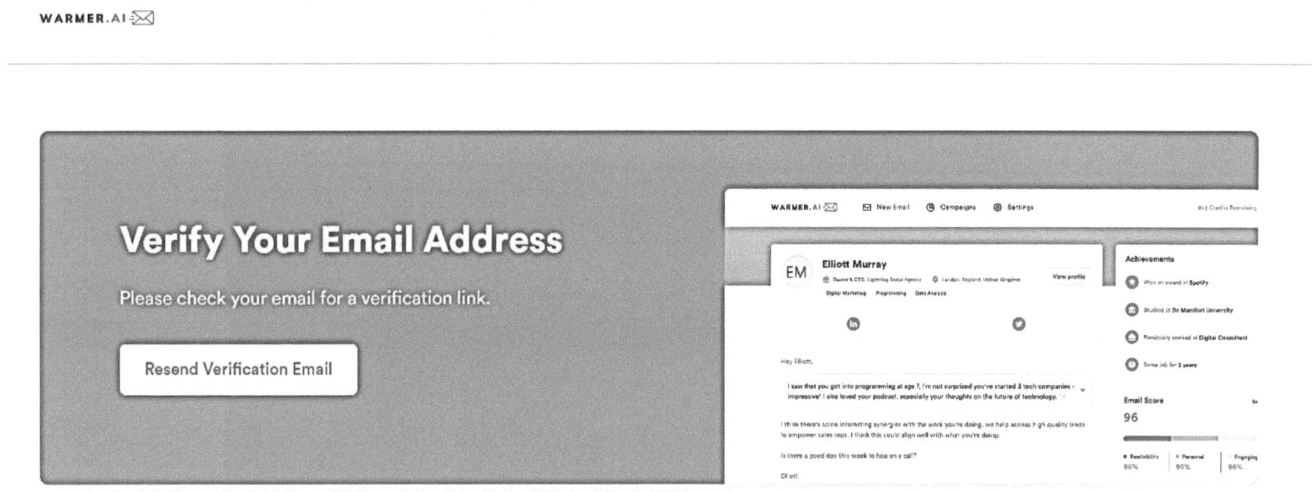

4. Now, to check your mail to send the verify link to click it and open this screen, welcome o warmer!. Click on next button.

Welcome To Warmer!
Watch this quick video to learn everything you need
New Email Wizard
What are we pitching?
Company name
Warmer
Website
Description
Add Identity
Next

5. Now to fill these entry details and click the add identity button. And it is optional also.

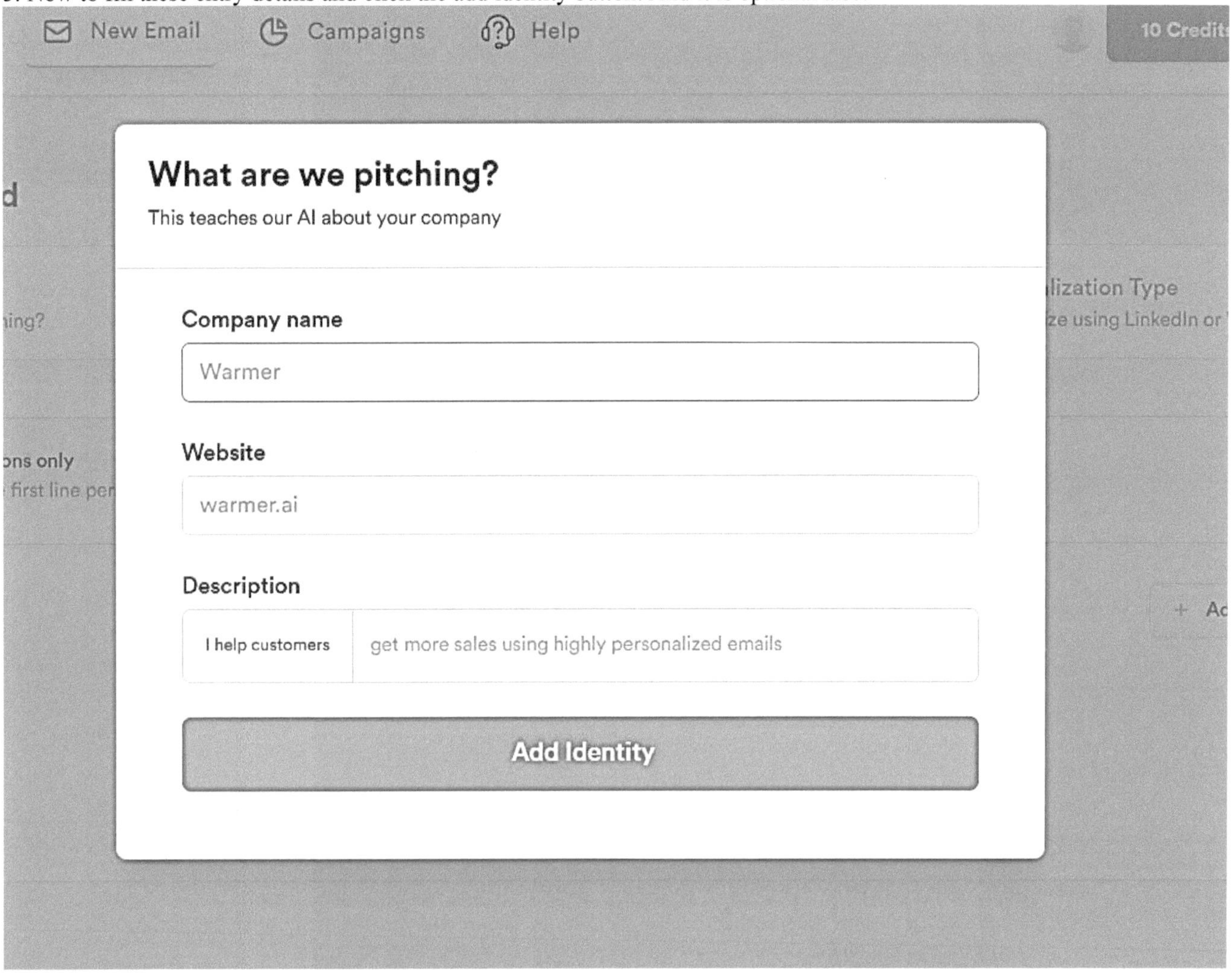

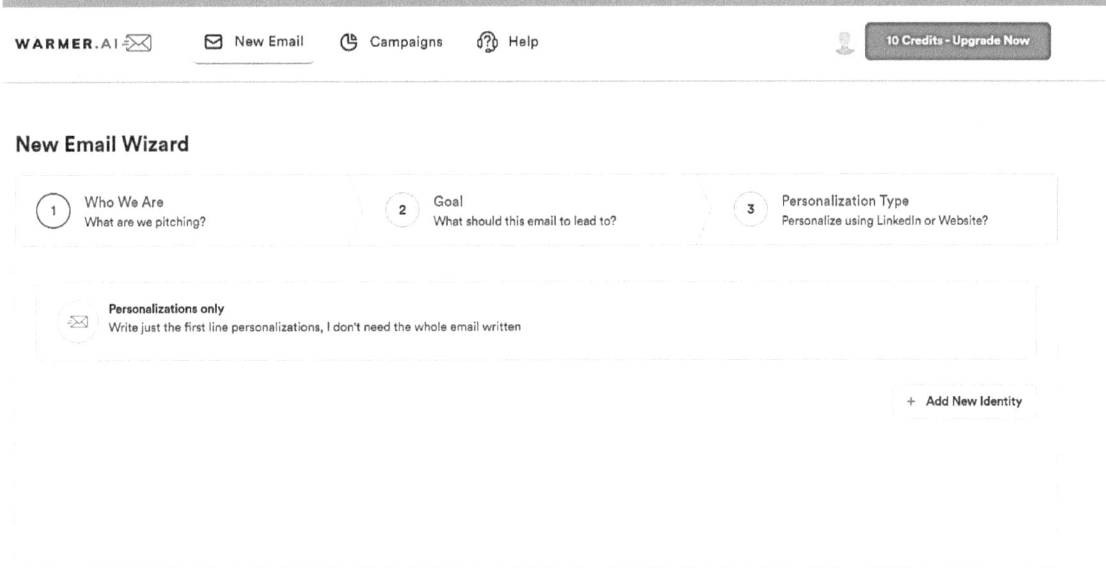

6. This is open a dashboard.

Exercise

Exercise 1 – MCQ

Q 1. What was the previous name of SecondBrain?

A. MagicChat
B. Chatfuel AI
C. AutoResponder
D. Conversica

Q 2. Which tool is NOT primarily focused on providing virtual assistance in content creation and social media management?

A. Chatfuel AI
B. Second Nature
C. Conversica
D. AutoResponder

Q 3. What is the main function of Kustomer?

A. Automated lead generation
B. AI-driven lead engagement
C. Natural language processing in communication
D. Customer support and sales prospecting

Q 4. What is AutoResponder specialized in?

A. Customer support and sales prospecting
B. Automated climate control solutions
C. Automatic replies for email communication
D. AI-driven lead engagement

Q 5. What is the primary focus of MagicForm?

A. Form creation and data collection
B. Automated lead generation
C. AI-driven lead engagement
D. Virtual assistance in content creation

Q 6. Conversica is known for:

A. Automated climate control solutions
B. Form creation and data collection
C. AI-driven lead engagement and conversation management
D. Customer support and sales prospecting

Q 7. What is the main focus of Candide in customer interactions?

A. Automated responses
B. Sentiment analysis using AI
C. Virtual assistance in content creation
D. Automated climate control solutions

Q 8. wARMER.ai is related to:

A. Customer support and sales prospecting
B. Automated climate control solutions
C. Virtual assistance in content creation
D. Automated responses

Q 9. What is the primary function of Chatfuel AI?

A. Automated responses
B. Form creation and data collection
C. Natural language processing in communication
D. Automated climate control solutions

Q 10. SecondBrain, previously MagicChat, is focused on:

A. Automated lead generation
B. AI-driven lead engagement
C. Automated responses in customer support interactions
D. Form creation and data collection

Exercise 2 – True/ False

Q 1. SecondBrain, previously known as MagicChat, is a Customer Support and Sales Tool.

Q 2. Chatfuel AI is primarily focused on providing virtual assistance in content creation and social media management.

3. Second Nature is a Customer Support and Sales Tool designed for natural language processing in communication.
4. Kustomer is a tool specifically designed for automated lead generation and sales prospecting.
5. AutoResponder is a Customer Support and Sales Tool specializing in automatic replies for email communication.
6. MagicForm is a tool primarily focused on form creation and data collection in customer interactions.
7. Conversica is known for its capabilities in AI-driven lead engagement and conversation management.
8. Candide is a Customer Support and Sales Tool that integrates AI for sentiment analysis in customer interactions.
9. wARMER.ai is designed for automated climate control solutions and is not related to customer support or sales.

10. SecondBrain, formerly MagicChat, primarily focuses on providing automated responses in customer support interactions.

Exercise 3 – Fill in the blanks

Q 1. Chatfuel AI is a customer support tool that specializes in ____________ responses through automated chat.
Q 2. Businesses use Chatfuel AI to create personalized and engaging ____________ with their customers.
Q 3. With Second Nature, sales teams can leverage AI to understand customer preferences and deliver targeted ____________.
Q 4. Kustomer is a comprehensive customer support platform that integrates ____________ into the customer service workflow.
Q 5. The tool is particularly useful for handling repetitive tasks in the ____________ stage of the sales funnel.

Exercise 4 – Match case

1. Second Brain (previously Magic Chat)	C. An AI-powered tool that streamlines customer interactions through chat.
2. Chat fuel AI	D. A tool specializing in automated responses and follow-ups in sales.
3. Second Nature	A. A platform designed to create a personalized sales experience.
4. Kustomer	B. A comprehensive platform for managing and analyzing customer interactions.
5. AutoResponder	E. A customer support platform that integrates automation into workflows.

Exercise 5 – One word answer

Q 1. What is the Innovation of SecondBrain?
Q 2. What is Streamlining of Chatfuel AI?
Q 3. What is the Automation in Second Nature?
Q 4. What is the Integration?
Q 5. What is the Versatile of MagicForm?

Exercise 6 – Small answer

Q 1. What does Chatfuel AI streamline?
Q 2. Focus of Second Nature in sales?
Q 3. What does Kustomer seamlessly integrate?
Q 4. Main focus of AutoResponder?
Q 5. Purpose of MagicForm?

Exercise 7 – Long answer

Q 1. What distinguishes SecondBrain, previously known as MagicChat, in the realm of customer support, and how does its AI-powered technology contribute to enhancing sales interactions?
Q 2. How does Chatfuel AI streamline customer interactions, and what role does it play in providing a seamless experience for businesses?

Answers

Exercise 1 – MCQ

Ans: 1 A, 2 B, 3 D, 4 C, 5 A, 6 C, 7 B, 8 B, 9 C, 10 C

Exercise 2 – True/ False

Ans: 1True, 2 False, 3 False, 4 False, 5 True, 6 False, 7 True, 8 True, 9 False, 10 True

Exercise 3 – Fill in the blanks

Ans: 1 Generating, 2 Interactons, 3 Recommendations, 4 Automation, 5 Outreach

Exercise 4 – Match case

Ans: 1 A, 2 C, 3 B, 4 E, 5 D

Exercise 5 – One word answer

Ans: 1 Personalization, 2 Chatbot, 3 Tailored, 4 Automation, 5 Forms

ONLINE RESOURCES

Practice Paper

Link https://forms.office.com/r/mHTaYzDzXq

QR Code

Video Content

Link:https://www.youtube.com/playlist?list=PLzlh_31VWEFroNjpEj1eykhiXHFUY9vmAhttps://www.youtube.com/playlist?list=PLzlh_31VWEFroNjpEj1eykhiXHFUY9vmA

QR Code

Chapter 11: HR and Recruiting Tools

11.1 Paradox

Paradox is an AI HR tool that aims to automate and streamline the recruiting process, from attracting candidates to hiring them. It offers several features, including a Conversational ATS (Applicant Tracking System), Conversational Career Sites, Conversational CX (Candidate Experience), and more.

Highlights

1. Their flagship product, the Conversational ATS (Applicant Tracking System), stands out as an applicant management solution that caters specifically to high-volume hiring managers and candidates in frontline positions.
2. The Conversational ATS also emphasizes candidate engagement and personalization.
3. Through 2-way texting, text-to-apply functionality, and chat-driven applications, candidates can easily interact with the system, ensuring a seamless and engaging experience.
4. The system adapts to candidates' preferred communication channels, such as SMS, WhatsApp, or Facebook Messenger, and allows them to conveniently answer s, complete screenings, and schedule interviews.

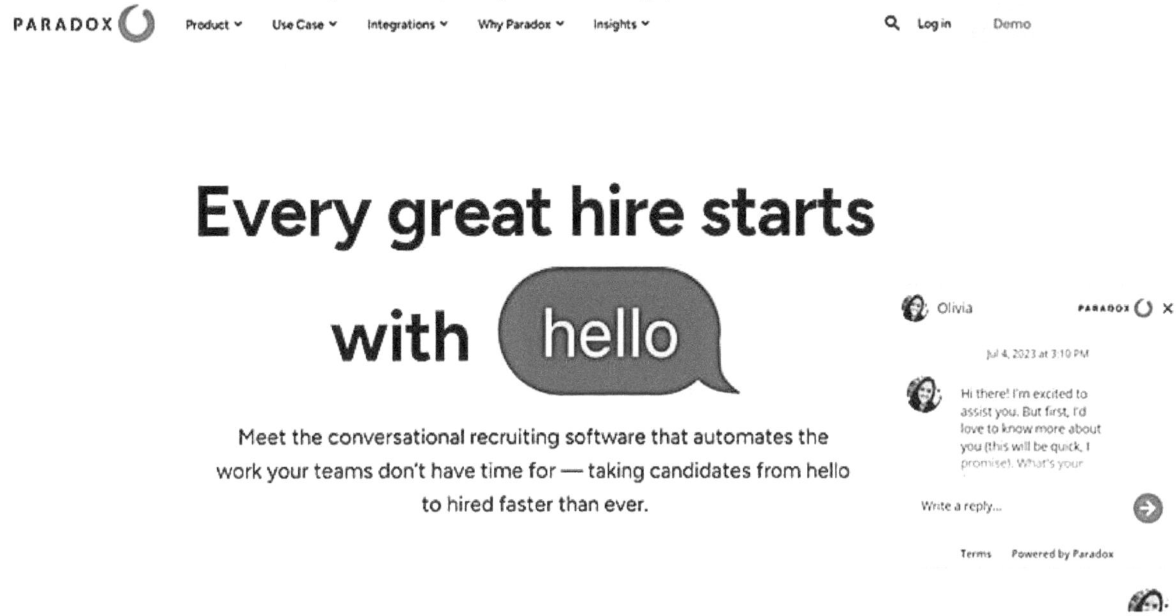

Paradox Key Features

1. **Conversational AI:** Paradox's unique selling point is their conversational AI tool Olivia, to whom you can delegate all your mundane HR tasks. Olivia would chat on your behalf with your job candidates and pass all the necessary information.
2. **Recruiting:** You can use Olivia for hiring in multiple ways. Candidates can use a job board to apply for an opening in your company and Olivia will start chatting with them the minute they click on the 'apply' button. You can also embed Olivia in your company's career site to bring candidates a tailored job opening based on their interests, experience, and responses to the conversation with Olivia.
3. **Interview scheduling:** You don't have to manually schedule interviews with candidates. Olivia syncs with your calendar and automatically takes care of this part for you. You can use it to schedule multi-location, multi-person, and other complex interviews. It also sends automatic reminders to job candidates and handles rescheduling with the candidate on its own.
4. **Screening**: When a candidate applies to a job opening and starts a conversation with Olivia, the candidate will be automatically screened against job requirements. If the candidate moves past the initial automatic screening, Olivia would also automatically schedule them for an interview.
5. **Events:** Olivia can be used as an event assistant for coordinating between event hosts and attendees. Instead of letting your guests sign up through an events page, Olivia can chat with them through text messages for registration, answering s, or sharing any information ahead of the event. This can be used for a variety of events including job

fairs, seasonal hiring, orientation, and recurring virtual events. Because Paradox supports native integrations for video conferencing, Olivia can also prompt qualified candidates to talk to recruiters on the spot.
6. Pre-employment assessment: You can use Traitify, Paradox's pre-employment assessment tool to acquire desired talent. What's interesting about this tool is that it gives its takers a visual, image-based test that takes less than two minutes to complete. Despite the brevity of the test, you can collect hundreds of personality data points about your potential employees.

11.2 Textio

1. Textio is an AI writing tool tailored to recruiters and HR professionals that analyzes and optimizes job descriptions. It uses advanced machine learning algorithms to identify language patterns that might be turning off potential candidates and suggests ways to rephrase your content to be more inclusive, engaging, and effective.
2. The tool helps you to remove gender bias and improve the diversity of your candidates ensuring that your job descriptions and emails are not only effective but also inclusive and welcoming to everyone.
3. Textio is an AI-powered writing platform that aims to enhance the quality of written content, particularly in the context of job recruitment. It relies on machine learning to analyze existing writing and develop lexical rules that can automate the writing process.
4. Despite the skepticism surrounding such tools, Textio is a testament to the growing influence of AI in our everyday tasks, marking a significant step in the quest to create machines that can replicate human-like thought processes.

Textio is a company that provides AI-powered tools to help HR and recruiting teams write more effective and inclusive content for attracting and retaining diverse talent. **Some of the tools that Textio offers are:**
1. Textio Score: This tool predicts how diverse your candidate pipeline will be based on the language you use in your job posts, emails, social posts, and other types of communication. It also gives you instant suggestions on how to improve your language and appeal to a broader audience.
2. **Bias interruption:** This tool highlights and helps you avoid using gendered phrases, racism, age bias, ableism, corporate clichés, and other forms of bias that might turn off potential candidates or employees.
3. AI safeguards: This tool ensures that your content is free of bias and errors, whether you write it yourself or generate it with AI. It also helps you maintain a consistent employer brand and tone across your communication channels.
4. Trackable analytics: This tool quantifies your progress in recruiting more inclusively and shows you the impact of your language choices on your hiring outcomes. It also helps you identify areas where you can make further improvements.

5. Extensions and integrations: This tool allows you to access Textio directly from your favorite platforms, such as Workday, Taleo, iCIMS, Greenhouse, SAP SuccessFactors, Oracle, LinkedIn, Outlook, and Gmail. You can also write at textio.com.
6. **Time-saving toolkits:** This tool provides you with a library of optimized job posts and templates that you can use to speed up your recruitment process, engage the right candidates, and reduce your overall cost-per-hire

How does Textio work?
Textio works efficiently on the following parameters. Take a look:
1. Textio's AI-powered analysis
Textio utilizes AI and natural language processing (NLP) algorithms to analyze text. It processes large amounts of data and identifies patterns, language usage, and contextual information to gain insights.
2. Predictive analytics
Textio's predictive analytics engine examines the analyzed data to predict the potential impact and effectiveness of written content. It provides suggestions and recommendations to improve the content's appeal, clarity, and overall engagement.
3. Language bias detection
Textio actively scans the text for potential bias, including gendered or exclusive language. It alerts users to any biased language and suggests alternative phrasing to promote inclusive and unbiased communication. This feature helps organizations foster diversity and equal opportunity in their messaging.
4. Real-time writing guidance
As users compose their text, Textio offers real-time guidance and feedback. It suggests enhancements, highlights potential issues, and provides alternative word choices or sentence structures to optimize the content's impact and effectiveness.
5. Performance tracking and analytics
Textio tracks the performance of written content over time. It provides analytics and metrics that measure factors like response rates, candidate conversion, and language impact. These insights enable users to understand the effectiveness of their writing and make data-driven decisions for content optimization.

Who uses Textio?
Textio has tons of clients, including big name companies. **For example, some of the brands that use Textio include names like:**
1. Johnson & Johnson
2. Cisco
3. Hulu
4. Tesco
5. Oracle
6. McDonald's
7. Ebay
8. American Express
9. Spotify

Here's a general step-by-step guide based on the typical use of Textio:
1. Sign Up or Log In:
2. Visit the Textio website.
3. Sign up for an account or log in if you already have one.
4. Explore Dashboard:
5. Upon logging in, you might be directed to a dashboard.
6. Familiarize yourself with the user interface and available features.
7. Create a Document or Job Listing:
8. Start a new document or job listing within the Textio platform.
9. Write or Paste Content:
10. Write or paste the content you want to improve. This could be a job description, email, or any other written material.
11. Receive Augmented Writing Suggestions:
12. Textio will use AI to analyze your text and provide real-time suggestions.
13. These suggestions may include improvements for clarity, tone, inclusivity, and effectiveness.

14. Optimize for Language and Tone:
15. Textio may provide insights on the language and tone of your writing.
16. It could suggest changes to make your communication more engaging or to target a specific audience.
17. Inclusive Language Recommendations:
18. Textio is known for providing suggestions to make language more inclusive, helping to avoid biased or exclusive terms.
19. Review and Edit:
20. Review the suggestions offered by Textio.
21. Edit your document based on the insights provided.
22. Export or Use within Platform:
23. Once you're satisfied with the optimized content, you can export it or use it within the Textio platform, depending on your needs.
24. Iterate and Refine:
25. Continue refining your content iteratively based on the feedback and suggestions from Textio.

11.3 HiredScore

1. HiredScore is an AI-powered tool that offers solutions for HR transformation in talent acquisition and talent management processes. Using explainable AI, automation, and deep integrations, HiredScore delivers proactive, action-driving recommendations to the right stakeholders at the right time.
2. The tool aims to help organizations achieve their HR transformation goals with transparency, quality, and real-time awareness.With HiredScore, users can automatically discover, score, and prioritize talent across all talent types, including leads, applicants, and candidates for any open role.
3. The tool also offers safe automation to optimize talent processes, removing bottlenecks and ensuring efficient, effective, and fair hiring practices.HiredScore enables strategic utilization of all workforce options for hiring and retention goals, allowing users to align workforce plans and discover the best talent irrespective of worker type.
4. The tool promotes ethical and compliant AI usage by providing bias audits, explainability, local compliance configurations, and privacy-centricity.Furthermore, HiredScore helps organizations make progress towards diversity and inclusion goals by seamlessly connecting DE&I goals to recruiter and manager processes.
5. The tool facilitates data utilization by integrating with most HR systems, third parties, collaboration platforms, and experience layers.HiredScore ensures a consistently unbiased review for every candidate, complying with governmental non-discrimination standards globally.
6. The tool minimizes compliance risk and complies with industry thought-leadership standards.Overall, HiredScore aims to provide innovative, safe, and effective AI solutions for HR teams worldwide, supporting data-driven recruiting processes and talent acquisition initiatives.

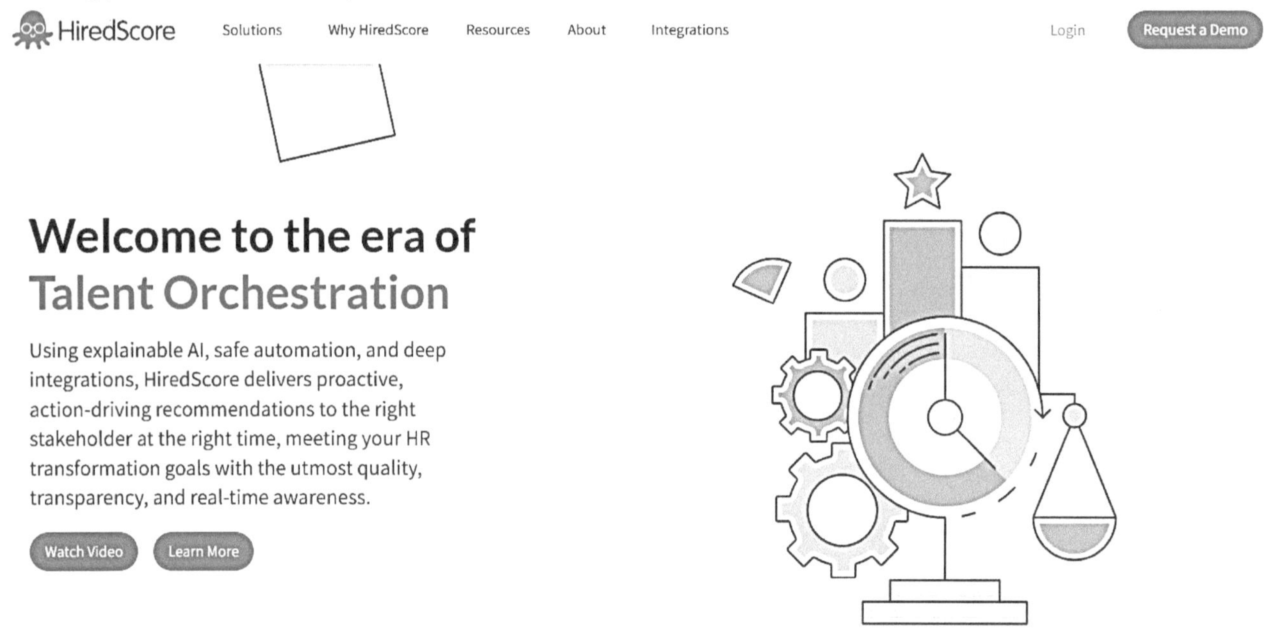

Features of HiredScore

1. Discover, Score, and Prioritize Talent: HiredScore allows you to automatically uncover the best talent, be it external, internal, flexible, or passive, and prioritize them effortlessly.

2. Augment Talent Processes with Safe Automation: The platform ensures that hiring teams, employees, and candidates collaborate in the most efficient, effective, and equitable manner.

3. Strategic Utilization of Workforce Options: HiredScore enables you to align your workforce plans with internal talent mobility, ensuring that the right talent is always matched with the right tasks.

4. Innovate with Ethical, Compliant AI: This proprietary AI not only provides unparalleled performance but also undergoes rigorous bias audits, offering complete transparency and privacy-centricity.

5. Seamlessly Connect DE&I Goals: Measurable progress is facilitated towards Diversity & Inclusion goals at every stage of your recruiting and internal promotion efforts, offering low-friction, highly satisfactory solutions.

HiredScore Use Cases

1. Effortless Lead and Applicant Prioritization: With HiredScore, you can instantly identify, match, and prioritize leads and applicants for any open role. Whether you're dealing with external candidates, internal talent, flex workers, or passive job seekers, the platform streamlines the selection process, saving you time and resources.

2. Enhanced Hiring Team Efficiency: Remove bottlenecks and keep your hiring teams, employees, and candidates working harmoniously. The safe automation ensures that the entire hiring process becomes more efficient, effective, and fair. This translates into quicker decisions and a better candidate experience.

3. Progress in Diversity & Inclusion Goals: Make measurable strides toward a more inclusive workforce at every stage of your recruiting and internal promotion efforts. Thesolutions are designed for low friction and high satisfaction, making them easy to adopt.

User Benefits:

1. Time-saving: HiredScore's ai algorithms automate various recruitment tasks, saving HR professionals significant time and effort in the hiring process.

2. Improved Quality of Hire: By leveraging data-driven insights, HiredScore enables organizations to make more informed decisions, resulting in higher-quality hires and reduced turnover.

3. Enhanced Efficiency: The platform streamlines the recruitment workflow, allowing HR teams to focus on strategic initiatives and improving overall efficiency.

Here's a general step-by-step explanation based on the typical use of HiredScore:

1. Integration with Applicant Tracking System (ATS):

- HiredScore seamlessly integrates with most major ATS platforms, allowing it to access and analyze candidate data directly within your existing recruitment workflow.

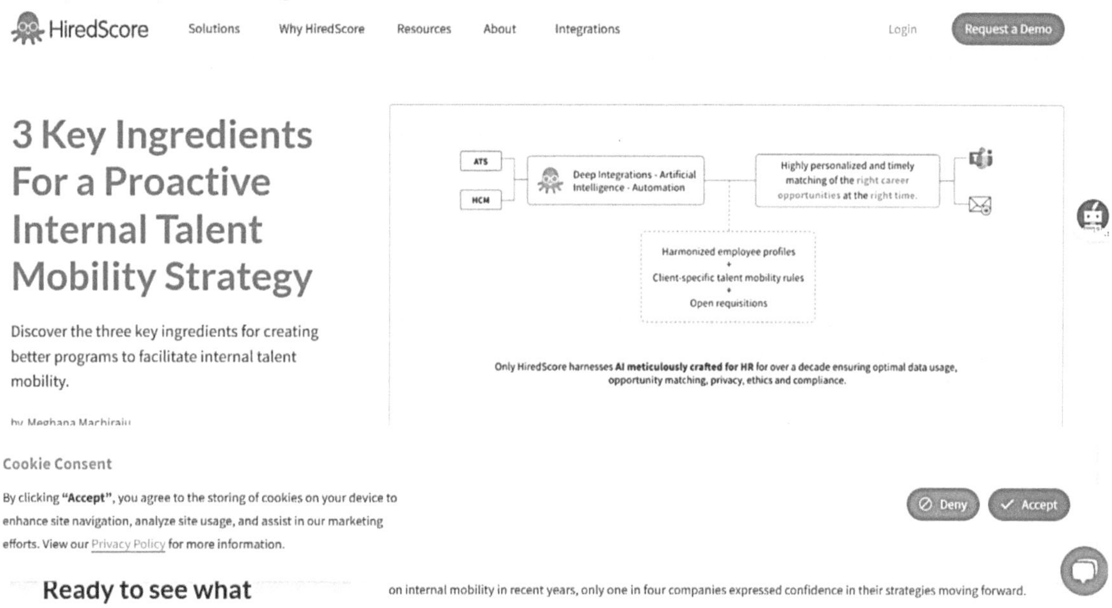

2. Candidate Data Collection and Analysis:

- HiredScore gathers a vast array of candidate information, including:
- Resume and application details (education, experience, skills)
- Online assessments and tests
- Social media profiles (if permitted)
- Past job performance data (from previous employers)
- It then applies its AI algorithms to analyze this data, identifying patterns and correlations that predict job success.

3. Candidate Scoring and Ranking:

- Based on its analysis, HiredScore assigns each candidate a score that reflects their predicted likelihood of success in the open role.
- It then ranks candidates based on their scores, helping recruiters quickly identify the most promising talent.

4. Bias Mitigation and Compliance:

- HiredScore incorporates features to mitigate bias and ensure compliance with regulations:
- It excludes sensitive personal information like race, gender, and age from its analysis.
- It conducts ongoing audits to detect and address potential biases in its algorithms.

5. Candidate Insights and Recommendations:

- HiredScore provides additional insights beyond scores:
- Strengths and weaknesses of candidates
- Potential areas for development
- Recommendations for interview s or assessment tasks

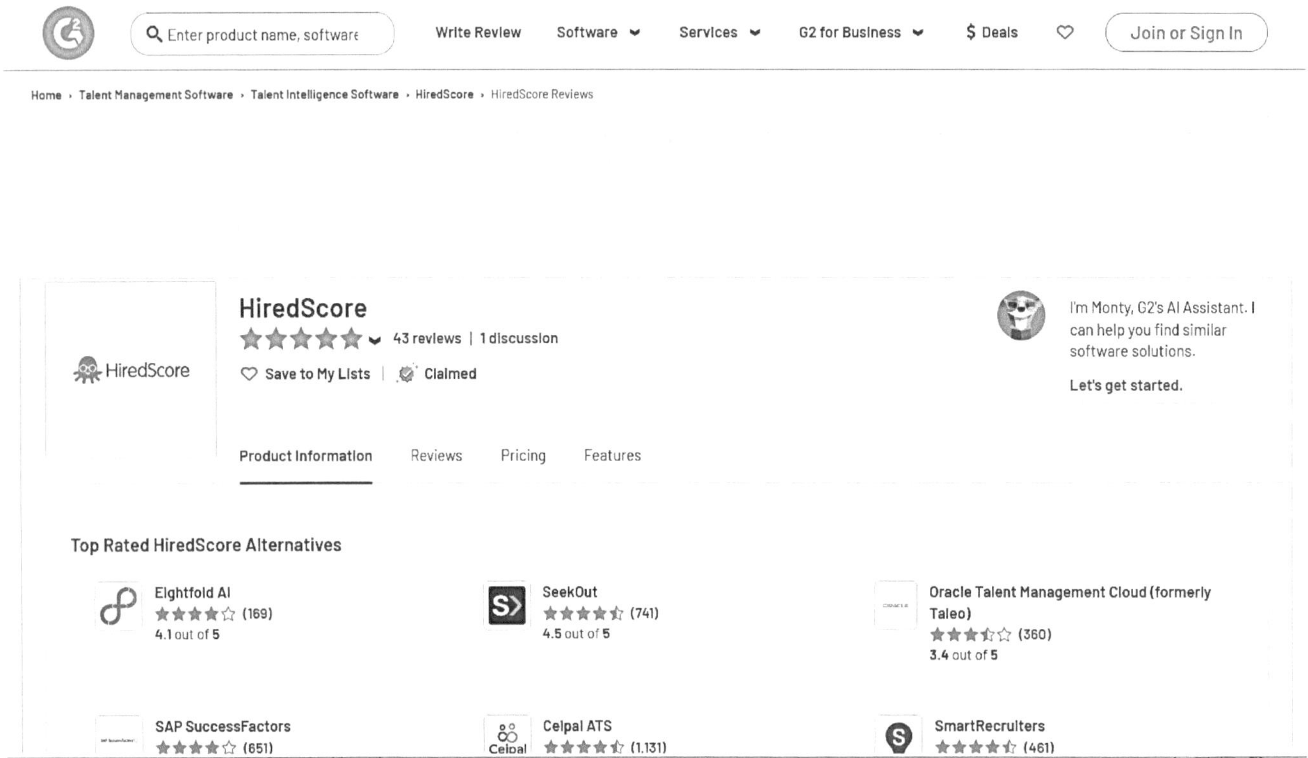

6. Customization and Optimization:

- HiredScore allows customization based on company-specific needs:
- Adjusting scoring models to align with organizational values and culture
- Setting benchmarks for different roles and departments
- Tracking and measuring the tool's effectiveness over time

7. Continuous Learning and Improvement:

- HiredScore's AI algorithms continuously learn and improve:
- Incorporating feedback from recruiters and hiring managers
- Analyzing new data to refine its predictions
- Adapting to changing job requirements and market trends

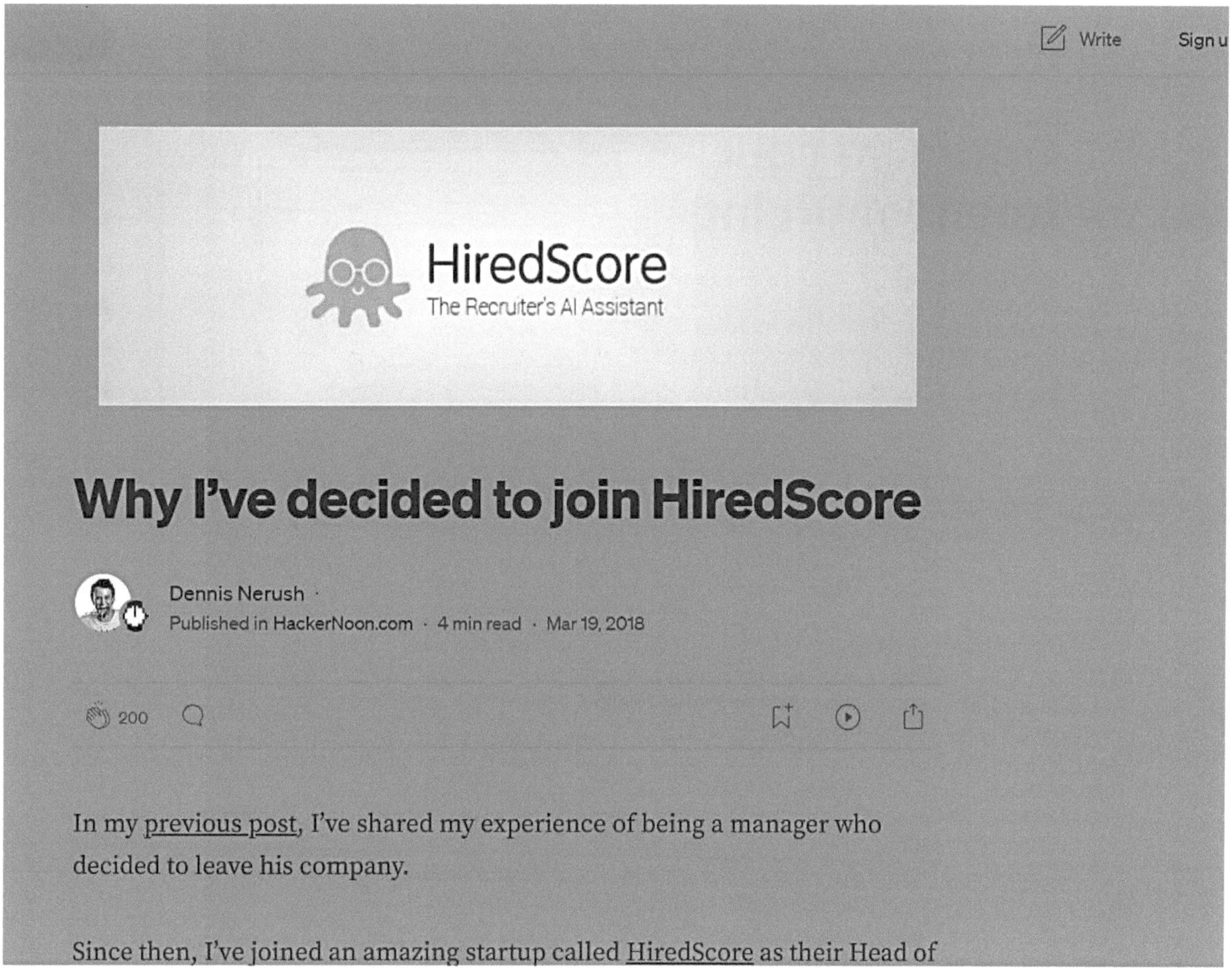

Write Sign u

HiredScore
The Recruiter's AI Assistant

Why I've decided to join HiredScore

Dennis Nerush ·
Published in HackerNoon.com · 4 min read · Mar 19, 2018

200

In my previous post, I've shared my experience of being a manager who decided to leave his company.

Since then, I've joined an amazing startup called HiredScore as their Head of

11.4 Attract

This platform utilizes an AI-powered search engine that enables HR professionals to uncover hidden candidate profiles from over 40 social platforms, providing access to an extensive talent pool. Its personalized search models cater to individual user requirements, ensuring accurate and relevant search results every time.

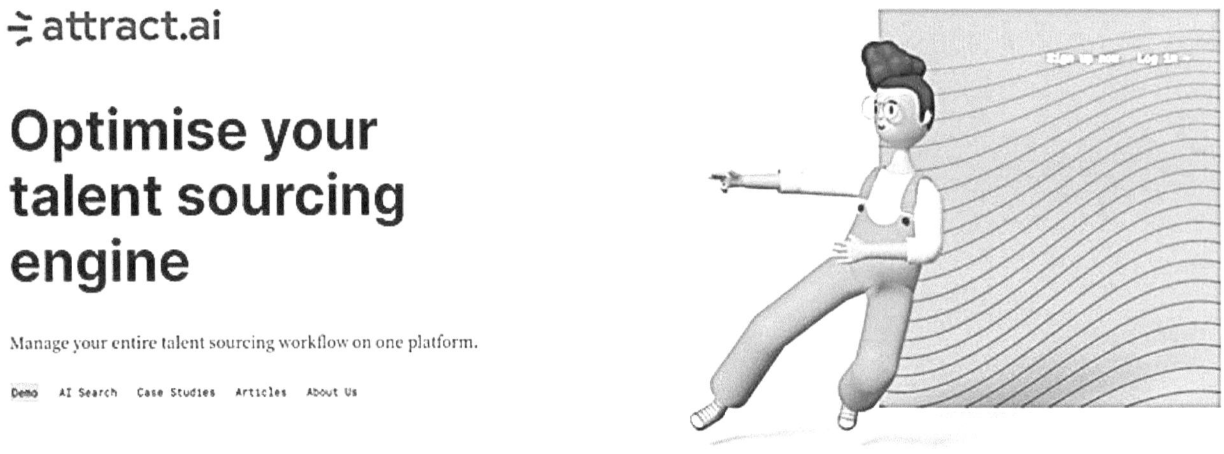

Key Features:

1. **Multiple Content Templates:** Offers a diverse range of templates, such as blog posts, product descriptions, social media captions, landing pages, emails, ads, and more.
2. **Customizable Input:** Allows users to specify product details, target audience, key messages, brand voice, desired length, and keywords to tailor content generation.
3. **AI-Generated Text:** Produces unique, original content based on user input and prompts, ensuring relevance and originality.
4. **Editing and Refining:** Provides built-in tools to edit and refine generated content, ensuring it meets specific requirements and brand standards.
5. **Publishing and Exporting:** Enables users to either publish content directly to websites or social media platforms or export it as text files for further use.

Visual Guide (Imagined Interface):

1. **Dashboard:** Displays active projects, templates, and account settings.
2. **Project Page:** Contains input fields, content preview, editing tools, and publishing/export options.
3. **Content Generation Panel:** Shows progress indicators and options to generate multiple variations.
4. **Editing Tools:** Text formatting, style adjustments, keyword highlighting, and collaboration features (if available).

Use Cases:

1. **Marketing Content Creation:** Generate blog posts, social media content, website copy, email marketing campaigns, and more.
2. **Product Descriptions:** Write engaging and informative product descriptions for e-commerce stores or product pages.
3. **Landing Pages:** Create high-converting landing pages to capture leads and drive sales.
4. **Ad Copywriting:** Craft compelling ad copy for various platforms, such as Google Ads, Facebook Ads, and social media ads.
5. **Internal Communications:** Generate internal emails, newsletters, and announcements for effective employee communication.

Benefits:

1. **Increased Content Production:** Generate content faster and more efficiently than traditional manual methods.
2. **Improved Content Quality:** AI ensures relevance, originality, and alignment with brand guidelines.
3. **Save Time and Resources:** Free up human resources for more strategic tasks.
4. **Experiment with Different Content Strategies:** Generate multiple content variations to test and optimize performance.

5. Reach Wider Audiences: Produce content for various platforms and channels efficiently.

Attract AI Tool: Step-by-Step Explanation
1. **Sign Up and Login:**
- Visit the Attract AI website (link unavailable) and create an account.
- Provide necessary details like email, password, and company name.
- Upon verification, log in to access the tool's dashboard.
2. **Create a New Project:**
- Click the "Create Project" button or similar option.
- Enter a descriptive project name and optional description.
- Select the desired language for your content creation.
3. **Choose Content Template:**
- Browse through various content templates, such as:
- Blog posts
- Product descriptions
- Social media captions
- Landing pages
- Emails
- Ads
- And more
- Select the template that aligns with your content needs.
4. **Provide Input Information:**
- Fill in the prompted fields with relevant information, such as:
- Product or service details
- Target audience characteristics
- Key messages or themes
- Brand voice and tone
- Desired content length
- Any specific keywords or calls to action
5. Generate Content:
- Click the "Generate Content" button (or similar) to activate AI.
- Attract AI will process your input and generate a unique piece of content based on your specifications.
- The generated text will appear within a text editor or preview panel.
6. Review and Edit:
- Carefully read the generated content to ensure it meets your requirements.
- Use the built-in editing tools to make any necessary adjustments, such as:
- Refining language
- Rephrasing sentences
- Adding or removing details
- Adjusting tone or style
7. Publish or Export:
- Once satisfied with the content, choose to either:
- Publish it directly to your website or social media platforms (if applicable)
- Export it as a text file (e.g., Word document, PDF) for further use
Visual Guide (Imagined Interface):
1. Dashboard: Displays your active projects, templates, and account settings.
2. Project Page: Contains input fields, content preview, editing tools, and publishing/export options.
3. Content Generation Panel: Shows progress indicators and options to generate multiple variations.
4. Editing Tools: Text formatting, style adjustments, keyword highlighting, and collaboration features (if available).

11.5 Effy

Effy.ai is a performance review and feedback management tool that simplifies the process with its ready-to-use templates, AI-generated insights, and comprehensive heat map analysis. It offers science-based templates, participant selection, and feedback integration with platforms like Slack and MS Teams. Effy.ai is GDPR- and CCPA-ready, trusted by teams at various organizations. Users praise Effy for its simplicity, customization options, attractive interface, ease of use, and integration capabilities. The tool allows for easy customization of reports and eliminates the need for manual Google Forms. Effy.ai offers a free plan and provides onboarding assistance.

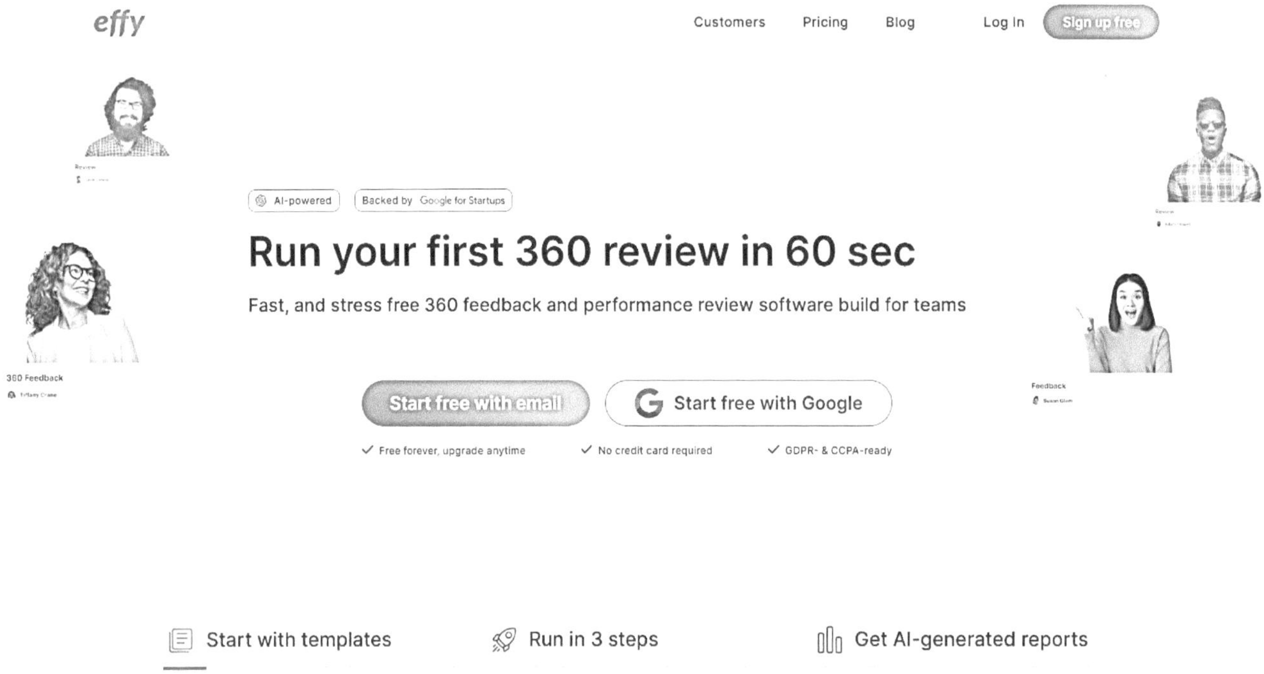

Potential Features:
Based on the glimpses available, some potential features of Effy AI include:
1. **Personalized Interface:** Adapts to your working style and preferences over time.
2. **Voice Commands:** Control Effy AI using natural language voice commands.
3. **Multiple Output Formats:** Generate content in various formats like text, images, code, and even audio.
4. **Integrated Tools:** Connect with other applications you use for a seamless workflow.
5. **Security and Privacy:** Focus on secure data storage and privacy protection.

Use Cases:
Effy AI's versatility potentially caters to individuals across various domains, such as:
1. **Writers and Creatives:** Generate ideas, overcome writer's block, and refine their work.
2. **Professionals and Students:** Write reports, analyze data, research topics, and manage projects efficiently.
3. **Busy Individuals:** Organize schedules, track tasks, and streamline daily routines.
4. **Anyone Seeking Inspiration and Assistance: Generate** content ideas, explore new perspectives, and receive reminders and prompts for personal growth.

Benefits:
If Effy AI delivers on its promises, it could offer several benefits, including:
1. **Increased Productivity:** Automate repetitive tasks and free up time for more important activities.
2. **Enhanced Creativity:** Spark new ideas and overcome creative roadblocks.
3. **Improved Organization:** Streamline tasks, manage deadlines, and stay on top of schedules.
4. **Personalized Support:** Receive customized assistance tailored to your specific needs and preferences.

1. Sign up for an account:
- Visit the Effy AI website (https://www.effy.ai/) and create a free account.

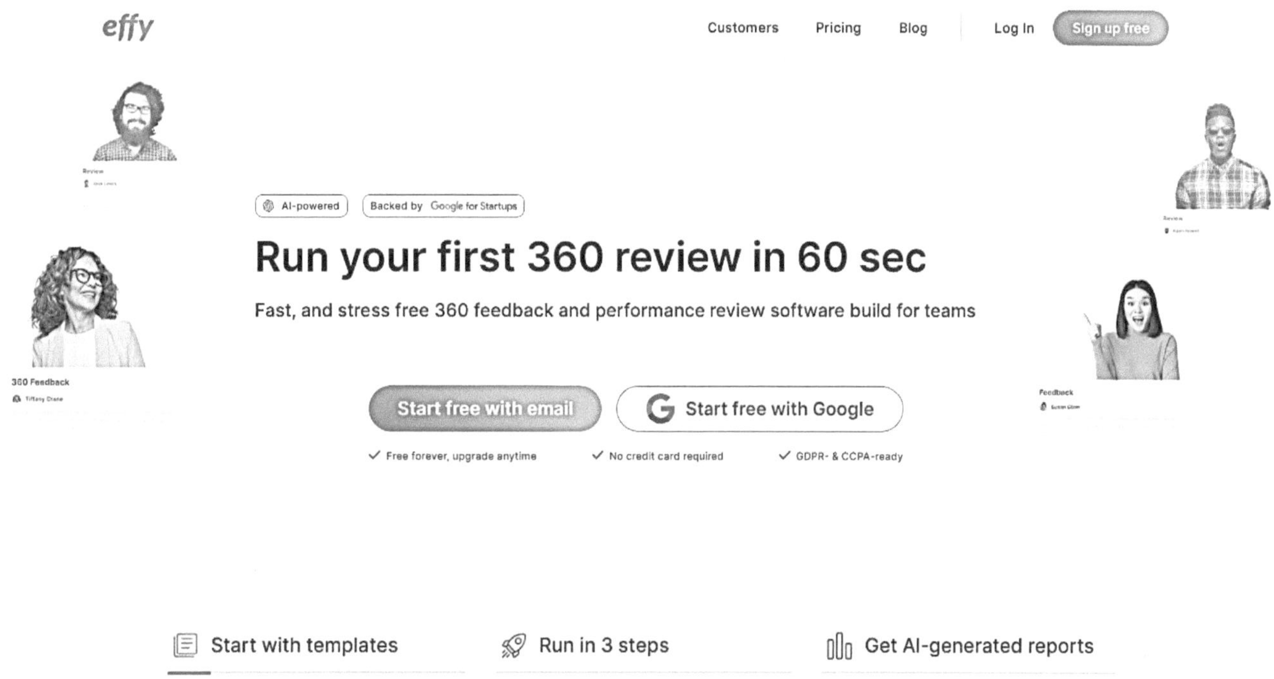

2. Select a template:
- Once logged in, you'll see a variety of templates to choose from, such as blog posts, social media captions, emails, ads, and more.

3. Choose your tone and keywords:
- Select the tone you want Effy AI to use (e.g., informative, persuasive, funny) and enter any relevant keywords or phrases.

4. Generate content:
- Click the "Generate" button and Effy AI will create multiple variations of text based on your selections.

5. Edit and refine:
- Review the generated text and make any necessary edits to ensure it aligns with your goals. You can also customize it further by adding your own input.

6. Download or share:
- When you're satisfied with the content, you can download it as a .txt file or share it directly to social media platforms.

Exercise

Exercise 1 – MCQ

1. Paradox is known for its expertise in:
A. Data visualization
B. Natural language processing
C. Chatbot-driven recruiting
D. Virtual reality integration

2. What is the primary focus of Textio in HR and recruiting?
A. Automated scheduling
B. Predictive analytics
C. Natural language processing for job postings
D. Virtual reality recruitment events

3. HiredScore is a tool specialized in:
A. Video interviewing
B. AI-driven candidate sourcing and screening
C. Employee engagement surveys
D. Resume formatting

4. What does the tool Attract primarily focus on?
A. Virtual reality integration in recruitment
B. Diversity and inclusion initiatives

C. Gamified assessments for candidates
D. Employee onboarding

5. Effy is known for its capabilities in:
A. Employee engagement surveys
B. Virtual reality recruitment events
C. Predictive analytics for hiring
D. AI-driven candidate sourcing

6. Paradox utilizes chatbot-driven recruiting for:
A. Employee engagement surveys
B. Virtual reality integration
C. Candidate sourcing and screening
D. Diversity and inclusion initiatives

7. What is the main function of Textio in the context of HR and recruiting?
A. Video interviewing
B. Natural language processing for job postings
C. Gamified assessments for candidates
D. Employee onboarding

8. HiredScore focuses on:
A. AI-driven candidate sourcing and screening
B. Diversity and inclusion initiatives
C. Employee engagement surveys
D. Virtual reality recruitment events

9. Attract integrates gamified assessments for:
A. Job applicants
B. Virtual reality recruitment events
C. Employee onboarding
D. Employee engagement

10. Effy's main emphasis is on:
A. Virtual reality recruitment events
B. Predictive analytics for hiring
C. Diversity and inclusion initiatives
D. Video interviewing

Exercise 2 – True/ False

Q 1. Paradox specializes in AI-driven candidate sourcing and screening using chatbot-driven recruiting.
Q 2. Textio focuses on video interviewing and virtual reality integration for HR and recruiting purposes.
Q 3. HiredScore is primarily known for its expertise in employee engagement surveys in the recruiting process.
Q 4. Attract places its main emphasis on diversity and inclusion initiatives in HR and recruiting.
Q 5. Effy is recognized for its capabilities in gamified assessments for job applicants during the hiring process.
Q 6. Paradox employs natural language processing to optimize job postings and enhance candidate engagement.
Q 7. Textio specializes in AI-driven candidate sourcing and screening for HR and recruiting.
Q 8. HiredScore integrates predictive analytics to enhance the efficiency of the recruiting process.
Q 9. Attract uses virtual reality integration for employee onboarding and training.
Q 10. Effy's primary focus is on virtual reality recruitment events to attract and assess potential candidates.

Exercise 3 – Fill in the blanks

Q 1. Paradox is a ____________ tool designed to streamline the recruitment process through innovative solutions.
Q 2. Paradox uses ____________ technology to engage with candidates in a natural and interactive manner.
Q 3. With Textio, recruiters can receive real-time ____________ to improve the effectiveness of their job descriptions.
Q 4. HiredScore's AI algorithms analyze candidates' skills and experiences to provide a ____________ assessment of their suitability for a role.
Q 5. With Attract, recruiters can build and manage a ____________ that showcases the company's culture and values.

Exercise 4 – Match case

1. Paradox	A. A tool that utilizes augmented writing technology.
2. Textio	B. An AI-driven platform for talent acquisition.
3. HiredScore	C. A recruitment software focusing on employer branding.
4. Attract	D. A tool that streamlines the recruitment process through conversational AI.
5. Effy	E. An AI-powered tool automating initial stages of candidate screening.

Exercise 5 – One word answer

Q 1. What are the Automation of Paradox?
Q 2. What Impact of Textio?
Q 3. What Approach in HiredScore?
Q 4. What is the Emphasis of Attract?
Q 5. What is the Specialty of Effy?

Exercise 6 – Small answer

Q 1. What is Paradox known for in HR and recruiting?
Q 2. How does Textio enhance job listings?
Q 3. What does HiredScore assist with in the talent acquisition process?
Q 4. What aspect does Attract focus on in recruitment?
Q 5. What does Effy automate in the candidate screening process?

Exercise 7 – Long answer

Q 1. How does Paradox utilize conversational AI in the recruitment process, and what specific role does its chatbot play in engaging with candidates?
Q 2. What role does HiredScore play in talent acquisition, and how does its predictive analytics feature assist recruiters in making informed decisions?

Answers

Exercise 1 – MCQ

Ans: 1 C, 2 C, 3 B, 4 B, 5 C, 6 C, 7 B, 8 A, 9 A, 10 B

Exercise 2 – True/ False

Ans: 1 True, 2 False, 3 False, 4 True, 4 False, 5 True, 6 True, 7 True, 8 False, 9 False

Exercise 3 – Fill in the blanks

Ans: 1 Conversational AI recruiting, 2 Chatbot, 3 Language suggestions, 4 Comprehensive, 5 Talent community

Exercise 4 – Match case

Ans: 1 D, 2 A, 3 B, 4 C, 5 E

Exercise 5 – One word answer

Ans: 1 Workflows, 2 Bias reduction, 3 AI- powered, 4 Candidate experience, 5 Scheduling

ONLINE RESOURCES

Practice Paper
Link https://forms.office.com/r/yBn8UUswxq
QR Code

Video Content
Link https://www.youtube.com/playlist?list=PLzlh_31VWEFqxBTQUzeR8S__5tvCydz-Y
QR Code:

Chapter 12: Future Trends in AI Tools

12.1 Continued Advancements in Natural Language Processing

Here are some continued advancements in NLP:

1. Transformer Architecture:

The introduction of transformer-based models, such as BERT (Bidirectional Encoder Representations from Transformers) and GPT (Generative Pre-trained Transformer), marked a significant breakthrough. These models excel in understanding context and have been pre-trained on massive datasets, enabling them to perform well on various NLP tasks.

2. Pre-trained Language Models:

Pre-trained language models, like GPT-3, have pushed the boundaries of what AI can achieve in natural language understanding and generation. These models are trained on diverse datasets and can be fine-tuned for specific applications, reducing the need for task-specific training from scratch.

3. Zero-Shot Learning:

Zero-shot learning capabilities in models like GPT-3 allow them to perform tasks without explicit training for those tasks. This means that the models can generate reasonable responses for tasks they were not explicitly trained on, showcasing a high level of generalization.

4. Multimodal NLP:

Advances in multimodal NLP involve combining text with other forms of data, such as images or audio. Models like CLIP (Contrastive Language-Image Pre-training) can understand and generate content based on both textual and visual inputs, leading to more comprehensive AI applications.

5. Contextual Embeddings:

Embeddings that capture contextual information have become standard in NLP models. ELMo (Embeddings from Language Models) and contextual embeddings in BERT are examples of how models consider the context of each word in a sentence, improving their understanding of meaning.

6. Efforts Toward Ethical AI:

There's an increased focus on making NLP models more ethical and unbiased. Researchers are working on developing techniques to mitigate biases present in training data and to ensure fairness and transparency in AI applications.

7. Conversational AI Improvements:

AI-driven chatbots and virtual assistants continue to improve in their ability to understand and generate human-like responses. This involves advancements in dialogue management, sentiment analysis, and the ability to handle more complex and nuanced conversations.

8. Domain-Specific NLP Models:

Tailoring NLP models for specific domains, such as legal, medical, or scientific, is an ongoing trend. These specialized models can better understand and generate content relevant to their respective fields.

9. Efficient Training Techniques:

Research is ongoing to make training large-scale language models more efficient. This includes techniques like knowledge distillation, model pruning, and quantization, which aim to reduce the computational resources required for training and deployment.

10. Real-Time Language Translation:

Advances in NLP contribute to more accurate and context-aware real-time language translation systems, breaking down language barriers in various applications.

12.2 Integration of AI in Emerging Technologies

The integration of AI in emerging technologies is a dynamic and rapidly evolving field, driving advancements and transformations across various industries. Here's a look at how AI is integrated into several emerging technologies:

1. AI in Edge Computing:

Edge computing involves processing data closer to the source of generation. AI is integrated into edge devices to enable real-time decision-making, reduce latency, and optimize bandwidth usage. This is particularly beneficial in applications like IoT devices, autonomous vehicles, and smart cities.

2. AI in 5G Networks:

AI plays a crucial role in optimizing and managing 5G networks. It assists in network planning, resource allocation, and dynamic optimization, enhancing overall network performance and efficiency.

3. AI in Quantum Computing:

Quantum computing, with its potential for exponentially faster processing, can benefit from AI algorithms. AI is used to optimize quantum algorithms, explore quantum machine learning, and improve the robustness and error correction capabilities of quantum computers.

4. AI in Robotics:

Integrating AI into robotics enhances the capabilities of robots. Advanced machine learning algorithms enable robots to learn from their environment, make decisions, and adapt to changing conditions. This is crucial for applications in manufacturing, healthcare, and exploration.

5. AI in Augmented Reality (AR) and Virtual Reality (VR):

AI enhances the user experience in AR and VR applications by enabling more realistic simulations and personalized content. Computer vision, natural language processing, and gesture recognition contribute to immersive and interactive experiences.

6. AI in Blockchain:

AI is integrated into blockchain technologies for various purposes, including fraud detection, smart contract optimization, and enhancing security. AI algorithms can analyze patterns, detect anomalies, and improve the efficiency of blockchain-based systems.

7. AI in Cybersecurity:

AI is used to strengthen cybersecurity by identifying and responding to cyber threats in real-time. Machine learning models can analyze vast datasets to detect unusual patterns and potential security breaches, providing a proactive defense against evolving cyber threats.

8. AI in Biotechnology and Healthcare:

AI is integrated into biotechnology for drug discovery, genomics, and personalized medicine. In healthcare, AI is used for diagnostics, predictive analytics, and patient care optimization. AI-driven robotic surgery is also gaining traction.

9. AI in Renewable Energy:

AI is applied to optimize the operation and maintenance of renewable energy systems. Predictive analytics, machine learning, and data-driven insights contribute to improving the efficiency and reliability of renewable energy sources like solar and wind.

10. AI in Agriculture:

AI technologies, including computer vision and machine learning, are integrated into agriculture for crop monitoring, pest detection, and precision farming. AI-powered systems help optimize resource usage and improve crop yields.

11. AI in Natural Language Processing (NLP) and Conversational AI:

In addition to traditional applications, AI is deeply integrated into voice-activated assistants, chatbots, and virtual agents. This enhances natural language understanding, enabling more sophisticated and context-aware interactions.

12. AI in Autonomous Vehicles:

AI algorithms are crucial for autonomous vehicles, enabling them to perceive their environment, make decisions, and navigate safely. Machine learning models contribute to the continuous improvement of vehicle autonomy through data-driven learning.

The integration of AI into emerging technologies is a multidisciplinary effort that involves researchers, developers, and industry experts collaborating to push the boundaries of innovation. This ongoing integration is expected to drive transformative changes across various sectors in the coming years.

12.3 Ethical Considerations in AI Tool Development

Ethical considerations in AI tool development are of paramount importance to ensure that artificial intelligence is deployed responsibly and respects human rights, fairness, transparency, and accountability. Here are key ethical considerations in the development of AI tools:

1. Fairness and Bias:

Issue: AI systems may inherit biases present in training data, leading to unfair or discriminatory outcomes.

Ethical Consideration: Developers should strive for fairness by identifying and mitigating biases in algorithms. Regular audits and diverse datasets can help address these issues.

2. Transparency:

Issue: Many AI models operate as "black boxes," making it challenging to understand their decision-making processes.

Ethical Consideration: Developers should prioritize transparency, providing explanations for AI decisions and ensuring that users, especially in critical domains, can understand the rationale behind AI-generated outcomes.

3. Privacy:
Issue: AI tools often process large amounts of personal data, raising concerns about privacy infringement.
Ethical Consideration: Developers must prioritize user privacy by implementing robust data protection measures, anonymizing data, and obtaining informed consent for data usage.
4. Accountability:
Issue: When AI systems make errors or exhibit biased behavior, it may be challenging to assign responsibility.
Ethical Consideration: Developers should establish clear lines of accountability, documenting decisions made during development, and ensuring mechanisms for oversight and accountability in case of unintended consequences.
5. Security:
Issue: AI systems may be vulnerable to attacks or manipulation, leading to malicious outcomes.
Ethical Consideration: Developers must prioritize security in AI systems, implementing robust cybersecurity measures, encryption, and continuous monitoring to prevent unauthorized access or tampering.
6. Explainability:
Issue: Users may not understand how AI models arrive at specific decisions, impacting trust.
Ethical Consideration: Developers should design AI models to be explainable, providing clear and understandable explanations of decisions, especially in critical applications like healthcare and finance.
7. Inclusivity:
Issue: Biases in AI systems can result in exclusion or discrimination against certain groups.
Ethical Consideration: Developers should prioritize inclusivity, ensuring that AI tools are designed to serve diverse user groups and are not biased against specific demographics.
8. Data Governance:
Issue: Inappropriate data collection and usage can lead to privacy concerns and ethical dilemmas.
Ethical Consideration: Developers should establish clear data governance policies, including guidelines on data collection, storage, and usage, ensuring compliance with relevant regulations.
9. Human-in-the-Loop:
Issue: Overreliance on automated decision-making may lead to unintended consequences.
Ethical Consideration: Developers should incorporate human oversight in AI systems, allowing human intervention and decision-making, especially in critical scenarios.
10. Environmental Impact:
Issue: Training large AI models can have a substantial environmental impact.
Ethical Consideration: Developers should consider the environmental sustainability of AI models, exploring energy-efficient algorithms and infrastructure.
11. Long-Term Impacts:
Issue: Unintended long-term consequences of AI deployment.
Ethical Consideration: Developers should conduct thorough risk assessments to anticipate and mitigate potential long-term impacts of AI technologies on society, the economy, and the environment.
Adhering to these ethical considerations helps ensure that AI tools are developed and deployed responsibly, fostering trust, fairness, and positive societal impacts. Ethical guidelines, standards, and frameworks, such as those from organizations like the IEEE or the Partnership on AI, can provide additional guidance for developers and organizations.

Exercise

Exercise 1 – MCQ

Q 1. What is the primary focus of "Continued Advancements in Natural Language Processing" in future AI trends?
A. Virtual reality integration
B. Enhanced decision-making
C. Improved data visualization
D. Advancements in language understanding

Q 2. In the context of AI tools, what does "Integration of AI in Emerging Technologies" primarily refer to?
A. Use of AI in traditional industries
B. Incorporating AI into new and evolving technologies
C. Ethical considerations in AI development
D. Data-driven decision-making

Q 3. "Ethical Considerations in AI Tool Development" primarily addresses:
A. Technological advancements in AI
B. The integration of AI in emerging technologies
C. Ethical challenges and responsibilities in AI development
D. Improving data visualization techniques

Q 4. What is a key area of improvement discussed in "Continued Advancements in Natural Language Processing"?

A. Predictive analytics
B. Fraud detection
C. Language understanding and processing
D. Virtual reality integration

Q 5. How does "Integration of AI in Emerging Technologies" contribute to the future of AI tools?
A. By emphasizing traditional technologies over emerging
B. By avoiding integration with new technologies
C. By incorporating AI into evolving and emerging tech
D. By solely focusing on data-driven decision-making

Q 6. What is a central theme discussed in "Ethical Considerations in AI Tool Development"?
A. Improving data visualization
B. Ethical challenges and responsibilities in AI development
C. Enhanced decision-making
D. Continued advancements in natural language processing

Q 7. Which area is specifically highlighted in the discussion of "Continued Advancements in Natural Language Processing"?
A. Fraud detection
B. Language understanding and processing
C. Virtual reality integration
D. Data visualization techniques

Q 8. What distinguishes "Integration of AI in Emerging Technologies" from other trends in AI tools?
A. A focus on traditional technologies
B. Avoidance of AI integration
C. Emphasis on predictive analytics
D. Incorporation of AI into new and evolving technologies

Q 9. In the context of "Ethical Considerations in AI Tool Development," what is emphasized regarding AI developers?
A. Increased use of virtual reality integration
B. Ethical challenges and responsibilities
C. Fraud detection techniques
D. Data-driven decision-making

Q 10. How does "Continued Advancements in Natural Language Processing" impact data analysis in AI tools?
A. By focusing on virtual reality integration
B. By enhancing language understanding and processing for improved data analysis
C. By avoiding advancements in language understanding
D. By emphasizing traditional data visualization techniques

Exercise 2 – True/ False

Q 1. Continued Advancements in Natural Language Processing" primarily focuses on improving language understanding and processing in AI tools.
Q 2. Integration of AI in Emerging Technologies" primarily involves avoiding the integration of AI into new and evolving technologies.
Q 3. Ethical Considerations in AI Tool Development" emphasizes the ethical challenges and responsibilities associated with AI development.
Q 4. One of the key areas discussed in "Continued Advancements in Natural Language Processing" is predictive analytics.
Q 5. Integration of AI in Emerging Technologies" primarily focuses on incorporating AI into traditional and well-established technologies.
Q 6. Ethical Considerations in AI Tool Development" primarily discusses technological advancements in AI rather than ethical challenges.
Q 7. In "Continued Advancements in Natural Language Processing," virtual reality integration is a central theme.
Q 8. Integration of AI in Emerging Technologies" avoids the incorporation of AI into new and evolving technologies.
Q 9. Ethical Considerations in AI Tool Development" emphasizes the use of virtual reality integration in AI tools.
Q 10. Continued Advancements in Natural Language Processing" contributes to the future of AI tools by enhancing language understanding and processing for improved data analysis.

Exercise 3 – Fill in the blanks

Q 1. The future of AI tools is expected to witness continued advancements in ____________ processing, enabling more nuanced and context-aware interactions.

Q 2. Integration of AI in emerging technologies like ____________ and ____________ is anticipated to redefine industries and user experiences.
Q 3. Ethical considerations in AI tool development are likely to lead to the incorporation of ____________ features, ensuring responsible and unbiased AI applications.
Q 4. As AI becomes more prevalent, the trend of ____________ AI is expected to gain momentum, allowing systems to learn and adapt in real-time.
Q 5. AI tools are anticipated to play a pivotal role in addressing global challenges, such as ____________ and ____________, through innovative applications.

Exercise 4 – Match case

1. Advancements enabling more nuanced interactions through language understanding.	A. Natural Language Processing
2. Redefined industries and user experiences through integration with AR and VR.	B. Application in Global Challenges
3. Incorporation of features ensuring responsible and unbiased AI applications.	C. Continual Learning
4. AI systems learning and adapting in real-time.	D. Explainability
5. Playing a pivotal role in addressing global challenges like climate change and healthcare.	E. Augmented Reality, Virtual Reality Integration

Exercise 5 – One word answer
Q 1. What approach to problem-solving is expected to increase with AI tools?
Q 2. What will enable efficient and data-driven decision-making through AI-powered processes?
Q 3. What will enhance safety, efficiency, and overall performance in various systems?
Q 4. What may lead to the development of standards and frameworks for responsible AI practices?
Q 5. What models are expected to be adopted for more sophisticated and personalized user experiences?

Exercise 6 – Small answer
Q 1. What's advancing in AI tools for more nuanced interactions?
Q 2. What's redefining industries and user experiences through integration with AR and VR?
Q 3. What feature is anticipated for incorporation to ensure responsible AI applications?
Q 4. What involves AI systems learning and adapting in real-time?
Q 5. What role are AI tools anticipated to play in addressing global challenges like climate change and healthcare?

Exercise 7 – Long answer
Q 1. As we navigate the future landscape of AI tools, what key trends are expected to shape the evolution of artificial intelligence, fostering responsible development, addressing global challenges, and redefining various industries?

Answers

Exercise 1 – MCQ
Ans: 1 D, 2 B, 3 C, 4 C, 5 C, 6 B, 7 B, 8 D, 9 B, 10 B

Exercise 2 – True/ False
Ans: 1 True, 2 False, 3 True, 4 False, 5 False, 6 False, 7 False, 8 False, 9 False, 10 True

Exercise 3 – Fill in the blanks
Ans: 1 Natural Language, 2 Augmented Reality, Virtual Reality, 3 Explainability, 4 Continual Learning, 5 Climate Change, Healthcare

Exercise 4 – Match case
Ans: 1 A, 2 E, 3 D, 4 C, 5 B

Exercise 5 – One word answer
Ans: Collaborative, Analytics, Autonomous, Regulatory, Federated

ONLINE RESOURCES

Practice Paper
Link: https://forms.office.com/r/kEamHidjGm
QR Code

Video Content
Link: https://www.youtube.com/playlist?list=PLzlh_31VWEFoNMiS7uUvACczKvKh-nTce
QR Code

Chapter 13: Auto caption, Art, Productivity, Music

13.1 Descript

Define: Descript is an AI-powered tool designed for audio and video editing, transcription, and collaboration. It allows users to create, edit, and publish multimedia content with ease, leveraging advanced AI capabilities for efficient and intuitive editing workflows.

Features:

1. Transcription:
Descript provides automatic transcription of audio and video content, saving users time on manual transcription efforts.
2. Text-Based Editing:
Users can edit audio and video content as easily as editing text, using a word processor-like interface for a more intuitive editing experience.
3. Voice Cloning:
The tool offers voice cloning capabilities, allowing users to generate synthetic voices that sound natural and can be used to replace or enhance audio recordings.
4. Overdub:
Descript's Overdub feature enables users to modify and edit spoken words directly, providing flexibility and control over the narrative.
5. Screen Recording:
Users can record and edit screen captures, enhancing the tool's versatility for creating tutorial videos, presentations, or any content requiring screen recording.
6. Collaborative Editing:
Descript supports collaborative editing, allowing multiple users to work on the same project simultaneously, streamlining collaboration among team members.
7. Publishing Options:
The tool provides various publishing options, allowing users to export their edited content to different platforms or formats, including podcasts and social media.

Benefits:

1. Time Efficiency:
Descript automates time-consuming tasks like transcription, saving users valuable time in the content creation and editing process.
2. User-Friendly Interface:
The word processor-like interface simplifies the editing process, making it accessible to users without advanced technical skills.
3. Flexible Editing:
The text-based editing approach offers flexibility and precision, allowing users to make edits easily and with a high degree of accuracy.
4. Voice Customization:
Descript's voice cloning and Overdub features provide users with the ability to customize and fine-tune the spoken content to match specific requirements.
5. Collaboration Efficiency:
Collaborative editing features enhance team productivity by enabling multiple contributors to work together seamlessly on the same project.
6. Multimedia Content Creation:
Descript supports a variety of multimedia content creation, including podcasts, video presentations, and screen recordings, making it a versatile tool for different applications.

Use Cases:

1. Podcast Production:
2. Content creators can use Descript for podcast production, automating the transcription process and editing audio content efficiently.
3. Video Editing:

4. Video editors can leverage Descript's text-based editing for precise control over spoken content in video projects, making the editing process more intuitive.
5. Voiceover Production:
6. Descript's voice cloning and Overdub features are useful for voiceover production, allowing users to generate or modify voice recordings for multimedia projects.
7. Collaborative Projects:
8. Teams working on multimedia projects, such as video production or podcast creation, can collaborate efficiently using Descript's collaborative editing features.
9. Educational Content Creation:
10. Educators and tutorial creators can use Descript to record and edit screen captures, creating engaging and informative educational content.

13.2 Captions.ai

Definition: Captions.ai is an artificial intelligence (AI) tool designed to generate descriptive and contextually relevant captions for images. Leveraging advanced natural language processing (NLP) algorithms, Captions.ai analyzes visual content and provides automated, human-like descriptions to enhance the understanding and accessibility of images.

Features:

1. **Image Analysis:** Captions.ai utilizes sophisticated image recognition algorithms to analyze visual elements within an image, identifying objects, scenes, and context.
2. **Natural Language Generation (NLG):** The tool employs NLG techniques to generate coherent and contextually relevant captions, ensuring that the textual descriptions align with the visual content.
3. **Context Awareness:** Captions.ai takes into account the context of the image, including relationships between objects, spatial information, and overall scene interpretation, resulting in more accurate and informative captions.
4. **Multilingual Support:** The tool often supports multiple languages, allowing users to generate captions in various languages to cater to diverse audiences.
5. **Customization Options:** Users may have the ability to customize the tone, style, or length of generated captions, providing flexibility based on specific content and branding requirements.

Benefits:

1. **Accessibility:** Captions.ai enhances the accessibility of visual content by providing descriptive captions, making it valuable for individuals with visual impairments or those relying on screen readers.
2. **Time Efficiency:** The tool automates the captioning process, saving time for content creators who would otherwise need to manually generate descriptions for each image.
3. **Consistency:** Captions.ai ensures consistent and standardized captions, reducing variations in the quality and style of descriptions across different images.
4. **Improved SEO:** Descriptive captions contribute to better search engine optimization (SEO) by providing search engines with additional context about the images on a website.
5. **Enhanced User Experience:** Users benefit from a richer and more informative experience when interacting with images, leading to increased engagement and understanding.

Use Cases:

1. **Content Creation:** Content creators can use Captions.ai to quickly and accurately generate captions for images, especially in scenarios where large volumes of visual content need descriptive text.
2. **Social Media:** Individuals and businesses can enhance the impact of their social media posts by using Captions.ai to automatically generate engaging and relevant captions for images shared on platforms like Instagram, Twitter, or Facebook.
3. **E-commerce:** Online retailers can improve the accessibility of product images by using Captions.ai to generate detailed descriptions, aiding customers in understanding product features and details.
4. **Educational Materials:** Captions.ai can be employed in educational settings to automate the process of adding descriptions to visual aids, making educational content more accessible to a diverse audience.
5. **Web Accessibility:** Website developers can integrate Captions.ai to ensure that images on their websites are accompanied by descriptive captions, complying with accessibility standards and regulations.

13.3 Playground Ai

Definition:

Playground AI is a platform or environment that serves as a virtual space for experimenting, testing, and developing various artificial intelligence (AI) models and algorithms. It provides a user-friendly interface and tools that enable individuals, researchers, and developers to explore and implement AI solutions without the need for extensive programming knowledge.

Features:

1. User-Friendly Interface: Playground AI typically offers an intuitive and easy-to-use interface, making it accessible to users with varying levels of expertise in AI and machine learning.

2. Code-Free Environment: It often allows users to experiment with AI models without writing extensive code, using drag-and-drop interfaces or pre-built components for model building.

3. Pre-trained Models: Many Playground AI platforms come with pre-trained models, enabling users to quickly test and deploy AI solutions without the need to train models from scratch.

4. Visualization Tools: Playground AI tools often include visualization features that help users understand and interpret the outcomes of their AI models, making it easier to analyze and refine results.

5. Collaboration Capabilities: Some Playground AI environments support collaboration, allowing multiple users to work on and share AI projects in real-time.

Benefits:

1. Accessibility: Playground AI makes AI experimentation accessible to a broader audience, including those without extensive programming or machine learning expertise.

2. Rapid Prototyping: Users can quickly prototype and test AI ideas, algorithms, and models, accelerating the development cycle and fostering innovation.

3. Learning Opportunities: It serves as an educational tool, allowing students and professionals to learn about AI concepts and applications in a practical, hands-on manner.

4. Cost-Efficiency: Playground AI often eliminates the need for significant computing resources, reducing the costs associated with setting up and maintaining AI development environments.

Use Cases:

1. Education: Playground AI platforms are commonly used in educational settings to teach AI concepts, enabling students to experiment with AI models in a controlled and supportive environment.

2. Prototyping and Testing: AI researchers and developers use Playground AI for rapid prototyping and testing of new algorithms or ideas before moving to more complex and resource-intensive environments.

3. Proof of Concept: It is often used to quickly demonstrate the feasibility of AI projects, allowing stakeholders to visualize potential applications and benefits.

4. Hackathons and Competitions: Playground AI is utilized in AI hackathons and competitions where participants can quickly experiment and build AI solutions within a limited timeframe.

5. Innovation Labs: Companies and research institutions use Playground AI in innovation labs to encourage creative thinking and the development of novel AI applications.

13.4 Adobe firefly

DEFINE:

Adobe Firefly is a free, web-based generative AI tool that helps spark creativity and streamline workflows for visual creators. It empowers anyone, from seasoned professionals to casual enthusiasts, to use natural language prompts and simple instructions to:

1. Generate images: Turn textual descriptions into unique visuals, illustrations, and even photorealistic scenes.
2. Modify existing content: Refine images, apply different artistic styles, or modify specific elements like colors or textures.
3. Create text-based content: Generate headlines, slogans, scripts, music, or even code based on your prompts.
4. Experiment with creative building blocks: Explore brushes, textures, patterns, and other assets to enhance your creations.

FEATURES:

1. Intuitive interface: Drag-and-drop functionality and natural language prompts make it easy to use, even for those with no AI experience.
2. Diverse outputs: Generate visuals in various styles, from cartoon characters to photorealistic landscapes, and text formats like poems or scripts.
3. Customization: Refine generated outputs with controls for adjusting details, colors, textures, and more.

4. AI-powered collaboration: Share projects with others and collaborate on edits and refinements within the Firefly interface.
5. Integration with Adobe Creative Cloud: Seamlessly export generated content to your favorite Adobe apps like Photoshop or Premiere Pro for further refinement.

BENEFITS:
1. Boosts creativity: Overcome creative block and explore new ideas by prompting AI to generate unexpected visuals and text formats.
2. Saves time and effort: Automate repetitive tasks like generating variations or experimenting with different styles, freeing up time for more focused work.
3. Democratizes creativity: Makes AI-powered content creation accessible to everyone, regardless of technical expertise.
4. Enhances collaboration: Foster teamwork and share ideas by co-creating within the Firefly platform.
5. Expands possibilities: Discover unexpected connections and explore new avenues in your creative projects.

USE CASES:
1. Graphic design: Generate mockups, logos, illustrations, and other visual assets for design projects.
2. Marketing and advertising: Create eye-catching visuals for social media, billboards, or product packaging.
3. Film and video editing: Generate storyboards, concept art, or even background scenes for video projects.
4. Product design: Explore prototypes, experiment with different styles, and visualize product iterations.
5. Music composition: Generate song lyrics, melodies, or even entire musical pieces based on your ideas.

13.5 Hotpot

Hotpot AI is a suite of AI-powered tools designed to make graphic design, image editing, and media creation more accessible, efficient, and affordable. It's developed by a company called Hotpot.ai, which aims to democratize creativity using AI.

Features:

1. Natural Language Processing (NLP): Hotpot leverages advanced NLP algorithms for understanding and interpreting human language.
2. Knowledge Base Integration: It integrates with extensive knowledge bases to enhance its information retrieval capabilities.
3. Predictive Analytics: Utilizes machine learning algorithms for predictive analytics, making it adept at forecasting trends and patterns.
4. Adaptability: Hotpot is adaptable to various domains, allowing users to tailor its functionalities based on specific needs.

Benefits:

1. Efficient Information Retrieval: Users can quickly retrieve relevant information from diverse sources, boosting productivity.
2. Predictive Insights: Businesses gain valuable insights through predictive analytics, aiding in strategic decision-making.
3. Versatility: Hotpot's adaptability makes it suitable for applications across industries, from customer support to market analysis.
4. Enhanced Communication: Natural language processing capabilities improve communication between users and the AI system.

Use Cases:

1. Customer Support Chatbots: Hotpot can be employed as a chatbot in customer support, offering instant responses and solutions.
2. Market Research: For analyzing market trends, Hotpot can process vast amounts of data and provide insights into consumer behavior.
3. Educational Assistants: In educational settings, Hotpot can assist students in researching topics and answering queries.
4. Healthcare Decision Support: By analyzing medical literature, Hotpot can assist healthcare professionals in making informed decisions.

13.6 tome.app

Definition:

Tome.app is an AI-powered presentation creation tool that streamlines the process of crafting visually compelling and engaging presentations. It harnesses natural language processing and machine learning to automate tasks, provide suggestions, and create polished content efficiently.

Key Features:

1. AI-Powered Outline Creation: Generate presentation outlines from simple text prompts or existing documents.
2. Page Generation: Automatically create multiple slide layouts based on your input, saving time and effort.
3. Visual Suggestions: Recommend relevant images and graphics to complement your content.
4. AI Edit: Refine text tone and style to match your desired messaging (e.g., persuasive, informative, neutral).
5. Real-Time Collaboration: Enable multiple users to work on presentations simultaneously.
6. Responsive Design: Ensure presentations adapt seamlessly to different devices and screen sizes.
7. Customization: Tailor presentations with themes, colors, fonts, and branding elements.
8. Interactive Elements: Incorporate links, videos, and other interactive features for engaging experiences.

Benefits:

1. Efficiency: Create polished presentations faster with AI assistance.
2. Creativity: Explore new ideas and content suggestions through AI-generated content.
3. Effectiveness: Craft more compelling and persuasive presentations with visual appeal.
4. Collaboration: Facilitate teamwork and streamline feedback processes.
5. Accessibility: Enable individuals with varying design skills to create professional-looking presentations.

Use Cases:

1. Business Presentations: Create pitch decks, product demos, company updates, and client proposals.
2. Marketing Campaigns: Craft engaging visual content for social media, email marketing, and landing pages.
3. Educational Purposes: Design engaging lesson plans, interactive lectures, and student assignments.
4. Content Creation: Produce visually appealing blog posts, website pages, and newsletters.
5. Personal Projects: Showcase portfolios, share ideas, and create personal presentations.

13.7 MusicLM

1. Definition:

MusicLM (assuming it's related to AI tools in music) could refer to a platform, software, or service that leverages artificial intelligence techniques for various applications within the music industry.

2. Features:

- **Automatic Composition:** AI algorithms can generate music compositions autonomously.
- **Music Recommendation:** AI can analyze user preferences to recommend personalized playlists or suggest new music.
- **Music Generation:** AI models can create new musical pieces, explore different genres, and even mimic specific artists' styles.
- **Genre Classification:** AI can classify and categorize music based on its genre, style, or other features.
- **Lyric Analysis:** Some tools may use natural language processing to analyze and generate lyrics.

3. Benefits:

- **Creativity Enhancement:** AI tools in music can inspire and augment human creativity, leading to novel compositions.
- **Efficiency:** Automated processes for tasks like composition and recommendation can save time for musicians and music enthusiasts.
- **Personalization:** AI can tailor music recommendations to individual preferences, providing a more personalized listening experience.
- **Exploration:** Musicians can use AI-generated suggestions to explore new genres and styles.

4. Use Cases:

- **Music Composition:** AI tools can compose music autonomously or assist musicians in the creative process.
- **Music Recommendation Platforms:** Streaming services use AI to recommend songs based on users' listening history and preferences.

- **Interactive Music Apps:** AI-powered apps that allow users to interact with and manipulate music in real-time.
- **Content Creation:** AI can be used to create background music for videos, games, or other multimedia content.

13.8 Soundraw

Definition: Soundraw.io is a web-based platform that leverages AI to generate royalty-free music and sound effects for various purposes. Users can create custom soundtracks, sound effects, and ambient noises without requiring musical expertise.

Features:

1. AI-powered Music Generation: Generate music in various genres, moods, and tempos with simple controls.
2. Customizable Loops and Instruments: Combine and tweak music elements like drums, bass lines, melodies, and harmonies to create unique soundscapes.
3. Sound Effects Library: Access a vast library of royalty-free sound effects for diverse use cases.
4. AI-powered Sound Design: Generate custom sound effects using descriptive keywords or by uploading reference audio.
5. Collaboration Tools: Share projects and collaborate with other creators in real-time.
6. Export and Integration: Export your creations in various formats and integrate them seamlessly into your projects.

Benefits:

1. Accessibility: Create professional-sounding music and sound effects without musical knowledge or expensive software.
2. Speed and Efficiency: Generate audio content quickly and easily, saving time and effort.
3. Variety and Customization: Access a vast range of musical styles and customize them to your exact needs.
4. Royalty-free Usage: Use your creations in personal and commercial projects without copyright issues.
5. Collaboration and Sharing: Work with other creators and share your work effortlessly.

Use Cases:

1. Video Production: Create soundtracks and sound effects for video projects, from YouTube videos to short films.
2. Podcast Production: Craft engaging intros, outros, and background music for podcasts.
3. Game Development: Create soundtracks and sound effects for video games.
4. Marketing and Advertising: Produce audio for commercials, presentations, and social media content.
5. Live Performances and Events: Generate background music and sound effects for live events.
6. Personal Projects: Create music for personal enjoyment, relaxation, or inspiration.

13.9 Boomy

1. Boomy.io for Social Media Content Creation:

Definition: Boomy.io is a web-based AI-powered platform that helps create engaging social media content for various platforms like Instagram, Facebook, YouTube, and TikTok.

Features:

1. Generates caption ideas and hashtags based on your chosen topic or image.
2. Provides content templates for different social media formats.
3. Analyzes your content's potential reach and engagement.
4. Offers scheduling and publishing tools for social media posts.

Benefits:

1. Saves time and effort in creating social media content.
2. Provides ideas and inspiration for engaging captions and hashtags.
3. Helps optimize your content for reach and engagement.
4. Simplifies social media management with scheduling and publishing tools.

Use Cases:

1. Content creators and social media managers.
2. Businesses and brands promoting themselves on social media.
3. Individuals looking to improve their social media presence.

2. Boomy Voice Assistant for Presentations:

Definition: Boomy is a voice assistant designed to help with creating and delivering presentations. It uses AI to analyze your voice and provide feedback on pacing, tone, and delivery.

Features:
1. Provides real-time feedback on your presentation delivery.
2. Suggests improvements to your pacing, tone, and word choice.
3. Offers practice sessions with virtual audiences.
4. Records and analyzes your presentations for later review.

Benefits:
1. Improves your presentation skills and delivery.
2. Boosts your confidence and stage presence.
3. Helps you create more engaging and impactful presentations.
4. Provides valuable feedback and practice opportunities.

Use Cases:
1. Public speakers and presenters.
2. Professionals who need to give presentations regularly.
3. Students and educators giving presentations in academic settings.

3. Boomy Music AI (hypothetical):
Definition: (This is purely hypothetical) Boomy Music could be an AI tool that helps with music creation, composition, or performance. Its specific features and functionalities would depend on its development and purpose.
Possible Features:
1. Generate melodies, harmonies, and rhythms based on user input or style preferences.
2. Provide real-time feedback on musical performance.
3. Suggest creative ideas for musical arrangements and compositions.
6. Help with music education and learning.

Potential Benefits:
1. Assist musicians and composers in their creative process.
2. Make music creation more accessible and engaging for everyone.
3. Provide valuable feedback and learning tools for musicians.

Use Cases:
1. Musicians and composers of all levels.
2. Music students and educators.
3. Individuals interested in exploring music creation.

Exercise

Exercise 1 – MCQ

Q 1. What is the primary function of Captions.ai?
A. Music composition
B. Image editing
C. Generating automatic captions for audio content
D. Artistic design

Q 2. Which tool is known for enhancing accessibility through automated captioning?
A. Descript
B. Hotpot
C. Playground Ai
D. Captions.ai

Q 3. What is the focus of Playground Ai in the realm of creative design?
A. Productivity enhancement
B. Artistic applications and visual design
C. Music composition
D. Auto captioning

Q 4. Which AI tool provides a dynamic environment for artistic exploration?
A. Boomy
B. Descript
C. Playground Ai
D. Adobe firefly

Q 5. How does Descript contribute to collaboration and productivity?
A. Visual design features
B. Audio-based features for content creation
C. Music composition tools
D. Automated captioning

Q 6. Which tool is recognized for streamlining the workflow of content creators and teams?
A. Hotpot
B. Descript
C. MusicLM
D. tome.app

Q7. In which domain does Boomy specialize?
A. Artistic design
B. Music composition and sound design
C. Automated captioning
D. Productivity enhancement

Q 8. What specific functionalities does MusicLM offer?
A. Auto captioning
B. Streamlining workflow
C. Music composition and sound design
D. Image editing

Q 9. What is the primary purpose of Soundraw?
A. Visual design
B. Automated captioning
C. Music composition
D. Productivity enhancement

Q 10. Which tool is associated with audio-based features for efficient content creation?
A. tome.app
B. Soundraw
C. Hotpot
D. Captions.ai

Exercise 2 – True / False

Q 1. Captions.ai primarily focuses on generating automatic captions for video content.
Q 2. Captions.ai contributes to accessibility by automating the captioning process for audio content.
Q 3. Playground Ai emphasizes artistic applications and creative visual design.
Q 4. Playground Ai primarily focuses on automated graphic design.
Q 5. Descript is recognized for enhancing productivity and collaboration through audio-based features.
Q 6. Hotpot is an AI tool designed to streamline project management workflows.
Q 7. Boomy is specifically associated with music composition and sound design.
Q 8. MusicLM focuses on enhancing productivity through collaboration tools for music production.
Q 9. Soundraw is an AI tool primarily used for visual design projects.
Q 10. tome.app is associated with audio-based features for efficient content creation.

Exercise 3 – Fill in the blanks

Q 1. __________.ai is an AI tool that focuses on generating automatic captions for audio content.
Q 2. Captions.ai contributes significantly to improving __________ for audio content through its automated captioning capabilities.
Q 3. Playground Ai stands out for emphasizing __________ applications and creative visual design.
Q 4. Playground Ai provides artists and designers with a platform for expressive __________ through innovative features.
Q 5. __________ is recognized for enhancing collaboration and productivity through its audio-based features.

Exercise 4 – Match case

1. Generate automatic captions for audio content	B. Captions.ai
2. Emphasize artistic applications and creative visual design	A. Boomy
3. Enhance productivity and collaboration through audio features	C. Playground AI
4. Efficient content creation with audio-based features	D. tome.app
5. Specifically associated with music composition and sound design	E. Descript

Exercise 5 – One word answer
Q 1. What is Captions.ai primarily focused on?
Q 2. What does Playground Ai emphasize in creative design?
Q 3. What aspect does Descript enhance in collaboration and work efficiency?
Q 4. In what field is Boomy specialized?
Q 5. What is the primary purpose of Soundraw?

Exercise 6 – Small answer
Q 1. Which tool specializes in generating automatic captions for audio content?
Q 2. What does Playground Ai emphasize in creative design?
Q 3. Which tool is recognized for enhancing collaboration and productivity through audio-based features?
Q 4. In what field is Boomy specifically associated?
Q 5. What is the primary purpose of Soundraw?

Exercise 7 – Long answer
Q 1. How does Captions.ai contribute to accessibility and user engagement by automating the captioning process for audio content, and what impact does this have on making audio content more inclusive?
Q 2. In what ways does Playground Ai stand out in the realm of creative design, emphasizing artistic applications and visual creativity, and how does it provide a dynamic platform for artists and designers to express their creativity through innovative features?

Answers

Exercise 1 – MCQ
Ans: 1 C, 2 D, 3 B, 4 C, 5 B, 6 B, 7 B, 8 C, 9 C, 10 A
Exercise 2 – True/ False
Ans: 1 False, 2 True, 3 True, 4 False, 5 True, 6 False, 7 True, 8 False, 9 False, 10 True
Exercise 3 – Fill in the blanks
Ans: 1 Captions, 2 Accessibility, 3 Artistic, 4 Creativity, 5 Descript
Exercise 4 – Match case
Ans: 1 B, 2 C, 3 E, 4 A, 5 E
Exercise 5 – One word answer
Ans: 1 Captioning, 2 Artistic, 3 Productivity, 4 Music, 5 Music

ONLINE RESOURCES

Practice Paper
Link https://forms.office.com/r/kEamHidjGm
QR Code

Video Content
Link: https://www.youtube.com/playlist?list=PLzlh_31VWEFqfL9uWbIzQyeKnWvtSj8yW
QR Code

Chapter 14: Viva Voce Questions

Q1: What is the role of AI in modern business according to the evolution discussed in various domains?
Answer: AI plays a critical role in enhancing efficiency, decision-making, and customer interactions across various business sectors, significantly transforming operations and competitive strategies.

Q2: Can you explain the key features of ChatGPT as outlined in your course?
Answer: Key features include its ability to understand and generate human-like text, support interactive conversation, and perform specific tasks like summarization, translation, and answering questions.

Q3: Describe a major impact of Bard AI in the industry.
Answer: Bard AI significantly impacts customer support and engagement by enabling more intuitive and efficient interactions, using its advanced natural language understanding capabilities.

Q4: What are the primary applications of Gemini AI Tool as mentioned in your study material?
Answer: Gemini AI Tool is primarily used for predictive analytics, risk assessment, and personalized customer experiences, leveraging its machine learning and data analysis capabilities.

Q5: Discuss the usefulness of GrammarlyGO for content creators.
Answer: GrammarlyGO assists content creators by providing real-time grammar, punctuation, and style suggestions, making their writing clearer, error-free, and more engaging.

Q6: What distinguishes GitHub Copilot in AI-driven coding tools?
Answer: GitHub Copilot stands out by offering code suggestions based on context, significantly speeding up the coding process and helping developers avoid common errors.

Q7: Explain how Otter.ai benefits meeting management.
Answer: Otter.ai enhances meeting productivity by providing real-time transcription, which facilitates better note-taking, information retrieval, and follow-up actions.

Q8: How does DALL.E 2 contribute to image design?
Answer: DALL.E 2 enables the creation of highly realistic and complex images from textual descriptions, broadening creative possibilities and reducing the need for manual graphic design.

Q9: What future trends in AI tool development were discussed in your course material?
Answer: Future trends include more sophisticated natural language processing, greater integration of AI with other emerging technologies, and heightened focus on ethical AI development.

Q10: How does AI influence customer support as mentioned in the course?
Answer: AI revolutionizes customer support by enabling automated, yet personalized responses, reducing response times, and allowing human agents to focus on more complex queries.

Q11: What advancements in AI writing tools have been significant?
Answer: Significant advancements include real-time editing assistance, content optimization for SEO, and style personalization, helping writers produce high-quality content more efficiently.

Q12: Discuss the impact of AI on video production tools as outlined in your studies.
Answer: AI has transformed video production by automating editing, enhancing video quality with AI-driven enhancements, and enabling synthetic media generation, which reduces production time and costs.

Q13: Can you describe how AI tools like Spinach improve meeting efficiency?
Answer: Spinach uses AI to summarize discussions, track action items, and even predict questions, making meetings more productive and ensuring critical information is highlighted.

Q14: What role does AI play in HR according?
Answer: AI streamlines HR processes by automating candidate screening, enhancing employee engagement through personalized interactions, and providing analytics for better workforce management.

Q15: How does GitHub Copilot adapt its suggestions to the coder's needs?
Answer: GitHub Copilot uses context from the existing codebase to offer relevant suggestions, learning from the user's coding patterns to improve its recommendations over time.

Q16: What are some ethical considerations in AI tool development?
Answer: Ethical considerations include ensuring fairness in AI decision-making, maintaining transparency in AI processes, and safeguarding user privacy and data security.

Q17: How does AI influence the development of customer support tools like Chatfuel AI?
Answer: AI enables tools like Chatfuel AI to provide automated yet highly personalized interactions, facilitating better customer engagement and satisfaction while streamlining support operations.

Q18: What features make GrammarlyGO a valuable tool for professional writers and marketers?
Answer: GrammarlyGO offers advanced features like tone detection, style guides, and plagiarism checks, which are essential for creating professional and unique content.

Q19: Explain the concept of 'AI in emerging technologies'.
Answer: AI in emerging technologies involves integrating AI with next-gen tech like IoT, blockchain, and quantum computing, creating more intelligent, secure, and efficient systems.

Q20: Describe the use case of AI in project management tools like ClickUp.
Answer: AI in ClickUp assists with automating task allocation, optimizing schedules based on project data, and predicting project risks, enhancing overall project management effectiveness.

YouTube Link for Viva Voce Questions:
https://www.youtube.com/playlist?list=PLzlh_31VWEFoOqdxccpUK1feLPYpiE-05

QR Code:

ADDITIONAL RESOURCES

Artificial Intelligence Tools Videos Playlist-
Link: https://www.youtube.com/playlist?list=PLzlh_31VWEFpjAkLEzK2HiiokXl8Cuaj2

QR Code:

YouTube Videos Playlists for all Microsoft Certifications Videos

Chapter 1
Link
https://www.youtube.com/playlist?list=PLzlh_31VWEFoGW10fGOcJlZBAhD9JtUwM
QR Code

Chapter 2
Link: https://www.youtube.com/playlist?list=PLzlh_31VWEFoLzaqayq06GM8O1ihO5enq
QR Code:

Chapter 3
Link: https://www.youtube.com/playlist?list=PLzlh_31VWEFoAEiQsraGzQlgT80FGJIce
QR Code:

Chapter 4
Link: https://www.youtube.com/playlist?list=PLzlh_31VWEFqpMMEpvwQ9-mh2my6hrM3d
QR Code:

Chapter 5
Link: https://www.youtube.com/playlist?list=PLzlh_31VWEFqEXMOclSf0Tt_udPnWJtr4
QR Code:

Chapter 6
Link: https://www.youtube.com/playlist?list=PLzlh_31VWEFqiIkmy_tBryzLuvz9y3ggp
QR Code:

Chapter 7
Link: https://www.youtube.com/playlist?list=PLzlh_31VWEFpNgaoIFXZU9f0R5q1nnruZ
QR Code:

Chapter 8
Link: https://www.youtube.com/playlist?list=PLzlh_31VWEFrapCfywmMKzhPPvZlnoEf5
QR Code:

Chapter 9
Link: https://www.youtube.com/playlist?list=PLzlh_31VWEFoiNJsDyhE2BAmPoSI5RCMs
QR Code:

Chapter 10
Link: https://www.youtube.com/playlist?list=PLzlh_31VWEFroNjpEj1eykhiXHFUY9vmA
QR Code:

Chapter 11
Link: https://www.youtube.com/playlist?list=PLzlh_31VWEFqxBTQUzeR8S__5tvCydz-Y
QR Code:

Chapter 12
Link: https://www.youtube.com/playlist?list=PLzlh_31VWEFoNMiS7uUvACczKvKh-nTce
QR Code:

Chapter 13
Link: https://www.youtube.com/playlist?list=PLzlh_31VWEFqfL9uWbIzQyeKnWvtSj8yW
QR Code: